THE EPIC HISTORY OF THE AMERICAN WEST

THE EPIC HISTORY OF THE AMERICAN WEST

FROM THE FIRST PEOPLES TO THE PRESENT

WILLIAM NESTER

FRONTLINE
BOOKS

THE EPIC HISTORY OF THE AMERICAN WEST
from the First Peoples to the Present

First published in Great Britain in 2025
by Frontline Books
An imprint of
Pen & Sword Books Ltd
Yorkshire - Philadelphia

ISBN 978 1 03613 375 7

A CIP catalogue record for this book is available from the British Library

Typeset by Lapiz Digital

Printed and bound in the UK by CPI Group (UK) Ltd,
Croydon, CR0 4YY.

Printed on paper from a sustainable source by
CPI Group (UK) Ltd, Croydon, CR0 4YY

Pen & Sword Books Limited incorporates the imprints of
Archaeology, Atlas, Aviation, Battleground, Digital, Discovery, Family
History, Fiction, History, Local, Local History, Maritime, Military,
Military Classics, Politics, Select, Transport, True Crime, Air World,
Claymore Press, Frontline Publishing, Leo Cooper, Remember
When, Seaforth Publishing, The Praetorian Press, Wharncliffe Books,
Wharncliffe Local History, Wharncliffe Transport, Wharncliffe True
Crime and White Owl.

For a complete list of Pen & Sword titles please contact
PEN & SWORD BOOKS LTD
47 Church Street, Barnsley, South Yorkshire, S70 2AS, England
E-mail: enquiries@pen-and-sword.co.uk
Website: www.pen-and-sword.co.uk
or
PEN & SWORD BOOKS
1950 Lawrence Rd, Havertown, PA 19083, USA
E-mail: uspen-and-sword@casematepublishers.com

CONTENTS

LIST OF PLATES

LIST OF TABLES

ACKNOWLEDGEMENTS

I would like to express my deep gratitude and pleasure at having had yet another opportunity to work with the outstanding publishing team of John Grehan, Lisa Hoosan, Stephen Chumbley, and Martin Mace, who were always as kind as they were professional.

PREFACE

The American West has intrigued me from my young boyhood. Since then I've read a thousand or so books, journeyed a couple hundred thousand miles, and written six books to explore the American West's far corners. Early, I learned the difference between the "legendary" and "real" West, and thereafter sought and savored the latter's complexities, contradictions, and paradoxes. I learned that a collection of related facts don't become history until someone knowledgeable and skilled explains their whats and whys. I learned that historians can interpret the same related facts in many ways. Then around 1990, the "New Western History" movement asserted an alternative explanation that highlighted class, racial, ethnic, religious, and gender conflicts and injustices downplayed by "Old Western" historians who emphasized the struggles of a series of explorers, trappers, traders, soldiers, settlers, ranchers, farmers, merchants, railroaders, miners, and entrepreneurs against nature and natives that resulted in the West's economic and political development.

The Epic History of the American West: From the First Peoples to the Present represents a synthesis of the best of New and Old Western history, and so is a unique, challenging, and, hopefully, inspiring contribution to the field. The book avoids hero and villain, exploiter and victim dichotomies. Instead, the emphasis is on the practical and moral dilemmas that fascinating groups and individuals faced as they asserted their conflicting interests against each other, first through prehistoric then historic time. All along, increasingly sophisticated and powerful technologies shaped how people tried to harness nature and subdue rivals. The American West today is an amalgam of sprawling, polluted cities with ever more diverse populations and swaths of magnificent mountains, canyons, plains, and deserts; vast agribusiness, stockyard, slaughterhouse, manufacturing, mining, and dam complexes and hardscrabble farmers, ranchers, laborers, and miners; an array of competing political parties, ideologies, interest groups, and ethnicities; Indian reservations that vary greatly in relative prosperity or poverty;

diminishing or depleted aquifers and rivers, lands uninhabitable from radioactivity and other deadly chemical toxins, and millions of acres of charred forests; tens of millions of unique individuals striving to realize their respective dreams; and countless novels, poems, plays, short stories, paintings, music, dance, and films that depict all that and much more.

INTRODUCTION

"Eastward I go only by force. But westward I go free. That way the nation is moving, and I may say that mankind progresses from East to West." (Henry David Thoreau)

Who doesn't thrill at images of the American West? Warriors with eagle headdresses atop swift ponies gallop across vast undulating plains; lean, wary, bearded mountain men set traps in icy streams; cowboys whoop it up in a saloon after a cattle drive; pioneer families in Conestoga wagons stoically head to the promised land of California or Oregon. And in today's West, who can resist the fun of attending a rodeo, powwow, reenacted O.K. Corral shootout, dude ranch, or Burning Man Festival? The American West symbolizes freedom, the right to reinvent oneself, to realize one's dreams. As such, the West epitomizes the American Dream's grandest version. Of course, those images obscure the American West's complex, paradoxical history, often as violent and unjust as it is inspiring and progressive.

What is the American West? Where does it begin and end? Who does it include and exclude? Historians endlessly debate those and countless related questions.[1] What is clear is that the American West is dynamically a direction, a frontier, a place, a process, an idea, and an identity whose relative weights vary through time.

The American West was first a direction. English settlers sailed west to North America to plant colonies that gradually expanded westward across the continent. Virginia's colonial charter granted it territory all the way to the Pacific Ocean. As for America's neighbors, Canada experienced a parallel westward moving frontier to the Pacific while Mexico's was northward whose far frontier is now within the American Southwest.

Of course, the West was also a place but that changed with time. For most of the colonial decades, the West lay from the tidal line to the Appalachian Mountains, and in the early republic, from the Appalachians to the Mississippi River. President Thomas Jefferson's

Louisiana Purchase in 1803 extended the West to the Rocky Mountain divide. Then the United States through diplomacy won the Northwest from Britain in the 1846 Oregon treaty, and through war won most of the Southwest from Mexico in the 1848 Treaty of Guadeloupe Hidalgo. The 1853 Gadsden Purchase from Mexico of a wedge of land below the Gila River completed the territory of what would become the lower forty-eight States.[2]

People headed west for many reasons that might include being pushed by exhausted soil, overcrowding, spiteful neighbors, and escape from debts or crimes, and pulled by the allure of a fresh start, getting rich, fertile soil, free land, liberty, adventure, and sheer wanderlust. For all that, the West was a safety valve for an increasingly populated East. Most of those who went west sought to recreate a better version of the society they left behind of church congregations, fraternal organizations, and political parties. A few sought solitude for themselves and their families. Daniel Boone was the quintessential frontiersman who spent years hunting and exploring alone or with a companion or two. He knew it was time to go West with his expanding family when he saw smoke curling from some new neighbor's cabin or just felt the restless need for more elbow room. He finally died near the Missouri River at the last homestead he and his family chopped from the surrounding wilderness. Patricia Limerick captured the paradox that haunted him and other westerners "of replicating the problems they had attempted to escape . . . Daniel Boone found civilization intolerable and escaped to the wilderness. His travels blazed trails for other pioneers to follow, and Boone found himself crowded out. His fresh start turned rapidly stale."[3]

"Frontier" and "Western" history overlapped for three centuries until the mappable frontier disappeared in 1890. The notion of "frontier" is central to American culture and identity. According to American history's "triumphantist" version, the West was charted, conquered, colonized, and developed by a series of explorers, hunters, trappers, traders, soldiers, entrepreneurs, ranchers, farmers, miners, lawmen, and railroaders. Heroic leadership was crucial to that process. The decisive acts of Meriwether Lewis, William Clark, Manuel Lisa, William Ashley, Jedediah Smith, Stephen Austin, Sam Houston, John Fremont, Zachery Taylor, Winfield Scott, George Crook, John Wesley Powell, and Nelson Miles, to name a few, decisively advanced the West's transformation from wilderness to civilization. Paul Hutton provided this insight: "Heroes are not born, they are created. Their lives so catch the imagination of their generation, and often the generations that follow, that they are repeatedly discussed and talked about. The lives of heroes are a testament to the values and aspirations of those who admire them. If their images change as time passes they may act as a barometer of the fluctuating attitudes of a society."[4]

The American West is also an idea and an identity imagined and developed by Americans over four centuries. The West was central to how Americans envisioned themselves. Hector Saint John de Crevecoeur vividly captured that essence: "What is this American, this new man? . . . Here individuals of all nations are melted into a new race of men whose labors and posterity will one day cause great changes in the world. Americans are the western pilgrims, who are carrying along with them the great mass of arts, sciences, vigor, and industry which began long since in the east . . . The American is a new man, who acts upon new principles."[5] Henry David Thoreau was among those inspired by the ideal West and westerner: "Eastward I go only by force. But westward I go free. That way the nation is moving, and I may say that mankind progresses from East to West."[6] Historian T.K. Whipple caught the aching longing that many felt for this idyllic West: "Our forefathers had civilization inside themselves, the wild outside. We live in the civilization they created, but within us the wilderness still lingers. What they dreamed, we live, and what they lived, we dream. That is why our western story still holds us."[7] The West is also a regional identity, a state of mind. Historian Clyde Milner argued that "the American West is an idea that became a place."[8] Westerners view themselves as exemplifying American cultural ideals of rugged individualism, self-reliance, courage, innovation, and enterprise.

***

Frederick Jackson Turner emphasized the West's frontier interpretation. He delivered what became the nation's most consequential scholarly paper at the American History Association meeting in Chicago amidst the 1893 World's Fair. "The Significance of the Frontier in American History" at once established a new historical discipline and way to understand it. He argued that the frontier was central, not peripheral, to America's political, economic, and social development. The frontier was the crucible within which Americans forged their national identity's core values of individualism, liberty, pragmatism, problem-solving, community, patriotism, and democracy. That emerged through the often violent struggle between "civilized" and "savage" peoples with the latter's inevitable and progressive conquest and transformation by the former. Turner emphasized the triumphant results of the frontier's transformation while saying little about the devastation of the tribes, wildlife, and landscapes. Studying the frontier was especially appropriate and poignant because the 1890 Census Bureau declared that it no longer existed. The book that best expresses Turner's interpretation is *Westward Expansion: A History of the American Frontier* written by Ray Billington and updated by Martin Ridge.[9]

Turner provided some profound insights into the past. By necessity, grassroots democracy did develop on the frontier. The Pilgrims drafted their "Mayflower Compact" that created a political system of rights and representation before they stepped ashore in 1620. Other isolated communities forged similar understandings to govern themselves and avoid the extremes of autocracy or anarchy. Of course, those ideas and practices originated in England, but in America far more people realized those democratic principles than in the country they left behind. Indeed, the Americans eventually rebelled against England and sought independence because their liberalism had become as deep-rooted as their identity as a separate nation.

Turner's thesis provoked plenty of critics. Earl Pomeroy, a University of Oregon professor, asserted a powerful rebuttal with his 1955 article, "Toward a Reorientation of Western History." He argued that America's frontier was originally part of Europe's overseas frontier and so American civilization must be understood as an extension and variation of western civilization. As such, "the westerner has been fundamentally imitator rather than innovator . . . He was often the most ardent of conformists."[10] The West was a backwater dependent on Washington policies and eastern finance.[11] Yet that backwater eventually developed into an economic and political powerhouse. Walter Nugget suggested how with this distinction: "In general, empires proved transient, and frontiers evolved into permanent societies."[12]

By the late 1980s, critics of the traditional version called themselves "New Western" historians to distinguish themselves from "Old Western" historians. New Westerners lambast the Old for celebrating rather than condemning past leaders, businesses, government policies, and popular attitudes; for emphasizing the West's economic, political, and cultural development while downplaying the human and ecological costs; and for spotlighting the feats of white male heroes and ignoring almost everyone else. They try to correct that by defining the West as a distinct region whose history persists through the present that spans urban as well as rural life; celebrates minority racial, ethnic, worker, sexual, and woman leaders and groups; emphasizes injustice, racism, massacres, exploitation, pollution, corruption, and waste while obscuring exemplary courage, exploration, entrepreneurship, economic development, and political progress; and lauds multiculturalism rather than Americanism. New Western historians explore the West with an interdisciplinary approach that includes with history related fields like sociology, economics, psychology, ecology, and Native American studies to expose long-neglected dimensions of the human experience. More than anyone, Patricia Limerick pioneered this approach with her 1987 book *Legacy of Conquest,* and the movement took off with the "Trails: Toward a New Western History" conference at Santa Fe in 1989.[13] The Western Historical Association's *Western Historical Quarterly* has been the key forum for debates.

Although critiques by New Western historians vary in emphasis, all echo Limerick's that "frontier" and "conquest" were synonymous: "the history of the West is the study of a place undergoing conquest and never fully escaping its consequences."[14] Conquest and "settler colonialism" led to the exploitation and devastation of tribes, species, and ecosystems. New Western historians identify a prevailing psychology that justified conquest. Humans tend to project their own worst flaws on their foes, accusing them of being aggressive, violent, greedy, and rapacious. They scapegoat hated and feared "others" while martyrizing themselves as innocent victims. The American frontier exacerbated that human tendency with its "might makes right," "to the victor go the spoils," "anything for a buck," and "survival of the fittest" mindset. Atop that was the notion that the tribes did not own the land they lived, hunted, and often farmed because they did not "improve" it but merely inhabited it communally without individual property deeds. Westerners justly took those lands because they developed them. During the frontier centuries, few Americans acknowledged the hypocrisy, injustice, and crime that dispossessed tribes of their lands. Images of Indians seesawed between noble savage and vile savage. One's distance from "real" Indians usually determined which prevailed. For instance, most Arizonian and New Mexican settlers would have gleefully lynched Apache leader Geronimo while President Theodore Roosevelt invited him to ride in his inaugural parade. The field of American Indian or Native American Studies in alliance with New Western historians explores the complex legacy beyond those stereotypes.[15]

Most New Western scholars defined the West as a region with four dimensions. First, was aridity or rainfall of twenty inches or less across the region from the 100th meridian in the central plains to the Sierra and Cascade Mountains; east of that was the Midwest or Southeast, west of that was the Far West of coastal California, Oregon, and Washington.

Second, was the federal government's vital role in conquering and developing the West. Third, was the exploitation of natural resources like water, gold, silver, copper, uranium, coal, natural gas, lumber, and petroleum. Fourth, was that exploitation's boom and bust cycle as investors initially reaped fortunes until they exhausted the resource, littering the West with ghost towns, abandoned mines, clearcut forests, depleted soils and grasslands, and polluted streams. Richard White captured that protean West as "a land and people constantly in the midst of reinvention and reshaping."[16]

New Western historians highlight the irony that the region that most celebrates "rugged individualism" depends the most on the federal government. Washington created the modern West by deploying the army to crush native resistance; subsidizing railroads and building dams, electrical grids, and expressways; passing laws like the 1862 Homestead Act and 1872 Mining Act that gave away resource-rich public lands; and establishing institutions like the Interior Department, Bureau of Indian Affairs, Army Corps of Engineers, Reclamation Bureau, Bureau of Land Management, Forest Service, and National Park Service to administer public lands. Without two centuries of massive federal interventions, the West would be sparsely peopled and exploited.

Gerald Nash argued that 1945 represented the West's weaning from dependence on the East and rising viability as a dynamic economic, political, and cultural region. But, paradoxically, that was possible only because of massive New Deal and World War II programs of dam and irrigation complexes, military bases, factory production, and the Manhattan Project for nuclear power.[17] The West's urban "sunbelt," especially southern California, now led the nation's development, while sprawling metropolises like Los Angeles, Seattle, San Diego, San Francisco, Salt Lake City, Las Vegas, Phoenix, Denver, Houston, Austin, Dallas-Fort Worth, Oklahoma City, Albuquerque, and Omaha dominated western regions.

Politics is synonymous with conflicts between individuals and groups and the power that each musters and wields to assert its respective interests. Power is both "hard" or physical like finance, weapons, institutions, and businesses, and "soft" or psychological like leadership, attitudes, ideologies, and aspirations. Politics and economics determine the lines drawn across maps and thereafter politics within and between those separate realms in the West like other regions. The West begins with the eastern borders of that north-south line of states including North Dakota, South Dakota, Nebraska, Kansas, Oklahoma, and Texas. The 100th meridian splits those states with tall grass prairies and farming eastward and short grass plains and ranching westward. Those ranching and farming interests give those states a common political outlook shared by other western states. Yet, defining the West's eastern border with those states is hardly a perfect fit. Does the Midwest extend into North Dakota, South Dakota, Nebraska, and Kansas or the South into Oklahoma and Texas, and if so how far? Some of those states like Texas, Oklahoma, and, recently, North Dakota harbor powerful fossil fuel interests, while Texas's diverse economy spawns countless rival interest groups.

Of course, more than powerful businesses determine politics. Identities and thus interests shaped by class, ethnicity, race, religion, or gender along with ideologies like liberalism, conservatism, environmentalism, and socialism just as profoundly affect politics.[18] Politically, the West is increasingly divided among "blue" or liberal states like California, Oregon, Washington, and New Mexico; "red" or conservative states like Texas, Oklahoma, Kansas, Nebraska, South Dakota, North Dakota, Wyoming, Montana, and Idaho; and "purple" or mixed states like Colorado, Arizona, and Nevada. As elsewhere across the United States, urban areas lean liberal, rural areas lean conservative, and suburbs split. In every western state, politics is an increasingly multistranded political tug-of-war among countless groups whose relative power greatly varies among issues.

***

The endless battles over nature's fate defines western politics more than any other issue. Historian Roderick Nash saw the relationship between Americans and the wilderness they encountered and transformed as central to the nation's history, development, and identity: "From the raw materials of the physical wilderness Americans built a civilization; with the idea or symbol of wilderness they sought to give that civilization identity and meaning."[19] Although Americans have always systematically consumed natural resources, the symbolism changed with time. For the first three or so centuries, nearly all Americans viewed nature in materialistic rather than aesthetic or spiritual terms, for the money and products they could make from it rather than the joy of simply reveling amidst it, and asserted the unregulated right to exploit natural resources that appeared endless. Alexis de Tocqueville observed during his 1831 visit that: "Europe is much preoccupied with the wilderness of America, but the Americans themselves scarcely think of it. The marvels of inanimate nature find them insensible, and they . . . perceive the admirable forests that surround them only at the moment at which they fall by their strokes. Their eyes are filled with another spectacle. The American people sees itself advance across this wilderness, draining swamps, straightening rivers, peopling the solitude, and subduing nature."[20] Government policies at once reflected and reinforced that attitude by underwriting nature's immediate exploitation even to the devastation of the soil, forest, water, and species rather than its sustained use indefinitely.

The Transcendentalist movement of painters and writers in the early nineteenth century provided an alternative view of nature that inspired the conservation and preservation movements later that century. The result was increasingly bitter prolonged political wars between them and those upholding materialist views. Gradually, as conservationists and preservationists acquired more followers, funds, and political skills, they pressured Washington and ever more state and local governments to adopt policies that either managed natural resources for just enough exploitation that let them continually replenish or to outright protect some swaths of nature from any commercial exploitation.

In no region has the political war of materialists versus conservationists and preservationists been fiercer than in the West. Powerful industries like mining, logging, petroleum, coal, natural gas, construction, real estate, and agribusiness allied with well-funded politicians and lawyers to fight conservationists and preservationists every step of the way; had laws and policies written to benefit themselves at public expense; and often "captured" the federal, state, and local bureaucracies that were supposed to regulate them. Global warming exacerbates these political struggles with worsening droughts, water shortages, and forest fires that devastate the West.

***

History explains related facts about a subject. One fact is that people act on their beliefs whether they are grounded in provable reality or fantasy. People embrace myths to explain themselves and their world. Richard White explained how vital that is: "Myths may be anti-history, but myths themselves are also historical creations . . . People create myths at certain times and places for certain purposes, and as these purposes change over time, the meanings of mythic stories also change." As for the American West, that "imagined by Americans has shaped the West of history, just as the West of history has helped create the West Americans have imagined."[21]

Americans once may have shared a similar mythology about the West, but that disappeared long ago into competing narratives.[22] That is most contentious among Old and New Western historians with their rival arrays of myths and anti-myths, types and anti-types. Each defends its own and debunks the other's. New Western historians have attracted their own critics. Gerald Nash blasted the "New Left ideology" for its "pronounced negative self-image of the nation's and the West's history, and became a dominant theme in the interpretation of the West as myth. It could be argued that it revealed more about this group of critics than about the myth itself."[23]

Symbols are the essence of myths. Although Americans may debate the meaning of their national myths, the symbols endure. Does any nation let alone region boast as many iconic symbols as the American West?[24] Indian chief, mountain man, cowboy, gunslinger, prospector, saloon gal, schoolmarm, homesteader, lawman, and cavalry officer are among the most vivid western archetypes. There are symbolic dates like September 23, 1806, when the Lewis and Clark expedition triumphantly reached St. Louis to complete its epic two and a half year exploration across the West to the Pacific Ocean and back, or May 10, 1869, when the golden spike was driven to complete the transcontinental railroad at Promontory Point, Utah. And there are the events and places that symbolize the American West's violent, unjust, tragic dimensions like Trail of Tears, Bosque Redondo, Sand Creek, Wounded Knee, Manzanar, Aurora High School, Greenwood District, and Alfred P. Murrah Building.

***

Historians face a dilemma that Carl Degler explained: "All historical interpretations are shaped by values. No interpretation can transcend the values that a historian brings to his or her own investigation of the past any more than historical figures at the time could escape their values."[25] Turner recognized that conundrum yet found a solution: "Each age tries to form its own conception of the past. Each age writes the history of the past anew with reference to the conditions uppermost in its own time . . . History, both objective and subjective, is ever becoming, never completed." He sought a comprehensive, systematic analysis: "In history, then, there is unity and continuity. Each age must be studied in the light of all the past."[26]

That principle guides *The Epic History of the American West: from the First Peoples to the Present*. In this book, the West is a vast, complex region of many regions where the notion of frontier was central for three centuries until its original meaning disappeared. Once a place of often violent struggle among rival groups, since 1890 the frontier has been a metaphor. The West, however, endures with incessant and increasingly diverse and divisive conflicts among rival business, class, religious, ethnic, racial, gender, and ideological groups. For any conflict, explaining the array of views and the dynamic among them is critical to understanding it. This book bridges the best of both traditional and revisionist views, and the dynamic between the American West's history and mythology.

Map 1: North America Tribes 1650.

Map 2: American Indian Tribes 1800.

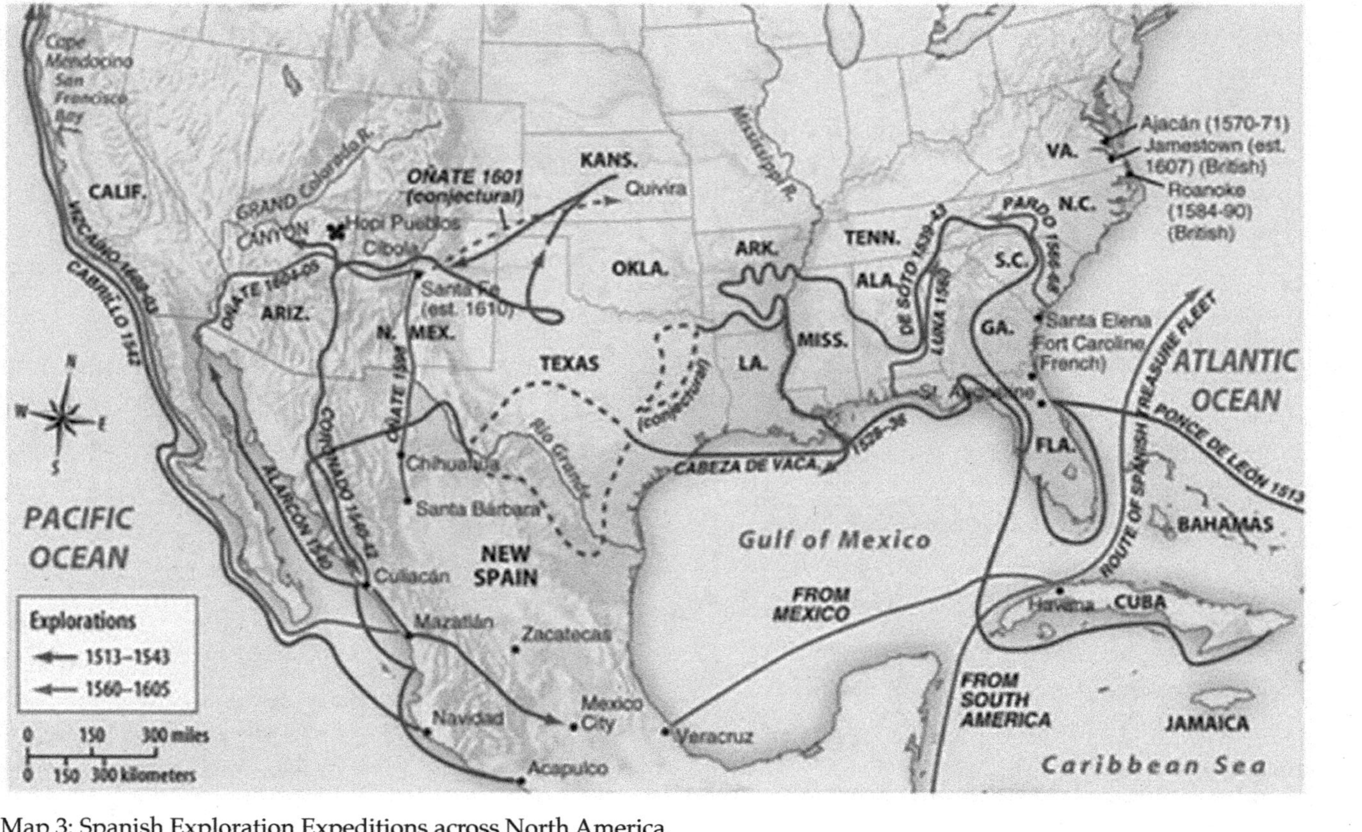

Map 3: Spanish Exploration Expeditions across North America.

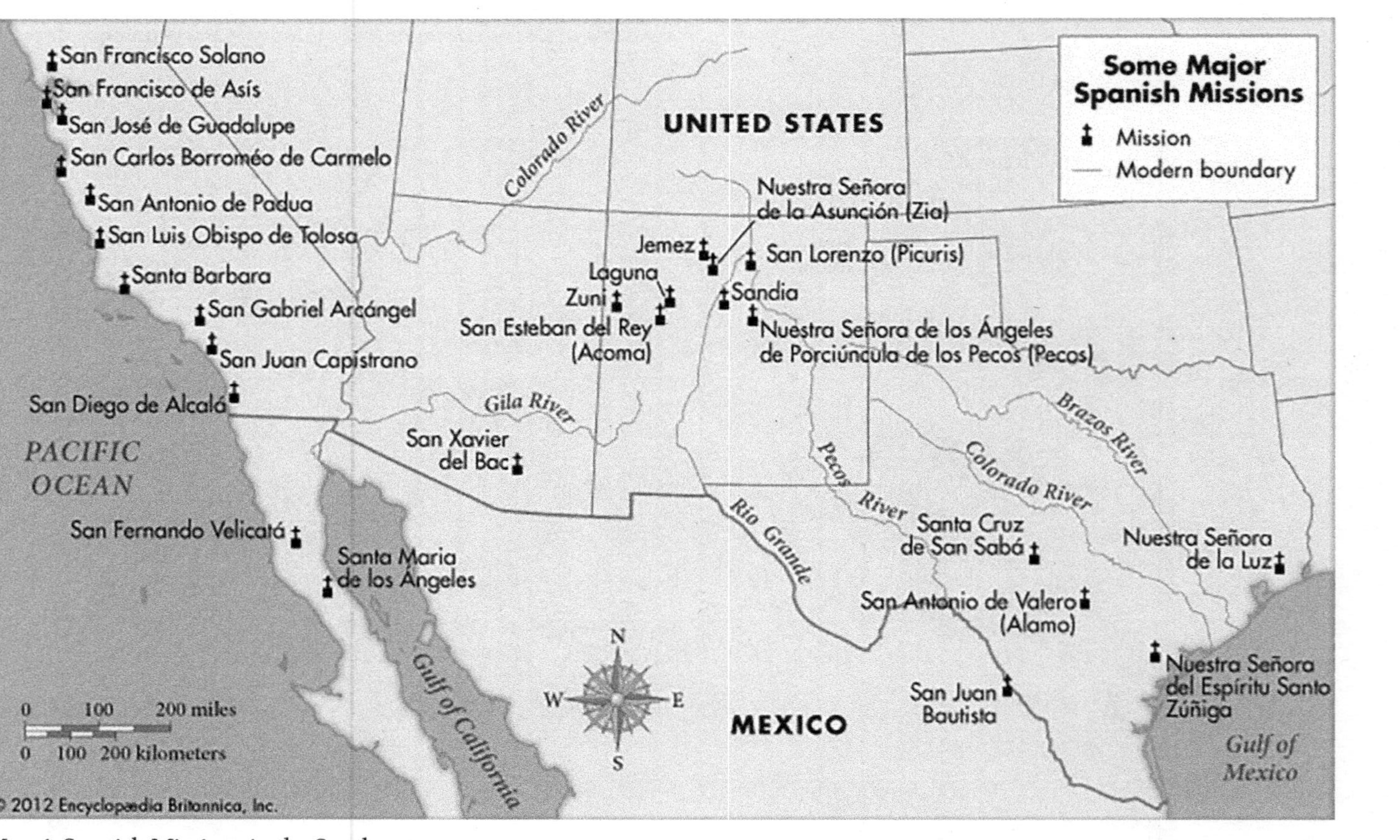

Map 4: Spanish Missions in the Southwest.

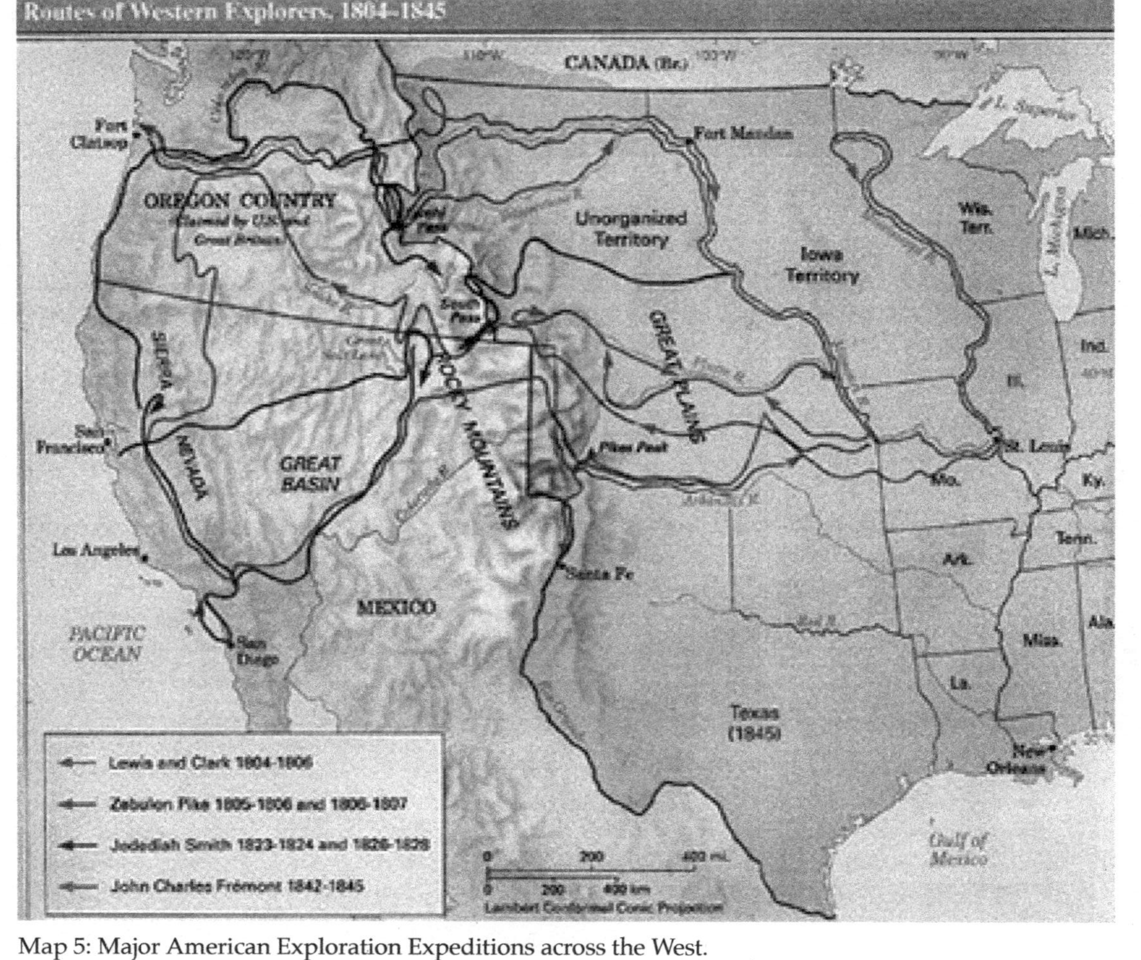

Map 5: Major American Exploration Expeditions across the West.

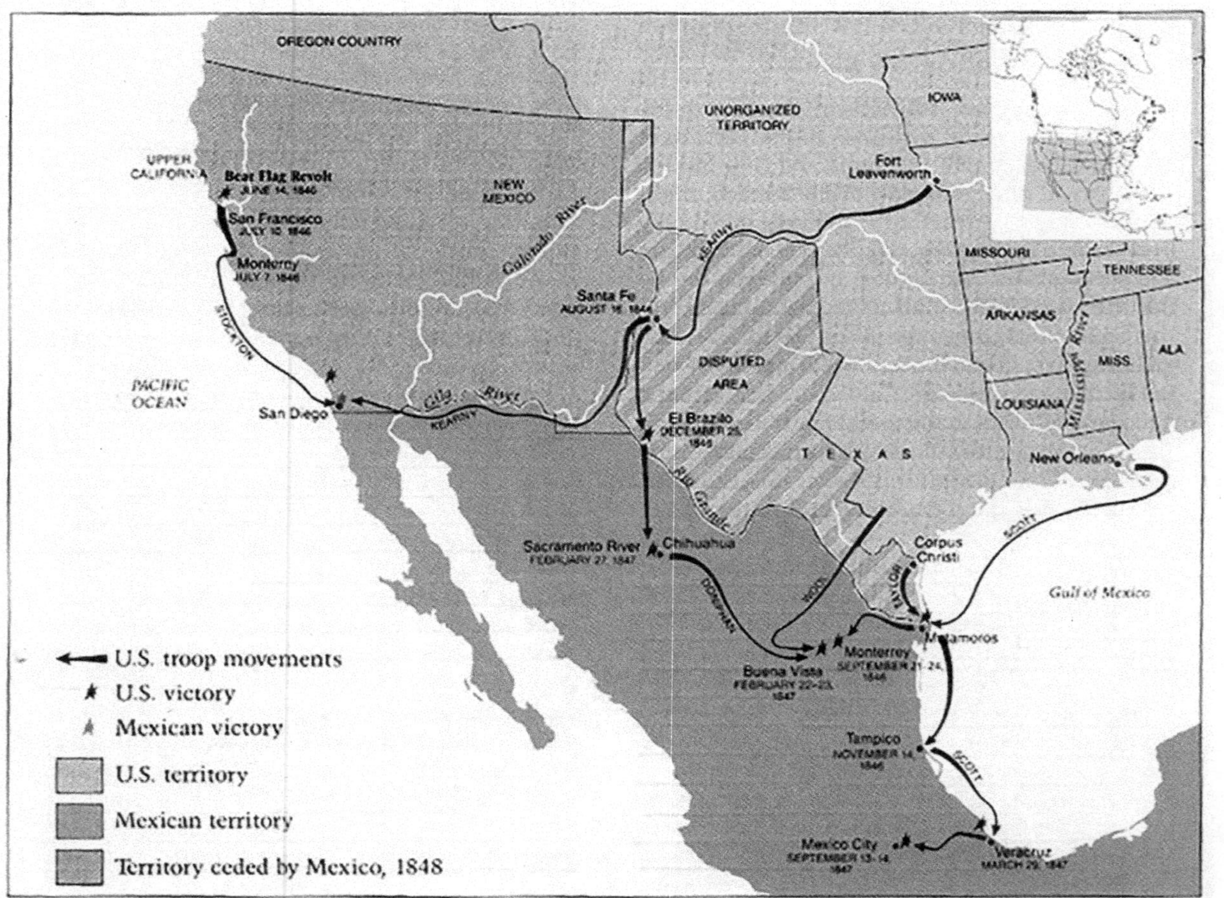

Map 6: The Mexican-American War.

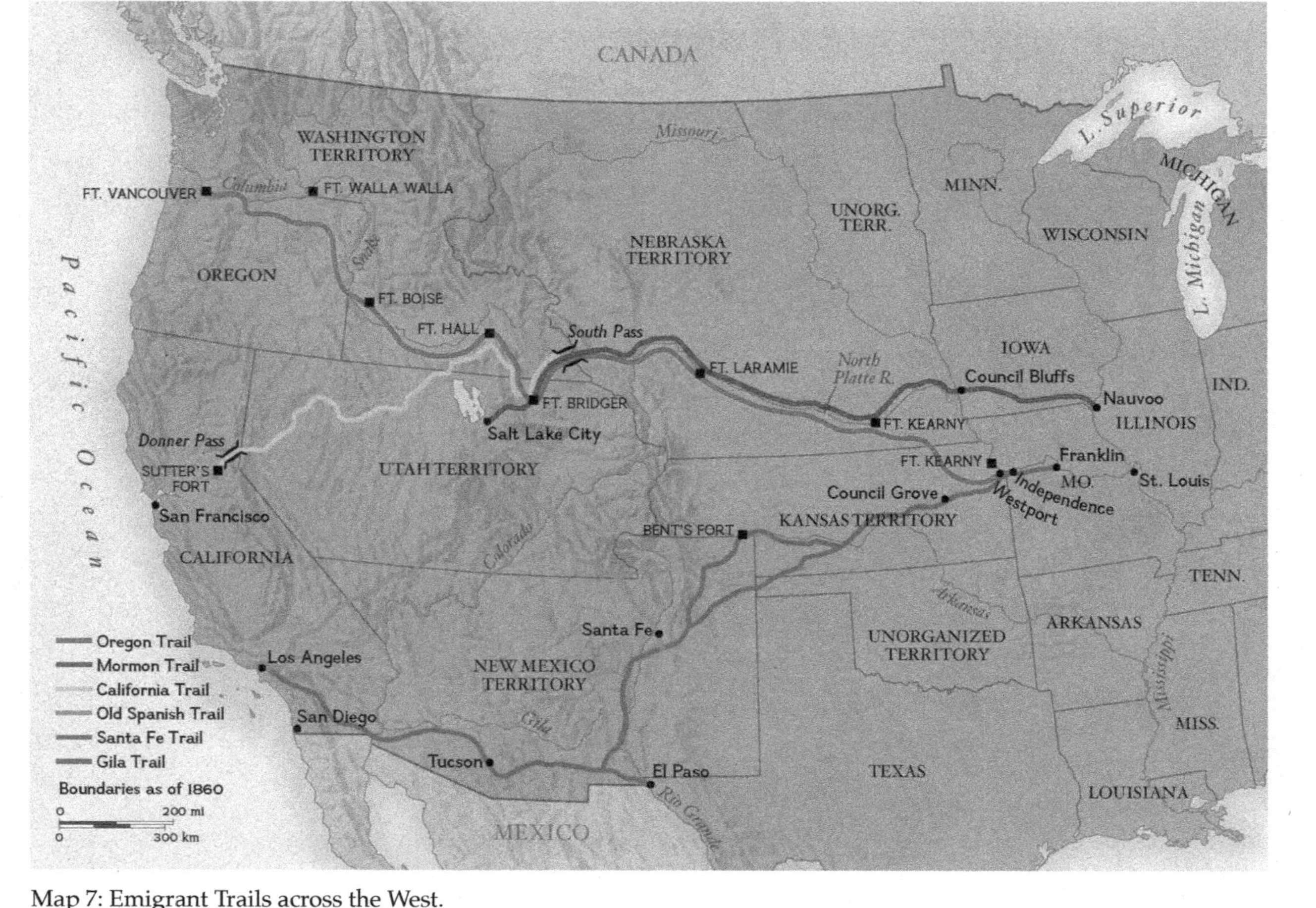

Map 7: Emigrant Trails across the West.

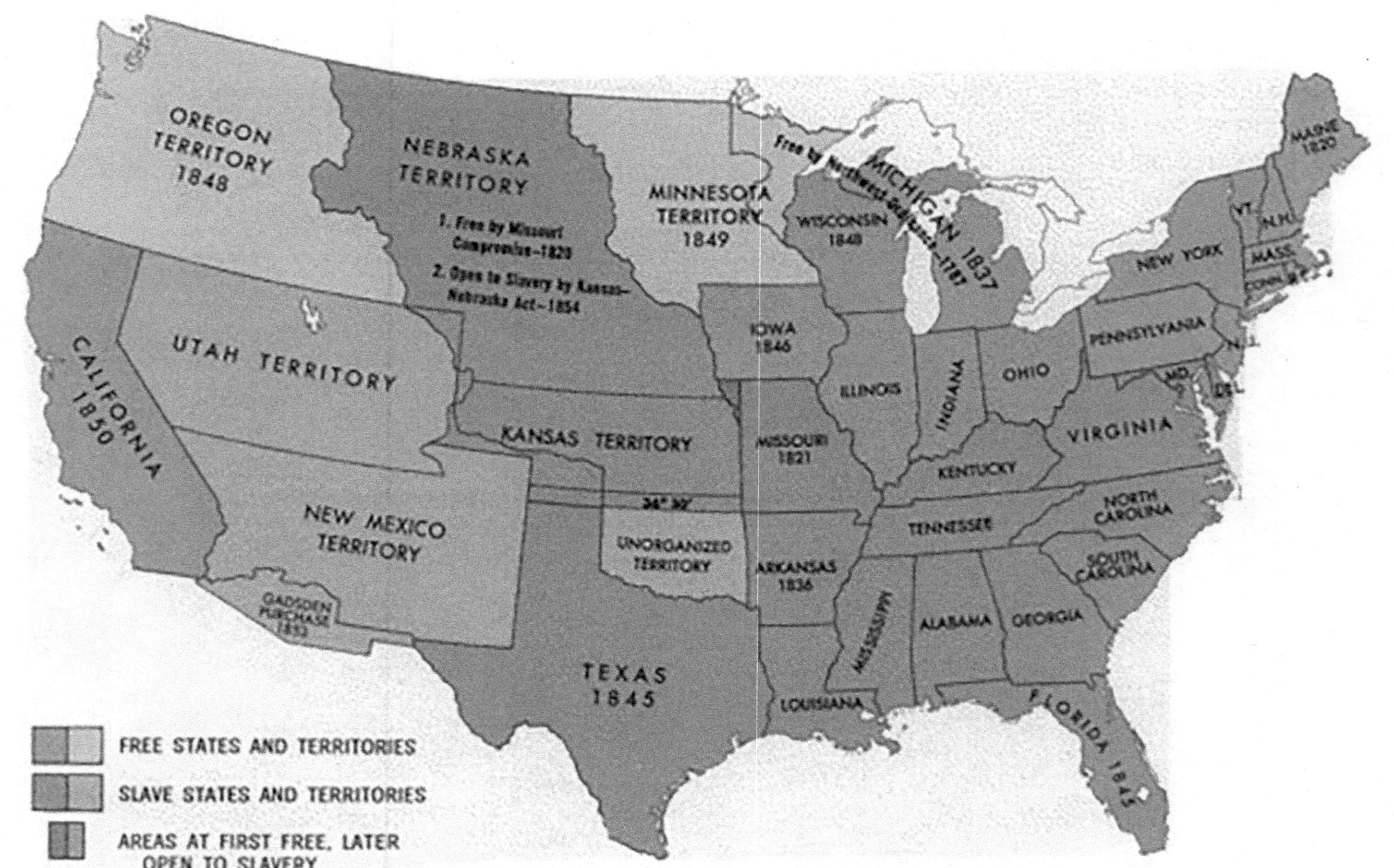

Map 8: Western Territories and States 1860.

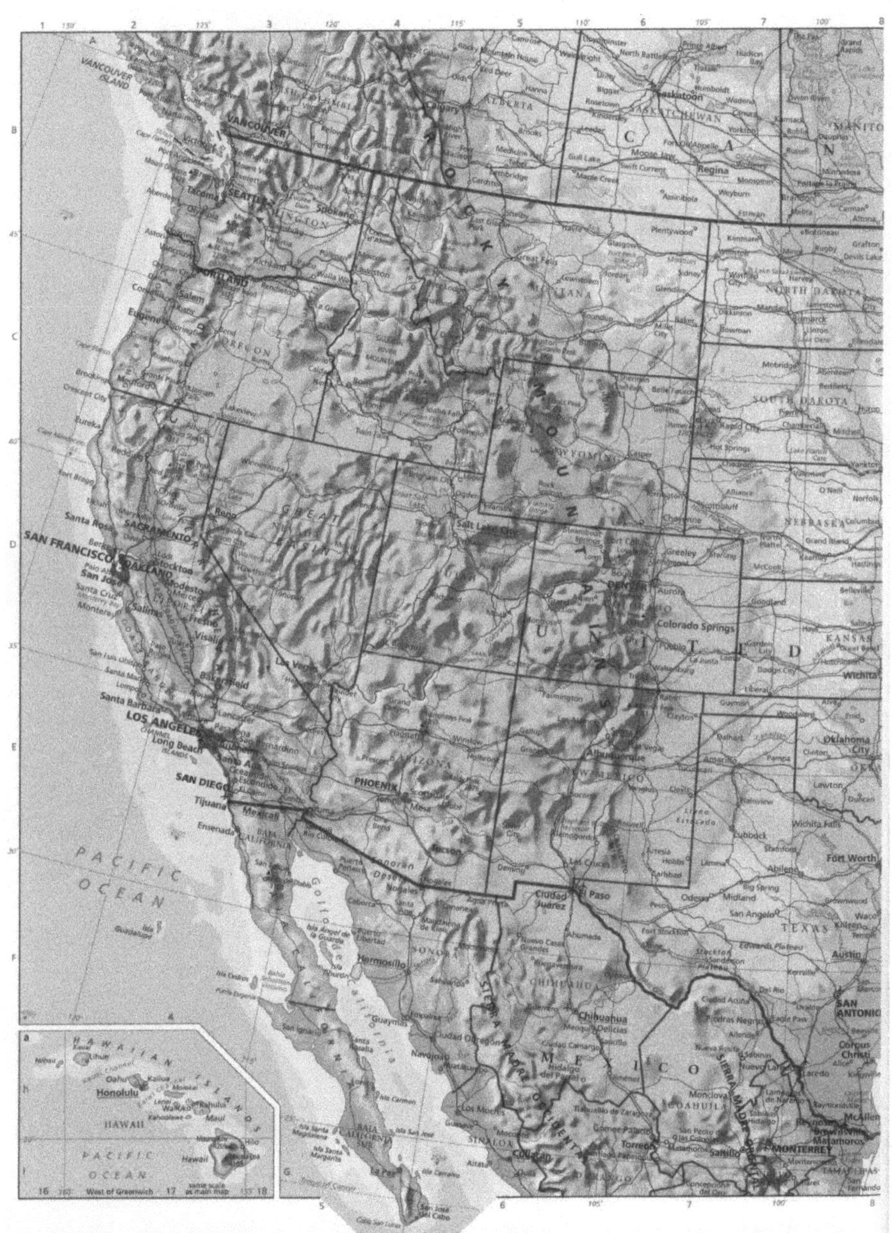

Map 9: The Contemporary West.

PART I: THE AMERICAN WEST BEFORE 1804

Chapter 1

REGIONS AND FIRST PEOPLES

> "No other section could compare with the Crow country, especially when it was untouched by white men. Its wealth in all kinds of game, grass, roots, and berries made enemies for the Crows, who, often outnumbered, were obliged continually to defend it against surrounding tribes." (Plenty Coups)

> "We did not think of the great open plains, the beautiful rolling hills, and the winding streams with tangled growth as 'wild.' Only to the white men was nature a 'wilderness' and . . . the land 'infested' with 'wild' animals and 'savage' peoples." (Chief Luther Standing Bear)

We will never know when the first people reached the Western Hemisphere.[1] People who hunt and gather for a living are light on the land and leave little behind beyond bones—those of the animals they killed and themselves—and those rarely last long. Stone weapons, tools, and ornaments do endure but finding them gets harder the older they are because nature has had more time to bury them. Until recently, most anthropologists believed the first groups arrived around 13,000 years ago during the last ice age when ocean levels lowered, opening a land bridge over the Bering Strait between Siberia and Alaska and then an ice-free corridor down North America's great plains. That may be when most made the slow journey following migrating animal herds but evidence mounts of earlier crossings. Mitochondrial DNA analysis of contemporary Indians confirms their Siberian origins with four groups accounting for 96.9 percent. One analysis estimates the original group immigrated 22,414 to 29,545 years ago. Yet radiocarbon dates at campsites in Yukon, New Mexico, and Monte Verde, Chile are respectively 40,000, 36,000, and 32,000 years old. A human site called Chukotka in northeastern Siberia dates to 35,000 years ago. If the Bering Strait was then submerged, they could only have canoed over it. After all, people reached Australia by boat 50,000 years ago. The linguistic diversity among indigenous peoples indicates that they have lived in the Western Hemisphere as long as Australia's aborigines.[2]

Just as debated is how many people inhabited North America and the Western Hemisphere when Columbus first visited in 1492. Estimates vary with the methodologies. Conservative figures include J.M. Mooney's 1,115,000 in North America and A.L. Kroeber's 900,000 in North America of 8,400,000 in the entire Western Hemisphere. William Devevan conceived 54 million with 4 million in North America where they spoke around 2,200 languages, with 200 north of Mexico, and thousands of dialects.[3]

Anthropologists divide Indians into four prehistoric eras based on their development levels with tools and weapons, the Paleolithic from 18,000 to 8000 BCE, Archaic from 8000 BCE to 1000 BCE, Formative from 1000 BCE to 300 CE, and Classic from 300 to 1500. For instance, during the Paleolithic era, two stone spearheads found in New Mexico, Clovis and Folsom, define separate sub-eras when Indians hunted mastodons, mammoths, long-horned bison, and sixty other giant beasts to extinction. They propelled their spears with an atlatl or wooden handle that increased its velocity and killing power. One hunting technique was stampeding a herd over a cliff. During the Archaic era, some groups created goods that combined practical and aesthetic needs like pottery with elaborate designs, 5,000-year-old copper jewelry from the Lake Superior region, 3,000-year-old decoy ducks woven from reeds from Utah, and necklaces of small, pierced round pieces of clam shells.

North America's 4 million or so inhabitants in 1492 split roughly equal east and west of the Mississippi River. They organized themselves into bands of clans or extended families. The availability of food determined where and how they lived, and their numbers. Populations expand with the diversity and stability of the food they eat. With steady food sources people lived in clusters of bands and moved only after they exhausted that area's arable soil, firewood, and game. Where food was meager, people lived in small nomadic groups that hunted and gathered their way across regions. The scarcer the food, the fewer a group's members and the further they had to journey searching for it. Food along the Pacific coast was abundant enough for people to live in the same place for generations. Virtually all bands domesticated dogs, which they often ate. Southwest bands domesticated turkeys.

Horticulturalists usually had more people than hunters and gatherers. Pueblo Indians in the Southwest and peoples from the Mississippi River valley east to the Atlantic coast cultivated crops.

Farming was usually women's work. They nurtured the three sisters—beans, squash, and corn—in the same mound as the corn served as a trellis for the beans and the broad leaves of the spreading squash retained moisture. Those crops originated in central Mexico around the time of the Olmec civilization from 1800 to 1000 BCE.

Whether a band was settled or nomadic, it usually had a headman or chief and council of elders that made vital decisions like resolving disputes among the people, allying with or warring against others, and going elsewhere if food dwindled. Some bands had separate peace and war chiefs. A chief usually acquired that status because others recognized his superior traits of wisdom, eloquence, courage, and generosity. A chief and his council reached decisions after long debates that forged a consensus that everyone more or less backed. Bands affiliated by language, religion, customs, intermarriage, and alliance can be considered tribes. A tribe's bands often gathered once a year when food was most abundant for ceremonies, trade, and intermarriage. Bands decimated by disease or war might become one.

Each band had an ethical system of right and wrong behavior. Hospitality was a core value. One gained status not by miserly amassing wealth but by generously giving it away. Parents guided their children's behavior with affection, moral stories, and encouragement. Children born out of wedlock were loved, not ostracized. Adolescent boys underwent a transition to manhood that involved instruction, praying, and fasting in a vision quest for one's animal spirit protector and guide. Adolescent girls had their own ceremonies for becoming women. For those who committed crimes, no formal system of punishments like fines, incarceration, whippings, or execution existed. Those who broke the rules might suffer ridicule for minor offenses, pressure to compensate victims for thefts, and, for murder, pay enormous amounts of gifts to the victims' family followed by banishment.

Taboos were few but powerful. Most tribes forbade incest. Many tribes prevented direct communication between mothers-in-law and sons-in-law, and fathers-in-law and daughters-in-law. Indians believed that menstruating women exuded negative power. During her period, a woman was forbidden to handle a man's weapons or spiritual objects, and had to isolate herself usually for four days with other menstruating women in a small lodge beyond the village.

A man who fancied a woman for marriage asked her father for her hand and then paid the price in gifts that he asked. Warfare and hunting accidents made women more numerous than men, so polygamy was a necessity. Wealthy men purchased as many wives as they could afford for their labor and sex, and their extra hands swelled his wealth. Many preferred to wed sisters because they usually got along much better than strangers. Most tribes viewed sexuality as naturally expressed not suppressed, and pre-marital sex was common. Divorce was easy, a simple declaration followed by the husband or wife moving elsewhere. Yet some tribes practiced a double standard for infidelity. A Comanche or Apache husband often cut off the nose of an unfaithful wife before banishing her. Most tribes understood and tolerated that some people were attracted to the same sex or wanted to change their gender. Males with female spirits were allowed to dress and behave like woman, a practice many tribes called Berdache.

One's identity was rooted in one's family and extended clan. Bands had societies or fraternities and sororities that conferred special identities along with duties for members and often had a spirit animal that protected them. Men and women had separate sweat lodges where they purified themselves and socialized. Storytellers entertained and informed listeners. Each tribe had an origin myth and annual celebrations for the changing seasons or good luck in war, hunting, and crops during which people drummed, danced, and sang. Peoples took pride in their refined crafts like baskets, pottery, porcupine quill or bead ornaments, painted designs on bison robes, war shields, and cliffs, petroglyphs on boulders, or carved red stone tobacco pipes.

War was common in most regions. Bands fought each other for resources, vengeance, and glory. Killings had to be avenged, which led to more killings. Enemies rarely sought to conquer or exterminate each other. Instead, young men gained status and wealth through raids that brought back scalps, loot, and captives while, ideally, suffering no losses. Most bands had warrior societies each with its own ceremonial lodge. Although every able-bodied man was expected to defend his village, only volunteers comprised raiding parties. A war chief or charismatic ambitious warrior might literally drum up recruits for a raid by drumming, chanting, and exhorting. On a raid, a member or even the leader might turn back if he experienced a bad omen that foretold defeat. After furtively approaching the enemy, a leader would whisper his plan of theft, charge, or ambush and encourage but not command his followers to execute it. At times, an overambitious warrior might ruin a plan by prematurely screaming a war cry and firing or charging. Captive women and children were integrated into the band while captive men were usually tortured to death but sometimes accepted as members after a harsh initiation period.

Indians saw themselves as part of the web of life, not detached and superior to it. Visible and invisible beings populated the earth. The interrelated unity of all living and non-living things was spiritual.

People had kinships with fellow living species and with spiritual entities. They beseeched spirits to lend them power for success in war, hunting, health, and courtship. Humans inhabited land but did not own it. Instead, they shared land with each other and all other species. Those who cultivated crops did so communally, deeply grateful as they borrowed arable patches of earth from Creator and local spirits. They spiritually embraced the animals that sustained them. They prayed for deer, bison, and other game to come and sacrifice themselves then thanked them after taking their lives. "Trickster" spirits could cause illness and even death, and had to be pacified. A prayer and a pinch of cornmeal or tobacco could entice a good spirit and appease a bad one. Shamans mingled the roles of priests, psychologists, and doctors. They acted as mediums between the spirit world and seekers, interpreted dreams and unusual phenomena, healed the sick and wounded, and conducted ceremonies for individuals, families, and the village.

Everyone had a spirit guide for protection. In most bands, young teenage boys went on vision quests where they isolated themselves usually on some distant height and prayed, mediated, and fasted until their spirit guide revealed itself. Men and women accumulated medicine bundles of sacred items that protected them. In many bands, a baby's umbilical cord was preserved in a beaded or quilled sack often shaped like a turtle and hung around one's neck to preserve one's link with one's mother and all other ancestors. Parents had a shaman conduct a naming ceremony for their child from days to months after its birth, depending on the band.

Indians believed that one's soul survived death. Ceremonies for the dead encouraged souls not to linger as ghosts but to journey to a remote spiritual realm. Most tribes buried their dead. Plains tribes wrapped their dead in buffalo robes and placed them on high wooden scaffolds or upper branches of cottonwood trees where wolves and bears could not reach them. Indians often mutilated their dead enemies because they believed that denied their souls heaven.

The American West is a region of regions, each with its distinct climate, landscapes, and natural challenges and opportunities for the peoples who lived there. In adapting to life in a region, those tribes inevitably shared characteristics distinct from tribes in other regions.

***

The Southwest is a dry region with vast low-lying deserts broken by soaring mountain ranges, escarpments, and mesas. The Sonoran and Chihuahuan deserts extend from Mexico north into Arizona and

New Mexico, respectively. An array of cacti dot the deserts with the Sonora's many-armed Saguaro the most spectacular, while juniper and pinon pines spread across higher elevations, and ponderosa pines and Douglas firs forest mountainsides from 7,000 to 10,000 feet. Only a few constant rivers flow through the region, notably the Colorado River that meanders through the Grand Canyon in northern Arizona then emerges to head south to the Gulf of Baja; the Rio Grande from north to south from Colorado's San Luis valley through central New Mexico before curling southeast to divide Texas from Mexico; and the Salt and Gila Rivers headwatered in southern New Mexico's mountains and flowing west before joining, then a hundred miles later mingling with the Colorado River. Wildlife is as relatively sparse as the water. Mountain lions and once wolves and jaguars roamed the deserts and mountains stalking big horn sheep, elk, mule deer, and javelins. A dozen types of rattlesnakes lurk across the region along with Gila monsters, colorful plump beady poisonous lizards. Scorpions and tarantulas scuttle across the earth during the night.

A series of distinct peoples inhabited the Southwest.[4] The earliest identified were two hunter-gather cultures, the Clovis people from 13,000 to 11,000 years ago followed by the Folsom people from 9,500 to 8,000 years ago, each named after the designs for their spear and arrow heads. Three sophisticated, populous, and sedentary cultures emerged later, Hohokam mostly in villages in the lower Gila and Salt River valleys in southern Arizona from 3500 to 1500 BCE; hunter-gatherer Mogollon in the upper Gila and Salt River valleys and the lower Rio Grande from 200 CE to 1450; and Anasazi in northern Arizona and New Mexico, southern Utah, and southwest Colorado from 900 to 1300. All three produced tightly woven baskets of yucca with intricate designs. Hohokam borrowed crops and irrigation, pottery techniques, building styles, temple platforms, and ball courts and rubber balls from central Mexican civilizations. They occupied Snaketown from 400 BCE to 1000 CE. Mogollon lived in pit houses with upright logs that held walls and roofs made of interwoven sticks. The Mimbres tribe of Mogollon produced slender pottery with intricate black and white paintings of animals, people, and mythical creatures. Anazasi mostly lived in villages in alcoves on cliffs reached by ladders that could be raised at night or when enemies approached. They nurtured crops in fields along the stream below. Anazasi pottery had black on white designs. Chaco Canyon was the most sophisticated Anazasi center with its complex of villages built from tightly fitted stones. Of them, Pueblo Bonita was the most elaborate with a crescent of 660 rooms where a thousand people lived around several plazas and two grand kivas. Elsewhere one of the largest villages was Cliff Palace at Mesa Verde with 200 rooms and 22 kivas. A drought from 1276 to 1299 destroyed the Anazasi and Mogollon civilizations and the survivors fled elsewhere.

Pueblo or "village" peoples descended from remnants of Anasazi and Mogollon peoples forced to migrate during that devastating drought. Most Pueblos lived in clusters of villages sharing the same language in the upper Rio Grande valley that included the Tanoan language group with the Tewa, Tiwa, Towa, and Piro languages, and the Keres language. For instance, the widely separated Taos, Picuris, Sandia, and Isela Pueblos speak Tiwa dialects. Three Pueblo peoples lived a hundred or so miles west of the Rio Grande. The Keresan-speaking village of Acoma was atop a steep mesa. The Zuni, with their unique language, had several villages 50 or so miles west of Acoma. The Hopi, who speak an Uto-Aztecan dialect, lived in villages atop three mesas within sight of each other 75 or so miles northwest of Zuni.

Pueblos enjoyed diverse and stable sources of food including irrigated crops like corn, beans, squash, and pumpkins, domesticated animals like turkeys and dogs, and game like rabbits and deer. They grew cotton to weave into clothing. Each Pueblo had its own styles of pottery and baskets with intricate designs. Socially Tiwa, Tewa, and Towa speakers are patrilineal while Hopi, Zuni, and Keres speakers are matrilineal; whoever is dominant owns the homes, fields, furnishings, tools, fetish bundles, and katsina effigies, and provides the key lineage for children. All Pueblos freely enjoyed sexuality. Many Pueblos buried umbilical cords of baby girls inside their homes beneath the grinding stone and that of boy babies outside in cornfields.

Every Pueblo is composed of often overlapping spiritual, kinship, healing, and war groups. Each group meets in a round or square stone kiva with some above and some below ground but all with a roof entrance and a ladder down below to the floor with a shipapu or hole symbolizing the earth's navel and a sacred bundle of fetishes. For instance, the Zuni have six kivas each associated with a different direction. Each season has ceremonies that seek harmony with and assistance from various gods. The most powerful gods are Sun Father and Earth Mother, and their offspring the Twin War Gods Elder Brother and Younger Brother who often fight or merge with each other. Women worshiped Corn Mothers as fertility goddesses for their own wombs and their crop fields. Katsina are gods that inhabit springs, mountains, canyons, clouds, lakes, thunderstorms, and ancient trees that Pueblos impersonate during ceremonial dances and represent with dolls that they placate with prayers and cornmeal sprinkles. Four is a sacred number for the Pueblo as for many other peoples. Most Pueblos believe there are four heavens and four undergrounds just like there are four directions, and have similar origin stories of forming below the earth and eventually climbing onto the surface.

Pueblos worship snakes among the gods because of their believed power to bring rain, their dual masculine and feminine nature, their living on and below the earth's surface, and their emulation of lightning as they slither in quick zigzags. Hopi have the most spectacular ceremony involving snakes. Each year for nine days, their rain inducing ceremony involves men capturing snakes in the desert, gripping them gently between their teeth, and bringing them to their kivas where they are ritually bathed. On the eighth day, there is a simulated marriage between a Snake Virgin Girl and a Snake Hero Boy. Antelope Society men stomp dance in the plaza to attract the gods. On the ninth day each kiva's members brings its snakes in their mouths to the central plaza, dance with them, then at night take them back to the desert and release them. Hopefully, the rains soon arrive to soak the crops and bring a bountiful harvest.

The Pueblo were not the Southwest's only historic horticulturalists. The Papago, Pima, and Yavapai lived along or near the Salt and Gila Rivers in southern Arizona, and the Havasupai, Walapai, Mojave, and Yuma lived along the Colorado River below the Grand Canyon. As for language, Piman speakers included the Pima and Papago, and Yuman speakers, the Yuman, Mohave, Havasupai, and Yavapai. Mohave were among the few tribes that ceremonially cremated their dead. Havasupai were renowned for the array of crops they cultivated like corn, beans, squash, tobacco, melons, and sunflowers supplemented by gathered fruits like mescal, cactus, yucca, and honey. Of these tribes, Pima created the most intricate baskets.

During the sixteenth century, aggressive nomadic Athapascan-speaking bands invaded the Southwest from the north and increasingly raided the Pueblo. Although popularly associated with the desert, most Apache are mountain people.[5] They eventually lived in six clusters of bands, Jicarilla in northern New Mexico's mountains, Mescalero in New Mexico's southeastern mountains, Chiricahua in southern New Mexico's Jemez Mountains, Western Apache in Arizona's Mogollon Mountains, and only the Kiowa Apache and Lipan flatland peoples respectively on the upper Arkansas River's high plains and on the Staked Plains. From their mountain strongholds Apache raided the Pueblo, Spanish, and later Americans, then withdrew with their loot and captives, confident that their enemies would not find them. Eventually the United States Army defeated each band, but usually only after using allied Apache warriors as scouts. Apache inhabited wickiups or domes of woven branches and reeds. Of their many gods, Ussen the Life Giver is most vital because his spirit pervades the world but Apaches seek power through rituals from a pantheon of Mountain Spirits or Gahan split among four groups for each direction. Annual celebrations included the Wheel Dance, Dance for the Sick, Night Dance, Devil's Dance, Protection from Ghosts Dance, Thank-Offering Dance, Rain Dance, and Death of Whistling Wind Dance, and as needed Dance for a Sick Woman and Dance for a Sick Child.

The Navajo, or Dine as they call themselves, settled in the region around the Hopi in northeastern Arizona where they adopted sheep raising, blanket weaving, and silver jewelry making from the Spanish. Like most Pueblo bands, the Navajo's origin story involves spirits guiding them up through a series of worlds beneath the earth to the surface where they finally flourished. Traditional Navajo live in six or eight sided log hogans and are matrilineal. Their shamans compose paintings on the earth of different colored sands to induce the gods, cure the sick, and exorcise bad spirits in at least fifty-eight distinct ceremonies. When a ceremony is over, shamans destroy the sand painting and deposit the remnants on the hogan's north side. The most elaborate healing ceremony is the nine-day Nightway with singing daily, sand paintings on each of the last four days, and dances where people represent different gods.

***

The Great Plains are the vast, mostly treeless region from central Texas to northern Montana east of the Rocky Mountains and west of the greater Mississippi Valley woodlands.[6] Rainfall diminishes and ground rises as one journeys west across the region with the earth a mile above sea level at Denver. Tall grass prairies give way to short grass plains. The hundredth meridian splits the Great Plains geographically and climatically with fewer than twenty inches of rain west of that line. Cottonwoods once grew thick in river valleys like the Missouri, Arkansas, and Red and their many tributaries, while grazing animals like pronghorn antelope, mule deer, elk, and thirty million bison flourished.

Tall grass prairie tribes included from north to south Cree, Ojibwe (Chippewa), Dakota Sioux, Ponca, Omaha, Oto, Kansa, Iowa, Missouri, Osage, Wichita, Quapaw, Caddo, and Tonkawa. Plains supported two different lifestyles. Sedentary tribes lived in large earth lodges with log frames in palisaded villages beside rivers, cultivated crops, and had annual bison hunts. Those tribes included the Mandan and Hidatsa on the upper Missouri River, the Arikara on the middle Missouri River, and the Pawnee in three villages along the Platte River. Nomadic tribes inhabited the high western plains, lived off bison, and lived in bison-skin tipis.[7] They included from north to south the Blackfeet, Gros Ventres (Atsina), Assiniboine, Crow, Lakota, Nakota, Cheyenne, Arapaho, Kiowa, and Comanche. Linguistically plains Indians were diverse with seven languages: "Siouan by the Crows, Dakota, Iowa, Kansa, Mandan, Missouri, Omaha, Osage, and Oto; Algonkian by the Arapaho, Blackfeet, Cheyenne, and Gros Ventre; Caddoan by the Arikara, Pawnee and Wichita; Kiowan by the Kiowa; Shoshonean by the Bannock, Comanche, and Shoshoni; and Athapaskan and Shahaptian by smaller tribal units."[8]

Relatively few people lived on the high plains before they obtained horses from the Spanish.[9] Until then bands used dogs to drag their few possessions on travois or crossed poles with a skin platform. They tried to follow bison herds and kill as many as they could. They used virtually every part of a bison for something: meat and offal for food; hides for clothing, moccasins, blankets, tipi covers, shields, drum heads, painting canvases, parfleche containers, and rawhide ropes; hoofs melted for glue; scrotums filled with pebbles for rattles; tails for whisks and whips; shoulder bones for shovels and saddle frames; bound ribs for sleds; small bones for knife and awl handles; wool for stuffing; stomachs for cooking pots and water containers; sinew for bowstrings and thread; dried dung to fuel fires; and skulls for spiritual symbols. It took six to twenty hides sewn together to make a tipi cover; thin long lodgepole pines stripped of bark and branches provided frames. Processing skins was long, hard women's work. A woman stretched the hide, staked the edges, scrapped off the flesh, then rubbed it with a mix of brains and ashes to soften it. Tipis usually faced east toward the rising sun and away from the prevailing winds, and were set in a protective circle with each warrior's best horse staked outside his lodge.

The most efficient bison-hunting tactic was stampeding a herd off a cliff. A band could spend weeks carving meat and peeling robes from the slaughtered animals. Another tactic was for men dressed in wolf skins and with bows and arrows to creep close to a herd and shoot bison, although at best they could usually only kill a few before the herd ran off. A third tactic was the surround, described by Weasel Foot, a Blackfoot: "After swift-running men located a herd of buffalo, the chief would tell the women to get their . . . travois. Men and women would go out together, and approach the herd from downwind so the animals would not get their scent and run off. The women were told to place their travois upright in the earth . . . The travois were spaced so that they could be tied together, forming a semicircular fence. Women and dogs hid behind them while two fast running men circled the herd . . . and drove them toward the travois fence. Other men took up their positions along the side of the route and closed in as the buffalo neared the enclosure. Barking dogs and shouting women kept the buffalo [back]. The men rushed in and killed the buffalo with arrows and lances."[10] All three methods were dangerous as bulls were as likely to charge as flee approaching hunters.

Most northern plains tribes held an annual Sun Dance with varying rituals. Sioux, Crow, and Hidatsa Sun Dances included self-torture while Arapaho, Kiowa, Ute, and Shoshone simply meditated and fasted. A Sun Dance usually unfolded over twelve days of celebration for all people and included a Buffalo Dance to draw them near and the last four Holy Days centered around those men who sought enhanced spiritual power. For that power, supplicants fasted, sang, drummed, blew eagle bone whistles, and danced around a sacred cottonwood tree to which they were attached by thongs and a skewer through their flesh. They could rest for brief periods in a nearby Sacred Lodge. As each received a powerful vision, he tore his body from his skewers.

Horses revolutionized life for nomadic plains Indians. Now a band could drag or pack far more goods, keep up with bison herds, and atop horses, men could race after bison and kill them with spears or arrows. Band populations swelled with the food, shelter, clothing, and other goods that dead bison provided. Francisco de Coronado and his men rode the first horses onto the plains in 1542 but the tribes they encountered got few strays and probably ate rather than tried to ride them. After Juan de Onate's expedition conquered the Rio Grande valley in 1598, the Pueblo peoples learned how to care for and ride horses. They got thousands of horses during their 1680 revolt. Neighboring tribes like the Apache, Ute, Kiowa, and Comanche stole or traded horses from the Pueblo. Gradually horses spread among the plains tribes by theft or trade and the number of horses steadily swelled. By the mid-eighteenth century, the nomadic tribes were all mounted.

Horses also revolutionized warfare as raiders journeyed quicker and further against their enemies.[11] Indeed, horses became war's primary object. The more horses a warrior stole, the greater his wealth and prestige. After the horse, the gun revolutionized hunting and warfare on the plains. The tribes got most of their muskets and munitions in exchange for furs from the French before 1763, and the British and

Americans thereafter. As in other regions, the purpose of war was not to exterminate or rout an enemy tribe, but to take as many of its horses, women, children, and other wealth as possible while not losing a single man. A warrior gained greater status by striking than killing an enemy warrior. Most men had a coup stick, a long pole with a curled end on which hung an eagle feather for each of his feats along with any scalps he had taken. For special occasions including battle, they wore headdresses with an eagle feather for each feat. From early adolescence boys were subjected to severe physical, mental, and spiritual training, became adept at wielding weapons, were superb horsemen, and could survive in the harshest weather and terrain. As in other regions, each tribe had its allies and enemies. Tribes that shared a common language often allied with each other like Cheyenne and Arapaho, Pawnee and Arikara, and Crow and Hidatsa. The adage "the enemy of my enemy is my friend" also encouraged some alliances. For instance, after warring against the Arapaho and Cheyenne for generations, the Sioux allied with them against their common enemy, the Americans.

Plenty Coups, a Crow warrior, lyrically extoled his homeland and the dilemma of living there: "The country belonging to the Crow was not only beautiful, but it was the very heart of the buffalo range of the Northwest. It embraced endless plains, high mountains, and great rivers, fed by streams clear as crystal. No other section could compare with the Crow country, especially when it was untouched by white men. Its wealth in all kinds of game, grass, roots, and berries made enemies for the Crows, who, often outnumbered, were obliged continually to defend it against surrounding tribes." He explained what finally devastated his tribe and others across the region: "The buffalo was everything to us. When it went away, the hearts of my people fell to the ground, and they could not lift them up again."[12]

The Sioux were the most powerful tribe on the central northern plains from around 1775 to 1890.[13] They were relative newcomers to the region, driven from the western woodlands in the eighteenth century by the Cree, Assiniboine, and Ojibwe with more guns. The westernmost Sioux bands, the Lakota, after acquiring guns and horses expelled the Cheyenne and Kiowas from the region around the Black Hills, believed to be sacred by all the tribes.

The word Sioux was actually a derogatory Ojibwe word that meant "Little Snakes." The Sioux considered themselves members of either the Lakota (Teton), Nakota (Yankton), or Dakota (Santee) groups of bands distinguished by dialects. The Lakota's Seven Council Fires included the Oglala, Hunkpapa, Sichangu (Brulés), Miniconjou, Oohenonpas (Two Kettle), Shihasapas (Black Feet), and Itazipchos

(Sans Arc), and lived in the high western plains with the Black Hills central. The Nakota included the Yankton and Yanktonai who lived between the Missouri and the James Rivers. The Dakota lived along the Minnesota River where they raised crops. The Lakota annually met in mid-summer for a council and Sun Dance but dispersed in different directions following buffalo herds the rest of the year.

Sioux had two types of societies, police or Akicitas of young war party veterans that kept order for dances and bison hunts, and civil or Nacas of chiefs who decided where to go and when to war. Every man was expected to practice the Four Virtues, bravery, fortitude, generosity, and wisdom. They had a very sophisticated cosmology. Wakan Tanka was the universal God composed of a four-level hierarchy of four gods, first the Supreme Gods including Chief God, Great Spirit, Creator, and Executive; Associate Supreme Spirits including Sun, Moon, Wind, Earth, and Sky; Kindred Gods including Buffalo, Bear, Whirlwind, and Four Directions; and Gods-like including Spirit, Ghost, Spirit-like, and Potency. Countless other spirits inhabited all living and nonliving entities. Many spirits were evil with Cyclone their chief, and lesser demons like Trickster, Witch, and Double-Faced Woman. The origins of life including humans came from the struggle between good and evil gods, called Controllers. Although good usually prevailed, evil could erupt at any time. Wakan Tanka sent Beautiful Woman to the Sioux to teach them, and White Buffalo Woman to women to protect and encourage them. Everyone had his or her own varying spiritual power or sicun. People sought favors from good gods and relief from bad gods through prayers, purifications, and sacrifices.

Comanche dominated the southern plains from around 1750 to 1874.[14] Their language was from the Uto-Aztecan family and they, like many tribes, called themselves the People (Nermernuh). Like the Sioux, they were relative newcomers. In the late seventeenth century, they split from Shoshonean peoples in the transmontane region and emigrated in thirteen bands to hunt bison between the Arkansas River, Staked Plains, Balcones Plateau, and Cross Timbers. Within a century they consolidated into three broad divisions from north to south—Yamparikas, Jupes, and Kotsotekas—each with several bands. Neither the tribe nor the divisions had a central council and bands rarely camped let alone fought together. Each band had from a hundred to several hundred warriors and a war chief, trail chief, and council of elders to make key consensual decisions of war or peace or where to go next. They allied with the Kiowa and Wichita, and mercilessly raided the New Mexican, Texan, and northern Mexico settlements along with the Pueblo,

Apache, Ute, Cheyenne, Arapaho, Pawnee, Kansa, Osage, Caddo, Tonkawa, Karankawa, and Jumano. Among plains tribes they were renowned for their horsemanship and accuracy with bows and arrows. Their weapon of choice was a 14-foot lance. They did not wear eagle feather bonnets but braided their hair on each side and greased it with bear fat or bison dung. Their war paint was black but they enjoyed adorning themselves with gaudy colors at other times. Men and women sported tattoos and never washed except for religious ceremonies. Although most plains tribes tortured to death captured men and gang-raped then enslaved captive women, the Comanche were especially notorious for doing so. Likewise, a Comanche husband was more likely to slice off the nose of an unfaithful wife than cuckolds of other tribes.[15]

***

The Transmontane or Plateau region is the Rocky Mountains' west side including parts of Colorado, Utah, Idaho, Oregon, and Washington.[16] From south to north the tribes included the Ute, Shoshone, Cayuse, Nez Perce, Flathead, Walla Walla, Yakima, Coeur d'Alene, Kalispel, Kutenai, and Spokane in six linguistic groups. Except for the Ute and Shoshone, salmon was a vital source of protein for those tribes that they caught and dried or smoked during the spring and fall migrations. They hunted deer and rabbits in sage covered flatlands and lower mountains, and elk higher up. They gathered camas bulbs, chokeberries, and huckleberries. Some tribes like the Ute, Shoshone, Nez Perce, Flathead, Kutenai, and Coeur d'Alene hunted buffalo on the high plains east of the Rockies. Most bands had summer and winter villages that took advantage of the most food and fuel sources in each season.

Nez Perce were the most numerous.[17] They lived in a dozen bands along the Salmon and Clearwater River valleys. They bred the spotted horse called the Appaloosa. Of all the tribes Lewis and Clark encountered, they found the Nez Perce the most honest and kind. The second largest tribe was the Ute, who lived in seven bands that hunted and gathered along river valleys in different regions of today's Colorado including the upper Rio Grande, San Luis, Umcompahgre, Yampa, and Uintah.[18] They fought the Apache and Navajo in the Southwest and the Comanche, Cheyenne, and Arapaho on the high plains. Their most important annual ceremonies were the Bear Dance in spring and Sun Dance in summer. Utes venerated bears as the wisest and fiercest animal. Ute culture was essentially a transmontane version of nomadic plains tribes.

***

The Great Basin is the vast region of broad deserts and numerous mountain chains between the Sierra and Wasatch Mountains and the Snake and Virgin Rivers. Water and food are scarce. Nearly all the Great Basin's small groups of hunter-gatherers were Paiute whose dialects were related linguistically to Shoshone.[19] Mono and Washo lived in the Sierra foothills. Many bands created petroglyphs by chipping out images of spirits and animals on black volcanic boulders. They wove long nets of yucca, erected them, and then drove rabbits into them. They ate the rabbits and made capes by sewing together the skins. They sheltered in half domed open-faced structures of reeds and branches. They made elaborately designed baskets and crude brown pottery.

***

Northwest coastal tribes lived in a verdant, forested region with the West's most rainfall; the Olympic Peninsula in northwestern Washington annually absorbs over a hundred inches.[20] Abundant food and a mild climate made Northwest tribes the West's most densely populated. The tribes included from north to south the Makah, Quinault, Chehalis, Chinook, Tillamook, Siuslaw, Coos, and Chastacosta along the coast, the Umpqua along the Umpqua River in southwest Oregon and the Klamath along the Klamath River in southeast Oregon. Most lived in clusters of villages at river mouths or upstream. They lived off salmon that they caught, dried, and smoked during the spring and fall migrations. They gathered blackberries, huckleberries, wild plums, wild cherries, crabapples, hazelnuts, and cranberries.

Coastal tribes constructed long red cedar dugouts with which they fished and hunted sea otters and whales. They built long houses of cedar planks in which many families lived together. At each entrance was a tall totem pole or upright log with carved effigies of gods atop one another. They wove elaborate waterproof baskets and hats. Most were hierarchical societies with hereditary chiefdoms atop noble, common, and slave classes. They had potlatches or celebrations for new chiefs, coming of age, funerals, marriages, and visiting delegations from other tribes during which chiefs and other wealthy men gave away their most valued possessions to others.

Warfare raged periodically among the tribes as they sought loot and slaves from each other. The Chinook were the most populous tribe spread among a couple score villages along the lower Columbia River valley up to Chelilo Falls.[21] They warred against surrounding tribes, enslaved their captives, pierced their own noses for ornaments, and flattened and elongated their heads by tightly wrapping a baby's tender growing skull within boards.

***

Of all the regions, California's tribes were the most linguistically diverse and yet also the most peaceful.[22] Coastal tribes like the Luiseno, Gabrielino, Chumash, Salina, Costanoan, Pomo, and Yuki enjoyed the most diverse food sources from the sea and nearby mountains. Central Valley tribes like the Tubatulabal, Yokuts, Miwok, Wappo, Maidu, Patwin, Wintun, Vana, Hupa, Shasta, and Karok hunted deer, elk, and other game in the Sierra foothills, fished in the rivers, and harvested acorns by pounding and leeching them into flour that they baked into flat bread. Each tribe had its own basket-making designs.

Chumash were the largest and most technologically advanced tribe.[23] They lived in villages along the coast mostly in present day Santa Barbara County. They fished and hunted whales from 25-foot boats constructed of planks corded together and caulked with petroleum. Their shamans went on vision quests in canyons and painted their experiences on the walls.

***

The so-called "Columbian Exchange" was the mingling of European and indigenous cultures from Christopher Columbus's 1492 voyage whereby the former reaped riches from colonialization at the latter's expense.[24] Trade, war, and conquest from the Spaniards and later the Americans would devastate or destroy every tribe from every region. Tragically, Indians shared a deadly vulnerability to the germs and viruses that European conquerors unwittingly hosted.[25] The result was a series of epidemics that killed up to 90 percent of some tribes. Smallpox was the deadliest disease but measles, typhoid, influenza, whooping cough, and cholera also killed countless Indians. Americans viewed those epidemics as godsends that assisted their conquests. For instance, an epidemic decimated the coastal New England tribes from 1616 to 1619. The Pilgrims built Plymouth at a deserted Pawtuxet village in December 1620, survived by eating its corn caches, then planted grain in its cleared fields in the spring. Smallpox ravaged the Cherokee in 1738, the Catawba in 1759, the Dakota in 1780, the Columbia River tribes during the early 1820s, and the middle Missouri River tribes in 1837.

Survivors mourned the deaths of not just their loved ones, but also their culture. The Indian view of nature was diametrically opposed to the nations that eventually overwhelmed them. Sioux Chief Luther Standing Bear explained those differences: "We did not think of the great open plains, the beautiful rolling hills, and the winding streams with tangled growth as 'wild.' Only to the white men was nature a 'wilderness' and . . . the land 'infested' with 'wild' animals and 'savage' peoples."[26] Kate Luckie, a Wintu medicine woman, deplored the devastation that Americans inflicted upon the land: "We don't chop down the trees. We only use dead wood. But the white people plow up the ground, pull up the trees, kill everything . . . How can the spirit of the earth like the white man?"[27]

Chapter 2

CONQUISTADORS AND MISSIONARIES

"They are fitted to be ruled and to be set to work, to cultivate the land and to do all else that may be necessary, and you may build towns and teach them to go clothed and adopt our customs." (Christopher Columbus)

"Who shall kill a Spaniard will get an Indian woman for a wife, and he who kills will get four women, and he who kills ten or more will get a like number of women." (Pope)

A series of innovations and visionaries led to the European discovery and conquest of the Western Hemisphere, including eventually the American West.[1] That began in the early fifteenth century with new ship designs like the deep-hulled caravel and carrack whose masts hoisted both rectangular and triangular sails that let captains capture more wind and sail faster with more cargo and sailors through rougher pounding oceans than the shallow-hulled galleys better suited to the relatively tranquil Mediterranean and Black Seas. The Ottoman Turks' conquest of the Middle East, culminating with Constantinople's capture in 1453, severed European trade routes that ultimately led to Asia's spice markets. Portuguese Prince Henry, called the Navigator, dreamed that one day his nation's merchants would sail south down the African continent and then eastward to the East Indies to buy spices like pepper, cinnamon, and cloves and carry them back to Europe for enormous profits. To facilitate that end, he gathered at his villa at Sangres, Europe's southwesternmost point, sea captains and engineers along with maps and books about distant seas, lands, and peoples. Annual voyages reached further down Africa's west coast, trading with various kingdoms and chiefdoms along the way. In 1487,

Bartholomew Dias reached the Cape of Good Hope and returned. In 1498, Vasco da Gama sailed around the Cape of Good Hope and across the Indian Ocean to Asia's markets.

Meanwhile, another visionary—Christopher Columbus—sought royal support to voyage westward to the East Indies.[2] He miscalculated that the East Indies were actually thousands of miles closer than traditional estimates of the distance. With the backing of Spain's King Ferdinand and Queen Isabella, Columbus commanded a three-vessel expedition that sailed westward in 1492. When Columbus and his men stepped ashore on a Bahaman island on October 12, 1492, they believed they had reached the East Indies and called the natives *Indios* that means either "Indians" or "In God." Columbus articulated a view of the natives that would determine their fate in the conquerors' hands: "They are fitted to be ruled and to be set to work, to cultivate the land and to do all else that may be necessary, and you may build towns and teach them to go clothed and adopt our customs."[3] He named the Caribbean Sea after the Carib Indians who inhabited many islands and were feared for their cannibalism.

During four voyages and colonization efforts in the Caribbean, Columbus eventually understood that he had discovered a "New World" previously unknown to Europeans. Spain's empire in the New World began when he brought 1,500 settlers on his second voyage from 1494 to 1496, and established Hispaniola, the island today split between the Dominican Republic and Haiti, as the first European colony in the Western Hemisphere. That empire would eventually expand across all of Central America, most of South America, and North America's southern tier.[4] During Columbus's last two voyages, from 1498 to 1500, and 1502 to 1504, he explored the coasts of Central America and northeastern South America. Expeditions by other conquistador leaders established colonies on Puerto Rico in 1508, Jamaica in 1509, and Cuba in 1511. Vasco Nunez de Balboa led 190 men across the Panama isthmus to discover the Pacific Ocean, that they called the South Sea, in 1515.

Until 1519, Spain's conquests were relatively easy because they faced disunited small bands of stone-age peoples overwhelmed by the invaders' "guns, germs, and steel."[5] The highly centralized, militant Aztec empire extended from Tenochtitlan, today's Mexico City, over most of central Mexico. In March 1519, Captain Hernando Cortez led 520 soldiers and sixteen horses ashore near the site of future Vera Cruz. Over the next two years, he and his men conquered the Aztec empire and its subject tribes. He did so by allying with tribes that hated the Aztecs for their imperial rule that included annually sacrificing thousands of people to the Aztec gods that inhabited the great pyramid in Tenochtitlan.

After Cortez, the person most vital for that conquest's success was a woman, Malintzin, called Malinche by the Spanish.[6] She was a slave that a chief gave Cortez. She rapidly learned Spanish and became Cortez's closest advisor, interpreter, and lover. Today she is a controversial figure for Mexicans and other Latin Americans. Some condemn her as a traitor. Others revere her as the literal and symbolic mother of the mestizo or mixed race (*la raza*) of Europeans and Indians after she bore Cortez's son.

For the Spanish, what became America's West was actually "North" as their expeditions landed along the Gulf Coast or trekked from Mexico to explore and eventually establish Florida, New Mexico, California, and Texas.[7] Juan Ponce de Leon and his men were the first Europeans to visit part of what became the United States when they stepped ashore somewhere on Florida's east coast in 1513. In Mexico, the Spanish established the Pacific port of Zacatula in 1522, and from there built vessels to explore up and down the coast. Among Indian legends circulating in northern Mexico was that of California, a beautiful island west of the continent. In 1532, Fortun Jimenez sailed from Zacatula and claimed to have spotted California. California appeared on maps as a jagged island off the mainland.

Panfilo de Narvaez and 400 Spaniards landed at Tampa Bay in April 1528 and from there thrashed through jungles and swamps along the coast in a desperate search for gold. They found no gold, only disease, starvation, and Indian attacks that steadily culled them. They eventually built boats and journeyed west along the coast but were driven ashore at Galveston Bay. By 1529, only four men survived, Alvar Nunez Cabeza da Vaca, a black slave Estevanico, and two others. Along the way, they heard tales of the gold-rich seven cities of Cibola. They reached Culiacan, a Spanish settlement in northern Mexico, in March 1536. Cabeza de Vaca wrote a fascinating account of his adventures.[8]

Hernando de Soto led 600 men to North America determined to find gold and establish a prosperous colony where Narvaez had failed. Instead, he and his men suffered the same fate. In May 1538, they landed at Tampa Bay to begin what became four years of exploring the Southeast. They did not starve because de Soto brought cattle and pig herds to sustain them as mobile food supplies. They got as far as stretches of the Savannah and Tennessee Rivers and up the Mississippi River nearly to the Ohio River and as far west as the Ozark Mountains and then down the Arkansas and Mississippi Rivers to the mouth; De

Soto died along the way. The 311 survivors built ships and sailed to Mexico.

Antonio de Mendoza became New Spain's viceroy at Mexico City in 1535. He organized and dispatched several expeditions to explore northward and find Cibola. That of 1539 included three men, Franciscan Father Marcos de Niza, another friar, and the guide Estevanico. They got as far as Zuni whose people killed Estevanico. Marcos and his companion returned to Mexico City with the claim that they had seen a golden city in the distance.

Menendez had Francisco Vasquez de Coronado head an expedition to Cibola. In February 1540, Coronado led 225 cavalry, 62 infantry, 800 Indians, 1,000 black slaves, and herds of cattle, sheep, pigs, and horses north from Compostela, with Marcos as his guide. He found no city of gold, let alone seven, but did learn of the golden city of Quivera in the heart of the Great Plains. In July 1541, they journeyed as far as the Wichita village in central Kansas, but its homes were made of reeds not gold. Back in the Rio Grande valley, he sent parties to explore in different directions, and one reached the Grand Canyon. All along, he had his troops brutally crush any Indian resistance; the Spaniards burned hundreds of men at the stake or cut off their right foot. Bitterly disappointed, Coronado led his men back to Mexico in spring 1542.

Mendoza dispatched Captain Juan Cabrillo to sail as far north as possible up the west coast. Cabrillo and his crew were the first Europeans to see California during a round-trip voyage from Navidad, Mexico in 1542. They reached San Diego in September and sailed all the way to Point Reyes where they turned back in November. Fog apparently obscured San Francisco Bay's entrance that they missed both ways.

Two Spanish expeditions had explored parts of the Philippine Islands, Ferdinand Magellan's in 1520 and Ruy Lopez de Villabos's in 1543. King Philip II had Miquel Lopez de Legazpi lead the conquest of the Philippines. The expedition sailed from Barra de Navidad on Mexico's west coast in 1564 and began the subjection of Cebu in 1565. Thereafter the Spanish expanded their control over other islands and founded their capital at Manila on Luzon in 1570. The Philippines became a key link in Spain's global trading chain that included Quandong, China and the Spice Islands westward and the Americas eastward. Each year a gallon filled with trade goods made the round trip between Manila and Acapulco.

Don Tristan de Luna y Arellano led an expedition that failed to sustain a colony in Pensacola Bay in 1559, Coosa Bay the next year, and then by his successor Angel da Villafane at Santa Elena in 1561. Word that a French expedition led by Jean Ribault had founded a colony in northern Florida prompted a Spanish expedition in 1565. Don Pedro Menendez de Aviles and his men wiped out Ribault's colony and established Saint Augustine on September 6, 1565. Saint Augustine was Spain's first permanent settlement in territory later acquired by the United States.

***

New Mexico was the second colony that Spain established in what became the United States.[9] Two exploring expeditions and an illegal attempt to found a colony preceded the settlement. In 1581, Francisco Sanchez Chamuscado left Santa Barbara in northern Mexico, ascended the Rio Grande valley, and explored as far north as Taos, west to Zuni, and east to the Pecos valley before returning. In 1582, Antonio de Espejo left San Bartolome and headed up the Rio Grande valley to Puaray in today's Albuquerque then northwest to the Hopi mesas and beyond to the region with today's Flagstaff, then east to the Pecos valley and down it to the Rio Grande and southwest to San Bartolome. In 1590, Gaspar Castano de Sosa led 170 people to Santo Domingo Pueblo and tried to settle there but Spanish authorities caught up and forced them to return because Sosa had no right to do so.

Juan de Onate led 130 soldiers and settlers, as many slaves, 20 Franciscan friars, 7,000 cattle, 1,000 sheep for wool, 1,000 sheep for meat, and 83 wagons packed with provisions from Santa Barbara in January 1598. In July, they reached Santo Domingo where Onate summoned thirty-one chiefs from the region's Pueblos and had them swear allegiance to Spain. The Pueblos surrendered to overwhelming Spanish power. He established Caypa as New Mexico's first settlement in 1599 then founded San Gabriel as the capital in 1600.

One tribe resisted the invaders. Captain Juan de Zaldivar's company of thirty-one soldiers stopped at Acoma for provisions on December 4, 1598. The Acomans attacked the Spanish after one of them raped a woman, and killed Zaldivar and twelve of his men. In January 1599, Onate retaliated by storming Acoma with 70 soldiers, slaughtering 800 of the inhabitants and indicting for murder the surviving 80 or so men and 500 or so women and children. The guilty verdict resulted in the Spaniards amputating a foot from any man 25 years or older and enslaving everyone for 20 years. The Spaniards intended that cruel mass penalty to deter other revolts. That worked for eight decades.

The Spanish nurtured relations with the Pueblos by fighting with them against their traditional enemies the Apache, Navajo, and Ute, and more recent enemies the Comanche and Kiowa. King Philip III declared New Mexico a crown colony in 1609. Governor Pedro de Peralta founded Santa Fe as New Mexico's capital in 1610. Two years later workers completed the Governor's Palace on the central square's north side. Santa Fe was 1,420 miles north of Mexico City. Mexico's viceroy dispatched a supply caravan up that Camino Real or Royal Road every three years. The round trip took eighteen months with six months going, six months distributing supplies and gathering products throughout the province, and six months returning. The caravan carried mostly sophisticated manufactured goods like guns, gunpowder, fancy clothing, clocks, scrap iron, sugar, chocolate, and indigo, and took back wheat, corn, beans, pelts, and livestock. The closest city to Santa Fe was Chihuahua, 555 miles away. Usually annual caravans arrived from Chihuahua. That tenuous and infrequent trade forced New Mexicans to be self-reliant and innovative.

***

The Spanish devastated the peoples they conquered. Perhaps 25 million people lived in central Mexico before the Spanish arrived. Within a century, epidemics and wars plunged the indigenous population to 730,000.[10] In New Mexico, violence and disease caused the Pueblo population to decline from around 60,000 in 134 villages when the Spaniards conquered the Rio Grande valley in 1598 to around 9,000 in nineteen villages two centuries later in 1790.[11]

If that genocide was inadvertent, Spain's ethnic cleansing was deliberate. The Spanish forced peoples to abandon their gods and instead worship the Christian God. The king rewarded his conquistadors with encomiendas or feudal fiefs that empowered the holder to exploit, tax, and punish all Indians inhabiting that land. The Catholic Church reinforced that suppression through its hierarchy of bishops, priests, and friars, institutions like the Inquisition, and religious orders like the Jesuits and Franciscans that established missions among the Indians. As elsewhere in the Western Hemisphere, marriages, mistresses, and rapes by Spaniards with native women produced an ever-larger mestizo population. The Spanish had a race-based hierarchy with pure Spaniards or espanoles at the top, mixed race people or mestizos next, pure Indians or genzaros below them, and Indian and African slaves at the bottom. Spaniards justified serfdom and slavery by distinguishing between "people of reason" (*gente de razon*) like themselves and "people without reason" (*gente sin razon*) like Indians, Africans, and children with the former having the right and duty to protect, nurture, control, and exploit the latter for their mutual benefit. Enforcing those relations was the government composed of the viceroy in Mexico City who ruled Mexico, which eventually included three provinces that later became part of the United States, New Mexico, Texas, and California; a governor and *audiencia* or court ruled each province and an *alcalde* or mayor each town, all appointed or approved by the king in Madrid.

Not everything the Spanish imposed on the indigenous peoples was negative. They enriched diets with crops like grapes, chiles, tomatoes, watermelons, apples, cherries, apricots, peaches, and pears; meats like chicken, sheep, beef, and goat; and milk and cheeses. They eased burdens with horses to ride, oxen to pull carts, and donkeys and mules to carry loads. Metal knives, pots, files, awls, needles, hammers, saws, made tasks easier and more productive.

Not all Spaniards mercilessly suppressed and exploited the Indians. Bartolome de Las Casas was a priest that accompanied the 1511 conquest of Cuba. In letters to kings and popes, he condemned the cruel treatment of the Indians. Pope Urban VIII officially declared that condemnation in 1537. King Charles V forbad enslaving Indians and abolished the encomienda in 1542. King Charles I brought Las Casas to Madrid to debate with others the nature and proper treatment of Indians in 1550. Las Casas chronicled the conquest's history in his 1552 book *The Destruction of the Indies*. The royal and papal edicts protecting Indians did little to alleviate their suffering. The Indians remained locked in a feudal system as serfs not slaves. To supplement their laborers, especially for plantations and mines, the Spanish bought ever more slaves from African rulers.

***

A miracle helped inspire Spain's initial attempts to colonize Texas. Sister Maria de Jesus de Agreda was a nun at the Immaculate Conception convent at Agreda in Spain.[12] During the 1620s, she mystically bilocated to west Texas's high plains where she called on various bands to convert to Catholicism. She reported her experiences to her superiors. Eventually word of her miraculous journeys reached Mexico's Archbishop Francisco Manzo y Zuniga who sent letters to missions in New Mexico asking the friars if they could verify her claims. In July 1629, fifty Jumano Apache Indians reached the Francisco convent at San Isleta, New Mexico and reported a Blue Lady had implored them to become Christians. That inspired Friars Juan de Salas and Diego Lopez to journey several hundred miles into west Texas where bands revealed their own Blue Lady visions.

Three decades passed before the first ambitious conquistador tried to conquer Texas.[13] In 1663, Juan de la Garza led a hundred men to the Rio Grande at Eagle Pass where the Cacaxtle tribe tried to prevent their crossing. Garza and his men killed over a hundred Indians and captured seventy. Garza decided to return with their captives as slaves. In 1675, Fernando del Bosque led ten soldiers and two priests into south central Texas to map the region and inform bands they encountered that they would later establish missions. They failed to do so. The 1680 Pueblo revolt delayed Spain's colonization of Texas for a couple of generations.

***

New Mexico's Spanish population reached 2,347 by 1680. They lived amidst 16,000 Indians who had at least nominally converted to Catholicism overseen by thirty-one priests. But the Inquisition's policies increasingly enraged the Pueblo peoples by purging their shamans, kivas, and kachinas. In 1675, the Inquisition arrested forty-seven shamans and executed three of them for heresy. Among those whipped and released was Pope, a charismatic and mystical San Juan shaman. Over the next five years, he organized a revolt against the Spanish. As an incentive, he promised that "who shall kill a Spaniard will get an Indian woman for a wife, and he who kills four will get four women, and he who kills ten or more will get a like number of women."[14] The Indians launched their attacks on August 11, 1680. By the time the Pueblo accepted a truce and the Spanish withdrawal on September 21, they had slaughtered 401 settlers and 21 friars. Governor Antonio de Otermin led the survivors to southern New Mexico where they established El Paso del Norte.[15]

The Pueblo liberation lasted 13 years. Pope and his followers destroyed anything associated with the Catholic religion and repelled Spanish attempts at reconquest in 1681 and 1687. After Pope died around 1688, the Pueblos split over whether to remain independent or invite back Spanish rule. Apache, Navajo, and Comanche attacks worsened. Diego de Vargas led 60 troops and 100 Indian allies to Santa Fe on September 13, 1692. He asked the Indians to submit in return for pardons for all rebels, abolition of encomienda serfdom, and imposition of repartimiento that required only a day or two of paid labor each week. The Indians refused. He returned with his men to El Paso but carried on long-distance negotiations with the Pueblo chiefs. After four of twenty agreed to submit, Vargas led 100 troops, 70 families, and 18 friars north up the Rio Grande valley to reestablish

Spanish rule in Santa Fe on December 16, 1693. It took years to subdue the other Pueblos and rebuild New Mexico's Spanish population and towns. New Mexico acquired the beginnings of a neighboring colony when Jesuit Father Eusebio Kino founded the mission of San Xavier de Bac just north of the present Arizona border in 1700. Other nearby settlements came decades later, the founding of Tubac in 1752, and Tucson and Terrenate in 1776

***

Meanwhile, the Spanish faced worsening rivalry for domination of North America and the Caribbean.[16] The French began exploring parts of North America three decades after Columbus and began their own conquest eleven decades later. In 1524, King Francis I dispatched Giovanni da Verrazano to explore and chart North America's east coast from Florida to Nova Scotia. In 1543, he had Jacques Cartier search for the fabled Northwest Passage to the Far East. Cartier's expedition sailed up the St. Lawrence River as far as the village of Hochelaga, today's Montreal, and rapids that barred his ships from further ascent. Ironically, he named those rapids La Chine, or China. Clearly, the Northwest Passage did not lie on that route. Cartier and his men returned to France to resupply. In 1535, Cartier sailed with five vessels to explore more of the St. Lawrence region and winter at the site later called Quebec. He led other voyages in 1541 and 1543. Religious wars and a succession crisis for the throne prevented any more French expeditions for nearly five decades.

Meanwhile, an intrepid English captain sought to capture the annual Acapulco-Manila galleon and other Spanish merchant vessels in the Pacific Ocean. Francis Drake and his crew aboard the *Golden Hind* became the second vessels to sail around the earth after Magellan's expedition and the first to see California after Cabrillo. They sailed in 1577, wintered at Point Reyes in 1578, and in September 1580 returned to London with their ship packed with riches looted during their voyage.

Henri IV authorized François Sieur de Pontgrave, assisted by Samuel de Champlain, to lead an expedition to Canada in 1603. They traded with the Indians at the Tadoussac River mouth on St. Lawrence Bay and established Port Royal on Nova Scotia in 1604 but sailed back to France in 1607. In 1608, Champlain returned to found Quebec and until his death in 1635, his decisive leadership was crucial to the colony's survival.[17] For thirteen decades, Canada slowly expanded in numbers mostly between Quebec and Montreal in the lower St. Lawrence valley, then with trading posts and missions at key points across the Great Lakes, and eventually down the Mississippi River. Yet Canada never flourished. Fish and furs were its only sources of wealth and revenues from those exports to France always fell short of paying for the supplies vital for Canada's survival. Louis XIV made Canada a royal province in 1663 but the extra attention, cash, and colonists could not break that dependence.

French explorers mapped swathes of North America. Medard Chouart, Sieur de Groseilliers and Pierre Radisson charted the Great Lakes from 1656 to 1666. From 1673 to 1674, with Indian paddlers, Louis Jolliet and Father Jacques Marquette journeyed from St. Ignace mission up the Fox River and over the divide to the Wisconsin River, then down the Mississippi River as far as the Arkansas River before they turned back. In 1681, Rene-Robert Cavelier, Sieur de la Salle led an expedition from Fort Miami at the St. Joseph River mouth over the divide to descend the Illinois River then Mississippi River to the Gulf of Mexico before returning. La Salle sailed to Paris where he received Louis XIV's permission to lead four ships packed with 400 settlers and supplies to establish the colony of Louisiana at the Mississippi River mouth in 1684. They missed the Mississippi and sailed west along the coast as far as Matagorda Bay, Texas, where they built Fort Saint Louis in January 1685. Disease, accidents, and Indian attacks steadily culled the settlers. La Salle's men rebelled at his autocratic rule and murdered him. Karankawa Indians wiped most of the French in 1687. Half a dozen survivors eventually trekked to Canada.

Word of the French settlement at Matagorda Bay provoked the Spanish to launch expeditions to seek and destroy it. In 1689, Alonso de Leon led 114 men from Coahuila to the lower Rio Grande valley then up the Texas coast to Matagorda Bay where they found the French settlement's ruins then returned. In 1690, Francisco de Llano led an expedition that sailed from Vera Cruz to Matagorda Bay to map the region and then sail back. Meanwhile, three priests and three soldiers trekked to the future site of Augusta in east Texas on the Neches River to found the mission of San Francisco de los Tejas among the Nabedache Indians. In 1691, Domingo de Teran de los Rios was appointed the first Texas governor. In March, he led an expedition from Monclova that reached San Francisco in June and Matagorda Bay in August where a supply ship awaited them. Teran then explored as far north as the Red River before returning to winter at the mission. In the spring, Teran led his men back to Mexico. A plague devastated the Indians at San Francisco and the survivors threatened the missionaries. In 1693, the Spanish abandoned the mission and returned to Mexico.

In 1698, an expedition founded Pensacola and eventually the Spanish set up a chain of missions at Indian villages across northern Florida between Saint Augustine and Pensacola.

Meanwhile, the French succeeded in establishing Louisiana. The first settlement came in 1688 when Henri Tonti founded Arkansas Post 20 miles up the Arkansas River from the Mississippi River. Pierre Le Moyne d'Iberville founded Fort Maurepas and Biloxi on the Gulf Coast in April 1699 and Mobile in 1702. In 1714, Louis Saint Denis founded Natchitoches on the Red River then with twenty-four men trekked across Texas to San Juan Bautista's mission and presidio on Mexico's side of the Rio Grande where Captain Diego Ramon arrested them for trespassing. Saint Denis ended up marrying Ramon's daughter and agreed to guide an expedition to establish missions in Texas. Jean Baptiste Le Moyne de Bienville founded New Orleans as Louisiana's capital in 1718.

The Spaniards viewed with alarm Louisiana's establishment between Mexico and Florida and Saint Denis's expedition to San Juan Bautista. They renewed their attempts to settle Texas and this time finally succeeded. Missions preceded settlements as priests founded twelve in southern and eastern Texas from 1713 to 1722. Six came from the 1716 expedition of Domingo Ramon guided by Saint Denis; the furthest east was San Miquel de los Adaes just 15 miles west of Natchitoches. The most important foundings were the mission of San Antonio de Valero by Father Antonio de San Buenaventura y Olivares on May 1 and the presidio of San Antonio de Behar as Texas's capital by Governor Martin Alarcon on May 5, 1718.

***

The worsening French threat to Texas and New Mexico provoked varying reactions by Spanish officials. New Mexican Governor Pedro de Villasur led forty-five troops and sixty Pueblo warriors toward the central plains in 1720. They reached a Pawnee village visited by French traders. Villasur demanded that they end their trade with the French. Enraged, the Pawnee attacked the intruders, and slaughtered Villasur and all his men except fourteen who eventually straggled back to Santa Fe.

Brothers Paul and Pierre Mallet journeyed with seven men from St. Louis to Santa Fe in 1739. Lieutenant Governor Juan Hurtado welcomed them and sent word to Mexico City for instructions. The viceroy granted permission for the French to trade if they returned with passports and permission from French authorities to do so. The

Mallet party headed east to the Canadian River, then down it to the Arkansas and Mississippi Rivers to New Orleans. Andre de la Bruyere led an expedition toward Santa Fe in 1741 but ran out of supplies and returned to New Orleans. Pierre Mallet and three men reached Santa Fe in November 1750, but the authorities arrested them and sent them to Mexico City where they may have died in prison. Jean Chapuis and Louis Feuilli led several men to Santa Fe in 1752, and they too were arrested and eventually ended up in a prison in Spain.

Meanwhile, Pierre Gaultier de Varennes, sieur de Verendrye, and his sons led the exploration of the eastern Canadian and northern American prairies. They established Fort St. Pierre on Rainy Lake in 1731, Fort St. Charles on Lake of the Woods in 1732, and Fort La Reine south of Lake Manitoba in 1738. Then from 1741 to 1743, they explored the northern plains as far as the Bighorn Mountains but did not found any permanent forts.

***

The French threat proved to be fleeting. France and Britain fought each other from 1754 to 1763, a struggle eventually joined by all the Europeans powers. Britain and its allies won that struggle, called the Seven Years War in Europe and the French and Indian War in America. French King Louis XV enticed Spanish King Carlos III into the war in 1761. The result was a disaster for Spain as British expeditions captured Havana, Cuba, and Manila, in the Philippines while a British and Portuguese army repelled a Spanish invasion of Portugal. That short war aggravated Spain's chronic financial problems. In compensation, Louis XV granted Carlos III title to New Orleans and the Louisiana Territory that stretched westward from the Mississippi River to the watershed high in the Rocky Mountains. Under the 1763 Treaty of Paris, Britain took Canada from France and East and West Florida from Spain.

Spain's northern frontier now extended between the Mississippi River and Pacific Ocean as far north as the Mississippi's northernmost tributary. Carlos III had General Cayetano, Marques de la Rubi, inspect the frontier and advise ways to bolster it. With a small escort, Rubi toured the frontier from 1766 to 1767. His report called for constructing a chain of presidios 40 miles apart from Laredo to the Gulf of California to protect New Spain; encouraging more settlers, farms and ranches in New Mexico and Texas; exterminating the Apache; and pursuing peace with the Comanche and Wichita. Spain never built the presidios or exterminated the Apache, inspired few emigrants, and negotiated only sporadic truces with the Comanche and Wichita.

***

Initially, enterprising Frenchmen contributed the most to Spain's expanded empire. Pierre Laclede Liguest headed the Laclede, Maxent, and Company or Louisiana Fur Company headquartered in New Orleans. In 1750, he led an expedition up the Mississippi River to found St. Genevieve on the west bank across from Kaskaskia. In 1764, he and his stepson Rene Auguste Chouteau founded St. Louis. Louis Blanchette founded Les Petite Cotes (Little Hills), later renamed St. Charles on the Missouri River's north bank 20 miles from the Mississippi in 1769.

St. Louis and St. Charles became starting points for exploration and trading expeditions up the Missouri River, with most at least partly financed by Chouteau. In 1783, Joseph Garreau reached the Arikara on the middle-Missouri and Jacque d'Eglise made it to the Mandan and Hidatsa a couple hundred miles further. Jacques Clamorgan received a Spanish charter to form the Company for the Exploration of the Missouri with a monopoly over the fur trade. Clamorgan tapped Baptiste Truteau to lead an expedition up the Missouri to the Mandan but the Teton Sioux turned him back, determined to act as intermediaries in any trade. In 1795, James Mackay got no further than the Omaha who stopped him but let him send his partner John Evans as far as the Mandan.

Pierre Vial was a fur trader who had traveled and lived among the Comanche, Wichita, Tawakoni, and Waco tribes in the southern plains. In 1786, Texas's governor asked Vial to mark a road from San Antonio, Texas to Santa Fe, New Mexico. With a comrade, he headed north to the Red River and then up it to its source in the high plains then across to Santa Fe, arriving in May 1787. That roundabout route was about 1,100 miles and took eight months. New Mexico's governor sent Corporal Jose Mares and three other men on the most direct route they could find which was around 710 miles after they arrived in April 1788. The governor then sent Vial with several other men east to Natchitoches then to San Antonio, and finally back to Santa Fe. That journey lasted from June 1788 until August 1789. In May 1792, the governor dispatched Vial with two comrades from Santa Fe to St. Louis. On the Arkansas River, Kansas Indians captured them, stole all their supplies, and took them to their village on the Kansas River. There three French traders ransomed the captives. Vial and his men reached St. Louis in

October. In June 1793, Vial and his men set off toward Santa Fe but via the Platte River where they traded with the Pawnee for horses and a guide. They entered Santa Fe in September. New Mexico's governor did not encourage others to tread those trails even though traders could bring far cheaper goods from New Orleans or even St. Louis than from Chihuahua. Chihuahua merchants pressured the viceroy to ensure that did not happen.

Comanche and Apache war parties plagued Texas and New Mexico, and often raided south through other provinces. They killed 820 New Mexican Spaniards from 1700 to 1849 and possibly 375 Texans from 1777 to 1794. At annual fairs in Taos, Pecos, and Picuris, Apache warriors brazenly rode in to ransom Pueblo and Spanish captives and sell livestock and other loot they had taken in earlier raids. Despite Indian depredations, New Mexico's population expanded from 9,722 including, 4,142 Spanish and 5,579 Indians in 1746 to 63,498 including 46,998 Spanish and 16,510 Indians in 1842. Swelling that population were 3,294 slaves taken from nomadic tribes from 1693 to 1846. Texas had only about 3,000 Spanish in 1820. No province suffered worse than Nueva Vizcaya where raiders murdered 1,674 people, captured 154, forced the abandonment of 116 haciendas and ranches, and stole 68,256 head of livestock from 1771 to 1776.[18]

***

Meanwhile, the Spanish established the province of Upper California. In January 1769, two expeditions set forth, one by land led by Captain Gaspar de Portola and Franciscan Friar Junipero de Serra, and the other by sea led by Captain Vicente Vila. The land party's advanced guard reached and founded San Diego on May 14. Father Serra established a mission there in July 1769. Portola founded Monterey as California's capital in March 1770. Before his death in 1784, Serra founded Carmel near Monterey in 1771, San Antonio and San Gabriel near Los Angeles in 1771, San Luis Obispo in 1772, San Francisco and San Juan Capistrano in 1776, Santa Clara in 1777, and San Buenaventura in 1782. His successors would eventually bring the number of missions to twenty-one, including Santa Barbara in 1782, Santa Cruz in 1797, and San Francisco de Solano at Sonora the last in 1823. As elsewhere, death accompanied California's conquistadors as diseases, forced labor, and despair killed more natives. The Indian population along the coast plunged from 72,000 to 18,000 between the conquest's beginning in 1769 and privatization of the missions in 1833, while that across California halved from 300,000 to 150,000 people.[19]

Franciscans Silvestre de Escalante and Atanasio Dominquez led an expedition from Santa Fe in hope of reaching Monterey in 1776, but they turned back in southern Utah. In 1779, Juan Bautista de Anza opened a route from New Mexico to California via the Gila River then across the southern Mohave Desert. He established a presidio and Franciscans two missions at the Yuma village on the southern Colorado River. The Yuma revolted and wiped out the missions and presidio in 1781.

Spain faced ever more intruders along the Pacific coast in North America. During his three voyages crisscrossing the Pacific, Captain James Cook reached Nootka Sound in 1778. There his crew traded trinkets for sea otter pelts and later reaped huge profits selling them in Quandong, China. Captain George Vancouver's expedition explored Puget Sound in 1792. American Captain Robert Gray discovered the Columbia River mouth, sailed up it 50 miles, and claimed that watershed for the United States in 1795. The Spanish sent their own expeditions to the region. Captain Juan Perez and his crew reached Nootka Sound in 1774 and he claimed that coastline for Spain. Captain Bruno de Hezeta and his crew charted the Quinault River mouth in Washington in 1775. Then, in 1789, Captain Estevan Martinez and his men captured three British merchant ships in Nootka Sound and brought them back to Mexico for trial on trespassing charges. That provoked a crisis with Britain that nearly led to war. Madrid and London diplomatically resolved that with the 1794 Nootka Convention whereby Spain yielded its claim to that Northwest Territory. The Russians established Fort Ross just 70 miles up the coast from San Francisco Bay in 1812. Spain never tried to capture that fort. Britain and Russia posed clear and present dangers to Spain's northwest empire. Yet there was a more insidious and worsening threat to New Spain, the Americans ever since they won independence.

Chapter 3

AMERICANS AND FRONTIERS

> "What could they see but a hideous and desolate wilderness, full of wild beasts and wild men . . . If they looked behind them, there was the mighty ocean which they had passed and was now a . . . gulf to separate them from all the civil parts of the world." (William Bradford)

> "The utmost good faith shall always be observed toward the Indians, their lands and property shall never be taken from them without their consent; and in their property, rights, and liberty, they shall never be invaded or disturbed unless in just and lawful wars authorized by Congress." (Northwest Ordinance of 1787)

America and Americans were conceived and developed on frontiers facing west. America's first West began on the Atlantic shore. With a royal charter, the Virginia Company established Jamestown, England's first permanent New World settlement, in 1607. From then to the 1803 Louisiana Purchase, Americans imagined a series of hazy Wests. Virginia's second charter in 1609 inspired the most far-reaching vision as James I granted the colonists land across the continent from the Atlantic to the Pacific. Wherever the West lay, countless people shaped its future without ever setting foot there. Most vital were Britain's kings, queens, army generals, sea captains, colonial governors, and entrepreneurs until 1776, and thereafter American congressmen, presidents, generals, and entrepreneurs.

Sixteen decades separated Jamestown's founding from the Declaration of Independence. During that time, the original hundred settlers expanded to 2,100,000 diverse mostly prosperous people; theocracy and communitarianism transformed into secularism and humanism; English subjects morphed into American citizens; each colony legalized slavery, although the population share varied among 2 percent in New England, 15 percent in the mid-Atlantic colonies, and

40 percent in the southern colonies; and colonial governments changed into thirteen state republics with elected assemblies and governors in a Confederation of the United States guided by Congress.[1]

The first two colonies, Virginia from 1607 and Plymouth from 1620, experienced horrendous hardships and mass death from disease, starvation, and violence. William Bradford, Plymouth's governor, expressed his community's grim and fearful outlook in this New World: "What could they see but a hideous and desolate wilderness full of wild beasts and wild men . . . and the whole country, full of woods and thickets, represented a wild and savage hue. If they looked behind them, there was the mighty ocean which they had passed and was now a . . . gulf to separate them from all the civil parts of the world."[2] That dread powerfully motivated settlers to convert wilderness into productive farms and villages as swiftly as possible.

Virginia lost hundreds of settlers and tens of thousands of pounds sterling for its investors during its first decade. Then John Rolfe developed a tobacco hybrid with large fragrant leaves that was relatively easy to cultivate. Farmers now had a cash crop to send to English merchants to pay for all the supplies they needed. In Plymouth, the fur trade with the Indians was their most viable business along with fish and lumber that underwrote vital imports from England. Another critical transformation for both colonies was abandoning their initial communal land ownership and labor, and embracing private property and enterprise. Gradually Virginia, Plymouth, and other colonies diversified their economies. The colonies eventually sold to England and English colonies in the Caribbean surplus goods like tobacco, rice, lumber, wheat, iron, dried fish, salt pork, salt beef, and rum along with beaver pelts from the northern colonies and deerskins from the southern colonies. Shipbuilding was the most advanced colonial industry. Slavery also helped develop each colony, although the impact varied with the portion of slaves in the labor force. To varying degrees, each colony prospered with a "triangular trade" whereby merchants exchanged their colony's surplus goods to English merchants for manufactured goods, of which most were sold in that colony but others were exchanged with West African kings and chiefs for their excess slaves that were sold largely to plantation owners in the southern colonies. Before independence, nine of ten Americans lived within 50 miles of the Atlantic, so the frontier economy was peripheral and subordinate to the seaborne economy.

Each of the eventual thirteen colonies developed a government with an assembly elected by men who met property and tax requirements, rights for freemen, and usually a monarch-appointed governor who formed a council of advisors from the colony's prominent members, although the assemblies of Connecticut and Rhode Island elected their governors. Americans largely governed themselves in relative isolation from Parliament and the monarchy 3,000 miles across the Atlantic in London.

The Mayflower Compact was the first explicit assertion of self-government by settlers. The men aboard the *Mayflower* sailing to the New World wrote and signed a contract that established an elected governing council and a chair among them that guaranteed their rights as English subjects on November 21, 1620. In January 1639, delegations from Connecticut towns met at Hartford to negotiate and sign the Fundamental Orders that established a General Court or assembly with four delegates elected from each town and a governor elected by those delegates.

Dissidents, however, suffered condemnation and banishment. In Massachusetts, Thomas Merton, a lawyer and poet, founded Merry Mount as a frontier community devoted to free enterprise, thought, speech, creativity, lust, and love. Plymouth's government had Morton arrested and exiled to England in 1628 and after he returned did so again in 1630. Massachusetts banished Roger Williams in 1635 and Anne Hutchinson in 1636 after each publicly espoused ideas that questioned the government's authority. Williams founded the colony of Rhode Island where all Protestant Christian sects could freely worship.

Victorious wars against indigenous peoples also crucially shaped colonial development. Fighting between Virginians and the local Powhatan tribe flared periodically nearly every year from 1607, but those annually killed numbered a score or so. Then on March 22, 1622, Powhatans launched a massive attack that slaughtered 350 of 1,200 settlers before the survivors drove them off. In 1637, war erupted between the Pequot tribe and the New England colonies of Plymouth, Massachusetts, and Connecticut, and ended with the Pequot devastated and submissive. In 1675, wars engulfed both the Chesapeake and New England frontiers. Virginia and Maryland fought and eventually crushed the Susquehannocks and allied tribes. The colonies of Massachusetts, Plymouth, Rhode Island, and Connecticut fought the Wampanoags, Narrangasetts, Nipmucks, and Abenakis with Chief Metacom, called King Philip, the most prominent Indian sachem or chief. The Indians slaughtered over 2,000 colonists and burned a dozen towns before the New Englanders mustered enough men to destroy them by slaughtering over 4,000 Indians and selling around 1,000 others as slaves to West Indian plantations. A few seventeenth-century Americans, most notably Miles Standish and Benjamin Church, mastered Indian-style warfare of secretly infiltrating enemy territory to attack villages or ambush approaching war parties.

Yet, despite the wars, most American relations with the tribes were peaceful and mutually profitable. Each eagerly exchanged goods it had in abundance for goods it desired. Americans mostly sought beaver pelts on the northern frontier and deerskins on the southern frontier, and for that swapped iron pots, hatchets, wool and linen clothing, glass beads, muskets, and munitions. Trouble arose when Americans sold rum or whiskey. Inebriated Indians gave away piles of pelts and skins for nothing more than fleeting derangement and splitting headaches. At times they got violent, fighting and even murdering each other or the traders. Alcohol impoverished rather than enriched Indians. In 1753, Iroquois chief Scarouady issued this plea: "Rum ruins us. We beg you to prevent its coming . . . When these Whiskey traders come, They . . . make us drink, and get all the furs that should go to pay the debts we have contracted for goods . . . by this means we ruin ourselves."[3]

***

For five decades, the Dutch empire divided the Chesapeake and New England colonies. In the Dutch West India Company's employ, Henry Hudson and his crew sailed up what the captain dubbed the Hudson River as far as the Mohawk River in 1609. He sought the fabled Northwest Passage to the Orient, but instead ran into rapids. He traded trinkets for furs from Indians before sailing away. Inspired by that discovery, a group of investors formed the New Netherlands Company with a government charter to colonize that land. They founded Fort Nassau near the site of future Albany in 1614, and bought Manhattan Island from the Leni Lenape in 1624 and established New Amsterdam at its southern tip.

Like other European imperialists in the New World, the Dutch played off rival tribes against each other to reap the most profits from both and occasionally fought wars to keep or extend their holdings. Dutch trade of guns with the Iroquois or Five Nations across central New York empowered that confederacy to fight a series of "beaver wars" against other tribes east into New England, north into Canada, and west as far as Illinois.

And, like the other European imperial powers, Holland's wedge of North American territory was part of an expanding global empire that competed with others for profitable markets and strategic sites. The Dutch and English fought three short naval wars for economic and strategic supremacy from 1652 to 1654, 1665 to 1667, and 1672 to 1676. An English expedition bloodlessly captured New Amsterdam in 1664, the Dutch retook it in 1673, and it reverted to England as New York with the 1674 Treaty of Westminster.

***

The English-speaking American frontier now ran from the Savannah River to the Kennebec River with most settlements within 50 miles of the coast. The Americans faced two other rivals for North America and each was far more resilient than were the Dutch. They fought three wars against the Spanish and their Indian allies, three wars against the French and their Indian allies, and two wars against all three.[4] The Spanish and Indian wars included Elizabeth's War (1585–1604), Cromwell's War (1655–60), and the War of Jenkin's Ear (1739–44). The French and Indian wars included the Huguenot War (1628–32), King William's War or the War of the League of Augsburg (1689–97), and King George's War or the War of the Austrian Succession (1744–8). Those against all three included Queen Anne's War or the War of the Spanish Succession (1702–13) and the French and Indian War or Seven Years War (1754–63). In nearly all those wars, the fighting consisted of raids by relatively small groups to attack isolated frontier villages or forts, ideally destroy them, then escape before overwhelming numbers of the enemy converged. Americans fought European-style sieges only at Cartagena in 1741, Oswego in 1756, Fort William Henry in 1757, Fort Frontenac in 1758, Fort Niagara in 1758, Montreal in 1760, and Havana in 1762, and open-field battles at Lake George Camp in 1755, Fort Carillon in 1758, and Belle Famille in 1759.

Only one of those wars was decisive and it was the last.[5] Previous wars did not roll back Spain's empire in East and West Florida or France's along the Great Lakes and Mississippi valley. By the mid-eighteenth century, thirteen economically dynamic American colonies with 2 million people had emerged along the east coast but were mostly cramped between the Atlantic and the Appalachian mountains. The French and British empires overlapped with conflicting claims in the upper Ohio River valley. Both sides were determined to seize the strategic forks where the Allegheny and Monongahela Rivers form the Ohio River.

George Washington was responsible for igniting the last, decisive colonial war between Britain and France in North America. In 1753, he was a 21-year-old major in Virginia's militia. He was a tough frontiersman as well as a member of one of Virginia's elite plantation and slave-owning families, having previously been a surveyor in the wilderness and investor in the Ohio Company that claimed 500,000 acres in the Ohio River valley.

Virginia Governor Robert Dinwiddie sent him to tell the commanders of three French forts linking Lake Erie and the Allegheny River that they were trespassing on the British empire and must withdraw to Canada with their men. With fellow frontiersman Christopher Gist as a guide, Washington made the thousand-mile round trip between Williamsburg and those forts in early winter. The French commanders were polite but warned Washington that it was the Americans who trespassed on French imperial lands and must depart. Nonplused, Dinwiddie had an expedition dispatched to build a fort at the Ohio Forks, promoted Washington to lieutenant colonel under Colonel Joshua Fry, and had them form a regiment to march to the forks. A French army forced the forty or so Virginians at the forks to surrender and withdraw, then established Fort Duquesne there. Washington assumed command when Fry died in a fall from his horse. He marched around 400 men on the trail toward the forks and established Fort Necessity at Great Meadows. Learning from Indian scouts that a French force was lurking a few miles away, he led forty of his men there and surrounded the camp. Someone fired a shot. Washington ordered his men to fire. They killed a dozen French and the rest surrendered except for one who fled to Fort Duquesne. A French force three times larger than Washington's surrounded the Virginians, opened fire, and threatened to wipe them out on July 3. Washington signed a surrender document on July 4, 1754.

When word of that fighting reached London and Paris, both kings mobilized their realms for war and dispatched reinforcements to their colonies. The fighting in North America between the British and French lasted until September 9, 1760, after three British armies converged on Montreal where Governor Pierre de Rigaud, marquis de Vaudreuil surrendered with the last French and Canadian troops. Until then the fighting was largely seesaw until a British expedition captured Quebec on September 13, 1759. Meanwhile, in 1756 the fighting spread to Europe with Britain, the Netherlands, and Prussia fighting France, Austria, and Russia, and, from 1762, Spain. Britain and its allies prevailed there too. That war spread to the West Indies, East Indies, West Africa, Argentina, and the Philippines, and in naval battles in the seas linking those distant lands. In the 1763 Treaty of Paris, Britain won Canada and Louisiana east of the Mississippi River from France and East and West Florida from Spain. France had transferred Louisiana along with New Orleans to Spain.

That war was decisive in North America because Britain for the first and last time committed overwhelming numbers of troops and warships there to win it. In all the previous colonial wars, the Americans had fought mostly alone. During this last war, each colony provided annual contingents of volunteer regiments that fought alongside regular British regiments. Lacking professional officers and training, the American regiments and leaders rarely distinguished themselves. The exception was Robert Rogers, who formed an elite ranger company in 1755 and each year added more companies until it formed a battalion. In that and two subsequent frontier wars he led around sixty raids and patrols deep behind enemy lines and fought with Indian tactics of rapid marches, ambushes, and escapes. Rogers was also a fine writer and thinker. He penned his twenty-eight "Rules of Ranging" that America's modern rangers use for operations, kept a thrilling journal of his adventures, and later created the intriguing play, "Ponteach, or the Savages of America, a Tragedy."[6]

***

Peace on America's frontier was fleeting. General Jeffrey Amherst, Britain's commander-in-chief in North America, provoked the newly conquered Indians of the Great Lakes region to revolt when he denied them the annual gifts, especially ammunition, that the French had given them.[7] The coalition of tribes in that war, called Pontiac's after the most prominent chief, initially captured eight frontier forts and besieged Forts Detroit and Pitt. Eventually armies with British regulars and American volunteers drove off the Indians and forced them to submit. King George III issued the Royal Proclamation of October 7, 1763, that sought to prevent future Indian wars by forbidding settlements west of the Appalachian Mountains.

The 1763 Proclamation deterred few frontiersmen from venturing west of the Appalachians to trap, hunt, and ponder sites for future settlements. Several score "long hunters" ranged through the future states of Kentucky and Tennessee over the next decade. James Harrod led thirty-one men to found Harrodsburg, Kentucky's first settlement, on June 16, 1774.

The vicious unprovoked murder of Mingo Chief Logan's family by frontiersmen provoked a war in the upper Ohio valley in 1774. Mingo avenged those deaths by leading raids on settlements. Virginia Governor John Murray, Earl Dunmore mobilized Virginia's militia into two columns that converged on the southeast Ohio tribes of Mingo, Shawnee, and Delaware. One column fought off an attack led by Shawnee Chief Cornstalk at Point Pleasant on October 10. The Virginians and tribal leaders ended the war with the Treaty of Camp Charlotte on October 14. That encouraged Richard Henderson, the Transylvania Company's president, to purchase lands between the Kentucky and Cumberland Rivers from the Cherokee for £10,000 worth of trade goods in the Treaty of Sycamore Shoals on March 14, 1775. He authorized Daniel Boone to lead thirty men to establish Boonesborough as Kentucky's second settlement on April 1. Boone had been a long hunter and would help lead Kentucky's defense during the independence war.[8]

The 1763 Proclamation was the first of a series of laws imposed by the king and Parliament over the next dozen years that eventually led to America's independence war and political revolution from 1775 to 1789.[9] For decades, British leaders increasingly feared that America's expanding population, economy, and nationalism would eventually lead those colonies to seek independence. They sought to thwart that by imposing taxes and troops on the colonists. In doing so, they unwittingly provoked what they most feared. Americans split among loyalists who accepted London's impositions, moderate patriots who lawfully protested with petitions and boycotts, and radical patriots like the Sons of Liberty who attacked British officials sent to enforce those laws. By 1773, London had rescinded all its taxes except one on tea, although it still kept several thousand redcoats in the colonies to preserve order. On December 16, several score radicals disguised as Indians swarmed aboard three vessels packed with tea in Boston harbor, and dumped the tea into the water. The British government reacted with what American patriots called the Intolerable or Coercive Acts that suspended Massachusetts' assembly, appointed General Thomas Gage the governor, sent more troops to Boston, and closed Boston harbor to all trade except food and fire wood until the colony paid for the destroyed tea. A separate law, the Quebec Act, extended Canada's border to the Ohio River thus depriving the northern colonies of their western land claims.

That provoked patriot leaders to convene a Congress of the colonies at Philadelphia in September and October 1774, during which the delegates agreed to boycott British goods, petition the king to suspend the Coercive Acts, establish committees of correspondence among themselves, and reconvene as Congress on May 10, 1775. Gage sent 800 elite troops to capture patriot leaders and supplies at Concord 16 miles west of Boston on April 19, 1775. Fighting erupted at Lexington when those redcoats opened fire on a militia company that stood in their way. The militiamen fled and the British marched on to Concord.

Militia companies converged on the redcoats and forced them to retreat to Boston, which they besieged.

Congress met in what became continual session until the war ended eight years later. Congress's most vital military decision was naming George Washington commander of the American army on June 19, 1775, and its most vital political decision was declaring independence for the United States of America on July 4, 1776. The war raged along both the settled eastern seaboard and wilderness frontier. During the war, although the Americans lost more battles than they won, two of their victories were decisive. The first came at Saratoga in upstate New York when an American army led by General Horatio Gates captured a British army led by General John Burgoyne on October 17, 1777. That encouraged French King Louis XVI to openly ally with the United States against Britain, and send over an army and navy to fight alongside the Americans. Washington led an army of American and French troops to bottle up General Charles Cornwallis at Yorktown, Virginia and force him to surrender on October 19, 1781.

Although the war persisted for two more years, the Americans had won it at Yorktown. Of the vicious fighting along the frontier, one American victory there was critical.[10] On February 25, 1779, General George Rogers Clark and his troops forced Colonel Henry Hamilton to surrender a British fort at Vincennes. That gave Americans a tenuous edge in the Ohio valley that let the diplomatic team led by Benjamin Franklin claim that territory for the United States in negotiations with the British. In the Treaty of Paris, signed on September 3, 1783, the British recognized American independence with a territory that extended west to the Mississippi River, south to Spanish East and West Florida, and north to midway through the Great Lakes of Superior, Huron, Erie, and Ontario, then a line eastward to the Atlantic Ocean.

***

Winning independence was the first stage in America's revolution. The second was establishing a viable national government. Congress was a weak government as each state had equal power, decisions had to be unanimous, the president annually elected by the delegates presided rather than governed, and Congress could raise money only from trade tariffs and was forbidden to impose taxes. During a convention at Philadelphia from May 25 to September 17, 1787, delegates from every state except Rhode Island debated and voted on the institutions and powers of a national government. The Constitution's preamble explains the new government's duties and its source of legitimacy:

"We the People, in order to form a more perfect Union, establish Justice, insure domestic tranquility, provide for the common defense, promote the general Welfare, and secure the Blessings of Liberty for ourselves and our Posterity, do ordain and establish this Constitution for the United States of America."

They designed a government with overlapping powers and duties among the president, Congress, and Supreme Court to encourage moderation and compromise. The delegates hoped that their civil, constructive behavior during the Convention would thereafter provide a model for politics at the federal, state, and local government levels. They overcame two divisions with compromises. States with large populations enjoyed the House of Representatives where their members were proportionate to their inhabitants while states with smaller populations enjoyed the Senate where each state had two members. Although the word slavery is not mentioned, three tenets acknowledged its existence that most delegates, including many slaveowners, abhorred. In state censuses held each decade, slaves were counted as three-fifths of a person for determining each state's number of representatives based on population; slaveowners could capture escaped slaves in other states including those that outlawed slavery; and the international slave trade could not be abolished before 1808.

The Constitution would become "the law of the land" after three-quarters of the state's assemblies ratified it. Alexander Hamilton, James Madison, and John Jay wrote 85 essays called the Federalist Papers to explain and promote support for the Constitution. The Constitution was ratified on June 22, 1788. Each state held popular elections for its representatives and each state assembly elected its two senators. The Electoral College unanimously chose George Washington to be president. Congress convened on March 4 and Washington was inaugurated president on April 30, 1789. Congress's priority was drafting a Bill of Rights as constitutional amendments to be ratified by the states. The Bill of Rights officially amended the Constitution on December 15, 1791.

Two interpretations of the Constitution soon emerged.[11] Hamilton, who was at the Convention, asserted that the Constitution empowered the federal government to do anything that it did not explicitly forbid. Hamilton wanted a muscular problem-solving national government that worked with the private sector to develop the economy and commanded an army and navy strong enough to deter foreign aggressors. Thomas Jefferson, who was ambassador to France when the Constitution was framed, favored a weak national government with powers confined only to what the Constitution explicitly stated while most power remained in the states whose militia and gunboats defended the country.

Another crucial issue was deciding how to dispose of the western territories. One by one, seven states with western claims surrendered them to the new federal government. Congress split those lands between the Northwest Territory that extended west from Pennsylvania to the Mississippi River and north from the Ohio River to the Great Lakes, and the Southwest Territory that extended west from Georgia, South Carolina, North Carolina, and Virginia to the Mississippi River and south from the Ohio River to the 35th Parallel and Spanish Florida. Three ordinances laid the foundation for America's frontier policy. The 1785 Ordinance had the Northwest Territory surveyed in thirty-six square mile townships to be divided into thirty-six sections of one square mile or 640 acres to be sold to the public for $640 or a dollar an acre or distributed to Independence War veterans. The 1787 Northwest Ordinance established a system for that territory eventually to be split first among five territories and then states. The federal government appointed a governor, a secretary, and three judges to govern the territory. The Ordinance had three especially progressive tenets; it outlawed slavery, required each township to maintain a public school, and protected Indians in their land and property. When a territory surpassed 5,000 American citizens, they could elect an assembly and send a representative to sit but not vote in Congress. When a territory surpassed 60,000 citizens, it could apply for statehood and write a constitution. The 1790 Southwest Ordinance extended the same process but allowed slavery.

The Northwest Ordinance upheld tribal rights: "The utmost good faith shall always be observed toward the Indians, their lands and property shall never be taken from them without their consent; and in their property, rights, and liberty, they shall never be invaded or disturbed unless in just and lawful wars authorized by Congress." The 1790 Indian Intercourse Act made the Northwest Ordinance's tenets on Indians policy across the United States. President Washington consistently called for peaceful, mutually nourishing relations with the tribes. In 1795, he got Congress to establish the Office of Indian Trade and the "factory" or federal trading post system to ensure fair prices and outlaw whiskey sales with Indians.

An ongoing debate was whether to sell public lands in large tracts to land companies or in small tracts to settlers.[12] A series of laws followed that regulated the size and price of public lands that varied depending on which side mustered more votes in Congress. The 1785 Land Ordinance made the smallest unit 620 acres for $620, a price only the rich could afford. That encouraged land companies to buy public lands and sell segments to homesteaders. Slow, sporadic sales caused Congress to lower the minimal purchase to 320 acres in 1796, lower the initial payment to half the total or $160 in 1800, and lower the floor to 160 acres in 1804. Those acts did encourage more sales with 3,374,843 acres bought in the Northwest Territory from 1800 to 1811.[13]

The latest frontier war threatened settlers in the Ohio River valley.[14] The Miami under Little Turtle and the Shawnee under Blue Jacket launched attacks into Kentucky and up the Ohio valley and inflicted two devastating, humiliating defeats on the army sent to crush them. They routed General Joseph Harmar and 500 mostly militiamen, killing 129 and wounding 94 at the battle of Kekionga on October 23, 1790, then devastated General Arthur Saint Clair's 1,200 troops, inflicting 933 casualties including 656 dead and 277 wounded at the battle of the Wabash on November 4, 1791. Washington appointed General Anthony Wayne to build a professional army at Fort Washington in Cincinnati, and lead it north to crush the northwest Indian alliance. It took Wayne three years to do so. As he built his army, he deployed it at a chain of forts built into Indian country. He defeated the Indian alliance at the battle of Fallen Timbers in the Maumee River valley on August 20, 1794. Under the Treaty of Greenville, signed on August 20, 1795, Little Turtle, Blue Jacket, and a score of other chiefs agreed to cede most of southern Ohio and a sliver of southeast Indiana to the United States.

The northwest Indians would not have resisted as long and successfully as they did without British weapons, munitions, advisors, and encouragement to resist the Americans. That aid mostly emanated from five forts—Detroit, Mackinac, Niagara, Oswego, and Maumee—that the British retained on American territory. They justified occupying those forts because Americans had not repaid all their pre-war debts to British financiers as required by the 1783 Treaty of Paris. The United States faced a worsening Indian coalition threat in the southwest that British agents and aid also abetted from Spanish territory. The Spanish and British had a common interest in containing America's frontier by intimidating or outright killing pioneers that ventured there. In 1793, Madrid closed the Mississippi River to American traders who had been shipping grain, lumber, salted meats, and other products to New Orleans and from there to foreign markets. That caused an economic crisis in Kentucky, Tennessee, Ohio, and western Pennsylvania. The Spanish also retained forts on American territory.

President Washington launched a diplomatic offensive to overcome those challenges. John Jay's treaty signed in London on November 19, 1794, required Britain to withdraw from forts on American territory, open British and West Indian markets to American traders, and pay for confiscations of American shipping and property in return for Americans to pay their debts to British financiers. Under the Treaty of San Lorenzo that Thomas Pickney signed on October 27, 1795, Spain agreed to open the Mississippi River to American traders for three renewable years, cede the Yazoo Strip, and abandon its forts in American territory. The Jay and Pinckney treaties advanced and secured America's frontier.

Yet another threat the United States faced was getting dragged into Europe's latest war. The French Revolution that began in May 1789 became increasingly radicalized. In 1792, France went to war against Austria, Prussia, and several smaller states, and declared itself a republic and a revolution without borders. In 1793, France executed its king and queen and declared war against Britain, Spain, and the Netherlands. Britain and France, the two greatest naval powers, imposed embargos against each other and captured neutral ships sailing to the other's ports. Scores of American ships, cargoes, and crews suffered confiscation. After signing the Jay treaty, Britain cut back its seizures of American merchant ships but depredations persisted by French naval and privateer captains. That led to a naval war between the United States and France from 1798 to 1800 that the Americans ultimately won. Napoleon Bonaparte, who seized power in a coup in November 1799, restored peace with the United States in the Treaty of Mortefontaine on September 30, 1800.

America's foreign trade steadily expanded to the ends of the earth and increasingly the continent's West Coast. The first American vessel bound for the Far East was the *Empress of China* that sailed from New York in 1784, reached Quandong (Canton), China the following year, and returned with a fortune for its investors. That inspired ever more entrepreneurs to outfit their own trade ventures. Voyages often lasted three years as captains stopped at ports along the way to exchange for products that they could profitably sell at other ports further along. Many vessels traded for hides and tallow at California ports and sea otter and beaver pelts from tribes along the Northwest coast before heading west across the Pacific to Hawaii and then China. Captain Robert Gray aboard the *Columbia* discovered the Columbia River, named it after his vessel, and claimed the region for the United States in 1795. In 1801, twenty of twenty-three vessels trading along the Northwest coast were American, two were British, and one was Russian. The homeport of most ships was Boston, causing Indians to call Americans "Bostons."[15]

***

Thomas Jefferson was a visionary.[16] He designed and had built by craftsmen and slaves a magnificent home atop Monticello, an 850ft hill overlooking Charlottesville. Eastward he could gaze across several score miles of mostly woodlands. Westward a few miles stretched the Blue Ridge Mountains that run northeast to southwest several hundred miles. In his mind, he looked beyond them 3,000 miles to the Pacific Ocean. He wanted America eventually to transform the Western Hemisphere into a prosperous, peaceful, democratic "empire of liberty": "Our confederacy must be the nest from which all America, North and South, is to be peopled."[17]

He had a dazzling political career as a delegate to Virginia's House of Burgesses then Congress, author of the Declaration of Independence, Virginia's governor, American ambassador to France, secretary of state, and vice president culminating in 1800, when he won the presidency. His most cherished project as president was to launch an exploration, scientific, and diplomatic expedition across the continent to the Pacific Ocean and then back. He had conceived that idea as a young man and first tried to realize it two decades earlier when he asked General George Rogers Clark to lead it, but it was stillborn for lack of money. He was chagrined to learn that Alexander Mackenzie of the Canadian Northwest Company first crossed the continent and reached the Pacific in 1793. In 1802, Jefferson got Congress to allocate $2,500 to outfit that Corps of Discovery, and selected Captains Meriwether Lewis and William Clark to lead it. There was only one catch. Spain owned the Louisiana Territory or the Mississippi River's western watershed that ran to the Rocky Mountains. He would have to obtain Madrid's permission for the Corps of Discovery to cross Spain's territory. Then he received words from his ambassador in Paris that France may have secretly purchased Louisiana.

That was true. In the Treaty of San Ildefonso, signed on October 1, 1800, France exchanged the Duchy of Tuscany and six warships to Spain for the Louisiana Territory. First Consul Napoleon Bonaparte did so because he wanted to revive France's New World empire that it had lost with the Seven Years War and the 1763 Treaty of Paris. He sent an army to crush the former slaves that had revolted and taken over Saint Dominique (Haiti), once France's most lucrative producer of sugar and other valuable tropical crops. But malaria and yellow fever decimated that army.

Rumors of France's takeover of Louisiana, especially New Orleans, alarmed Jefferson. On April 18, 1802, he wrote Robert Livingston, America's ambassador to France, that: "There is on the globe one single spot, the possessor of which is our natural enemy, it is New Orleans through which they produce of three eighths of our territory must pass to market . . . France, placing herself in that door, assumes to us the attitude of defiance."[18] Then Jefferson learned that on October 18, 1802, Louisiana's governor had closed the Mississippi River to American trade. He got Congress to appropriate money for New Orleans' purchase and sent James Monroe to Paris to negotiate. Monroe and Livingston were astounded when they offered to buy New Orleans and Foreign Minister Charles Talleyrand-Perigord replied that they could purchase the entire Louisiana Territory. They signed a treaty on April 30, 1803, whereby France transferred the Louisiana Territory to the United States for $15 million. Talleyrand graciously and presciently remarked that: "You have made a noble bargain for yourselves and I suppose you will make the best of it."[19]

PART II: THE FRONTIER AMERICAN WEST 1804–1848

Chapter 4

EXPLORERS AND TRADERS

> "The Indians have in no case obeyed the command to multiply and replenish the earth, and they cannot stand in the way of others doing so." (Marcus Whitman)

> "Oh, this is a life I would not exchange! ... There is such independence, so much free uncontaminated air ... I breath free without that oppression and uneasiness felt in the gossiping circles of a settled home." (Susan Shelby Magoffin on the Santa Fe Trail)

> "The amount of death among them is plainly told by the number of newly made graves ... Sad is their fate, buried here in this wild of wastelands, where not a mark will denote their last resting place far from loved ones." (William Swain)

Spanish, French, and American officials ceremonially transferred southern Louisiana to the United States at New Orleans on December 20, 1803, and northern Louisiana at St. Louis on March 8, 1804. That freed the way for the Corps of Discovery.[1] President Thomas Jefferson wrote Captain Meriwether Lewis that: "The object of your mission is to explore the Missouri River, and such principal streams of it, as, by its course and communication with the waters of the Pacific Ocean ... [that] may offer the most direct and practicable water communication across the continent." They should map prominent geographical features there and back. As for Indians, the Corps must "treat them in the most friendly and conciliatory manner which their own conduct will admit; allay all jealousies of the object of your journey; satisfy them of its innocence; make them acquaintance with the position, extent, character, peaceable and commercial disposition of the United States; of our wish to be neighborly, friendly, and useful to them, and of our disposition to a commercial intercourse with them."[2] He was to note each tribe's numbers, range, sustenance, disposition, allies, enemies, language, and customs. Finally, he was to record and collect samples of all animals, plants, and minerals.

Lewis spent months preparing for the journey by accumulating and sending supplies, studying maps, picking the minds of geologists and botanists, and learning navigation and surveying skills. The expedition wintered at Camp Dubois beside Wood Creek on the Illinois side of the Mississippi River across from the Missouri River mouth. After the United States officially took title to Louisiana, the Corps journeyed to St. Charles 20 miles up the Missouri River.

Lewis, Clark, and around forty-five soldiers, hunters, and boatmen along with Clark's slave York embarked aboard a keelboat and two pirogues and headed up the Missouri River from St. Charles on May 21, 1804. Over the next two and a half years, the Corps journeyed to the Pacific Ocean and back, stepping ashore at St. Louis on September 26, 1806. Along the way, Lewis and Clark conducted diplomacy with around 70 tribes and discovered over 200 new plants and animals.[3] They lost only one man who died from a burst appendix. They had only one fight with Indians when Blackfeet tried to steal the rifles of Lewis and four other men; the explorers killed two Blackfeet and the others fled.

They first wintered with the neighboring Mandan and Hidatsa tribes, which let them build a nearby palisade and cabins. There the captains sent back the keelboat packed with all the stuffed and live animals, plants, fossils, and reports they had gathered so far. They also hired Toussaint Charbonneau, a French Canadian, as an interpreter; accompanying him was his pregnant wife Sacagawea, a Shoshone captured by a Hidatsa raiding party a couple of years earlier. As soon as the snow melted, they resumed their journey aboard pirogues as far as Three Forks where they headed into the mountains. Along the way, Sacagawea gave birth to a healthy boy. With extraordinary luck, they encountered Sacagawea's band, which traded them horses and gave them a guide to cross the Rockies. Beyond the mountains, they left their horses with the Nez Perce, built pirogues, and headed down the Snake and Columbia Rivers.

Awestruck, they first gazed at the Pacific Ocean on November 7, 1805. The captains decided to winter at the Columbia River mouth hoping that a ship might appear and resupply them. They let everyone in the Corps, including York and Sacagawea, vote on which bank to reside. That was the first recorded time a woman and a black man voted. To their disappointment no ship appeared. The Corps' establishment of Fort Clatsop helped solidify America's claim to the region begun by Captain Grey with his 1795 discovery.

They began paddling up the Columbia River on March 23, 1806, and after six months of mingled toil and exhilaration reached St. Louis. Along the way, Lewis had that fatal battle with the Blackfeet and Charbonneau, Sacagawea, and their son stayed at the Mandan and Hidatsa villages. News of the expedition's successful journey thrilled and inspired the nation. Jefferson named Lewis Upper Louisiana's governor and Clark Indian Superintendent at St. Louis. Tragically, Lewis, who suffered from manic depression, died from a likely self-inflicted gunshot wound on the Natchez Trace in October 1809. The Corps' official report did not appear until 1814 after President James Madison had scholars Nicolas Biddle and Paul Allen edit it. The Corps of Discovery was the most famous and important of the army expeditions that mapped the West during the nineteenth century.[4]

***

The Lewis and Clark expedition opened the way for the West's fur trade era, with two subsequent phases. The first was dominated by beaver pelts taken mostly by trappers in the Rocky Mountains from 1807 to 1840, along with bison robes taken mostly by trade with Missouri River tribes increasingly important.[5] Bison robes dominated the second phase from 1840 to 1885. Beaver pelts and bison robes served different needs. Pelts had short and long hairs; once separated, the short hairs were made into felt for top hats. Robes made excellent blankets, especially for sleigh goers in winter, and leather belts in machinery. Other commercial furs included otter, muskrat, weasel, raccoon, mink, deer, elk, bear, wolf, sable, and marten, although together they were a fraction of the market value and volume of beaver and bison.

The pelt era had two peak phases, one from 1807 to 1812, and another from 1822 to 1834. In between was a hiatus caused by the 1812 War and postwar depression. Pelts varied in price that peaked around $6 each at St. Louis in 1830 then steadily declined as silk became more popular than felt for hats. That shift was fortuitous because over-trapping rendered beaver increasingly scarce. Robe prices stayed steady at around $3 each at St. Louis.

Indians supplied one quarter of the pelts and nearly all the robes from 1807 to 1840. As in other regions, American and other foreign traders and trappers exploited, distorted, and expanded existing tribal trade networks across the West. That led to varying tensions with the tribes. Relations ranged from mostly friendly with the Mandan, Hidatsa, Nez Perce, Cheyenne, and Crow to perennial war with the

Blackfeet and Gros Ventres. But a raiding party from any tribe might steal a trapping party's horses or kill isolated trappers.

Trappers were either "engagees" who received a salary and supplies for taking, processing, and giving all pelts to their employer or "free" who supplied themselves and sold their pelts to whoever paid the highest price or had the most vital goods to trade. The best trapping seasons were late fall when beaver fur thickened and the streams and lakes were still ice-free, and early spring after snowmelt when beaver fur was still thick. Generally, a trapper had half a dozen traps that he set during late afternoon at places along a stream or lake frequently by beaver, then checked the next morning to see if he caught anything. To lure beavers, he put a drop of castoreum oil from their gland on a stick stuck in the water near the trap. Ideally, the beaver triggered the trap as he sniffed the scent and drowned as he struggled to escape. The trapper skinned the pelt, then stretched and tied it within a willow hoop with sinew lashed through holes punched around the edge, and finally scrapped the pelt of all meat. Pelts were stacked and pressed in hundred-pound bound packs.

Free trappers or mountain men are among the West's icons, celebrated for their survival, hunting, trapping, fighting, and exploring skills, their buckskin clad appearance, and either their taciturn or boisterous behavior. Mountain man faced near constant danger. One of four died from Indians, grizzlies, frostbite, starvation, heatstroke, rattlesnakes, accidents, or brawls. An analysis of 312 mountain men found that around half or 50.7 percent were Anglo-Americans, 25.7 percent were French-Americans and French-Canadians, and the rest were an array of other nationalities or tribes. Nearly two-thirds or 63.4 percent were trappers, 23.9 percent were clerks, leaders, and partners, and 12.7 percent were hunters, guides, interpreters, and boatmen. Journals or letters exist from one of five among them. They averaged 15 years in the West, with 17.8 percent eventually settling in the Northwest, 16.2 percent in St. Louis or Kansas City, 14.8 percent in California, 13.8 percent in Taos, and 12.8 percent in the northern Rockies.

Many married Indian women who provided labor, sex, usually children, and sometimes love. A mountain man who sought a desirable wife bought her from her father after haggling over her price in horses and other goods. Married trappers tended to be richer than bachelors, although wives usually displayed that wealth through bangles, rings, ribbons, and other "foofaraw" and "gewgaws." Divorce was easy. A husband could simply dump his wives' possessions outside the tipi or sell her to someone else. Those who stayed with their wives suffered the stigma of being a "squaw man" and their children "half breeds" if they returned to the settlements. "Respectable" folks shunned them. Living with his wife's people usually meant no privacy and constantly hosting her relatives. The average marriage with Indian women lasted 15 years and 41 percent of the time ended with the mountain man's death. Those who settled in New Mexico or California usually married Mexican women. One in five never married.[6]

***

Manuel Lisa dominated the Missouri fur trade from 1807 to 1812.[7] In April 1807, he headed up the Missouri River with forty-two men and supplies packed aboard a keelboat. They ascended the Missouri to the Yellowstone River then up it to the Bighorn River where he established Fort Manuel and dispatched his men to trap the region. In April 1808, they descended with pelts worth $9,000 in St. Louis. That success attracted investors including William Clark, Andrew Henry, and Auguste and Pierre Chouteau to the Missouri Fur Company that Lisa founded in 1809. Lisa and Henry led 172 men in keelboats up the Missouri River, established Fort Mandan at the Mandan village and reestablished Fort Manuel at the Bighorn. Lisa's most valuable man was John Colter who had accompanied the Corps of Discovery and stayed in the mountains to trap. Alone or with small parties, he explored much of the Three Forks and Yellowstone regions. Henry led a party over the divide to Three Forks where they built a fort. Blackfeet war parties stalked Henry and his trappers in 1810 and killed five. Henry abandoned the post and returned with his men and furs to St. Louis. Nonplused, Lisa led profitable expeditions in 1811 and 1812.

Meanwhile at the continent's east end, John Jacob Astor transformed himself from rags to riches and became America's first millionaire.[8] He was born in Germany and at age 21 arrived in New York to seek his fortune in 1783. He first sold flutes then worked as a butcher but in 1784 got a job in a fur company. Within a year, he was buying and selling furs on his own in New York, Albany, Montreal, and London. He founded the American Fur Company in 1808 and ruthlessly crushed rivals by underselling them and either bankrupting or buying them out, and extended his operations across the Great Lakes and eventually across the continent. He diversified his wealth through real estate deals in New York City, his headquarters, and elsewhere. At his death in 1848, he bequeathed to his heirs an estate worth $20 million, or more than half a billion dollars today.

Not everything Astor touched turned to gold. He was a high stakes gambler. His riskiest was trying to capture the Northwest fur trade.

In 1810, he formed the subsidiary Pacific Fur Company that launched two expeditions, one across the continent and the other around the Western Hemisphere to converge at the Columbia River mouth. Both eventually led to disaster.[9]

Captain Jonathan Thorn commanded the supply ship *Tonquin* that departed New York on September 8, 1810, and reached the Columbia River via Cape Horn on March 22, 1811. The overland party had not arrived so the expedition sailed up the coast trading with the tribes. Thorn was a violent martinet who alienated the partners and crew alike. On Vancouver Island, he smacked an Indian chief who was a tough bargainer. The chief angrily left with his men but returned smiling the next day ready to trade. After the Indians boarded, they pulled clubs and hatchets from beneath their robes and slaughtered everyone aboard. A sailor detonated the gunpowder magazine that killed virtually all the Indians. The sole American survivor was ashore, and eventually escaped to Astoria with horrifying news of what happened.

Wilson Hunt led sixty men, including botanists John Bradbury and Thomas Nuttal, on three keelboats from St. Louis on October 22, 1810, and five weeks later, they established a winter post at the confluence of the Missouri and Nodaway Rivers. Hunt returned to St. Louis for more supplies and men. Manuel Lisa was also planning his own expedition for 1811, and was determined to get upriver first. The result was a race in which Lisa and his keelboats steadily caught up to Hunt and his men on their keelboat despite their 21-day head start. Both parties reached the Arikara tribe's villages on June 12. There Hunt and Lisa competed to buy horses. By July 12, Hunt had eighty-two horses and he led his men west across the plains; Bradbury and Nuttal lingered with the Arikara before returning to St. Louis. Along the way, Hunt discovered South Pass, a broad plain across the Continental Divide, lost horses and three men, ran short of supplies, and eventually split into two groups. The first reached the Columbia River mouth on January 18, 1812, and began building Fort Astoria. Hunt and the second arrived on February 15. Hunt dispatched his men in parties to trap and trade throughout the region. The supply ship *Beaver* dropped anchor at Astoria on May 11. They gathered around thirty-five packs of pelts. In early June, Hunt dispatched Robert Stuart with several men east with a report to Astor.

Three challenges combined to doom the Pacific Fur Company. A storm sank the third supply ship, the *Lark*. The British Northwest Company had launched its own expedition of seventy-four men led by John McTavish to cross the continent, descend the Columbia

River, and capture the fur trade. After the United States declared war against Britain on June 12, 1812, the Admiralty dispatched a warship to take Astoria.

Leaving Duncan McDougall in charge, Hunt sailed with the *Beaver* to the Hawaiian Islands to trade. On October 8, 1813, McTavish and his men reached Astoria. McTavish informed McDougall that a British warship would soon arrive, and offered to buy them out with the men free to join the Northwest Company or return home. McDougall agreed to sell his beaver pelts for $2 a pound and sea otter pelts for $0.50, fractions of what the Chinese at Quandong would have paid. McTavish renamed Astoria Fort George. The Northwest Company established trading posts at key confluences up the Columbia River valley.

Astor's Pacific Fur Company was a financial loss and the war with Britain suppressed his American Fur Company operations and profits in the Great Lakes and upper Mississippi River valley regions. However, after the war, American Fur Company profits steadily rose until by the early 1820s, Astor was ready to launch his latest grand plan, this time systematically to take over the trans-Mississippi fur trade. Meanwhile, the United States and Britain diplomatically resolved their conflict over who had the best claim to the Northwest with an 1818 treaty that established joint occupancy.

***

Louisiana Territory's acquisition inspired American visionaries, merchants, and adventurers to want more. They especially eyed New Mexico's markets. Those efforts eventually led to the Santa Fe Trail, but not before numerous failed expeditions with many suffering confiscated goods and prison stints.[10]

William Morrison, a merchant at Kaskaskia, Illinois, sent Baptiste LaLande and Jose Gervais with trade goods atop packhorses to Santa Fe in 1804. They headed first to the Pawnee villages in the Platte River valley to trade and hire guides for the journey, and they reached Santa Fe in autumn. But LaLande did not return to Kaskaskia with the profits. Instead, he settled in Santa Fe and lived off them.

President Jefferson's latest ventures also fell short. He got Congress to sponsor an expedition led by William Dunbar and George Hunter up the Red River to explore its headwaters in October 1804 but Osage Indians blocked their way. Instead, Dunbar and Hunter headed up the Ouachita River in Arkansas before returning. In 1806, Jefferson got Congress to allocate $5,000 for Captain Thomas Sparks, botanist

Thomas Freeman, and twenty-four other men to embark from Fort Adams up the Red River. At their 635th mile, Spanish cavalry forced them to turn back.

General James Wilkinson, Upper Louisiana's governor, dispatched Lieutenant Zebulon Pike with twenty-three men from St. Louis, first to visit the Osage in western Missouri followed by the Pawnee in the Platte River valley, then south to the Arkansas River and up it to its source, then south to the Red River's source, down it to the Mississippi, and up it back to St. Louis.[11] Wilkinson, who was a paid spy for Spain, secretly sent word about the expedition to his handlers. That round trip would have been within American territory. Instead, Pike led his men over the divide into the upper Rio Grande valley in Spain's empire, where they built a fort in February 1807. Pike sent a man to Santa Fe to determine whether the expedition would be welcomed. New Mexico's governor dispatched a hundred dragoons to capture the intruders. Outnumbered five to one, Pike prudently surrendered. The Spanish conveyed him and his men first to Santa Fe then Chihuahua and finally to Nacogdoches in east Texas where they were released.

Meanwhile, the latest enterprising Americans headed to Santa Fe. Jacques Clamorgan was a St. Louis merchant whose company traded with tribes up the Missouri River. In August 1807, he led a dozen men southwest and reached Santa Fe in November. The governor let them trade their goods and proceed to Chihuahua. Clamorgan and his men eventually returned to the United States via Natchitoches by late spring 1808. An eight-man party led by Reuben Smith, a former army lieutenant, left St. Genevieve on December 20, 1809, but Spanish dragoons arrested them and took them to Santa Fe. Their penalty for trespassing was to labor in the Santa Rita copper mines for two years. They were released and reached Natchitoches in April 1812. That same month a nine-man party led by Robert McKnight with packhorses laden with $10,000 worth of trade goods arrived in Santa Fe. Spanish authorities arrested, tried, and convicted them of trespassing and confined them to prison. A royal decree freed them and other foreigners in Spanish prisons in May 1820. Joseph Philibert led eighteen men on a trapping and trading expedition to New Mexico's Sangre de Cristo Mountains in April 1813. Spanish soldiers captured them but this time the court released them after confiscating their goods. They returned to St. Louis on July 29, 1815. Auguste Chouteau and Julius De Mun were business partners who sought permission to trade and trap in New Mexico. On September 10, 1815, they led forty-six men from St. Louis toward the Arkansas River headwaters. De Mun journeyed to Santa Fe where officials rejected his request. They returned with forty-four packs of beaver pelts to St. Louis after repelling a Pawnee attack along the way. Chouteau and De Mun led another trapping expedition to the upper Arkansas watershed in 1816, but Spanish troops arrested and brought them to Santa Fe where officials confiscated their goods and released them after two months in prison.

Spain cut a deal that relieved it of a financial and political burden just two years before it lost its continental empire. On February 22, 1819, Secretary of States John Quincy Adams and Luis de Onis, Spain's ambassador, signed the Adams-Onis Treaty whereby Spain ceded East and West Florida to the United States, and they defined their border to extend from the Gulf of Mexico up the Sabine River to the 32nd degree north to the Red River and up it to the 100th meridian then north to the Arkansas River and up it to the 42nd Parallel then west to the Pacific Ocean. The United States paid indirectly for Florida by compensating American investors with $5 million of claims against Spain and its subjects.

Mexico officially won independence on February 24, 1821, when General Augustin de Iturbide issued his Plan of Iguala. A decade of war had devastated Mexico's population and economy. Mexico desperately needed infusions of money, entrepreneurs, and settlers, especially on the northern frontier. The government announced that Mexico was open to international trade, investment, and immigrants.

William Becknell was an enterprising frontiersman and 1812 War veteran. He was on his farm at Franklin, Missouri near the Missouri River when he learned that Mexico's government had opened the country and resolved to get there first. He bought $300 worth of trade goods, inspired seventeen other adventurers to join him, and they embarked on the 865-mile journey to Santa Fe on September 1, 1821. Becknell had masked their expedition as a hunting excursion on the plains with a *Missouri Intelligencer* newspaper advertisement but soon explained his true goal. They had no maps to follow, just a direction, and with enormous fortitude, instinct, and luck reached Santa Fe in November. Governor Facundo Melgares warmly welcomed Becknell and his men, and let them stay and sell their goods. Becknell earned $6,000 in Spanish coins for his investment. He reinvested some of that in more goods for a return journey the next year, this time with twenty-one men and wagons. Inspired by Becknell's success, ever more entrepreneurs launched their own trading ventures to Santa Fe and most profited.

***

Robert Fulton worked on designs and prototypes for steamboats for 15 years before building one powerful enough to steam up the Hudson River from New York to Albany in 1807. Steamboats revolutionized transportation and thus the economy. They held a hundred times more cargo than a keelboat and were ten times faster up and down stream. A hundred pounds of cargo carried from Louisville to New Orleans cost $5 on a keelboat and $0.25 on a steamboat. The first steamboat on western waters was the *New Orleans*, constructed at Pittsburgh in 1811. Its namesake was its first destination. The first steamboat docked at St. Louis in August 1817. The first steamboat to journey up the Missouri River got as far as Franklin in May 1819. By May 1839, shipyards had constructed 378 steamboats for western rivers, 130 at Pittsburg, 83 at Cincinnati, 22 at Wheeling, and the rest elsewhere for an average cost of $25,000 and combined cost of $9,480,000.[12]

President James Monroe authorized a mission for Colonel Henry Atkinson to pack 1,126 troops aboard four steamboats and ascend the Missouri River to the Yellowstone River mouth, and build a fort there. The expedition embarked in May 1819, but got no further than a dozen miles above Council Bluffs where Atkinson had his troops found Cantonment Missouri, later renamed Fort Atkinson. During the winter, scurvy killed more than 200 men. Nonetheless, Atkinson's expedition inaugurated steamboat transportation on the Missouri River.[13]

Major Stephen Long led nineteen troops from Fort Atkinson in June 1820, with orders to head west up the Platte River to the Rocky Mountains then south as far as the Red River then down it back to civilization. They thought they found the Red River but instead it was the Canadian River that led them back to the Arkansas River, which they followed east to the settlements. In his report, Long pronounced the region "almost wholly unfit for cultivation" and labeled his map the "Great American Desert." The region's only value was "as a frontier . . . to serve as a barrier to prevent too great an extension of our population westward, and secure us against the machinations or incursions of an enemy that might otherwise be disposed to annoy us in that part of our frontier."[14]

***

The West's second peak beaver fur era, from 1821 to 1834, overlapped and was developed by what some historians have deemed a national era of "expectant capitalists" led by "rags to riches" "self-made men." By the 1820s, America had transformed from an elitist into a populist nation as states dropped their property qualifications for voting and running for public office, and entrepreneurs took advantage of greater opportunities to get rich. Richard Hofstadter defined an "expectant capitalist" as "a hardworking ambitious person for whom enterprise was a kind of religion . . . the master mechanic who aspired to open his own shop, the planter or farmer who speculated in land, the lawyer who hoped to be a judge, the local politician who wanted to go to Congress, the grocer who would be a merchant."[15] Of course, such men had been in America since Jamestown, but the chance of them realizing their dreams was better than ever by the 1820s.

More than anyone Andrew Jackson, the president from 1829 to 1837, epitomized and inspired that transformation.[16] The six previous presidents more or less were born into affluence and enjoyed good educations, with four from Virginia and two from Massachusetts. Jackson was born into poverty in South Carolina and most of his family died during the Independence War. As a young man, he headed west to Tennessee and there by enterprise, courage, and determination transformed himself into a lawyer, rich plantation owner, militia general, congressman, senator, and finally president. His greatest fame was as the ruthless general who crushed the Creek Indians in central Alabama and the British at New Orleans during the War of 1812. Jackson had a hair-triggered temper and sense of honor. He killed one man in a duel and bore a bullet near his heart from another. He advocated a presidency unbound by most legal and moral restraints, an army and navy powerful enough to deter or devastate any foreign or domestic enemies, and abolition of the United States Bank and any federal policies that promoted infrastructure, industries, science, and education.

For the fur trade, from 1807 to 1813, Manuel Lisa and John Jacob Astor personified "expectant capitalists" long before Andrew Jackson symbolized the type. In the early 1820s, two men exceeded all others in reviving the beaver pelt trade and opening the West for exploitation, William Becknell for the Santa Fe trade and William Ashley for the Rocky Mountains.

***

William Ashley was a Missouri entrepreneur who revolutionized the fur trade and accelerated the West's development by inaugurating the first rendezvous in the heart of the Rockies in 1825.[17] He led a supply train to the site where trapping parties and Indian bands gathered. The annual rendezvous lasted until 1840 when plunging beaver pelt prices rendered it unprofitable.[18] Previously, Ashley, after reaching Missouri in 1805, invested in lead mining, gunpowder making, and real estate, and was an adept politician who became a justice of the peace, militia general, and lieutenant governor. But by 1822, his businesses had failed and he was deep in debt. Rather than cutback and payoff, he doubled down, now determined to reap a fur fortune from the West. He faced cutthroat competition from the Missouri, Columbia, and French Fur Companies that competed for the Missouri River trade by building trading posts at river junctions and launching their own trapping parties into the Rockies.

Ashley formed a partnership with Andrew Henry and on credit they bought two keelboats and packed them with goods. On February 13, Ashley issued this advertisement in the *Missouri Gazette*: "To enterprising young men. The subscriber wishes to engage ONE HUNDRED MEN to ascend the Missouri River to its source, there to be employed for one, two, or three years—For the particulars enquire of Major Andrew Henry, near the lead mines in the county of Washington, (who will ascend with, and command the party) or to the subscriber near St. Louis." Each recruit would receive munitions and could keep half the furs he trapped.

That appeal and deal inspired around 130 adventurous young men to sign up. Henry led about half of them up the Missouri on April 3, followed by Ashley with the rest a month later. Henry's party reached the Yellowstone in September and constructed Fort Henry as a base. After Ashley's joined them in October, the leaders dispatched trapping parties in different directions. Ashley then returned to St. Louis to sell what furs they had gathered and organize next year's expedition. Blackfeet war parties harassed Henry and his men throughout the winter and into the spring, killing half a dozen trappers.

Ashley borrowed more money, bought more supplies, hired more men, packed them into a keelboat, and headed upriver in March 1823. On May 30, they anchored near two Arikara villages. Ashley planned to buy horses from the Arikara and send a party west across the plains while he continued upstream with the rest aboard the keelboat. Instead, the Arikara attacked and killed fifteen of his men. He withdrew to an island downstream and sent word to Colonel Henry Leavenworth at Fort Atkinson downstream above the Platte River. Atkinson led most of his 6th Infantry that with Ashley and his men and rival Missouri Fur Company leader Joshua Pilcher and his men defeated the Arikara and reopened the river.

Ashley then implemented his plan. He selected Jedediah Smith to lead his land party. Over the next seven years, Smith's expeditions mapped swaths of the far West, including two to California.[19] He was renowned for his courage, intelligence, honesty, modesty, and vision. Tragically, he suffered two attacks that wiped out most of his men, one by the Mohave on the Colorado River and the other by Umpqua in southern Oregon in 1828. A grizzly mauled him near the Black Hills. A Comanche war party killed him on the Cimarron River in 1830.

Meanwhile, Ashley and Smith eventually joined Henry's men on the Yellowstone then fanned out in trapping parties across the Rockies. In spring 1824, Ashley returned with that year's furs to St. Louis. Before leaving, he told his field leaders that he would bring supplies by horseback to a rendezvous at Horse Creek near the upper Green River on July 1, 1825. Around 120 men attended that first rendezvous and Ashley departed with around fifty packs worth $48,000 in St. Louis.

At the 1826 rendezvous, Ashley sold out to Jedediah Smith, David Jackson, and William Sublette. The partners divided their duties. Jackson would lead trapping parties in the northern Rockies; Sublette would head back and forth with the supply caravan to rendezvous and beaver packs back to St. Louis markets; and Smith would explore for new beaver rich regions.

The partners faced a rival in the northern Rockies. After taking Astoria in 1813, the Northwest Company expanded trading and trapping in the region until 1821 when the Hudson Bay Company acquired it, and expanded further. The regional headquarters was Fort Vancouver on the Columbia River across from the Willamette River mouth. John Mcloughlin was the factor or director from 1825 to 1832. Peter Ogden led annual trapping brigades through the Northwest as far as northern California, the Great Basin, and northern Rocky Mountains. The strategy was to create a "fur desert" by trapping out streams before Americans could exploit them.[20]

Smith, Jackson, and Sublette reached a crucial decision at the 1830 rendezvous. They decided to get out of the mountains while they were ahead and alive. They emulated Ashley who recognized that it was more profitable and less dangerous to sell goods to fur companies than lead them in the field. They sold their company to Jim Bridger, Thomas Fitzpatrick, Milton Sublette, Henry Fraeb, and Jean Baptiste Gervais who called their partnership the Rocky Mountain Fur Company. That new company faced fierce competition in the northern Rockies not just from the Hudson Bay Company but increasingly from a new rival.

***

After his Pacific Fur Company failed, John Jacob Astor spent a decade reaping riches from the Great Lakes fur trade and New York real estate.

Yet he could not shake his dream of dominating the fur trade across the continent. In 1822, he formed the American Fur Company's Western Department with Kenneth McKenzie in charge. Astor worked out with McKenzie a two-stage strategy of conquest. First, McKenzie would take over the Missouri River buffalo robe trade by building posts on each tribe's land and underselling rival companies. Next, he would dispatch trapping parties that eventually squeezed out the Rocky Mountain Fur Company. McKenzie established his headquarter at Fort Union, which his men built at the confluence of the Yellowstone with the Missouri in 1829 and from there dispatched the first American Fur Company trapping expedition to the Rockies. Steamboats plied back and forth between St. Louis and American Fur Company trading posts up the Missouri.[21]

During a business trip to Europe in 1832, Astor wrote this warning to his partner Pierre Chouteau in St. Louis: "I very much fear beaver will not sell well. It appears that they make hats of silk in place of beaver."[22] The American Fur Company's 25-year charter expired in 1833. Rather than renew it, he sold the American Fur Company's Northern Department to its director Ramsay Crooks and its Western Department to Pierre Chouteau and Bernard Pratte in 1834.

Smallpox lurked aboard the American Fur Company steamboat that journeyed up the Missouri River in 1837, and spread at each Indian village and trading post to Fort Benton. The result was mass death for the tribes, with the Mandan, Hidatsa, and Arikara suffering the worst, with nine of ten people dead. Four Bears, a Mandan chief, expressed his rage at the source of the smallpox epidemic that destroyed his people: "I have loved the Whites . . . I have Never Wronged a White Man . . . I have always protected them . . . And how have they repaid it! With ingratitude . . . I do pronounce them to be a set of Black hearted Dogs . . . think of your Wives, children, Brothers, Sisters, Friends, and . . . all you hold dear, are all Dead or Dying, with their faces rotten . . . and rise all together and Not leave one of them Alive."[23] Four Bears died later that day.

***

Over time, as coin dwindled in New Mexico, American traders accepted more pelts, robes, and bison tongues in payment. Free trappers reaped about a quarter of pelts from the West in the Southwest, with most congregating at Taos between expeditions.[24] William Wolfskill led trapping parties down the Rio Grande to El Paso in 1822 and 1823, then with partner Ewing Young up the Rio Grande and over the divide into the San Juan River in 1824. After rescuing the governor's daughter from Comanches, father and son Sylvestre and James Pattie got the right to trap the Gila River in 1824 and Sylvestre to operate the Santa Rita copper mine in southern New Mexico in 1826 while James returned to the Gila River. The Patties led a party as far as Santa Catalina Mission in California but Mexican officials arrested and jailed them in San Diego. In 1830, Sylvestre died in prison but James was released and eventually returned to his Ohio home. Two trapping parties reached California and managed to evade arrest in 1830, one led by Young and the other by Wolfskill. Of the free trappers, Joseph Walker ranged the furthest, lasted the longest, and provided the most skilled leadership.[25] He led two expeditions to California and gazed in wonder at Yosemite Valley in 1833.

***

Senator Thomas Benton of Missouri proposed a bill that mapped and formed a standard route for the Santa Fe Trail. On March 3, 1825, President James Monroe signed the bill that appropriated $10,000 for surveying and marking the road, and $20,000 for negotiating the right to cross from tribes along the way. In 1827, the army completed that task and built Fort Leavenworth on the Missouri River's west bank 30 miles upstream from Independence.

Ever more wagon trains followed the Santa Fe Trail. Independence became the jumping-off town for the 770-mile trail in 1827. From 1837, Westport on the Kansas River competed with and eventually surpassed Independence as the starting point. At the Arkansas River, traders faced a tough choice. They could angle southwest to the Cimarron River route, which was shorter and quicker but water and grass were scarce while Comanche war parties often lurked along the way. Or they could follow the Arkansas River upstream to the Rocky Mountain foothills then head south over Raton Pass, a route longer, rockier, and harder on wagon wheels. From 1824, New Mexico's governors imposed increasingly onerous and arbitrary "taxes" on the American traders that peaked with Manuel Armijo's $500 fee on each wagon in 1839.

Susan Magoffin, who accompanied her merchant husband Samuel down the Santa Fe Trail in 1846, was "delighted with this new country, its people." She embraced the kind-hearted New Mexicans and their lifestyle of plaza strolls, leisurely meals, and joyful fandangoes. Among the customs she adopted, "it is truly pleasant to follow after the Mexican style, which is after dinner to close the shutters and take a short siesta; it both refreshes the mind and body, one is then prepared, without fatigue, of the morning's labors, to go about the duties of the evening." She marveled at the elegant dress of the ladies "in silks, satins, ginghams . . . embroidered crape shawls, fine rabozos—and decked with . . . huge necklaces, countless rings, combs, bows . . . and . . . colored handkerchiefs." She followed a female friend's advice for how to deal with seductive men: "punish them for their misconduct, spoil them for their good deeds." The only custom she did not like was how the sexes separated at most gatherings to talk among themselves. She preferred the American custom of mixed socializing.[26]

Merchants competed for trade with the upper Arkansas River Cheyenne and Arapaho bands. Brothers Charles and William Bent and Ceran Saint Vrain established Fort William at Big Timbers 25 miles east of the Purgatoire River mouth in 1831. John Gantt and Jefferson Blackwell founded Fort Cass in the Rocky Mountain foothills in 1832. The Bents and St. Vrain built a second fort three miles east of Fort Cass. They built Bent's Fort near the mouth of Fountain Creek and present day La Junta, Colorado in 1833. After they drove Fort Cass out of business, they abandoned their other two posts and concentrated their operations at Bent's Fort.

***

American claims to the Columbia River valley appeared a pipe dream after the Northwest Company and a British warship took over Astoria in 1813. Nonetheless, James Monroe's administration was able to negotiate a treaty with Britain for joint occupancy of the Northwest in 1818. A few visionaries promoted America's settlement of the Northwest. In 1820, John Floyd, a Virginia congressman, sponsored a resolution calling for a special committee to "inquire into the situation of the settlements upon the Pacific Ocean and the expediency of occupying the Columbia River." That resolution passed and Floyd chaired the committee that produced an annexation bill but it lost by 100 to 61 votes in 1823. Most congressmen viewed the Northwest as too remote and American interests there too limited for annexation.

Hall Kelly was a Massachusetts schoolteacher who also dreamed of America's takeover of the Northwest. He understood that the nation's claim was only as strong as the number of boots on the ground there. In 1831, he founded the "American Society for Encouraging the Settlement of the Oregon Territory" that lobbied Congress for funds to underwrite emigration but failed to get any backing. Hall and fifty others formed a "Joint Stock Trading Company" to raise money for an expedition. Among them was an entrepreneur bold enough to lead the way.

Nathaniel Wyeth was a Boston businessman whose most lucrative money-making operation was harvesting ice from New England ponds in winter for sale to town and city people with ice storage cellars. Like Astor, Wyeth's strategy for establishing a settlement in Oregon included one expedition crossing the continent and another reaching the Columbia River by sailing around the Western Hemisphere. In March 1832, he headed with thirty-one men to Independence, Missouri, where William Sublette agreed to let them join his caravan to that year's rendezvous at Pierre's Hole west of the Teton Mountains. There Wyeth's party joined Milton Sublette's trapping brigade that took them as far as the Hudson Bay Company post of Walla Walla. By then, Wyeth had only eleven men left as the others either turned back east or joined other trapping parties. Wyeth and his men reached Fort Vancouver where John McLoughlin cordially welcomed him. He learned that his ship had sunk along the way. Wyeth returned to Boston where, in 1833, he formed the Columbia River Fishing and Trading Company. By 1834, he had raised enough money to dispatch another ship and organize another land party. At rendezvous, he learned that Thomas Fitzpatrick, whom he had contracted to supply him, had sold his goods to the Rocky Mountain Fur Company. Undaunted, he led his men further west and established the trading post of Fort Hall then headed on to Fort Vancouver. This time his supply ship arrived and he established Fort William at the Willamette River mouth. The inexperienced traders at Fort William and Fort Hall failed to make enough money to cover expenses so Wyeth had to sell out to the Hudson Bay Company.

Protestant missionaries competed as fiercely for "pagan" souls as fur companies did for pelts and robes.[27] Methodist Jason Lee and his nephew Daniel Lee were the first missionaries to travel the Overland Trail and settle in Oregon. They established a church at French Prairie 60 miles up the Willamette River valley in 1834. Not to be outdone, Presbyterians dispatched Elkanah Walker, Cushing Ells, Marcus and Narcissa Whitman, and Henry and Eliza Spaulding who journeyed with a trading brigade to the 1836 rendezvous. As the first white women to travel that trail, Narcissa and Eliza astonished the mountain men and Indians attending. The missionaries split up with Walker and Ells founding a mission among the Spokan at Tshimakain, the Whitmans with Cayuse and Walla Walla at Waiilatpu, and the Spauldings with the Nez Perce at Lapwai. The Whitmans' only child drowned. They overcame their sorrow by eventually adopting eleven white and mixed-blood orphans.[28]

Meanwhile, inspired by published reports by missionaries in the Willamette Valley, other groups of settlers headed west on the Overland Trail. Dr. Elijah White led a wagon train of fifty settlers there in 1842. Over a thousand settlers reached Oregon in 1843 and the number swelled steadily each year thereafter.

Emigrants unwittingly carried diseases with them that afflicted tribes along the way. In 1847, a measles epidemic ravaged the Cayuses, killing many, with most victims children. The Cayuse noticed that American children suffered measles but rarely died. They feared that the Americans somehow deliberately spread measles to the Cayuse to weaken them and take their land.

Whitman scoffed at Indian complaints that he and other settlers were stealing their land and killing their children. As for land, he insisted that Indians lost the right to it by failing to develop it: "When a people refuse or neglect to fill the designs of Providence, they ought not to complain at the results. The Indians have in no case obeyed the command to multiple and replenish the earth, and they cannot stand in the way of others doing so."[29] The Cayuse murdered the Whitmans and ten other settlers in November 1847.

***

Religion inspired the settlement of another western region, Salt Lake valley. No group of western settlers provoked more political, theological, and legal controversy than did the Mormons.[30] The founder, Joseph Smith, was a devout Christian who intensely prayed daily and had a series of divine revelations in his teenage years and early twenties. In 1820, when he was 14, he envisioned God and Jesus telling him that he should establish a new church because the existing sects had failed to realize their divine teachings. In 1823, Angel Moroni led Smith to the golden plates of the *Book of Mormon* on Hill Cumorah near his hometown of Palmyra, New York. Moroni let Smith translate the hieroglyphics behind a curtain to two friends who were scribes. That translation was published in 1830. The *Book of Mormon* revealed that Indians were descendants of a lost tribe of Israelites. Mormons believe they are "Church of Jesus Christ of Latter Day Saints" who represent Jesus's true teachings.

Smith's first congregation had six members. In 1831, they established a church at Kirkland, Ohio that steadily grew in numbers. Their investments in various enterprises went bankrupt during the Panic of 1837, and they fled their angry creditors for Missouri. There they suffered discrimination and violence by fearful neighbors who called them heretics. Governor Lilburn Boggs actually declared them "enemies" to be "exterminated or driven from the state, if necessary, for the public peace."[31] In 1838, they fled to Illinois, where they established Nauvoo on the Mississippi River. By 1844, 15,000 Mormons had congregated there and in towns throughout the region.

Once again, local people and politicians opposed the Mormons' theology and swelling population, wealth, and political power. In 1843, Smith declared that Mormon leaders could practice polygamy with as many wives as they could support. In 1844, Smith announced his candidacy for president in that year's election and promised to abolish slavery, reduce the number of congressmen, and annex Mexico and Canada. A dissident Mormon group established the *Nauvoo Expositor* newspaper and criticized Smith, his theology, and his political views. Smith led a mob that destroyed the press and most copies of its first issue on June 7. The editors fled to Carthage where they asked authorities to arrest Smith on a litany of felonies. The militia marched to Nauvoo, arrested Smith and his brother Hyrum, and brought them to the jail at Carthage where a mob lynched them on June 27, 1844.

Brigham Young became head of the Council of Twelve Apostles that governed Mormons.[32] He established a truce with Illinois's government and prepared Mormons to emigrant to a remote western sanctuary. They began their trek in 1846 and established a winter camp north of Omaha. The advanced guard led by Young followed the Overland Trail to Salt Lake valley, arriving on July 24, 1847. Young sent back word for the others to follow.

***

The Overland Trail with branches to Oregon and California developed fully during the 1840s.[33] The first successful crossing came in 1841 by the Western Emigrant Society founded by Captain John Bartleson and John Bidwell. They were inspired by a letter from their friend Dr. John Marsh, who had emigrated to California and had a flourishing ranch in Central Valley. Bartleson and Bidwell attracted around fifty settlers. Starting on May 18, they traveled as far as Soda Springs, Utah with a missionary party led by Father Pierre Jean De Smet and guided by mountain man Thomas Fitzpatrick. From there, with a series of Indian guides, they eventually reached California via Bear River, the Humboldt River, Sonora Pass over the Sierra Mountains, and down the Stanislaus River to Central Valley. On the Humboldt, they abandoned their wagons and put their necessities on packhorses and mules. They reached Marsh's ranch on November 5. Word of their successful passage encouraged countless others.

Traffic along the Overland Trail naturally began with relatively modest numbers. At least 18,847 completed the journey to one of three destinations from 1841 to 1848, with 2,735 reaching California, 11,513 Oregon, and 4,500 Mormons reaching Utah. That stream became a flood after word spread in the east of the gold strike in California. At least 296,259 people followed the Overland Trail from 1849 to 1860, including 200,335 to California, 53,062 to Oregon, and 42,862 to Utah.[34]

There were three popular "jump offs" along the Missouri River, Independence, St. Joseph, and Council Bluff whose legs eventually joined the Overland Trail along the Platte River. Most people took a steamboat to one of those towns where they bought a wagon, draft animals, and supplies, and joined a group. Each group elected a wagon master. Nineteen of twenty people survived the journey. Tragically, they had to bury several thousand along the trail who died from disease, accidents, murder, or Indians. Cholera was the deadliest disease. The worst natural calamity afflicted the "Donner Party" that got a late start on the trail and bogged down in steadily deepening snow on the Sierra Mountains' east side in 1846. By the time a relief party reached them early the next year, forty-two had died and forty-seven others survived largely by cannibalism. Indian attacks were relatively rare. From 1840 to 1860, 362 emigrants and 426 Indians died fighting each other, of which nine of ten perished west of South Pass mostly along the Snake River, Humboldt River, and Applegate routes. Mormons actually inflicted the worst atrocity when the Nauvoo Legion murdered 120 members of a wagon train and kidnapped eighteen children at Mountain Meadows in September 1857. Livestock suffered far worse than people. One emigrant counted carnage along the way that totaled 4,960 horses, 1,061 mules, 3,750 oxen. Another counted 787 abandoned wagons.[35] Forty-niner William Swain observed "the amount of death among them is plainly told by the . . . newly made graves . . . Sad is their fate, buried here in this wild of wastelands, where not a mark will denote their last resting place far from loved ones."[36]

***

California needed enterprising emigrants. That need became more urgent in 1812, when the Russians established the Fort Ross colony to gather sea otter and beaver pelts just 90 miles north of San Francisco. To entice settlers, Mexico's government established the 1824

Colonization Act, amended in 1828, that granted anywhere from 4,428 to 48,708 acres of land to anyone with the means of livestocking it. The government eventually issued over 700 grants. The one in California with the biggest economic and political impact went to Swiss-born John Sutter. In 1839, he abandoned his wife and children for a Central Valley land grant centered on the American River that he called New Helvetia with Sutter's Fort the center for ranching, farming, and trading ventures. Sutter bought Fort Ross, which chronically lost money, from the Russians in 1841.

Americans received many land grants. Trappers and sailors were the first to arrive. Overland expeditions included Jedediah Smith's in 1826 and 1827, James Pattie's in 1828, Ewing Young's in 1830 and 1831, and Joseph Walker's in 1833. American merchant ships traded along the coast for cowhides and tallow that might take two or three years before the hull was packed and they returned to their homeports. Some vessels made the round trip between American east coast port and California ports while for other vessels the west coast was a stage of what was often a two- or three-year round-the-world trading voyage. Whalers often stopped at ports like Monterey and San Diego to replenish their water and food.

Hundreds of American and other foreign sailors and trappers stayed in California, married Mexican women and started farms or businesses. From 1842, a growing number of overland emigrants reached California and applied for land. By 1845, Americans numbered about one of ten among 7,500 California settlers.[37] Although they were a minority, most swiftly acquired economic and political power by converting to Catholicism, marrying young women from prestigious families, and starting lucrative businesses. Richard Dana, who spent over a year and a half on California's coast working on a merchant ship, contrasted the dynamism of American immigrants with the turpitude of Mexicans: "Having more industry, frugality, and enterprise than the natives, they soon get all the trade into their hands. They usually keep shops, in which they retail the goods purchased in larger quantities from our vessels, and also send a good deal into the interior, taking hides in pay which they again barter with our vessels. In every town on the coast there are foreigners engaged in this type of trade, while I recollect but two shops kept by natives." He noted that Americans were the mayors of Monterey and Santa Barbara. He lauded Monterey's deep bay, rich soil, temperate climate, and abundant water but lamented that "nothing but the character of the people prevents Monterey from being a great town . . . The men are thriftless, proud, and extravagant, and very much given to gaming, and the women have but little education, and a good deal of beauty, and their morality . . . is none the best." In one tense standoff between Americans and Mexicans over a murder, he observed that the "Kentucky hunters with their rifles were a match for a whole regiment of hungry, drawling, lazy half-breeds."[38] Fortunately, no violence then ensured. But in 1846, some of those Americans would revolt and help conquer California along with the rest of the Southwest for the United States, fulfilling a recently coined notion of America's "manifest destiny" to expand to the Pacific Ocean.

Chapter 5

WARRIORS AND PEACEMAKERS

> "The American claim is, by the right of our manifest destiny to overspread and to possess the whole of the continent which Providence has given us for the development of the great experiment of liberty and federative self-government." (John O'Sullivan)

> "Spare me then, my Father; let me enjoy my country . . . we have everything we want—we have plenty of land if you will keep your people off of it." (Pawnee Chief Sharitarish)

> "Treaties were expedients by which ignorant, intractable, and savage people were induced without bloodshed to yield what civilized people had a right to possess by virtue of that command that the Creator delivered to man upon his formation—be fruitful, multiply, and replenish the earth and subdue it." (Georgia Governor George Gilmer)

Publisher John O'Sullivan invented the term "Manifest Destiny" and most succinctly asserted it in his *New York Morning News* on December 27, 1845: "The American claim is, by the right of our manifest destiny to overspread and to possess the whole of the continent which Providence has given us for the development of the great experiment of liberty and federative self-government."[1] Manifest Destiny was the latest avatar for American continental ambitions asserted since Virginia's colonial charter granted by James I two and a half centuries earlier, followed by John Winthrop's "City on a Hill," Thomas Jefferson's "Empire of Liberty," and James Monroe's "Doctrine."[2] Through a mostly deft mix of diplomacy and war, a series of presidents achieved that dream by 1848.

The United States fought six wars between 1803 and 1848. Two were traditional nation-state wars against Britain from 1812 to 1815 and Mexico from 1846 to 1848. The others were Indian wars. Three were east of the Mississippi against the Seminole in Florida from 1816 to 1818, and from 1835 to 1842, and against the Fox and Sac in 1832. The only and first Indian war west of the Mississippi was against the Arikara in 1823. Then there was a war Americans fought against Mexico but without Washington's official sanction, the Texas War of Independence in 1835 and 1836. Finally, there were non-wars like the Burr conspiracy and the removal of eastern tribes to reservations in the west that might have led to war had key leaders chosen differently.

Of those wars, only that against the Seminole was fought exclusively in the east and had no significant impact on the West. The Fox and Sac war, known as Black Hawk's War, began when that chief led his people from their exile west of the Mississippi to reclaim lands east of the river. Only the Arikara war was fought in the West and it had critical consequences. The 1812 War had only a few western skirmishes but vital implications for the West. The Mexican War was an exclusively western war largely caused by the results of the earlier Texas independence war and was the most vital war for the American West.

***

Every war has its own unique reasons for why it happened, how it was fought, and what the results were. Yet, Indian wars usually followed a pattern from Jamestown's founding in 1607 to the final battle at Wounded Knee in 1890.[3] The infiltration of trappers, hunters, and settlers onto a tribe's territory led to worsening tensions. The murder of one or more people by one side provoked vengeance by the other. Violence swiftly escalated in scale. Warfare was merciless as each side committed atrocities against the other's old men, women, and children. The Indians often scored initial victories but defeat was inevitable. After defeating the tribe or tribes, the government imposed a treaty whereby the vanquished ceded more land and either had a smaller reservation or moved to a new reservation where the pattern soon began again.

A core justification for American conquest of Indian lands was that "savages" had no notion of private property, did not "improve" it, and thus had no legal right to it. Duwamish Chief Sealth poetically expressed the universal Indian reaction at American demands to purchase their land: "How can you buy or sell the sky—the warmth of the land? The idea is strange to us. We do not own the freshness of the air or the sparkle of the water . . . We know the white man does not understand our way . . . .The earth is not his brother but his enemy . . . There is no quiet place in the white man's cities . . . The Indian prefers the soft sound of the wind darting over the face of a pond, and the smell of the wind itself cleansed by a midday rain, or scented with a pinon pine . . . When the last red man has vanished from the earth, and the memory is only the shadow of a cloud moving across the prairie, these shores and forests will still hold the spirits of my people."[4]

All along, most Americans projected tendencies for greed, violence, and deceit onto hated Indian others. They saw themselves as victims of Indian aggressors, not as aggressors against Indians. Some cynically called for taking Indian lands by any means, regardless of how peaceful a tribe might be. President Thomas Jefferson sought to seize Indian territory by subterfuge: "We shall push our trading houses, and be glad to see the good and influential individuals among them run into debt, because . . . when these debts get beyond what the individuals can pay, they become willing to lop them off by a cession of land . . . by this way our settlements will gradually circumscribe . . . the Indians, and they will in time either incorporate with us as citizens of the United States or remove beyond the Mississippi . . . As to their fear . . . our strength and their weakness is now so visible that they must see we have only to shut one hand to crush them."[5] Ironically, that strategy made war likely.

Pawnee Chief Sharitarish made this plaintive plea when he visited President James Monroe in Washington in 1822: "My Great Father—I have travelled a great distance to see you. I have heard your words . . . and I will carry them to my people . . . The Great Spirit made us all . . . You love your country—you love your people—you love the manner in which they live, and you think your people brave. I am like you . . . I love my country—I love my people—I love the manner in which we live, and think myself and warriors brave. Spare me [and] . . . let me enjoy my country . . . we have everything we want—we have plenty of land if you will keep your people off of it."[6] Of course, that chief's plea was something that no American president could accept.

***

Aaron Burr and James Wilkinson are among American history's most despicable characters.[7] Each was venal, corrupt, duplicitous, and ultimately a traitor. Wilkinson secretly swore allegiance to Spain on August 22, 1790, and thereafter took regular payoffs as a Spanish spy. Burr was notorious for challenging Alexander Hamilton to a duel and then killing him after Hamilton fired in the air as a harmless symbolic act of honor. In 1804, Burr was vice president and Wilkinson was Louisiana's governor and the army's senior general. They began conspiring to provoke a rebellion among settlers in the Ohio and Mississippi River valleys to form a new country with themselves its leaders. Over the next two years, they secretly enlisted followers. To help finance the plot, Burr took payments from British ambassador Anthony Merry and Spanish official Carlo Martinez de Irujo y Tacon. In February and March 1806, Burr recruited in the Ohio valley in hope of leading the revolt later that year. Joseph Daviess, Kentucky's federal attorney, learned of his efforts and warned President Jefferson. Unaware that Wilkinson was a co-conspirator, Jefferson asked him to investigate. Fearing that he would be implicated, Wilkinson confirmed to Jefferson that Burr was plotting rebellion. Jefferson had Burr arrested and put on trial at a federal court in Richmond, Virginia with Chief Justice John Marshall presiding. On April 1, 1807, the court acquitted Burr of treason and filibustering charges. Congress investigated similar charges against Wilkinson in 1809 but an army court martial acquitted him in 1811.

Another American cabal actually succeeded briefly in conquering a realm, this one in Texas. Mexicans revolted against Spain in September 1811. Most Americans approved that rebellion against royal authority, recalling their own independence struggle and preferring a weak neighboring Mexico in need of trade, investments, and settlers to Spain's closed empire. An expedition launched from American soil but renounced by President James Madison's administration tried to aid Mexico's rebels.[8] On August 8, 1812, Bernardo Gutierrez de Lara, Augustus Magee, and their 130-man Republican Army invaded Texas and over the next year nearly conquered it. They captured Nacogdoches and San Antonio, forced Governor Juan de Salcedo to surrender his army after routing it at the battle of Salado on April 1, declared independence for Texas on April 6, and issued a constitution for the new country on April 17, 1813. But divisions split the invaders at the height of their success. Magee died suspiciously and Jose de Toledo's faction forced Gutierrez to return to the United States. General Jose Arredondo's army routed the Republicans at the battle of Medina River on August 18, 1813, recaptured Republican-held towns, and executed 327 rebels. A quarter century would pass before another revolt led to Texas independence.

***

When the United States acquired Louisiana in 1803, Americans were still struggling to consolidate control over their territory east of the

Mississippi. To do so, they needed another dozen years capped by a war against Britain and allied Northwest and Southwest Indians. The British exacerbated conflicts with those tribes by supplying them arms and encouraging them to unify and war against the Americans.

Tecumseh was a brilliant Shawnee chief who, with his brother Tenskwatawa or the "Prophet", sought to push back the American frontier.[9] Tenskwatawa was the latest Indian prophet whose visions caused him to call on Indians to purify themselves of their dependence on American goods and customs before exterminating the Americans. In August 1811, Tecumseh journeyed to the Southwest to rally those tribes. When he was gone, William Harrison, Indiana Territory's governor and militia general, led an army against Prophetstown on Tippecanoe Creek. Before dawn on November 7, Tenskwatawa sent the warriors against the invaders but the troops repelled the attacks. Tenskwatawa led his people west to safety. Harrison had his troops burn the village then returned to Vincennes, the territorial capital.

***

President Madison asked Congress for a war declaration against Britain on June 1, 1812.[10] Congress complied with the House of Representatives voting 79 to 49 and the Senate 19 to 13 in favor, and he signed it into law on June 18. What provoked that war declaration?

Americans had endured nearly three decades of British arming and instigating Indian attacks on the frontier and two decades of British seizures of American ships, cargoes, and sailors at sea. The British asserted those policies to enhance their national security. They sought to contain America's frontier expansion with Indian resistance. After Britain went to war against revolutionary France in 1793, Whitehall issued Orders In Council for the navy to confiscate vessels and their cargos from neutral countries trading "contraband of war goods" to France, and impressed or kidnapped sailors who could not prove they were not British for service in the Royal Navy. British naval captains treated Americans disdainfully. That contempt and aggression peaked with an unprovoked attack by HMS *Leopard* against USS *Chesapeake* in American waters that left four Americans dead and seventeen wounded on June 22, 1807. President Jefferson reacted by asking Congress to declare not war but the first of several trade embargos against not just Britain but other European states. He had hoped that severing American trade with Britain would force it to accept American demands to stop its depredations. Instead, the embargos devastated America's economy from its previously thriving ports and far inland.

In Congress, War Hawks like Henry Clay of Kentucky advocated war with the goal of conquering Canada.

That war was a disaster for the United States as Americans suffered a series of debacles. The British captured or routed American troops at Mackinac, Detroit, Queenston, Raisin River, Bladensburg, and Fort Niagara. America's most humiliating defeat came on August 24, 1814, when a British army marched into undefended Washington City and burned the White House, Capitol, and other public buildings. The Americans did win a few battles. They repelled British campaigns against Fort Meigs, Fort Stephenson, Baltimore, and Plattsburg. General Winfield Scott trained his troops in close-order drill and defeated redcoats at Chippewa and Lundy's Lane near the Niagara River. America's navy partly redeemed the army's mostly inept leadership, organization, and fighting skills. Americans warships defeated twice as many British warships as they lost in battle. Commodore Oliver Perry's squadron battered an entire British squadron into surrender at the battle of Put-in Bay in Lake Erie on September 10, 1813.

Most vitally, the Americans crushed the Northwest and Southwest Indian alliances. On October 5, 1813, General Harrison's army defeated a British and Indian army at the Thames, where Tecumseh was killed and his followers scattered. In several campaigns from August 1813 to August 1814, Tennessee General Andrew Jackson's army devastated the Creeks in central Alabama and forced them to cede 23 million acres to the United States with the Treaty of Fort Jackson, signed on August 9. He then marched to Pensacola to intimidate the British into sailing away from that Spanish port. The greatest American victory came at New Orleans, where Jackson's army defeated an invading British army led by General Edward Pakenham on January 8, 1815, and forced it to retreat from American territory. Tragically, that battle occurred after the peace Treaty of Ghent was signed on December 24, 1814. The treaty simply restored the situation before the war by requiring each side to return what little territory it had taken. But with the tribes devastated, American settlement of the Northwest and Southwest accelerated and spread across the Mississippi River, especially up the Missouri River valley.

***

For two centuries, Americans struggled with a fundamental moral contradiction. White Americans demanded ever more liberties and rights for themselves while denying them to the African Americans who lived among them, with nine of ten of them slaves. Over the decades since Americans won independence, tensions steadily rose between free and slave states. The Constitution accepted slavery as legal and let each state determine whether to accept or reject it. The nation's population increased faster in the northern free states and so that region enjoyed more representatives in Congress. The Senate was split eleven each between free and slave states. Slavocrats or those who backed a slavocracy or slave-based political, economic, and social system feared that eventually free states would outnumber them and a majority of senators could abolish slavery for the United States. Many northerners feared that if a majority of states had slavery, they could pass a law requiring all states and western territories to legalize slavery.

A political crisis erupted in 1819 when Missouri's territorial government submitted to Congress a constitution and request that Missouri become a state. Northern politicians amended the constitution to restrict slavery in Missouri. That provoked an uproar by slavocrats in Missouri and other slave states. Eventually Kentucky congressman Henry Clay, himself a slaveowner, devised a compromise whereby Missouri would be slave state, Maine would be a free state, and a line drawn west from Missouri's southern border allowing all future states to be free above and slave below that line. Congress passed that bill on March 3 and President James Monroe signed it on March 6, 1820. Although the 1820 Compromise preserved the nation's union, animosities between the regions persisted.

A potential source of national unity came on December 2, 1823, when President Monroe issued what was soon called the Monroe Doctrine that declared the entire Western Hemisphere off limits to European imperialism. Secretary of State John Quincy Adams actually authored that doctrine in reaction to both an extraordinary opportunity and threat that followed the collapse of Spain's empire and the emergence of weak new nation-states eager for foreign trade, investments, and immigrants. Enterprising Americans could profit enormously from that opportunity while the reimposition of colonial rule by Spain backed by France, Russia, or other great powers could extinguish that opportunity. With the same interest, the British government actually asked the Monroe administration to issue a joint declaration. Adams recognized that Americans could better protect their own national security interests with a separate declaration. America's army and navy was then miniscule and could not deter, let alone defeat, any European power determined to plant colonies in the Western Hemisphere. Only Britain with the world's greatest navy could and would do that. So with the Monroe Doctrine, the United States acted like a great power in words without having to pay its exorbitant costs.

***

The United States fought its first war west of the Mississippi River in 1823.[11] That war was against the Arikara tribe with two adjacent palisaded villages on the middle Missouri River. The Arikara were farmers who lived in earth lodges and supplemented their diets with annual bison hunts on the surrounding plains. They struggled to profit from their position by pressuring fur trade expeditions heading up and down river to trade with them. The companies were happy to do so but rejected Arikara demands that they be the intermediaries for other tribes across the region. The Arikara especially wanted to limit the growing power of their worst enemy, the Teton Sioux, whose war parties stole their horses, destroyed their crops, killed their warriors, and captured their women and children.

William Ashley's 70-man expedition arrived before the Arikara villages in late May. Tensions were high. A few weeks earlier Arikara warriors had killed two Missouri Fur Company employees near Fort Recovery downriver. Ashley had around twenty-five men camp on the beach near the lower village while the rest of his men remained aboard a keelboat anchored mid-river. His plan was to supply the land party with horses bought from the Arikara and then those men would head west across the plains to trade and trap before eventually uniting with the keelboat party that traded its way up the Missouri and Yellowstone Rivers. Tragically, on the evening of June 1, two men got in a fight over a woman in the village. One escaped to camp while the Arikara killed the other. On the morning of June 2, the Arikara attacked and routed the land party, killing fifteen.

Ashley withdrew to an island near the Cheyenne River mouth and sent a plea for help to Colonel Henry Leavenworth who commanded the 6th Infantry at Fort Atkinson on the Missouri River a score of miles above the Platte River mouth. Leavenworth embarked upriver with 230 troops marching ashore with supplies and cannons packed aboard a keelboat. Along the way, Ashley and his men, Joshua Pilcher and fifty employees of the rival Missouri Fur Company, and over 700 Teton Sioux warriors joined Leavenworth's expedition.

The expedition arrived before the Arikara villages on August 9. The Sioux attacked Arikara in the outlying crop fields and killed a dozen. The next day, Leavenworth had his gunners bombard the lower village while his company of riflemen and the trappers sniped at Arikara firing back from within the palisade. The Arikara suffered around fifty killed over two days of fighting. On August 11, the Arikara asked for a truce and talks. Leavenworth negotiated a treaty that required the Arikara to restore the horses they had killed and supplies they had stolen from Ashley and never again attack Americans or impede their voyages up or down river. That night the Arikara fled onto the plains and eventually sheltered with a Pawnee village on the Platte River. On August 15, Leavenworth led his men back downriver, as did Pilcher who had his men burn the two villages contrary to Leavenworth's order to preserve them. Soon Ashley realized his plan of a mounted land party west and his keelboat upstream to converge in the Rockies. That war devastated the Arikara and deterred another Indian war on the Missouri until 1863.

***

Not everyone who went West did so willingly. President Andrew Jackson was determined to purge all Indians from the eastern United States.[12] He worked with congressional leaders to devise and pass the Indian Removal Act that empowered the president to negotiate treaties with eastern tribes to exchange their lands for lands in Indian Territory, today's Oklahoma and southern Kansas. The Senate voted 28 to 9 and the House 102 to 97 in favor, and Jackson signed that law on May 28, 1830. Jackson offered this justification: "Can it be cruel in the Government, when, by events which it cannot control, the Indian is made discontented in his ancient home—to purchase his lands, to give him a new and extensive territory, to pay the expense of his removal, and support him a year in his new abode? How many of our own people would gladly embrace the opportunity of removing to the West on such conditions."[13]

The Jackson administration negotiated ninety-four treaties with tribes from 1829 to 1837. Typically, officials pressured and usually bribed each tribe's chiefs to sign away their homelands. To facilitate removal and future relations with Indians, Congress established the Office of Commissioner of Indian Affairs in 1832, reorganized as the Indian Affairs Bureau in 1834, and regulated commerce with Indians with the Trade and Intercourse Act of 1834

The Southwest tribes of Cherokee, Creek, Choctaw, and Chickasaw were called the "civilized tribes" because they had adapted American customs, private landownership, and slavery. The Cherokee were the most advanced with a democratic government, diverse, prosperous businesses, productive farms, public schools, and frame houses. In 1830, "the 15,000 members of the tribe owned 22,000 cattle, 1,300 slaves, 2,000 spinning wheels, 700 looms, 31 grist mills, 10 saw mills, 8 cotton gins, and 18 schools."[14] Sequoyah invented a Cherokee alphabet and published the newspaper *Cherokee Phoenix*.

The Cherokee faced a worsening crisis after gold was discovered on their land in 1828. Georgia's government claimed that land was the state's, and sought to drive the Cherokee from it, with January 1,

1830, the deadline. Governor George Gilmer admitted the cynicism whereby "treaties were expedients by which ignorant, intractable, and savage people were induced without bloodshed to yield what civilized people had a right to possess by virtue of that command that the Creator delivered to man upon his formation—be fruitful, multiply, and replenish the earth and subdue it."[15] Rather than go to war, the Cherokee went to court. Chief Justice John Marshall wrote the opinions for *Cherokee Nation v. Georgia* (1831) and *Worcester v. Georgia* (1832), describing tribes as "domestic dependent nations" in the former and exempt from state laws in the latter. That did not restrain Jackson who infamously declared, "the decision of the Supreme Court has fell still born."[16]

Elias Boudinot, a Cherokee newspaper editor, protested the absurd justifications for removal: "It appears that the advocates of this new system of civilizing the Indians are very strenuous in maintaining the novel opinion that it is impossible to enlighten the Indians, surrounded as they are by the white population, and they will assuredly become extinct unless they are removed . . . .Where have we an example in the whole history of man of a Nation or a tribe, removed as a body from a land of civil and religious means to a perfect wilderness in order to be civilized."[17] Under the 1835 Treaty of New Echota, a group of Cherokee chiefs agreed to lead their people west, but others refused and remained in remote Smokey Mountain valleys where their descendants live today.

Around 60,000 eastern Indians were forced onto the "Trail of Tears" from 1830 to 1850. How many died from disease or starvation along the way is impossible to determine with numbers ranging from 400 to 4,000. Two tribes initially defied attempts to drive them to the western prairies but eventually succumbed.

Black Hawk led his Fox and Sauk people east of the Mississippi River into Illinois to plant crops in their former farmlands in April 1832. President Jackson had the army coordinate offensives with Illinois's militia to converge against the invaders. Black Hawk's warriors defeated those forces in a series of battles until an army led by General Henry Atkinson cornered and crushed them at Bad Ax on the Mississippi River on August 2. The Seminole in Florida also resisted in wars from 1835 to 1842 and 1855 to 1858. The United States eventually won those wars, resulting in more Seminoles sent to an Oklahoma reservation. Nonetheless, a band of Seminoles managed to remain in the Florida everglades much as a Cherokee band did in the Smoky Mountains.

***

Mexico won independence from Spain in 1821 but a decade of war had devastated the country, leaving one of ten Mexicans dead and the economy half its previous size.[18] Mexico desperately needed enterprising immigrants and financial investments. What they initially got instead was a dictatorship. General Augustin Iturbide's faction took power in Mexico City on September 27, 1821, and declared Iturbide emperor on May 19, 1822. He was so inept and corrupt that a liberal faction led by Guadalupe Victoria forced him to abdicate on March 19, 1823. The coalition declared Mexico a republic and enacted a constitution modeled after the United States' with a president, congress, and supreme court on October 4, 1824.

Victoria served as the first president from October 10, 1824 to March 31, 1829. Asserting control over and strengthening the frontier was a priority. The government joined Texas with neighboring Coahuila to make one state and designated New Mexico and California territories with appointed governors. The 1824 Colonization Law promised immigrant families free land and a four-year tax holiday. The 1825 Colonization Law required a household head to declare that he was Catholic and pay a small fee over six years for title to 177 acres of farmland and 4,428 acres of pastureland. The law encouraged large-scale colonization by rewarding leaders or empresarios that brought 100 families with large land grants.

Moses Austin applied for a grant but died before he could realize it. His son Stephen Austin, eventually celebrated as the Texas republic's key founder, received three contracts to bring 900 families to Texas.[19] In all, Mexico granted fifteen contracts for 5,450 families by 1828. Meanwhile, thousands more people immigrated hoping to find land after they arrived. Soon Americans far outnumbered Mexicans and many of them were slaveowners. President Vicente Guerrero declared slavery's abolition on September 15, 1829. Austin succeeded in lobbying the Texas-Coahuila government to grant a loophole whereby slaveowners officially liberated their chattel but then forced them to sign contracts making them lifelong indentured servants.

Meanwhile, two presidents tried to buy Texas from Mexico, but Mexico's government indignantly rejected each offer. John Quincy Adams instructed Ambassador Joel Poinsett to offer $1 million in 1827, and Andrew Jackson had him offer $5 million for Texas, New Mexico, and California in 1829. After the second try, President Anastasio Bustamante demanded that Jackson recall Poinsett. Jackson complied.

Mexico's government passed a law on April 6, 1830, that forbad further American immigrants. Americans violated that law as they had earlier ones as settlers continued to stream into Texas. With Austin presiding, Texan leaders convened a "Consultation" at San Felipe and on October 1, 1832, agreed to pressure Mexico City to grant Texas its own statehood, cut tariffs on imports, permit slavery, and repeal the law forbidding new American immigrants. They sent a petition to the government but received no reply. On April 1, 1833, the Consultation reconvened to make the same requests and this time dispatch Austin to lobby the government. Mexico City grudgingly repealed the ban on American immigrants in November 1833.

To reassure potential immigrants, the state of Coahuila y Texas passed a law in 1834 that pledged, "no person shall be molested for religious or political opinions provided the public order is not disturbed."[20] General Antonio Lopez de Santa Anna took power in a coup on June 12, 1834, dismissed Congress, and suspended the constitution. He had Austin arrested and imprisoned for eighteen months before releasing him. In September 1835, General Martin de Cos, Santa Anna's brother-in-law, led 1,200 troops from Matamoras on the Rio Grande north to impose martial law on Texas.

By then, 35,000 Americans, including 3,000 slaves, lived in Texas, and outnumbered the 3,500 Mexicans by ten to one.[21] The first skirmish erupted at Gonzales on October 2, when 140 Texans refused to surrender a cannon to a Mexican captain with 100 dragoons. The Mexicans retreated after suffering two dead and one wounded and the Texans no casualties. After Cos led his army into San Antonio, around 600 Texans led by Austin besieged them from October 12 to December 11, during which over 150 Mexicans and 35 Texans died in the fighting. Austin and Cos reached an agreement that the Mexican troops would withdraw to Mexico and not return. Meanwhile, the Consultation met at San Felipe and on November 7, the delegates proclaimed that they would become independent if the constitution was not restored, would raise an army to defend Texas, and would reconvene on March 1, 1836.

Fifty-seven delegates gathered at Washington on the Brazos on March 1. Learning that Santa Anna with several thousand troops had crossed the Rio Grande, they voted to declare independence and have Sam Houston command the Texan army on March 2. Houston was an extraordinary character, a heroic Creek War veteran and charismatic politician who served as a Tennessee congressman and governor but was also an alcoholic with a failed marriage who resigned as governor and headed West for a fresh start.[22] They drafted a constitution that established an elected congress, appointed court system, and president with a three-year non-renewable term. They also legalized slavery. The two advanced Texan forces included around 200 under Colonels William Travis and Jim Bowie at the Alamo, a former walled monastery outside San Antonio, and 400 under Colonel James Fanin at a former walled monastery outside Goliad.

The advance guard of Santa Anna's army first reached San Antonio and began a siege of the Alamo on February 23.[23] Eventually, Santa Anna surrounded the Alamo's garrison with 2,000 troops. Among the defenders was David Crockett, a celebrated Tennessee bear hunter, storyteller, showman, and one time Congressman. When he lost reelection, he famously told the voters that they could "go to hell, I'm going to Texas."[24] The final assault came just below dawn on March 6. Attacking from all four sides, the Mexicans overwhelmed the Texans, killing nearly all of them but losing as many as 600 troops then or over the siege.

The Alamo swiftly became an exalted symbol of the nation's manhood fighting to the death for the noble cause of freedom, America's Thermopylae. Of course, that is the mythic version celebrated by popular culture, novels, songs, and movies. Critics point out that the liberties and opportunities that Texans fought for did not extend to their slaves. Likewise, Crockett's fame was mostly due to shameless self-promotion rather than any extraordinary achievements, and the most reliable first-hand account of the Alamo reveals that he did not die fighting but surrendered and was executed with six others who gave up. Nonetheless, most Americans understandably prefer the Alamo's mythic rather than historic version.[25]

Santa Anna then marched after Houston who commanded the main Texan army. Outgunned, Houston led his 800 men eastward along with thousands of settlers who fled the Mexican advance. At the San Jacinto River, Houston halted and awaited Santa Anna. On April 20, Santa Anna arrived with 1,500 troops and set up camp. Houston ordered an attack that routed the Mexicans, killed 630 and captured 730 including Santa Anna. On May 14, Texas President David Burnet and Santa Anna signed two treaties. Under the public treaty, Santa Anna agreed to a truce and withdrawal of his army from Texas. Under the secret treaty, Mexico would essentially recognize an independent Texas with a border on the Rio Grande, and accept bilateral trade. Mexico's government repudiated Santa Anna and his treaties but did not immediately order the army to reinvade Texas.

The Texas Congress and President Houston agreed to request annexation by the United States in November 1836, but delayed a formal submission. Andrew Jackson had been America's president since 1829. Although he favored annexation, he knew that would provoke a political crisis as northern states protested admission of a slave state without an offsetting free state. As compensation to free states, he offered to purchase California north of the 38th Parallel for $3.5 million but Mexico's government refused. He formally endorsed Texan independence on March 3, 1837, the day before he ceded the presidency to Martin Van Buren. The Texan ambassador to the United States formally submitted the annexation request to Van Buren on August 4, 1837. Worried about the political uproar by free states, Van Buren refused to endorse it and Texas withdrew its request in October.

***

Meanwhile, independent Texas suffered devastating Comanche attacks that killed scores of settlers and captured dozens of women and children. Texas Rangers provided the chief defense.[26] Austin founded the Rangers as ten men who patrolled the frontier in 1823, and the provisional government expanded them to 300 men in 1835. Each man supplied his own weapons and horse in return for monthly pay in money, food, and shelter, all minimal. By 1844, virtually all rangers had .45 caliber Colt revolvers which gave them the edge in an Indian fight. The trouble was tracking and catching up to war parties before they reached their villages on the distant plains.

In that merciless war, the Texans killed the most Comanches through an act of deceit. Mook-war-ruh led sixty-five Comanche including a dozen chiefs, women, and children to San Antonio for peace talks on March 19, 1840. With them were only two captives, one a child and the other a teenage girl who had been mutilated and repeatedly raped. That infuriated the Texans who quickly agreed to lure the Comanche into a building, dubbed the Council House, and hold them as hostages until other bands released their captives. During talks, violence erupted in which thirty-three Comanche including all the chiefs and warriors along with women and children were killed, thirty-two women and children were captured, and seven Americans died. The Texans sent word to other bands that they would execute their captives if the Comanche did not release all Americans that they held. Comanche bands responded by murdering their captives while Buffalo Hump led a raid that killed over twenty-five Texans, burned scores of homesteads, and ran of hundreds of horses. The Texans eventually released their captives.

***

Houston pressured Washington by giving the impression that he would seek annexation by Britain. That pressure worked. President

John Tyler submitted an annexation resolution to Congress. The House of Representatives voted 120 to 98 in favor on January 25, 1845, the Senate 27 to 25 in favor of an amended version on February 27, and the House 132 to 76 in favor of that amended version on February 28. Tyler signed the resolution on March 1, 1845, three days before he left office. The next president was eager to implement that policy.

No president asserted Manifest Destiny more decisively than John Polk from 1845 to 1849.[27] He was determined to take the Northwest from Britain and the Southwest from Mexico, ideally by diplomacy but by war if necessary. In the worst scenario, that high stakes gamble would have plunged the United States into war simultaneously against Britain and Mexico, a war the Americans would likely have lost. A mix of skilled statesmanship and luck bloodlessly won the Northwest from Britain but the Polk administration went to war against Mexico.[28]

Word that the United States would annex Texas enraged Mexico's government. In May 1845, the government announced that it would recognize Texan independence if its government did not let another country annex it. The United States formally annexed Texas on July 4, 1845. Mexico responded by severing diplomatic relations with the United States. On December 10, 1845, Congress approved a resolution establishing Texas as a state by votes of 141 to 56 in the House and 31 to 14 in the Senate. Polk signed the resolution on December 29, 1845.

***

Meanwhile, the Polk administration pressured Britain to cede the Northwest initially as far north as the 48th Parallel in southern Alaska. Polk enjoyed a vast hard power edge over Britain in the negotiations. Over 6,000 Americans had emigrated to Oregon by 1845 and they outnumbered the 750 British settlers by nine to one. Fort Vancouver was the Hudson Bay Company's regional headquarters headed by John McLoughlin at the Willamette River mouth on the Columbia River. In 1845, McLoughlin essentially ceded the region to the Americans when he shuttered Fort Vancouver and relocated his headquarters 300 miles north to the tip of Vancouver Island and the city of Victoria's future site. The Americans and British finally agreed to extend the existing border on the 49th Parallel that extended to the Rocky Mountain divide westward to the Pacific Ocean where it dipped beneath Vancouver Island, which Britain would retain. The Senate ratified that treaty by 41 to 14 votes on June 15, 1846.

***

Polk sent John Slidell to Mexico City with an offer to buy New Mexico and California for as much as $30 million but successive presidents Jose Herrera and Mariano Paredes refused to speak to him. To pressure Mexico, on January 13, 1846, Polk had War Secretary William Marcy order General Zachery Taylor to march his 3,550 troops from Corpus Christi on the Nueces River 160 miles south to the Rio Grande. Taylor and his men reached the Rio Grande on March 24.

One critical dispute between the Americans and Mexicans was Texas's southern border. The Americans insisted that it extended to the Rio Grande while the Mexicans countered that it ended at the Nueces River. The Mexicans believed that Taylor's army invaded their country when it crossed the Nueces River. General Pedro de Ampudia commanded the 5,000-man Mexican army at Matamoros on the Rio Grande a dozen miles upstream of the Gulf of Mexico. On April 11, he sent Taylor an ultimatum that war would result unless he withdrew with his troops toward the Nueces River within 24 hours. Taylor politely refused. On April 15, considering Mexico was now at war against the United States, he sent word to Commodore David Connor who commanded a flotilla at the Rio Grande mouth to begin a blockade. General Mariano Arista succeeded Ampudia as the army commander. On April 23, he dispatched General Anastasio Torrejon with 1,660 cavalry upriver and then across. Learning of that act, Taylor sent Captain Seth Thornton with sixty-three cavalry to scout. Torrejon ordered his cavalry to charge, and they killed sixteen Americans and captured the rest.

Taylor sent a courier by steamboat to Polk to report that the Mexican army had invaded Texas and overwhelmed Thornton and his men, then left 500 troops at Fort Texas on the Rio Grande and withdrew to Port Isabel for supplies and reinforcements. On May 8, Arista led his army across the river and besieged Fort Texas.

In Washington, Polk and his cabinet debated whether to ask Congress for a war declaration and if so on what grounds. On May 8, Slidell arrived at the White House to reveal all the belligerence, corruption, and intransigence he endured in Mexico. On May 9, the courier appeared with word that Mexico had initiated the war with an invasion and attack on American forces. Polk sent Congress a war declaration that the House of Representatives approved by 173 to 14 and the Senate 40 to 2 on May 11. Polk, his cabinet secretaries, and General Winfield Scott, the army commander, quickly reached a consensus on strategy and asked Congress to appropriate money for all needed troops and supplies.

Taylor advanced with his army from Port Isabel to trounce the Mexican army at Palo Alto on May 8 and Resaca de Palma on May 9. Arista withdrew his battered army south of the Rio Grande, abandoned Matamoros, and withdrew upriver. Mexico City replaced Arista with Ampudia. Taylor received orders and eventually enough troops and supplies to pursue along with his promotion to major general. Taylor marched his army up the Rio Grande to Camargo, where he established a supply base, then led most of his men toward Monterrey, which they captured on September 24 after a series of combats from September 21. Taylor had the opportunity to surround and force the Mexican army to surrender. Instead, hoping that a conciliatory gesture might induce peace, he agreed to a two-month truce that let Ampudia withdraw with his army first to Saltillo then to San Luis Potosi.

Meanwhile, Polk assigned General Stephen Kearney the mission of organizing an army at Fort Leavenworth and leading it along the Santa Fe Trail to conquer New Mexico. With 1,600 troops, Kearney departed on June 30 and marched unopposed into Santa Fe on August 18. New Mexico's population of Mexicans, Pueblo Indians, and foreigners was 65,000 in 1846.[29] Among the Americans was Charles Bent who had traded in the region for two decades and founded Bent's Fort on the Arkansas River. Kearney appointed Bent governor then headed with 300 cavalry down the Rio Grande with orders to journey to California and assist its conquests. On October 6, Kearny and his men encountered Christopher "Kit" Carson and nine companions heading east. Carson reported that California was already in American hands.

After becoming president, Polk issued standing orders to America's consul, Thomas Larkin, at Monterey, California and naval captains patrolling the West Coast to capture that province as soon as they learned that the United States and Mexico were at war. Polk's policy was not new. His predecessor had issued similar orders. On October 18, 1842, Commodore Thomas Jones acted on a rumor of war to land marines at Monterey, announce America's takeover, and replace the Mexican flag with the Stars and Stripes. After learning that peace prevailed, he apologized profusely to California's authorities and withdrew.

If all had gone according to plan, the White House had an American force in California ready to take over if war erupted with Mexico. Captain John Fremont was Manifest Destiny's greatest flagbearer.[30] He became popularly known as the "pathfinder," but is better understood as the "mapmaker" since he mostly followed trails blazed by Indians, trappers, or emigrants. He led five expeditions that mapped swathes of the West in 1842, 1843–4, 1845–8, 1848–9, and 1853–4. He spearheaded

California's conquest during the Mexican War. He married Jessie Benton, the daughter of powerful Senator Thomas Benton of Missouri. Jessie actually rewrote his reports to appeal to the public. He got rich from a California gold mine and became one of California first senators in Congress. In 1856, he was the Republican Party's first presidential candidate, although he lost. Jessie excited crowds by appearing beside him at campaign rallies. They were a power couple a century before the notion was coined. He was an inept general during the Civil War. He later lost his fortune through speculation and sometimes fraudulent dealings. Fremont's character and career spanned the best and worst of human nature and westerners.

Before embarking on his 1845 expedition, Fremont met Polk and Benton at the White House. They did not keep records of what transpired, but apparently the three agreed that Fremont should linger in California as long as possible and cooperate with American naval captains anchored at California ports in a war with Mexico. On October 30, 1845, Polk sent Lieutenant Arnold Gillespie to inform America's warship captains, Larkin, and Fremont to prepare to implement long-standing instructions for California's conquest as soon as they learned from a reliable source that war had begun.

Previously, Fremont and sixty-two frontiersmen left St. Louis on June 1 and straggled into Sutter's Fort in today's Sacramento, California on December 9, 1845. John Sutter was a Swiss immigrant who California's governor in 1839 granted a vast estate along the American River in Central Valley, where he established a fort and farm with crops and pasturelands surrounding present day Sacramento. After resupplying his men from Sutter's storehouse, Fremont led them to San Jose then went alone to Monterey where he met Larkin and Governor Jose Castro. Castro ordered Fremont and his men to leave California as soon as possible. Instead, Fremont withdrew with his men to Gavilan Peak 25 miles away and raised the American flag on March 6, 1846. In doing so, Fremont essentially committed an act of war. Castro gathered the militia, approached Fremont's camp, and repeated his demand to depart. Fremont finally did so on March 9, and for the next two months slowly headed north toward Oregon, fighting Indians along the way.

Meanwhile, Gillespie had journeyed all the way to Mazatlán, Mexico where he met Commodore John Sloat, gave him Polk's instructions, and they steamed to Monterey to confer with Larkin. Gillespie then headed north on horseback to find Freemont and caught up at Klamath Lake on May 9. Fremont eagerly led his men back to California.

Mariano Vallejo was northern California's largest landowner. His home at Sonoma had a growing number of American neighbors. Believing that war had erupted, Ezekiel Merritt and William Ide mobilized thirty-two other Americans to capture Vallejo and declare California's independence on June 15. They fashioned a flag with a grizzly bear on it that inspired their act to be called the "Bear Flag Revolt." They sent a request to Fremont, who was then at Fort Sutter, to lead their revolt. Fremont agreed. Together Fremont's expedition and the rebels numbered 134 tough frontiersmen. They captured San Francisco then rode to Monterey, entering unopposed on July 19. General Castro fled with his men to Los Angeles.

Commodore John Stockton arrived with warships to replace Sloat. Fremont and Stockton devised and implemented a plan to take over California with troops overland and marines occupying key ports all the way to San Diego. The conquest was nearly bloodless. Stockton announced California's annexation and appointed Fremont governor on August 17. Fremont then sent his scout Kit Carson and nine men east with a report to Washington. Mexican officials Andres Pico and Jose Flores led a revolt of 300 militia in Los Angeles in September, besieged San Diego, and defeated Kearney and his cavalry at San Pasqual on December 6. Eventually, the American forces overwhelmed the Mexicans in California. Under the Treaty of Cahuenga, signed on January 15, 1847, Pico surrendered with his men.

New Mexico also experienced an initial American conquest followed by a revolt that the Americans had to crush. On January 19, 1847, a mob murdered Governor Bent and fifteen other Americans in and around Taos. Colonel Sterling Price marched with 353 troops from Santa Fe, scattered a rebel forces at a village called Canada then wiped out the rest at Taos Pueblo on February 3. The fate of New Mexico and California now lay in the war's outcome far south in Mexico.

Polk sought to end the war by instigating a coup that overthrew Mexico's government and negotiating peace that ceded New Mexico and California to the United States for $30 million. Antonio Lopez de Santa Anna, Mexico's former president, was then in exile at Havana, Cuba. Through intermediaries, Polk got Santa Anna to agree to that deal and let him sail through the American blockade at Vera Cruz. Santa Anna had no intention of honoring his promise. He reached Mexico City where he supported the government and received command of the Mexican army at San Luis Potosi. On December 24, Mexico's Congress elected Santa Anna president.

Taylor reported that the vast distance from Monterrey to San Luis Potosi (320 miles) and from San Luis Potosi to Mexico City (260 miles) made the capital's conquest all but logistically impossible. Polk was choleric when he learned that Taylor had granted Ampudia a truce rather than forced him to surrender. He ordered Taylor to discard the truce and resume his advance. He sent two other columns into northern Mexico, General John Wool with 1,300 troops from San Antonio and Colonel Alexander Doniphan with 850 troops from Santa Fe. He then had Taylor divert 3,000 troops under General Robert Patterson to capture Tampico assisted by Commodore Connor's flotilla. Each column achieved its objectives. Patterson occupied Tampico while Doniphan and Wool eventually joined Taylor, Doniphan after routing Mexican forces near El Paso and Chihuahua. Those reinforcements did not reach Taylor when he desperately needed them.

Taylor advanced with 4,500 troops to the heights of Buena Vista, 100 miles southwest of Monterrey by early January 1847. Santa Anna marched with 20,000 troops north from San Luis Potosi, but lost 5,000 to desertion, disease, and exhaustion by the time he arrived before Taylor on February 21. Yet the Mexicans still outgunned the Americans by three to one and nearly defeated them in a series of attacks on February 22 and 23. In the end, superior American tactics, morale, and fighting ability routed the Mexicans. Santa Anna had only 10,000 troops left when they straggled into San Luis Potosi on March 9.

Polk finally accepted Taylor's assessment that logistically marching his army to Mexico City was a non-starter. Instead, he approved General Scott's plan to land an army at Vera Cruz and march to the capital in the bootsteps of Hernando Cortez's conquistadors more than three centuries earlier. Scott's armada packed with 8,500 troops landed on beaches south of Vera Cruz then arched north to cut off the city on March 9. Vera Cruz's commander surrendered on March 27, after a week's bombardment by American batteries.

Scott began his march to Mexico City in early April. Santa Anna with 15,000 troops blocked the way at Cerro Gordo. Scott's army outflanked and routed the Mexicans on April 17, resumed their advance and marched unopposed into Puebla on May 15. Scott's army rested three months at Puebla, awaiting supplies and reinforcements to replace troops lost through battles, disease, and the departure of volunteer regiments whose enlistments had expired.

The army numbered 12,000 troops when Scott resumed the advance in early August. After entering Mexico City valley, Scott conducted a brilliant campaign that outflanked Santa Anna's army at the twin battles of Contreras and Churubusco on August 20, at Molino del Rey on September 7, and at Chapultepec Castle on September 13, causing

Santa Anna to flee with his army's remnants north up the valley. Scott led his troops into Mexico City on September 14.

***

The news of one victorious battle and campaign after another delighted most Americans. However, Congress and the public split over what territory, if any, to take from Mexico, and whether slavery should be allowed there. Although Mexico had abolished slavery in 1824, southern politicians demanded that slavery be reinstated in any acquired lands, with some slavocrats insisting that the United States take all of Mexico. David Wilmot, a Pennsylvania congressman, three times attached to bills what was called the Wilmot Proviso that forbad slavery in any territory taken from Mexico. Each time the House of Representative passed the bill with the proviso but the Senate, with most members sympathetic to slavery, stripped it out of their versions.

Polk sent Nicholas Trist, a State Department official, to negotiate a peace treaty with the Mexicans. Manuel Pena y Pena, the latest president, ousted Santa Anna as the army's commander but refused to make any concessions in peace talks with Trist, fearing he would be overthrown if he did. Meanwhile, Scott governed Mexico City, requisitioning taxes and provisions from the population. Impatient with the diplomatic stalemate, Polk recalled Trist. Trist refused to leave and instead warned Pena that his successor would demand even more from Mexico. Pena finally agreed to Trist's terms.

Under the Treaty of Guadeloupe Hidalgo, signed on February 2, 1848, the United States paid Mexico $15 million and assumed $3.5 million of Mexican debts to American investors in return for Mexico recognizing America's annexation of Texas and ceding the provinces of California and New Mexico to the United States. The 529,017 square miles cost forty-eight cents an acre. The Senate ratified the treaty by 38 to 14 on March 10. To fight the war, the eventual bill to American taxpayers totaled $101 million including veteran pensions, with the army and navy costing $74 million and $27 million, respectively, which with the treaty's $28.2 million brought the total to $129 million. As for manpower, 116,119 Americans served in the army during the war including 42,587 regulars and 73,532 volunteers. Of them 1,192 died in combat, 529 from wounds, and 11,155 from disease or 12,876 altogether, the highest death ratio of any American war. Another 4,102 suffered combat wounds, 9,754 were discharged for injuries, and 9,207 deserted. Probably at least

50,000 Mexican troops and civilians also died directly or indirectly from the war.[31]

James Gadsden, America's ambassador to Mexico, negotiated a treaty whereby the United States bought a triangle of land below the Gila River between Mesilla and the Colorado River for $10 million on December 30, 1853. The Senate ratified the treaty by 33 to 12 votes on April 25, 1854. With the Gadsden Purchase, the United States completed its present-day territory for eventually forty-eight states.

Chapter 6

ARTISTS AND WRITERS

> "I set out with the determination of reaching . . . every tribe of Indians . . . and bringing home faithful portraits of their principal personages, both men and women, views of their villages, games, and full notes on their character and history." (George Catlin)

> "The West of which I speak is but another name for the Wild; and . . . in Wildness is the preservation of the World." (Henry David Thoreau)

> "I love the woods, and ye relish the face of man . . . I'm form'd for the wilderness; if ye love me, let me go where my soul craves to be ag'in!" (Natty Bumppo)

America's high culture budded steadily for two centuries before blossoming in the early nineteenth century. From the beginning, writers expressed themselves through histories, essays, autobiographies, and poetry. Likewise, craftsman created increasingly beautiful and sophisticated furniture and silverware. As for architecture, initially the saltbox house was ubiquitous in established villages and the log cabin on the frontier. Among tens of thousands of immigrants were a trickle of trained artists who painted portraits and taught students. During the eighteenth century, large Georgian, Palladian, and Christopher Wren style houses, public buildings, and churches replaced saltboxes and chapels, with Charles Bulfinch, Benjamin Latrobe, and Thomas Jefferson the greatest architects. French émigré Pierre L'Enfant designed the elaborate street network for the new capital, Washington City. Furniture was increasingly elegant and elaborate Chippendale-style, and some austere yet elegant Shaker-style. New fine crafts appeared like tall clocks and long rifles along with new folk crafts like quilts and rocking chairs.

America's frontier or West inspired the most interesting early literature. John Smith and William Bradford wrote the best respective accounts of the Jamestown and Plymouth colonies, Indian customs and relations with them, and the natural world. America's first literary genre was the "captivity narrative," harrowing morality tales of settlers captured by "savages" but with faith, courage, and perseverance they survived until they were liberated; as such they experienced a Christ-like near death, descent into hell, then resurrection. The best-written and most profound were Mary Robinson's *Narrative of the Captivity and Restoration of Mrs. Mary Robinson* (1682) and John Williams's *The Redeemed Captive* (1707). The only notable colonial attempt at fiction set on the frontier was the play *Ponteach, or the Savages of America* (1766), written by Robert Rogers, the acclaimed Ranger war leader. *Ponteach* is a surprisingly sympathetic and vivid portrayal of Ottawa Chief Pontiac during the Indian War from 1763 to 1764 in the Old Northwest. As for western history, John Filson celebrated Daniel Boone as the archetypical frontier explorer, adventurer, and hunter happiest alone in wilderness in a long essay appendixed to his *The Discovery, Settlement, and Present State of Kentucke* (1784). Interviews with Boone provided most of the substance for his largely factual account. Boone genuinely liked and respected the Indians with whom he at times traded, hunted, resided, fought, and killed.

***

Two brilliant American-born painters appeared in the mid-eighteenth century, John Copley and Benjamin West, although eventually they migrated to London. Two of West's paintings addressed frontier events. His "Death of James Wolfe" (1770), depicts an American Ranger and an Indian among those crowded around the mortally wounded general at the battle before Quebec. His "Penn's Treaty with the Indians" (1771) dealt with frontier diplomacy. Other American painters like Gilbert Stuart, Charles Peale, Rembrandt Peale, Raphaelle Peale, and Thomas Sully were nearly as good and stayed in the United States to paint iconic portraits of America's revolutionary and early republic leaders. John Trumbull created a series of history paintings of America's War for Independence that eventually decorated the Capitol. John Vanderlyn's "Murder of Jane McCrae" (1804) was the first sophisticated painting that depicted a frontier tragedy. One sculptor, Italian émigré Enrico Causici, carved a sandstone relief titled "Daniel Boone Struggling with the Indian" (1827). Meanwhile, John Audubon spent years traveling around the United States painting its birds. He published his results in a series of portfolios called *Birds of America* from 1827 to 1839, that depicted 497 species, 25 of which he discovered, in 435 color plates.

America's landscapes evoked sublime feelings in sensitive viewers. Thomas Cole founded the first distinct American art subject, style, and theme with what was soon called the Hudson River School.[1] Cole and colleagues like Asher Durand, Jasper Cropsey, Sanford Gifford, George Inness, and Frederic Church produced stunning landscapes in the northeastern United States, with Lake George a favorite. The parallel Luminist School with John Kensett, Robert Salmon, Fitz Lane, and Martin Heade depicted mostly tranquil ports, beaches, and salt marshes. A third group including William Mount and Henry Inman painted common folks like farmers, storekeepers, and children working, socializing, or idling.

Hudson River School painters at once inspired and were inspired by the Transcendentalist philosophy developed by Ralph Emerson and Henry Thoreau. Transcendentalists saw divinity in nature. Thoreau expressed his philosophy's essence in these lines: "I wish to speak a word for Nature, for absolute freedom and wildness as contrasted with a freedom and culture merely civil—to regard man as an inhabitant, or a part and parcel of Nature, rather than a member of society . . . The West of which I speak is but another name for the Wild; and . . . in Wildness is the preservation of the World."[2] Asher Durand captured Transcendentalism's literary and artistic essence in his "Kindred Spirits" (1848) of painter Thomas Cole and poet William Bryant standing atop a cliff amidst wilderness.

What could be called the Frontier School of American painting emerged around the same time.[3] The most common image was of Indians. Samuel Seymour and Titian Peale accompanied Major Stephen Long's 1819 expedition in a vast circle that included parts of the Missouri River, Platte River, front range of the Rockies, Canadian River, Arkansas River, and Mississippi River. Each made scores of sketches of the Indians, wildlife, and landscapes they encountered along the way. Charles King painted beautiful portraits of 150 Indian chiefs who came to Washington to visit "the Great Father" from 1821 to 1837. He provided illustrations for the book, *A History of the Indian Tribes of North America* that appeared in three volumes between 1836 and 1844.

George Catlin first trained to be a lawyer but eventually realized that he loved art more. He studied painting at the Philadelphia Academy and during the 1820s mostly painted portraits in eastern cities. In 1830, he journeyed to St. Louis where Indian Superintendent William Clark was among those who sat for him. Clark's adventure tales of his trek to the Pacific and back inspired Catlin's true calling: "I set out with the determination of reaching . . . every tribe of Indians . . . and bringing home faithful portraits of their principal personages, both men and women, views of their villages, games, and full notes on their character and history."[4] He joined a trading expedition up the Missouri River to Fort Union in 1832. He accompanied Colonel Henry Leavenworth's expedition across the southern plains to the Wichita Mountains in 1835. In 1836, he visited and wrote about the pipestone quarry in western Minnesota where Indians mined the soft red stone that they shaped into pipe heads. Geologists later named the stone Catlinite for his discovery. He ventured again up the Missouri River in 1837. By 1840, he had "visited forty-eight tribes . . . and . . . brought home safe . . . 310 portraits in oil."[5] Among his best were "Buffalo Bull, Head Chief Blackfeet" (1832) and "A Pretty Girl" (1832). His "Pigeon's Egg Head, Assiniboine" (1837) depicts in the same painting two back to back versions of the chief, in full Indian dress on one side and American dress with a top hat, umbrella, and cane on the other.

Catlin tried to sell his collection to the federal government as the foundation for a national Indian museum but never succeeded. Instead, he opened "Catlin's Indian Gallery" in New York in 1837. He took his collection for display in a London gallery from 1840 to 1845. In 1844, he published *Letters and Notes on the Manners, Customs, and Condition of the North American Indians*. Later he published *Amongst the Indians: A Book for Youths* (1857) and *Last Rambles Amongst the Indians of the Rocky Mountains and the Andes* (1867). Joseph Harrison, president of a locomotive manufacturing company, bought Catlin's collection in 1852 and his widow later donated it to the federal government.

Catlin reveled in his western experiences and deeply respected and enjoyed being with Indians. He explained "that the Indians' misfortune has consisted chiefly in the ignorance of their true native character and disposition . . . inducing us to look upon them in no other light than that of a hostile foe." Instead, he found them "by nature, a kind and hospitable people . . . no Indian ever betrayed me, struck me a blow, or stole from me a shilling's worth of my property. And thus in these little communities . . . I have often beheld peace and happiness."[6] He was the first American publicly to advocate a "magnificent park" that protected tribes and their lands from commercial exploitation and private ownership: "What a beautiful and thrilling specimen for America to preserve and hold up to the view of her refined citizens and the world in future ages! A nation's Park, containing man and beast in all the wild and freshness of nature's beauty."[7]

Alfred Miller's visit to Catlin's Indian Galley inspired him to become an artist and head west to paint his own versions of the peoples and landscapes. He studied art at L'Ecole des Beaux Arts in Paris then moved to New Orleans where he opened a gallery. In 1837, he met English lord William Stewart who was organizing an expedition to explore the West. Miller accompanied Stewart across the plains and into the Rockies to that year's rendezvous. Among his most striking paintings were panoramic "Fort Laramie," disturbing "Lost Greenhorn," sensuous "Indian Women Swimming," and romantic "The Trapper and his Bride," all painted around 1845.

Karl Bodmer accompanied Prince Maximilien von Wied in his America journey from 1832 to 1834 that climaxed with their ascent of the Missouri River from 1833 into 1834. Eighty-two of Bodmer's paintings illustrated Wied's book, *Travels in the Interior of North America*, and provided vivid images of Indians as portraits and within landscapes. Bodmer's most vivid paintings included "Buffalo Dance of the Mandan," "Mato-Tope, a Mandan Chief," "Interior of the Hut of the Mandan Chief," "Abdih-Hiddisch, a Minitarre Chief," "First Chain of the Rocky Mountains above Fort McKenzie," "Bison Dance of the Mandan," and above all "Fort McKenzie, August 28, 1833" when he witnessed an Assiniboine war party attack a Blackfoot village just outside the fort.

Two artists joined John Fremont's expeditions. Charles Preuss was a topographer and illustrator who produced some stunning images of jagged mountains and bleak landscapes in the report published in 1845. Richard Kern accompanied Fremont's 1846–7 and 1848 expeditions and later painted landscapes of those journeys, some harrowing like "Robidoux Pass" and others sweeping like "Taos Valley" and "Sutter's Fort" all from 1848.

Three other artists produced memorable works. Captain Seth Eastman painted Indians when he was posted at Fort Snelling near Minneapolis from 1841 to 1848. His wife Mary wrote *Dakota Life and Legends of the Sioux* (1849). He later taught drawing at the West Point Military Academy. Thompkins Matteson's "The Last of the Race" (1847) shows an Indian family on a barren shore forlornly gazing out to sea. Charles Deas painted vivid frontier scenes, sensually of a young man grasping a beautiful unconscious young woman on a galloping white horse fleeing towering flames in "Prairie Fire" (1847), iconically of a bearded trapper in a red shirt, grasping his rifle, and looking warily back over his shoulder while atop a black horse in "Long Jake, the Rocky Mountain Man" (1844), and disturbingly of a wild-eyed trapper and a warrior on horses gripping each other as they plunge off a cliff in "The Death Struggle" (1845). In 1848, a judge committed Deas to a New York insane asylum where a heart attack killed him 20 years later.

The United States developed cultural institutions that collected and inspired art in the late eighteenth and early nineteenth centuries. Philadelphia led the way with the American Philosophical Society and Academy of Natural Sciences founded respectively in 1743 and 1812. Charles Peale opened Peale's Museum, America's first art and natural history museum, in Philadelphia in 1784 that became the American Academy of Fine Art in 1805. Not to be outdone, New York intellectuals and artists established the American Academy of Fine Arts in 1802 and the Literary and Philosophical Society in 1814. In Washington City, Thomas McKenney, the Commissioner for Indian Affairs from 1824 to 1830, commissioned artist Charles King to paint chiefs that visited the capital and displayed them in his "Indian Gallery." James Smithson, a British scientist, bequeathed his estate worth $500,000 to the United States "for the increase and diffusion of knowledge." Congress formally accepted that inheritance in 1836 but spent the next decade debating what to do with it. On August 10, 1844, President James Polk signed the law establishing the Smithsonian Institution. Creative Americans would fill the Smithsonian and other cultural institutions with ever more profound artistic, literary, and scientific works with many depicting the West.

***

During the early nineteenth century, American literature about the West was not as prolific or profound as the array of paintings. Memoirs remained the most potent writings about the West. Meriwether Lewis and William Clark kept journals of their epic journey that were later published. A number of mountain men wrote accounts of their experiences that varied in veracity and literary merit including James Pattie, Osborne Russell, George Nidever, Joe Meek, Jim Beckwith, Warren Ferris, Zenas Leonard, Jim Clyman, and Kit Carson. Thomas Farnham and Alfred Robinson were traders who sojourned in California and wrote books about their experiences. Susan Shelby Magoffin kept a diary of journeying with her merchant husband on the Santa Fe Trail that was published after her death. John Fremont and his wife Jessie wrote the best-selling reports on his 1842 and 1843–4 expeditions.

Four memoirs were especially well written and insightful, Washington Irving's *A Tour of the Prairies* (1835), Richard Dana's *Two Years Before the Mast* (1840), Josiah Gregg's *Commerce of the Prairies, or the Journal of a Santa Fe Trader* (1844), and George Ruxton's *Life in the Far West* (1848). The West fascinated Irving who wrote two history books, *Astoria* (1836) and *The Adventures of Captain Bonneville* (1837). Of the memoirs, Dana's *Two Years Before the Mast* sold the best. He was born into a prominent Boston family whose father and namesake founded the *North American Review*. He was briefly a student of Ralph Emerson. He dropped out of Harvard when measles harmed his eyesight and to restore his vision became a sailor aboard the merchant ship *Pilgrim* bound for California, beginning the two years before the mast that he wrote about. He eventually became a lawyer and served as a Massachusetts state assemblyman.

As for fiction, James Fenimore Cooper led the way West. He set his five novels called the "Leatherstocking Tales" on the American frontier with its hero the skilled woodsman and reluctant Indian fighter Natty Bumppo. Of them, only *The Prairie* (1827) takes place west of the Mississippi River with an aged Bumppo aiding other struggling settlers while deploring their devastation of the land and wildlife. Cooper himself never journeyed there but relied on second-hand accounts to write this novel. Of all the passages in his novels, this declaration by Bumppo best expressed the spirit that drove adventurous men west: "I love the woods, and ye relish the face of man . . . I'm form'd for the wilderness; if ye love me, let me go where my soul craves to be ag'in!"[8]

Beyond Cooper, frontier fiction was scarce and frivolous. Davy Crockett was a renowned Tennessee bear hunter, Creek War veteran, storyteller, and Congressman.[9] He celebrated himself in his mostly true *A Narrative of the Life of David Crockett* (1834) and inspired James Paulding's play *Lion of the West* (1831) and Robert Bird's novel *Nick of the Woods* (1837), although both changed the hero's name and told tales that never happened. Charles Averill's *Kit Carson, Prince of the Gold Hunters* (1849) used that famed mountain man's name for a fantasy set in the West, the first by him of seventy other hack novels. Carson was a genuine frontier hero of extraordinary hunting, scouting, and Indian fighting skills, and despised the nonsense written about him.[10]

Yet, in one tragedy, reality ironically mirrored fiction. Carson scouted for an army company pursuing a Jicarilla Apache war party that massacred a family of settlers on the Santa Fe Trail and enslaved the wife Ann White. They caught up too late. The Apache murdered Ann and fled. Carson was enraged at "the treatment she had received from them . . . brutal and horrible." Near Ann's ravished body, he found Averill's novel, "the first of the kind I had ever seen, in which I was represented as a great hero, slaying Indians by the hundred." Among his fictional feats was rescuing a woman kidnapped by Indians. Carson bitterly reflected that, "Knowing that I lived near I have often thought that as Mrs. White read the book, she prayed for my appearance and that she would be saved. I did come but I lacked the power to persuade those that were in command over me to follow my plan for her rescue."[11]

PART III: THE FRONTIER AMERICAN WEST 1849–1890

Chapter 7

WARRIORS AND PEACEMAKERS

> "They employed the art of deceiving, misleading, decoying, and surprising the enemy with great cleverness. The celerity and secrecy of their movements were never excelled by the warriors of any country. They had courage, skill, sagacity, endurance, fortitude, and self-sacrifice of a high order." (General Nelson Miles)

> "I have come to kill Indians and believe it is right and honorable to use any means under God's heaven to kill Indians. Kill and scalp all, big and little." (Colonel John Chivington)

> "I am tired of fighting. Our chiefs are killed . . . The old men are all dead . . . It is cold and we have no blankets. The little children are freezing to death . . . My heart is sick and sad. From where the sun now stands I will fight no more, forever." (Nez Perce Chief Joseph)

The army's duties expanded with America's frontier from the Rocky Mountain divide to the Pacific coast by 1848. Nearly every year from then until 1890, the United States warred against one or more tribes.[1] From 1848 to 1861 alone, the army fought around 200 skirmishes.[2] In 1845, there were fifty-six military posts with only twelve west of the Mississippi. The number of frontier forts peaked at around a hundred in 1880. Most forts were poorly built, manned, and supplied. A garrison's strength naturally varied with the threat it was supposed to deter or defeat. A company might suffice in a region with relatively peaceful or sparse Indians, while several companies might be assigned to forts in regions with hostile tribes. A regiment's companies usually only assembled for Indian campaigns.[3]

The initial post-Mexican War army included four artillery, eight infantry, and three cavalry regiments, to which Congress added two infantry and two cavalry regiments in 1853. Cavalry and infantry regiments had ten companies and artillery regiments twelve companies and official strengths varied with 559 for infantry, 652 for cavalry, and 748 for artillery regiments; actual numbers were from two-thirds to half those authorized. The initial cost of raising a cavalry regiment with all the horses and equipment was around $1,500,000 and thereafter cavalry regiments cost nearly twice as much to maintain as infantry regiments, from $500,000 to $600,000 compared to $250,000 to $300,000 annually. Likewise, cavalry took two or three times longer to train than infantry as troopers had to learn how to care for and ride their horses, then maneuver in formation.[4]

The Mexican War produced a generation of veteran officers who a dozen years later would fight on both sides during the Civil War. Meanwhile, they mostly served at dreary frontier posts across the West. Although the Mexican War boosted the skills of officers at command, combat, logistics, and survival, little could be done to improve the quality of recruits, which tended to be abysmal. The army took what volunteers they could with few standards or questions. Recruits mostly were failures in other occupations, immigrants fresh off the boat, or criminals who sought a temporary refuge. Privates received $7 a month in the infantry and artillery, and $8 in the cavalry through 1854 and thereafter $11 and $12, respectively. Poor sanitation and food caused sicknesses that annually hospitalized soldiers an average three times and killed one of thirty-three. Punishments for offenses were severe. A soldier could be flogged for being late for assembly, drunk, brawling, theft, or disobeying orders, and shot for sleeping on duty, striking an officer, or desertion. Given all that, historian Robert Utley found that: "Desertion, discharge, and death produced an annual turnover of about 28 percent . . . [In] June 1853, as a typical example, the authorized size of the Army was 13,821, the actual size was 10,417; and of the 8,342 officers and men in units stationed on the western frontier, 6,918 were actually at their posts, or an average of 124 for each of the 54 stations in the western command."[5]

Although three of four frontier soldiers were infantry, fighting western Indians was largely a cavalryman's duty. Infantry might defend posts and trudge alongside supply trains to protect them, but only cavalry could possibly catch up to Indian raiders on swift horses or even villages on the move. Combat was rare even for cavalry. Frontier wars tended to follow a pattern. Columns of converging troops spent weeks or months searching for enemy bands, might fight skirmishes and rarely a battle or two, then finally find and destroy a village. With their food and munitions exhausted, the Indians eventually submitted.

Man for man Indians were superior to Americans as fighters. Although most Indians continued to rely for weapons on traditional bows and arrows or clubs, many were remarkably well-supplied with an eclectic collection of firearms obtained from trade or capture. Like most soldiers, Indians could not afford the luxury of frequent target practice but were probably better shots. Indian ponies were inured to sparse prairie grass while large cavalry mounts had to be grain fed. Not surprisingly, Indians usually evaded their pursuers. General Nelson Miles appreciated the warfare practiced by his Indian foes: "The art of war among the white race is called strategy, or tactics; when practiced by the Indians it is called treachery. They employed the art of deceiving, misleading, decoying, and surprising the enemy with great cleverness. The celerity and secrecy of their movements were never excelled by the warriors of any country. They had courage, skill, sagacity, endurance, fortitude, and self-sacrifice of a high order."[6]

Although war parties might number from one man to several hundred, Indians fought largely as individuals, competing with each other to perform the bravest acts. War leaders did not so much command as inspire. Attacks were planned by consensus among the leading warriors, although that did not guarantee that everyone would strictly follow the plan. Many an ambush was spoiled by warriors so eager for personal glory that they fired or charged alone, thus warning the quarry.

Most tribes tortured to death any men they captured and gang-raped and enslaved any women. Peace treaties usually included a clause that required defeated tribes to free any captive women and children. That was usually a terrible dilemma for released women who suffered the stigma of having been sex slaves, often had half-Indian children, and many bore mutilations and tattoos inflicted on them by their captors. Few husbands took back their wives. Captive children taken young often forgot English and also were scarred and tattooed. They suffered rejection, bullying, and taunts. Quannah Parker was the son of Cynthia Anne Parker, captured during a Comanche raid on their family's homestead in 1838. She bore him and other children as the wife of Chief Peta Nawkohee. Quannah became a Comanche chief.[7]

***

The first post-1848 Indian crisis was in California where the gold rush resulted in ever more death and destruction inflicted by miners against the natives. President Millard Fillmore assigned three commissioners to negotiate treaties with California's tribes. From March 1851 to January 1852, they concluded eighteen treaties with 139 bands that designated reservations and promised over $1 million in annuities spread among them. Yet the Senate refused to ratify those treaties as most senators objected to the cost and assumed those bands were not entitled to any land. Without protection, California's Indian population plummeted from 150,000 in 1845 to 30,000 by 1870. Disease and starvation caused most deaths but vigilantes, militiamen, and the army killed at least 4,500 California Indians from 1848 to 1880. Although the perpetuators claimed self-defense, the reason nearly always was to purge them from their land that could yield profitable minerals, lumber, crops, or livestock. California's 1850 Act for the Government and Protection of Indians actually permitted debt peonage that empowered loaners to force debtors to work for them until they paid what they owed. Gangs enslaved Indians and sold them to miners, farmers, and ranchers. California's Indians were easy to conquer because most lived in small bands with no warrior tradition.[8]

The army failed to keep peace between settlers and Indians. General Ethan Hitchcock explained the dilemma facing him and other commanders: "The whites go in upon Indian lands, provoke the Indians, bring on collisions, and then call for protection, and complain if it is not furnished, while the practical effect of the presence of troops can be little else than to countenance and give security to them in their aggressions; the Indians, meanwhile, look upon the military as their friends, and implore their protection." General George Crook revealed the crimes committed against California's Indians that he witnessed as a young lieutenant: "It was of no infrequent occurrence for an Indian to be shot down in cold blood, or a squaw to be raped by some brute. Such a thing as a white man being punished for outraging an Indian was unheard of."[9]

The army committed several of those massacres. After Indians killed two American merchants who had severely exploited them, Lieutenant John Davidson led an expedition that attacked a Wappo village in northern Napa Valley and killed around thirty-five in late December 1849. Pit River Indians of northern central California attacked a topographical expedition led by Colonel Edward Stevenson and killed Captain William Warner in September 1849. Captain Nathaniel Lyon led the retaliatory campaign that attacked and slaughtered 60 to 400 Pomo people at Clear Lake on May 15, 1850, and perhaps 150 more Pomo on the Russian River on May 25.[10]

***

President Fillmore assigned two former mountain men, David Mitchell, the Superintendent of Indian Affairs, and Thomas Fitzpatrick, the

Upper Platte River agent, to convene a peace council for the northern plains tribes. The Fort Laramie peace council lasted from September 1 to 21, 1851, and eventually included around 10,000 Sioux, Cheyenne, Arapaho, Assiniboine, Gros Ventres, Crow, Shoshone, and Mandan. The Fort Laramie Treaty designated territories for each tribe and required the United States to keep peace among them in return for which they granted Washington the right to build forts and roads on their lands and for Americans to traverse their lands. In addition, Washington would annually divvy $50,000 worth of trade goods among the tribes for ten years, but could withdraw any portion to a tribe that violated the peace. Fitzpatrick then negotiated a similar treaty with the southern plains Comanche, Kiowa, and Apache bands at Fort Atkinson on July 27, 1853. The treaty required Washington to split $10,000 annually among those tribes for a decade. From March 15 to June 5, 1854, various commissioners negotiated treaties with the tribes living in the high grass prairies and woodlands, some long-term residents like the Oto, Osage, Omaha, Missouri, and Iowa and others recent arrivals like the Delaware, Piankeshaw, Miami, Shawnee, Wea, and Peoria. The treaties reduced or consolidated each tribe's holdings so they fit more tightly together in return for more annuities.

***

Despite all the diplomacy, treaties, and annuities, peace on the plains did not last long. Fort Laramie guarded the Overland Trail along the North Platte River. The soaring number of migrants heading west worsened tensions with neighboring tribes. First Lieutenant Hugh Fleming commanded Fort Laramie. His deputy, Second Lieutenant John Grattan, was a hothead eager for any excuse to war against Indians, boasting that he could wipe out a village with a company of infantry and a howitzer. That excuse came on August 18, 1854, when a migrating Mormon demanded compensation for his stray cow butchered by an Indian at Chief Conquering Bear's nearby Brule Sioux village. Fleming gave Grattan permission to lead thirty troops and two howitzers to the village the next day. Conquering Bear refused to give up the accused but promised to pay for the cow after the annuities arrived. Grattan ordered his troops to open fire. The fusillade killed Conquering Bear but the enraged Sioux overwhelmed and wiped out Grattan and his men. Led by Chief Little Thunder, the Sioux packed up their village and fled north.

Although news of the Grattan massacre horrified the nation, the army was unable to muster an expedition until the next year. Colonel

William Harney led 600 cavalry and infantry from Fort Kearney in April 1855. Of course, by then any trail leading to the Brule was obliterated. Believing that they faced no danger, Little Thunder and his 250 people eventually returned to the region, and in September were camped at Ash Hollow, not far from the Transcontinental Trail. Learning of their presence, Harney quick-marched his troops there and attacked on September 3. The soldiers killed eighty-five, wounded five, and captured seventy women and children while suffering four killed, seven wounded, and one missing. Little Thunder and around 125 people escaped.

Over the next half year, Harney dispatched friendly Indians to Lakota Sioux chiefs, including Little Thunder, calling for peace talks at Fort Pierre on the Missouri River. The talks lasted from March 1 to 5, 1856, and resulted in a treaty whereby chiefs agreed to stop fighting, appoint head chiefs who would be responsible for restraining warriors and negotiating with the government in return for a resumption of annuities. That war no sooner ended than the next began, this one over a horse.

A Cheyenne band came to Upper Platte Bridge in April 1856. Captain Henry Heth ordered his troops to arrest three Cheyenne accused of stealing a horse. When they resisted, the troops killed one and arrested another. The Cheyenne fled but retaliated with attacks on emigrants that killed one and terrified others. Washington did not authorize an expedition until 1857. At Fort Kearney, Colonel Edwin Sumner received orders to pursue the Cheyenne with his 600 troops. They caught up at the Solomon River on July 9. Sumner ordered a charge and his men killed four Cheyenne while suffering two dead and eight wounded. He and his troops marched on to burn the abandoned village. The Cheyenne escaped. That ended the campaign.

The Comanche dominated the southern plains.[11] Raids by the Comanche and their Kiowa allies against Texas frontier settlements in 1857 prompted a campaign by Captain John "Rip" Ford and 200 Rangers from Fort Belknap. Ford and his men attacked a Comanche camp on the Canadian River near Antelope Hills on May 12. In the seven-hour battle, the rangers killed seventy-six warriors and routed the rest, the first time the Comanche had suffered a serious defeat.

That only enflamed the Comanche and Kiowa who retaliated with raids against the Texas settlements, Santa Fe Trail, and "civilized tribes" in Indian Territory. Chief Buffalo Hump's war parties inflicted the most death and destruction. Major Earl Van Dorn led 225 troops and 135 Indian allies from Fort Belknap in pursuit. On October 1, they attacked Buffalo Hump's village camped near a Wichita Village. Buffalo Hump was then negotiating with Fort Arbuckle's commander. The troops killed 56 warriors, routed the rest, captured 300 horses, and burned the lodges. The war subsided during the winter then resumed the following spring. On April 30, 1859, Van Dorn and his men departed Fort Radzinski to search for and destroy Comanche villages. On May 13, 1859, one of his companies attacked a Comanche village at Crooked Creek, killed forty-nine warriors, captured thirty-two women and five men at the cost of two soldiers and four allied Indians killed, and nine soldiers wounded. Although Van Dorn and his troops returned triumphantly to their fort on May 30, the raids continued.

The war persisted into 1860. Three columns converged on Comanche and Kiowa country, Major John Sedgwick's from Fort Riley, Captain Samuel Sturgis's from Fort Cobb, and Major Charles Ruff's from Fort Union, each numbering several hundred troops. Each column fought a series of skirmishes with bands before eventually returning to its base. The Comanche and Kiowa continued to raid the Texas frontier for the next four years with little retaliation as civil war engulfed the United States.

***

Although little known today, fighting between Americans and Jicarilla and Mescalero Apache and Ute in New Mexico's Sangre de Christo and White Mountains was bloodier and more destructive than the campaigns against the Plains Indians during the 1850s.[12] From 1849, the Jicarilla and Ute stole horses, cattle, and sheep from ranches and wagon trains plodding the Santa Fe Trail, and murdered pioneer families. Those tribes resisted attempts by New Mexico's territorial governors James Calhoun and William Lane to force them to surrender their homelands and move to reservations headquartered at Taos and Abiquiu. From 1854 to 1861, the region's commanders at Forts Union, Stanton, Buchannan, Breckinridge, and others launched expeditions to pursue raiders and search for their villages. On March 5, 1854, a cavalry company led by Lieutenant David Bell surprised Jicarilla Chief Lobo Blanco's war party and wiped it out. Jicarilla Chief Chacon and his warriors ambushed Lieutenant John Davidson's cavalry company, killing twenty-two and wounding thirty-six on March 30. Those were just the opening engagements. Hundreds died on both sides over the next half dozen years. The fighting spread to the Chiricahua Apache bands living in the upper Gila River and the Western Apache in the Mogollon Mountain regions, the Yuma and Mohave in villages along the Colorado River, and the Navajo in the region around Canyon de

Chelly. Chiricahua Chiefs Mangas Colorado and Cochise were the most brilliant Indian leaders. Kit Carson played a prominent role first as a scout then as a lieutenant colonel of volunteers. Commissioners negotiated six treaties with various tribes but each proved to be merely a truce as fighting soon resumed. The war sputtered to a close in 1861 as the United States army faced invasion by a Confederate army.

***

The army also fought Northwest Indians during the 1850s.[13] American miners and ranchers spread up the Rogue River region, taking land from and murdering Tolowa and Takelme people that lived there. In August 1853, Shasta Indians from northern California raided Rogue River settlements and killed several people. Civilian leader Joseph Lane mustered volunteers and, backed by Captain Bradford Alden's 4th Infantry company, led a campaign that defeated the Indians on August 24. Under the Treaty of Table Rocks, the region's tribes agreed to surrender their lands and move to a reservation. Captain Andrew Smith established Fort Lane to maintain order in the region. In early October 1853, Smith learned that civilians planned to attack a local band and urged the chiefs to shelter in the fort. The chiefs and warriors did but left their noncombatants behind. A mob murdered twenty-three women, children, and old men on October 8. That provoked a regional uprising that lasted until June 1854 when army and volunteer forces subdued those bands and escorted them to the Coast Reservation. During the fighting 33 soldiers, 17 volunteers, 27 settlers, and around 100 Indians died.[14]

Isaac Stevens and Joel Palmer, the respective governor of Washington Territory and Indian Superintendent of Oregon Territory, were determined to prevent future wars. They convened a council with the Cayuse, Umatilla, Walla Walla, Nez Perce, Yakima, and Palouse tribes at Walla Walla on the Snake River in May 1855. The treaty designated a specific territory and annuities for each tribe. Stevens and Palmer negotiated similar treaties with the Pend d'Oreilles, Flathead, Spokane, Coeur d'Alenes, and Blackfoot tribes later that summer.

That peace was brief. In September, a group of miners raped and murdered two Yakima women and a baby. A Yakima war party slaughtered the miners and later killed Indian agent Andrew Bolon when he came to investigate. Major Granville Haller pursued with eighty-four troops from Fort Dalles. Yakima Chief Kamiakin and his warriors surrounded and besieged the soldiers at Toppenish Creek, killing five and wounding seventeen while losing two dead and two wounded before they fled on October 5. District commander Major Gabriel Rains marched with 350 regulars and 400 volunteers into Yakima territory, but Kamiakin and his warriors defeated several of his contingents and he withdrew to Fort Dalles. Those victories inspired thirteen other tribes eventually to revolt across the Columbia basin and Puget Sound.

General John Wool superseded Rains in command in November 1855. Headquartered at Fort Vancouver, he deployed reinforcements to forts throughout the region where each district commander wielded them against the local tribes. In 1856, the result were plenty of pursuits, occasional skirmishes, and one key battle. On July 17, Lieutenant Colonel B.F. Shaw and 400 troops defeated around 300 Cayuse, Umatilla, and Walla Walla, killed 40 and burned a village in the Grande Ronde Valley. Governor Stevens sent couriers to the tribes for a peace conference. In September, they met at Walla Walla but the warriors attacked Stevens and his escort. The war continued until October 1858. Each year converging army columns devastated and forced more tribes to submit with treaties that forced them onto reservations. Kamiakin and a few followers fled to Canada.

***

Meanwhile, a series of controversial and violent acts worsened relations between people in free and slave states that would result in civil war.[15] Congress unwittingly exacerbated regional tensions by passing the Kansas-Nebraska Act on May 25, 1854. Democratic Senators Stephen Douglas of Illinois and David Atchison of Missouri crafted that bill to express popular sovereignty, or the right of people in a territory or state to determine the policies that directly affected them. The Kansas-Nebraska Act voided the 1820 Missouri Compromise that drew a line westward from Missouri's southern boundary with future states free above and slave below that line. The Kansas-Nebraska Act let settlers in those territories decide whether slavery would be legal or not. Of the two territories, Nebraska's small population had virtually no slaves and was unlikely to attract many more slaveholders. Kansas, however, was up for grabs. That territory extended westward from Missouri and slaveholders in search of rich, abundant soil needed merely to head for the setting sun.

The Kansas-Nebraska Act outraged northern abolitionists and free soilers alike, respectively those who favored ending slavery or limiting its extension. The New England Emigrant Aid Society, founded by abolitionist Eli Thayer in April 1854, helped 1,240 of 4,208 New

Englanders who moved to Kansas by that decade's end. Migrants to Kansas from other states included 6,331 from New York and 40,929 from Ohio, Indiana, and Illinois. During that same time, 20,481 people from Missouri, Kentucky, and Tennessee moved to Kansas. By 1860, Kansas held 107,206 people of whom most were free soilers.[16]

Despite overwhelming numbers of free-soil settlers, Kansas officially was a slave territory until 1861. Free soilers outnumbered but did not outgun slavocrats during those years. Slavocrats made up with blatant cheating and bullying what they could not muster in numbers. President Franklin Pierce appointed slavocrat Andrew Reeder the territory's governor. Reeder held an election for representatives to a territorial assembly on March 30, 1855. At that time only 8,501 white people including 5,128 men and 3,373 women along with 242 slaves and 151 free blacks lived in Kansas. Women and blacks could not vote. Nonetheless 6,318 votes were cast, of which a later investigation found that 4,908 were fraudulent, stuffed by slavocrats to dominate the assembly then draft and pass a constitution. Reeder approved the constitution that limited officeholders to slavocrats and outlawed any speaking or writing against slavocracy.[17] Free soilers and slavocrats respectively dubbed each other "Border Ruffians" and "Jayhawkers."

Free soilers led by Charles Robinson and James Lane held their own convention at Topeka in October 1855, and unveiled a constitution that forbad slavery on November 11. An election by Kansans ratified that constitution on December 15, 1855. In January 1856, free soilers elected representatives to an assembly. On March 4, the Topeka assembly sent Congress an appeal to accept their constitution and grant Kansas statehood. Congress deadlocked as the House approved the free soil constitution and the Senate the slavocrat constitution. Meanwhile, slavocrat Judge Samuel Lecompte convened a grand jury dominated by fellow slavocrats who indicted free state officials for treason.

Violence erupted between them in 1856. On May 21, Samuel Jones led 300 slavocrats into Lawrence where they destroyed the printing presses of two newspapers, looted shops, and burned the hotel and home of free soil leader Charles Robinson. The violence spread to Congress when on May 23, Representative and slavocrat Preston Brooks of South Carolina savagely beat with a cane Senator and free soiler Charles Sumner of Massachusetts. Incensed by those atrocities, radical abolitionist John Brown led six accomplices, including four of his sons, to murder five slavocrats at Pottawatomie Creek on May 25. By 1861, the war for "Bleeding Kansas" had cost over 200 lives and $2 million in destroyed property.

Slavocrats convened a convention in Lecompton that produced a constitution that legalized slavery permanently in 1857. Free soilers boycotted the referendum. The result was that slavocrats approved the Lecompton Constitution and sent it to Congress for ratification. Slavocrat President James Buchannan accepted the Lecompton Constitution but a majority in the House of Representatives rejected it. Kansas's statehood lay in abeyance until after the Civil War began. Meanwhile, the respective populations of Kansas and Nebraska rose from 107,206 to 364,399 and 28,841 to 122,993 from 1860 to 1870.[18]

***

Mormons established an empire they called Deseret throughout the Southwest with Salt Lake City the capital and trails linking towns that extended as far as San Bernadino, California, Tempe, Arizona, Mormon Station, Nevada, and Fort Bridger, Wyoming.[19] By 1856, they numbered 22,000 and made the desert bloom through an extensive irrigation system that watered an array of crops and livestock. They enriched themselves by selling or exchanging items to settlers heading to California or Oregon. They eagerly traded desperately-needed flour, salt pork, salt beef, and wagon wheels to passersby in return for relatively cheaply-priced items like furniture, clothing, plows, and worn-out horses or oxen. They also reaped profits by charging exorbitant fees for ferry and bridge crossings of rivers. Brigham Young ruled Deseret.[20] Young was not just an extraordinary political and spiritual leader; he had twenty-seven wives and fifty-six children.

President Millard Filmore sought to coopt rather than confront Young and the Mormons by appointing Young Utah Territory's governor in 1850. But he also appointed non-Mormons Perry Brocchus and George Stiles as federal judges for Utah Territory. Young mobilized a secret vigilante group called the Danites or Avenging Angels that murdered several federal officials and terrorized others into fleeing Utah Territory. The result was war.[21]

President Buchanan replaced Young with Alfred Cumming as governor and dispatched 2,500 troops led by Colonel Albert Johnston to impose federal rule on Utah in 1857. Young mobilized the Nauvoo Legion against the American army and withdrew Mormons from outlying settlements to Salt Lake City. Raiders drove off the army's horses and burned its supply train. In September, the Nauvoo Legion led by John Lee surrounded an Oregon-bound wagon train and forced the pioneers to surrender. After they laid down their arms, the Mormons murdered 120 men and women, and took 18 children for adoption by would-be parents. Washington never prosecuted anyone for that Mountain Meadow Massacre.[22] Instead, Buchannan cut a deal with Young to accept federal officials and troops in Utah in return for a blanket pardon for any alleged crimes on June 12, 1858. That ended the "Mormon War" but not the controversy over Mormonism.

***

Buchannan was eager to set aside the distant Mormon conflict because tensions between northern free and southern slave states were soaring. Two events exacerbated regional animosities in 1857 and 1858, respectively the Supreme Court's Dred Scott decision and John Brown's attempt to inspire a slave revolt at Harpers Ferry.

Dred Scott was a slave who accompanied his master, Dr. John Emerson, to stints at Fort Armstrong in free state Illinois in 1836 and Fort Snelling in free territory Minnesota in 1837.[23] They returned to their home in St. Louis in 1838 and Emerson died in 1846. Scott sued Emerson's widow Irene for freedom for himself, his wife, and two children on the "once free, always free" idea that slaves were liberated when they lived in free states. Irene Emerson sold Scott and his family to her brother, John Sanford. The lawsuit was officially called Dred Scott versus Sandford because a clerical error misspelled Sanford's name. Scott actually won the first round in the federal circuit court in St. Louis but lost when Sanford appealed. The case went to the Supreme Court. On March 6, 1857, Chief Justice Roger Taney submitted the seven to two ruling against Scott, with the justification grounded on slavocracy's core principles. He argued that Scott had no standing because he was not a citizen, and he was not a citizen because he was black. Scott's residence in a free state did not end his slavery. Slaves were property and could not be taken from their masters without due legal process. Congress had no power to limit or end slavery anywhere. The Dred Scott decision outraged northern free soilers and abolitionists alike.

John Brown's attempt to provoke a slave uprising at Harpers Ferry, Virginia outraged slavocrats.[24] On the night of October 16, 1858, Brown and his twenty-one followers captured the Harpers Ferry arsenal, intending to distribute the arms to slaves for a revolt. Instead, President Buchanan had Colonel Robert E. Lee lead eighty troops to surround the arsenal. In the assault on October 18, the troops killed ten of the rebels and captured seven while six escaped. Brown was among those who were captured, tried, and executed for insurrection.

***

Four candidates competed for the presidency during the 1860 election.[25] None favored the national abolition of slavery but Abraham Lincoln and his Republican Party advocated preventing slavery's spread to the western territories. Lincoln won with a plurality of votes or 39.8 percent and 180 electoral votes to the Southern Democratic Party's John Breckinridge with 18.1 percent and 72, Constitutional Union Party's John Bell with 12.6 percent and 39, and Northern Democratic Party's Stephen Douglas with 29.5 percent and 12.

That prompted slavocrats in eleven southern states to secede from the United States, starting with South Carolina on December 20, 1860, followed by Mississippi, Florida, Alabama, Georgia, Louisiana, Texas, Virginia, Arkansas, North Carolina, and Tennessee. Delegates from the first seven met at Montgomery, Alabama, and on February 8 formed the Confederate States of America with a constitution, congress, and Jefferson Davis as president. On April 12, Confederate batteries opened fire on Fort Sumter, a federal fort in the bay at Charleston, South Carolina; the garrison surrendered the next day. Lincoln called for 75,000 volunteers to suppress the rebellion. Davis called for 100,000 volunteers to resist. The other six states seceded and joined the Confederacy.

***

The Civil War was America's most catastrophic period.[26] The war lasted four years before Union forces finally crushed that rebellion. The dead officially numbered around 620,000 but recent estimates reveal 750,000 people probably died directly or indirectly. Even the lower figure is higher than the dead of all other American wars combined. Rampaging armies and raiders left trails of destroyed towns, farms, railroads, and bridges in their wake.

The West did not escape that death and destruction. The Civil War in the West included United States army campaigns against rebels and Indians.[27] The only major Confederate campaign in the West was the two-stage invasion of New Mexico and Arizona in late 1861 and into 1862 that ended with the Union army's reconquest of the region. The only other invasion was by the terrorist gang led by William Quantrill and William "Bloody Bill" Anderson that murdered 182 men and boys, and burned 185 buildings in Lawrence, Kansas on August 21, 1863. In contrast, Indian rebellions erupted in nearly every region of the West after tribes saw regular troops depart from local forts to fight back east. Militarily the West's campaigns were a sideshow to the eastern campaigns where the war was decided. Indeed, the Civil War's scale of troops, bloodshed, logistics, and geographic expanse dwarfs all the Indian wars that preceded, accompanied, and followed the Civil War. Yet every Indian war was catastrophic to the tribes along with the thousands of settlers and soldiers who fought them.

When the war began about 5 million people or 14 percent of America's 31 million people lived west of the Mississippi River and 80 percent of them in states lining that river. Elsewhere about 380,000 lived in California, 62,500 in Oregon, 11,000 in Washington, 604,000 in Texas, 107,000 in Kansas, 28,000 in Nebraska, 93,000 in New Mexico, 40,000 in Utah, 34,500 in Colorado, 6,000 in Arizona, and 6,000 in Nevada. As for Indian Territory, later called Oklahoma, 55,000 "civilized" Indians along with 3,000 slaves lived there. In the West only Texas joined the Confederacy while the other territories and states stayed in the United States. However, with its large slave population, most of Indian Territory's people sided with the rebels. During the war, Washington reorganized vast swaths of the West by establishing Colorado Territory and Dakota Territory in 1861, Nevada Territory in 1861 and statehood in 1864, Idaho Territory and Arizona Territory in 1863, and Montana Territory in 1864.

After the war erupted, frontier commanders received War Department orders to abandon Forts Lancaster, Stockton, Davis, Quitman, and Bliss in Texas; Smith, Gibson, Washita, and Cobb in Indian Territory; and Buchanan and Breckinridge in southern New Mexico Territory. Texan troops captured and later exchanged Federal troops withdrawing from forts across that state but troops from the other forts reached safety.

***

Colonel Edward Canby commanded the Department of New Mexico.[28] Defending the Rio Grande valley were Forts Fillmore and Craig, 40 and 163 miles north of El Paso respectively. Other posts included Fort Marcy near Santa Fe, Fort Sumner in the Pecos River valley, Fort Stanton in the Sacramento Mountains, Fort Union on the Santa Fe Trail, and Fort Wingate on Rio San Jose. Lieutenant Colonel Christopher "Kit" Carson commanded New Mexico's volunteer regiment.[29]

The Confederacy established the Department of Texas with General Earl Van Dorn its commander at San Antonio in April 1861. Van Dorn dispatched Lieutenant Colonel John Baylor with 300 troops to occupy Fort Bliss near El Paso and attack Fort Fillmore in New Mexican Territory if possible. In July, Baylor invaded New Mexico. Major Isaac Lynde abandoned Fort Fillmore and withdrew toward Fort Stanton.

Baylor and his men caught up and forced Lynde to surrender with his 500 troops on July 25. Baylor dispatched troops to occupy Tucson and on August 1, proclaimed the Confederate Territory of Arizona that included New Mexico with Messila its capital.

General Henry Sibley superseded Baylor in command of now 2,500 troops and fifteen cannons in January 1862, and led his army up the Rio Grande valley in early February. Canby had 3,800 troops at Fort Craig when the invaders approached on February 16. When Sibley tried to bypass the fort on February 21, Canby blocked the rebel passage of the Rio Grande at Valverde 10 miles upstream. The rebels repelled an attack then counterattacked, routing the Union troops; each side suffered several hundred casualties. Sibley and his men resumed their march north on February 23, entered undefended Albuquerque and Santa Fe then headed up the Santa Fe Trail in early March.

Colonel John Slough and 1,300 mostly Colorado volunteers defended Glorieta Pass. On March 26, Sibley's troops attacked but the Union troops repelled them. Slough sent Major John Chivington with 500 troops through the mountains around the rebel lines to destroy their supply train on March 28. That forced Sibley to withdraw first to Santa Fe, then, with Slough in pursuit, eventually all the way back to El Paso. At Fort Craig, Canby made no attempt to block the rebel retreat.

Meanwhile, in California 17,000 volunteers joined eight infantry and two cavalry regiments and nearly all served in posts across much of the far West, replacing regular troops that had been called east. Two columns headed east in spring 1862. General James Carleton led the "California Legion" of 2,350 troops from San Diego. On April 15, the advanced guard skirmished with a rebel patrol at Picacho Pass 50 miles northwest of Tucson, the Civil War's westernmost clash. The column marched into Tucson on June 7 and reached the Rio Grande on July 4. After his column entered Santa Fe in September 1862, Carleton received command of New Mexico Territory. Elsewhere, Colonel Patrick Connor led 1,000 troops from Sacramento east along the California Trail to garrison forts in Nevada, Utah, Wyoming, and Idaho.

As with other tribes across the West, Apache and Navajo took advantage of the Civil War to attack American settlements, wagon trains, and mines. The Mescalero launched their raids after the Americans abandoned Fort Stanton in their territory. General Carleton had Lieutenant Colonel Kit Carson lead 500 New Mexican cavalry to reoccupy Fort Stanton then push on against the Mescalero while Colonel Joseph West converged against them from Messila. In a skirmish in the Guadeloupe Mountains, troops killed Chief Manuelito, eleven warriors, and a woman. That encouraged the Mescalero to come to Fort Stanton and accept peace. Carleton established Fort Sumner on the Pecos River east of the mountains and had the 400 Mescalero placed on a nearby reservation called Bosque Redondo. Carleton then sent Carson with 1,000 troops against the Navajo in June 1863. Carson established a supply depot at Fort Wingate then marched northwest 40 miles to establish Fort Canby as an advanced position. Carson's strategy was to capture Navajo horse and sheep herds and destroy their crops to force them to submit. Along the way, his troops killed 66 Navajo and captured 8,793 in 155 skirmishes until the last band surrendered by December.[30]

Carson and his troops escorted the Navajo from their homeland in the "Long Walk" 400 miles east to Bosque Redondo where they had to live alongside their enemies, the Mescalero. Outnumbered and bullied, the Mescalero fled the reservation for their former White Mountain homeland. The Navajo sent petitions protesting their wretched conditions and requesting their return to their homeland to Washington. In 1867, Congress commissioned General William Sherman and Samuel Tappan to meet with the Navajo and negotiate a treaty that addressed their grievances. Under the treaty signed on June 1, 1868, the Navajo were allowed to go home.

An invasion of miners into the upper Gila River region around Pinos Altos in 1862 provoked Mangas Colorado and Cochise to lead their Chiricahua warriors against them. General Joseph West had his troops capture Mangas Colorado under a false white flag then encouraged his soldiers to torture and murder the chief on January 18, 1863. Detachments defeated war parties in several skirmishes with dozens of Apache killed. Fabled mountain man Joseph Walker led thirty-four miners into central Arizona where they struck gold and founded Prescott in early 1863. Warm Springs Apache led by Chief Victoria and the Yavapai warred against the invaders. Carleton's strategy against this expanded war was to ring hostile tribes with forts from which expeditions invaded their territory. The war's results were lopsided. During 1863 and 1864, the Indians killed 41 soldiers and 34 civilians, wounded 45 soldiers and 17 civilians, and captured 29,879 stock but suffered 664 killed, 227 wounded, 8,793 captured, and 49,722 stock captured.[31]

***

Shoshone and Ute bands raided wagon trains, settlements, and mines in late 1862. Colonel Patrick Conner led a column from Fort Bridger against Shoshone Chief Bear Hunter's band that held a captured boy. Bear Hunter released the boy and sent word that he wanted peace after his warriors skirmished with Connor's troops in Cache Valley. That did not end the war. Upon learning that Shoshone had killed several prospectors, Connor pushed on to the village in the Bear River valley and attacked on January 27, 1863. The troops slaughtered 224 men, women, and children, captured 160 women and children, and 175 horses, and burned 70 lodges, while suffering 14 dead and 53 wounded. That victory earned Connor promotion to brigadier general. Ute raids provoked a retaliatory expedition. On April 15, 1863, Lieutenant Colonel George Evans and 170 cavalry fought around 200 Ute warriors led by Chief Little Soldier in Spanish Fork Canyon. The troops routed the Indians, killing around 30 while losing one dead and two wounded. That inhibited further Ute attacks. Regional Indian Superintendent James Doty followed up those victories with messages calling on the Ute, Shoshone, and other transmontane tribes for peace. By late 1863, Doty had secured agreements with all that region's tribes.

***

The bloodiest Indian war amidst the Civil War was fought mostly in Minnesota.[32] Washington made Minnesota a territory in 1849 and a state in 1858, while the population soared from 6,072 in 1850 to 171,072 in 1860. The four-band Dakota or Santee Sioux lived in the Minnesota River valley. Under the 1851 treaty, the Dakota accepted a reservation 20 miles wide and 150 miles long split between upper and lower agencies with $3,000,000 paid over 50 years. In 1853, the army established Fort Ridgely 10 miles below the Lower Agency near New Ulm. Under the 1858 treaty, the Dakota sold the north bank's 10-mile stretch and split the reservation's south side among 80 acres for each family head in return for $266,880 and annuities of food, tools, and other necessities.

The reservation faced starvation in 1862. With a mix of incompetence, corruption, wartime shortages, and bad harvests, Washington failed to deliver the annuities. On July 14, during talks between chiefs and agents, sutler Andrew Myrick scornfully rejected the Dakota request that he sell them food on credit, declaring, "So far as I am concerned, if they are hungry, let them eat grass or their own dung."[33] Four Dakota teenagers robbed and murdered five settlers on August 17. When Chief Little Crow and the tribal council learned of those crimes, they chose to wipe out the region's soldiers and settlers rather than surrender the suspects. Over the next month, warriors killed around

500 settlers along with 77 regular and 29 volunteer soldiers, while troops killed around 150 Dakota and captured over 2,000; Myrick was among the dead, his mouth stuffed with grass. The defenders of Fort Ridgely, New Ulm, and Fort Abercrombie on the Red River repelled attacks. Governor Alexander Ramsey had Colonel Henry Sibley lead 1,400 Minnesota volunteers up the Minnesota River valley against the Dakota. The battle of Wood Lake on September 23 was decisive. The Dakota lost about 35 killed but by now had expended virtually all their ammunition. By September 26, most chiefs and 1,300 people submitted, released 269 captives, and eventually were incarcerated at Fort Sibley. Others, including some led by Little Crow, fled to Teton Sioux bands on the plains east of the Missouri; war parties from those bands began raiding isolated forts and settlements across the region.

A five-man federal government commission established on September 28 indicted 392 prisoners on murder and rape charges, and found guilty and condemned to death 303. President Lincoln carefully studied each conviction and reduced the condemned to thirty-nine. Sibley commuted the sentence of one of them. On December 26, 1862, thirty-eight Sioux were hanged at Mankato, Minnesota, the largest mass execution in American history. On March 3, 1863, Congress authorized the transfer of the Dakota along with 1,950 Winnebago, of whom some had joined the uprising, to new reservations on the middle Missouri River. Before that could happen the army had to crush that region's now hostile Sioux bands.

General John Pope, the regional commander, launched two columns against the Yanktonai bands in June 1863, Sibley's 3,000 troops from Fort Ridgley and General Alfred Sully's 1,200 troops from Fort Randall on the Missouri River. The ultimate objective was Devil's Lake where the hostile tribes were reported to be massing. Sibley's men skirmished with warriors at Big Mound on July 20, Dead Buffalo Lake on July 26, and Stoney Lake on July 28 then marched to the Missouri River to await Sully. When Sully did not appear Sibley and his men headed back to Fort Ridgley. Meanwhile, Sully led his troops up the Missouri River valley beyond Fort Pierre then angled southeast to fight Inkpaduta's Sioux band at Whitestone Hill on September 3; the soldiers killed around 200 and captured 250 mostly women and children while losing 22 dead and 38 wounded. The column then headed southwest to establish Fort Sully on the Missouri River. Elsewhere Little Crow was killed during a horse-stealing raid into Minnesota. Neither column reached Devil's Lake.

Two columns searched for hostile bands in the summer of 1864, Sully's 1,700 troops from Sioux City and Colonel Minor Thomas's 1,000 troops from Fort Ridgley. Sully's skirmished with Sioux at Killdeer Mountain on July 28 and Badland on August 9, while Thomas's failed to find any band. Short of supplies, Sully led his men to Fort Berthold, most of the way harassed by warriors. The bands split. Some submitted and eventually were settled on reservations along the middle Missouri River. Most migrated west of the Missouri River to the Powder, Yellowstone, and Little Missouri River valleys.

Three army columns marched through the heart of Lakota Sioux country in July 1865 with the plan to converge in the Rosebud River valley on September 1. Colonel Nelson Cole's from Fort Kearney and Colonel Samuel Walker's from Fort Laramie to join in the Black Hills while General Patrick Connor's from Fort Laramie followed the Bozeman Trail toward the Powder River. Connor's troops constructed Fort Connor on Crazy Woman Fork of the Powder River. After garrisoning the fort, Connor marched to the Tongue River and attacked Black Bear's Arapaho village. Most Arapaho escaped to shelter with a Cheyenne Band. Meanwhile, Cole and Walker met on the Belle Fourche River on August 18. Morale and supplies were low, and the commanders agreed to withdraw to their respective posts. The campaign accomplished nothing important and merely exacerbated animosities.

***

The 1858 Pike's Peak gold rush brought a flood of miners, merchants, and settlers to a stretch of the Rocky Mountain Front Range centered on Denver, founded in 1859. By 1860, 34,277 people lived in Colorado Territory. Trails along the Republican, Smoky Hill, and Arkansas Rivers were the most direct routes from Missouri. Others arrived via the Overland Trail that followed the Platte River with a branch that veered southwest along the South Platte River. The army protected the region with Forts Leavenworth, Kearney, Riley, Larned, and Lyon.

Word of the Sioux uprising in Minnesota and the northern plains inspired Sioux, Cheyenne and Arapaho bands on the central plains and Comanche and Kiowa bands on the southern plains to revolt. The initial raids struck wagon trains, stagecoaches, ranches, and relay stations along the Platte, South Platte, Republican, Smokey Hill, and Arkansas River valleys in 1864.

Colorado Governor John Evans issued on June 27 a demand that all bands adhere to the 1851 and 1861 treaties they had signed and journey to the nearest army post. Virtually all bands ignored that demand and condemned Washington and the territorial governments for violating those treaties. Only Black Kettle's Cheyenne and Little Raven's Arapaho bands complied. On September 28, Black Kettle met with Evans, Colonel John Chivington, and other officials, and declared his dedication to peace.[34] Black Kettle and his people camped for a couple of weeks beside Fort Lyon commanded by Major Edward Wynkoop, who shared rations with them. Then in early November, they moved 40 miles north to Sand Creek where American and white flags fluttered from poles beside the chief's tipi.

During the summer of 1864, army columns departed from forts across the region but failed to find and destroy any hostile villages. Those included General Thomas Mitchell's from Fort Larned, Colonel Samuel Sumner's from Fort Kearney, and General James Blunt's from Fort Leavenworth. Colonel John Chivington commanded the Colorado District headquartered at Denver. In November, he departed with 575 Colorado volunteers and this vow: "I have come to kill Indians and believe it is right and honorable to use any means under God's heaven to kill Indians. Kill and scalp all, big and little."[35]

Chivington was an ordained Methodist "hellfire and damnation" preacher with political aspirations who rangled a colonel's commission after the Civil War erupted. His decisive actions during the battle of Glorieta Pass made him famous. He had recently lost a bid for election to the House of Representatives and hoped a victory would revive his political career. Unable to find any hostiles, Chivington targeted Black Kettle's peaceful band. On the morning of November 29, Chivington ordered a "take no prisoners" attack that slaughtered around a hundred people, mostly women and children; Black Kettle escaped with a hundred others. Among the survivors was George Bent, the son of William Bent and Cheyenne Owl woman. In his memoir, he recalled that when the bluecoats attacked: "The Indians all began running, but they did not seem to know what to do or where to turn. The women and children were screaming and wailing, the men running to their lodges for their arms and shouting advice and directions to one another . . . We ran up the creek with the cavalry following us, one company on each bank . . . and the dry bed of the creek was a terrible sight: men, women, and children lying thickly scattered on the sand, some dead and the rest too badly wounded to move."[36]

Chivington's "victory" provoked condemnation when reluctant participants revealed that the troops had massacred a peaceful village. In January 1865, Congress's Joint Committee on the Conduct of the War opened an investigation. After weeks of hearing testimonies, the Committee's report concluded that: "Chivington . . . deliberately planned and executed a . . . dastardly massacre . . . Having full knowledge of their friendly character . . . he took advantage of their incomprehension and defenseless condition to gratify the worst passions . . . He surprised and murdered in cold blood the unsuspecting men, women, and children . . . who had every reason to believe they were under the protection of the United States authorities."[37]

Only one column actually found and attacked a hostile village during that war. With 71 Ute and Jicarilla scouts ahead, Colonel Kit Carson led 260 cavalry, 75 infantry, two howitzers, and a supply train from Fort Bascom east along the Canadian River on November 12 and they struck Kiowa Chief Little Mountain's village on November 25. The warriors fought off the assault as the women, children, and old men fled to a nearby Comanche village. After burning the village, the troops pursued a few miles to Adobe Walls where over 1,400 Comanche and Kiowa warriors attacked. The howitzers kept the Indians from overwhelming the defenders. Carson's troops killed or wounded around fifty Indians while losing six killed and twenty-five wounded. The next day, Carson withdrew back up the valley, reaching Fort Bascom on December 12.

Army columns vainly searched for hostile bands on the central plains in 1865. Meanwhile, Spotted Tail's Sioux and Roman Nose's Cheyenne attacked Julesburg and nearby Fort Rankin on the South Platte River on January 7, and killed fourteen soldiers and four civilians, while suffering several dead and wounded. Raids elsewhere killed around 50 soldiers and civilians and ran off 1,500 cattle.

One by one, hostile bands with dwindling munitions and food surrendered in return for promises that treaties would resolve injustices. The southern tribes met with commissioners where the Little Arkansas River joined the Arkansas River on October 4. Commissioners signed separate treaties with tribes on October 14, 17, and 18, 1865, whereby the chiefs ceded all land between the Arkansas and Platte Rivers and accepted reservations in Indian Territory. Later most warriors from those tribes repudiated the treaties.

***

An estimated 270,000 Indians split among 125 bands inhabited the West in 1866.[38] Most bands were in a reservation system that included sixty-one agencies and fourteen superintendencies overseen by the Bureau of Indian Affairs administered by the Interior Department. Corruption permeated the Indian Bureau and reservation system. Indian rings included federal officials and contractors that either supplied shoddy overpriced goods or outright stole annuities designated for the tribes and sold them for profit. Indian Bureau directors appointed to purge the corruption made little progress. The theft of all or part of a tribe's annuities and the little goods and food that did arrive provoked many revolts.

The army was at war with one or more tribes every year from 1866 to 1886. To fight those wars, the army split the nation into divisions each with a commander. The West had the Division of Missouri with headquarters at St. Louis and the Division of Pacific with headquarters at San Francisco, with the Continental Divide between them. Divisions were split among departments. Many Indian wars sprawled across departments and some across divisions and so required coordination of strategy and logistics among their respective headquarters. The War Department included the divisions of Adjutant General, Inspector General, Judge Advocate General, Quartermaster, Subsistence, Medical, Pay, Ordnance, and Corps of Engineers.

Washington swiftly demobilized the million-man army after the Civil War. During the post-Civil War era from 1865 to 1891, the army averaged around 25,000 troops among forty-five infantry, ten cavalry, and five artillery regiments respectively with ten, twelve, and twelve companies. Four regiments, the 9th and 10th Cavalry and the 24th and 25th Infantry were "colored," with black troops and noncommissioned officers and white officers. The esprit, combat record, and reenlistment rates of these regiments surpassed most other regiments. Indians dubbed them "buffalo soldiers" for their black wooly hair and brown skins. American frontier commanders deployed allied Indians as translators, scouts, and fighters. In 1866, Congress authorized the army to organize 1,000 Indians into companies for six months of service and $13 a month pay. Most acclaimed was Captain Frank North's Pawnee scout company.[39]

The basic fighting unit was the infantry or cavalry company; cavalry companies were called troops from 1883. A regiment's companies rarely campaigned or fought all together. Companies were scattered in isolated posts across the West and were responsible for patrolling vast stretches of territory. Cavalry companies averaged fifty-eight men, infantry companies forty-one men, and artillery companies forty men. In some campaigns, state or territorial volunteer units augmented regulars.

A regiment had a colonel, lieutenant colonel, major, and a captain, first lieutenant, and second lieutenant for each company. Promotions were all but frozen in the postwar army. Most lieutenants needed from 24 to 26 years to make major, and 33 to 37 years to make lieutenant colonel. Virtually all officers were demoted from the field ranks (brevets) they had earned during the Civil War. Annual salaries ranged from $3,500 for colonels to $1,400 for second lieutenants.

The quality of troops was poor. Half of privates were foreign-born. Each year from 25 to 40 percent of the ranks disappeared from desertion, discharge, or death. Only about 1,000 men reenlisted annually. Veterans with one or more five-year terms numbered less than one in three men or 7,000 of 25,000 troops. The army lacked stringent recruitment or training standards. Most men had never fired more than a handful of cartridges before they faced warriors trying to kill them. There was little esprit de corps. Most men enlisted for the regular if meager food, clothing, shelter, and stipend. Annual pay ranged from $274 for sergeants to $166 for privates.

A soldier mostly faced prolonged boredom and squalor broken by bouts of drinking, gambling, and whoring in a saloon or brothel near his fort. Venereal diseases topped the sick list. Troops spent more time with shovels, saws, and hammers than rifles, and were often deployed to build forts, bridges, or telegraph lines, cut timber or hay, make adobe, or repair equipment. Standard rations were hardtack, salt pork, and coffee. Penalties for even minor infractions could be brutal including whippings and jail, and execution for desertion or striking an officer.

The infantry wielded a Springfield rifle retooled in 1873 to breech-load a copper cartridge with the caliber reduced from .58 to .50. The cavalry had several firearms including the .50 Spencer seven-shot, the single-shot .50 caliber Sharps, and the 1873 single-shot .45 Springfield carbine. From 1872, the standard sidearm was the .45 caliber Colt revolver. Cavalry sabers were useless for warfare and confined to ceremonial occasions. Artillery for Indian campaigns usually included 12-pounder mountain howitzers. A few howitzer shells usually scattered large groups of Indians and kept them from charging. Artillery was less effective against villages since a bombardment rather than surprise attack usually let the people escape.

Despite decades of experience, the army failed to develop an Indian fighting doctrine. Military doctrine emphasized conventional nation-state type warfare. It was a field commander's responsibility to adopt strategy and tactics for fighting a highly mobile, hit and run guerilla war with Indians. The standard strategy was to build army posts across territories to encircle and intimidate the region's tribes. There were around a hundred posts scattered across the trans-Mississippi West between 1865 and 1890. Even so, there were rarely enough troops to blanket a region to the point where tribes did not revolt.

The major campaign strategy was to launch several columns into hostile territory hoping that one or more would locate and destroy Indian villages. That usually occurred in winter when Indians were less mobile and alert. The troops would kill anyone in the crossfire as long as resistance continued and sometimes after the warriors fled, burn the village, shoot any captured horses, and herd survivors to a reservation. Those attacks were rare. A column usually lacked the ability to track and report back on villages and war parties. Some commanders, most notably General George Crook, used Indian scouts, mule trains, and hand-picked army units to wage the mobile warfare needed to track down and defeat nomadic bands. Typically, cavalry rode to battle and dismounted to fight on foot with every fourth man holding the horses for his three comrades.

As in any war, victory depended as much as the ability to supply units in the field as on their combat prowess. By 1869, the Union Pacific Railroad spanned the West, greatly easing the army's ability to supply campaigns north and south of those tracks. The Missouri River provided a relatively rapid means of shipping goods by steamboat to a dozen or so forts upstream as far as Fort Benton in Montana Territory. No other western river east of the Rockies was navigable. Supplying troops elsewhere required large numbers of wagons, draft animals, and teamsters.

Supply concerns slowed army advances to a crawl. Although many regiments were cavalry, their speed was limited to the wagon train that supplied their needs. Cavalry and infantry companies respectively required three and one six-mule wagons. Forage had to be hauled because cavalry horses could not solely subsist on native grasses. Even then, horses often expired from lack of enough fodder and water, and the rough terrain. Most supplies were bought and shipped by civilian contractors, many of whom were corrupt and sold the army shoddy goods and spoiled food.

***

The war against the Sioux that began in Minnesota in August 1862 spread across the northern plains to the Bighorn Mountains in 1866. A visionary unwittingly exacerbated that conflict. John Bozeman pioneered a 500-mile route from Virginia City, Montana to the Overland Trail in 1863 that ran from the Yellowstone River south along the Bighorn Mountains eastern side and then across the high plains to the Platte River. The Lakota Sioux bands along with Cheyenne and Arapaho bands lived in that region and resented the intruders. Red Cloud was the most prominent Sioux war chief.[40] War parties killed around 50 of 3,500 people who traversed that trail from 1863 to 1866.[41]

To secure that route, Colonel Henry Carrington led 700 infantry up the Bozeman Trail in June 1866 with orders to reinforce Fort Reno (formerly Fort Connor), and begin constructing Fort Phil Kearny on August 3 and Fort C. F. Smith on August 12. Carrington was an inept leader with no command or combat experience. He failed to prevent Sioux war parties from blocking people heading to Montana. From July to December, the Sioux killed ninety-six soldiers and fifty-six civilians, and wounded a hundred others.

Sioux attacked a woodcutting party outside Fort Phil Kearney on December 21. Carrington sent Captain William Fetterman and his eighty-two men to drive off the attackers but warned him not to go beyond Lodge Trail Ridge. Oglala Sioux Chief Crazy Horse led a party that taunted Fetterman just beyond rifle shot then rode away.[42] That enraged Fetterman who led a charge after them. Around a thousand Sioux surrounded and slaughtered Fetterman and his men.

The war stalemated. The Indians could not overrun the forts and the army could not catch and defeat the warriors or destroy their villages. Troops detached outside forts to cut hay or wood did repel massive attacks during the Hayfield and Wagon Box battles on August 1 and 2, 1867. Nonetheless, the Indians won that war, although their victory was fleeting.

Commissioners signed a series of treaties at Fort Laramie in 1868, with the Brule Sioux on April 29, the Crow on May 7, the northern Cheyenne and Arapaho on May 10, and Red Cloud's Ogallala Sioux on November 6. The United States recognized Lakota territory as a "Great Sioux Reserve" north of the North Platte River, east of the Big Horn Mountains, and west of the Missouri River. The Lakota promised never to kill or capture any Americans and to accept any railroads, stagecoaches, and migrants that crossed their territory. Any Americans or Indians accused of murder or theft would be arrested and delivered to American courts for trial and possible conviction. The army would abandon its Bozeman Trail forts. The troops completed their evacuation during the summer of 1869 and the Indians gleefully torched the forts after they marched away.

Yet, like countless other treaties, the 1868 treaty was a temporary truce rather than a lasting peace. Americans and Indians alike disregarded the treaty's boundaries and other requirements. Few of the bands agreed to the stipulation that they draw supplies at their reservation agencies on the Missouri River. The Indians preferred the high plains where buffalo still roamed to the Missouri valley where few survived. Warriors from most bands continued to alternate drawing supplies and stealing horses or killing isolated groups of traders, miners, or settlers.

***

War again engulfed the central and southern plains in 1867, and persisted off and on until 1875.[43] The army essentially caused that war first by being too passive and then too aggressive. Scalp and horse raids along the Smokey Hill and Arkansas continued despite the 1865 treaties binding those tribes to stop them. Territorial governors demobilized their volunteer regiments after the Civil War, while the regular regiments that replaced them were fewer and depleted by desertion. The army exacerbated animosities by banning licensed traders who sold guns and ammunition to peaceful Indians in July 1866. Then, amidst negotiations between commissioners and chiefs in 1867, the army tried to intimidate the restless tribes by dispatching an expedition into the region.

General Winfield Hancock led 1,400 troops that included Colonel George Custer's 7th Cavalry from Fort Larned in early April to a Cheyenne and Sioux village 35 miles west on Pawnee Fork. Fearing they would be massacred like the people at Sand Creek, Cheyenne Chiefs Roman Nose and Tall Bull blocked the way with their warriors and demanded that Hancock halt. Hancock complied but warned the chiefs that they either had to surrender and return to the reservation or fight. That night the Sioux and Cheyenne abandoned their village and fled. The next morning Hancock ordered the village burned and dispatched Custer to pursue the Indians and escort them to a reservation. Custer led his men over much of western Kansas and eastern Colorado but failed to find the refugees.

Incensed that the bluecoats had destroyed their village, the warriors attacked wagon trains, stagecoaches, and small army posts throughout the region. The army officially ended the campaign in September to encourage the bands to attend a peace conference near Fort Larned in October. Under the Medicine Bow treaties of October 21 with the Kiowa and Comanche, October 22 with the Kiowa Apache, and October 28 with the Cheyenne and Arapaho, those tribes agreed to end their raids and return to their reservations.

Disgruntled with reservation conditions, Cheyenne and Arapaho warriors haunted the Smokey Hill River Trail, attacking wagon trains and ranches, and killing seventy-nine civilians from August through October 1868. Colonel Alfred Sully led a column from Fort Riley in early September. Although Indians skirmished with him, he was unable to bring them to a decisive battle. Cheyenne Chief Roman Nose and several hundred warriors besieged Captain George Forsythe and his fifty-man scouting company on Beecher Island from September 17 to 19. The soldiers finally drove off the Cheyenne after killing Roman Nose and thirty-two others while losing six dead and fifteen wounded.

Major Eugene Carr's column entered the field in early October but searched in vain for hostile villages. The troops withdrew to their post with winter's onset. Their repose was brief.

General Phil Sheridan planned a winter campaign to destroy the hostile bands in their lodges by four converging columns, Custer's from Fort Supply, Colonel George Evans's from Fort Bascom, Carr's from Fort Lyon, and Captain Emmet Crawford's from Fort Larned. Custer's was the first to draw blood when his column found and attacked Black Kettle's Cheyenne village on the Washita River on November 27. His troops killed 103 men, women, and children including Black Kettle and over 800 horses, and captured 53 while suffering 22 dead. Custer then withdrew as warriors massed from nearby Comanche, Kiowa, and Arapaho villages. Crawford's column bogged down in deep snow and rolling hills then struggled back to Fort Bascom. Evans marched down the Canadian River valley, left behind his plodding infantry and wagons at Monument Creek, and hurried on with his cavalry. He attacked and destroyed a Comanche village at Soldier Spring on December 22. Carr's column failed to find any villages and suffered terribly from frostbite and lack of forage. The campaign succeeded in intimidating the Indians to return to their reservations. Thereafter the Comanche and Kiowa rarely raided north although they kept attacking the Texas frontier.

Carr led his men from Fort Lyon in early May to find and destroy Tall Bull's Cheyenne village whose warriors continued to harass the Smokey Hill and Platte River Trails. After a skirmish at Spring Creek, Carr marched to Fort McPherson to refit and welcome Major Frank North's 150 Pawnee scouts. Resuming the field they found and attacked the Cheyenne at Summit Springs, killing fifty-two and capturing seventeen women and children on July 21. Some Cheyenne escaped but most surrendered.

***

President Ulysses Grant was determined to forge lasting and just peace with the tribes. In his inaugural address on March 4, 1869, he declared: "The proper treatment of the original inhabitants of this land—the Indians—is one deserving of special study. I will favor any course toward them which tends toward their civilization and ultimate citizenship."[44] Congress responded on April 10, by authorizing the president to form a ten-man Board of Indian Commissioners to devise and implement a policy to fulfill his vision. Grant filled the commission with humanitarian Christians of various denominations, with General Ely Parker, a Seneca and his aide, as chair, and Vincent Colyer, a prominent Quaker and philanthropist, as secretary. The commission assigned different Christian sects that volunteered to oversee tribes and purge corruption and incompetence from the Indian Bureau, reservations, and annuities. Congress essentially eliminated tribal sovereignty with the 1871 Indian Appropriation Act: "No Indian nation or tribe within the territory of the United States shall be acknowledged or recognized as an independent nation, tribe, or power with whom the United States may contract by treaty, but no obligation of any treaty lawfully made and ratified with any Indian nation or tribe prior to March third eighteen hundred and seventy-one shall be hereby invalidated or impaired."

The massacre of an innocent Indian band by American troops appalled enough congressmen to enact those policies, although not enough to launch an investigation. Members of Piegan Blackfoot Mountain Chief's band killed two settlers in the upper Missouri River. Major Eugene Baker and his troops failed to catch that band. Instead, on January 23, 1870, Baker ordered his troops to attack Chief Heavy Runner's peaceful Piegan band. The troops killed as many as 220 mostly women and children and captured 240, while only one soldier died. Unlike the Sand Creek massacre, there was no army or congressional investigation and Baker escaped any indictment or even formal rebuke for ordering mass murder.[45]

***

The Modoc lived in northeastern California and fiercely defended their territory by attacking American intruders during the 1850s and 1860s.[46] However, in 1864, Chief Captain Jack reluctantly signed a treaty that surrendered most of their land and confined them to a reservation with the Klamath, who resented their presence. Captain Jack led his people back to their homeland in 1865. Complaints about the Modoc by the region's growing number of settlers led Indian Superintendent Thomas Odeneal to try to force them to return to the reservation. On November 29, 1872, fighting erupted between Modoc and troops sent to escort them. The Modoc fled to the Lava Beds, a maze of eroded stone and for five months defeated assaults against them, killing sixty-eight and wounding seventy-five soldiers and Indian scouts while suffering only five killed and three wounded. General Edward Canby massed troops around the stronghold and tried to negotiate the Modoc's surrender. During talks on April 11, 1873, Captain Jack and other chiefs killed Canby and a commissioner. Eventually the Modoc ran out of food and ammunition. Captain Jack surrendered with 155 Modoc on May 29. Captain Jack and three other chief were tried, found guilty, and hanged for murder, while the other Modoc were placed on the reservation. The campaign cost $500,000 while the land that the Modoc homeland was worth only $10,000.[47]

***

Comanche, Kiowa, and Cheyenne again went to war in early summer 1874.[48] The first attack came on June 27 against a group of buffalo hunters at Adobe Walls on the Canadian River. The hunters repelled the assault and managed to reach safety with the news. General Sheridan's plan was for five columns to converge against bands across the region. He had messengers inform the bands to return to their reservations by August 4 or else be destroyed. Most bands defied the warning. Summer heat, lack of water, and plagues of locusts made the campaign a living hell for all participants. The army scored several victories in the autumn as the columns of Nelson Miles, Randall Mackenzie, and George Buell each burned a village although most inhabitants fled. The relentless pursuit and lack of buffalo caused the bands one by one to surrender or return to their reservations by June 1875. This time the peace was permanent. The southern plains tribes never warred again.

***

The army dispatched annual expeditions into Sioux country between 1871 and 1873 to protect a surveying party plotting a route for the Northern Pacific Railroad. In August 1873, Custer's 7th Cavalry repelled two attacks by Sitting Bull's Hunkpapa, inflicting around forty casualties while suffering a dozen.[49] Although the 1868 Fort Laramie Treaty set the Black Hills squarely in Sioux territory, in July 1874, Custer led his troops to reconnoiter that region. The expedition returned in August with word that there was gold in those hills. That provoked a gold rush in 1875 as thousands of miners and merchants surged into the region, quickly set up towns like Deadwood, and began reaping fortunes from the streams.

Commissioners offered to buy the Black Hills but the Sioux refused to sell. Determined to take the Black Hills, the Grant administration contrived a war to do so.[50] The White House issued a warning through the agencies that all Sioux had to return to their reservation agency headquarters by January 31, 1876, or else be considered hostile. The deadline passed with virtually all bands still in their winter camps on the high plains. The army planned an offensive to crush the bands with three converging troop columns. The commanders failed to coordinate their offensives and the Indians defeated each. On March 1, General George Crook and his 900 troops marched north from Fort Fetterman for the Powder River valley. Although he found and attacked a Cheyenne village on the upper Powder River, nearly all the inhabitants fled to Crazy Horse's Oglala village. Short of supplies and buffeted by blizzards, Crook withdrew his men to Fort Fetterman. On March 30, Colonel John Gibbon's 450 troops marched from Fort Ellis along the Yellowstone River east toward Sioux country. On May 17, General Alfred Terry and Custer led 925 troops from Fort Abraham Lincoln west up the Yellowstone valley. By May 29, Crook had resupplied his troops and headed back toward the Powder River valley.

Of the three columns, Crook's first fought the enemy. On June 17, a thousand Indians led by Sitting Bull, Crazy Horse, and Gall attacked as the troops crossed Rosebud Creek. The battle lasted most of the day until Crook retreated with his men toward his supply base at Goose Creek. The Indians killed twenty-eight and wounded fifty-six troops while suffering thirty-six dead and sixty-three wounded. On June 21, Terry, Gibbon, and Custer met aboard a steamboat on the Yellowstone River to coordinate a two-pronged campaign. Scouts located the hostile bands concentrated on the Little Bighorn River. Custer would march up the Rosebud River valley and over the divide to the Little Bighorn above the village while Terry and Gibbon marched up the Bighorn River valley then Little Bighorn valley. Each would attack his end of the village on the same day.

Custer and his men reached the divide between the Rosebud and Little Bighorn Rivers on June 24. Fearing he had been discovered and the bands would depart, he planned to attack the next morning, June 25. He split his 600 troops into four columns with two, one led by himself, attacking the village from different directions while the third remained in reserve and the fourth protected the mule supply train. The village may have sheltered as many as 10,000 people including 2,500 warriors from half a dozen bands. Led by Crazy Horse and Gall, the Sioux and their Cheyenne and Arapaho allies swarmed from the village, wiped out Custer and his column, drove off the other column, which retreated to the third column and then to the mule train guard where they fought off repeated attacks. The warriors killed 262 and wounded 55 soldiers and scouts while suffering 31 warriors, six women, and four children killed and scores wounded.[51] The bands then fled in different directions. Two days later the column of Terry and Gibbon rescued the 7th Cavalry's remnants. Word of the "Custer massacre" stunned the nation, especially since Americans were celebrating the centennial of their independence.

Generals Crook and Terry massed reinforcements and supplies with the plan to converge against the hostiles. Colonel Wesley Merritt led troopers from Fort Sully on July 10, and they skirmished with a Cheyenne war party at War Bonnet Creek on July 17. During August's first week, the regiments of Colonels Elwell Otis and Nelson Miles landed at Rosebud Creek and joined Terry's command. There were skirmishes at Slim Buttes on September 9, Cedar Creek on October 21, and Ash Creek on December 18. The biggest victory came on November 25, when Colonel Ranald Mackenzie's troops destroyed Dull Knife's Cheyenne village, killing 40 and wounding 120 people while losing seven dead and 26 wounded.

During the winter, Miles' troops guarded the Yellowstone River fords while Crook's column traversed the Belle Fourche and Little Missouri valleys before withdrawing. Miles defeated an attack by Crazy Horse at Wolf Mountain on January 8, 1877, then withdrew to winter quarters. Sitting Bull and his band escaped to Canada while the rest of the bands surrendered during 1877, starting with Crazy Horse at the Red Cloud agency on May 6. Agency police killed Crazy Horse when he resisted arrest on September 5.

Cheyenne Chiefs Dull Knife and Little Wolf led around 300 of their people north from their Oklahoma reservation on September 9, 1878, hoping to join Sitting Bull. On October 23, Dull Knife and part of his band surrendered near Fort Robinson and were imprisoned there. They refused to return to the reservation and broke out on January 9, 1879. The pursuing soldiers killed or captured most of them but Dull Knife and a few reached Sitting Bull's band. On March 25, 1879, the army caught up to Little Wolf's band, forced it to surrender, and imprisoned it at Fort Keough. Sitting Bull led his people back to the United States and surrendered on July 19, 1881.

***

Treaties signed in 1855 and 1863 bitterly split the Nez Perce.[52] Around half the tribe accepted those treaties and a reservation on the Clearwater River. Four bands, with Joseph, White Bird, Looking Glass, and Toohoolzote the most prominent chiefs, remained in the Wallowa valley and resisted pressure to yield their land and move to the reservation. That pressure peaked in November 1876 when a five-man commission led by General Oliver Howard met Joseph but he refused to give up. In

May 1877, Howard reappeared with a 30-day deadline with which to comply or be forcibly moved. The soaring tensions led three warriors to murder four traders who had cheated them on June 13 and 14. That emboldened other Nez Perce to kill another eighteen nearby settlers on June 15. Although Joseph opposed those killings, he agreed with the other chiefs that they should flee eastward rather than submit.

What followed was an epic journey as the Nez Perce fought off converging columns of troops over 1,170 miles and five months. The Nez Perce began with around 250 warriors and 500 women, children, and old men. Along the way they suffered 133 dead and 94 wounded, while killing 180 and wounding 146 pursuers at the battles of White Bird Canyon on June 17, Clearwater River on July 11 and 12, Big Hole on August 9, Camas Meadows on August 19 and 20, Canyon Creek on September 13, and Bear Paw Mountain from September 30 to October 5. A column led by General Nelson Miles finally cut them off at Bear Paw Bear Mountain just 40 miles from the Canadian border and the fighting and siege lasted six days. White Bird escaped with 233 Nez Perce to Canada.[53]

During a truce, Joseph handed his rifle to Miles and explained: "I am tired of fighting. Our chiefs are killed . . . The old men are all dead . . . It is cold and we have no blankets. The little children are freezing to death . . . My heart is sick and sad. From where the sun now stands I will fight no more, forever."[54] General William Sherman lauded the Nez Perce's military and moral prowess: "The Indians throughout displayed a courage and skill that elicited universal praise; they abstained from scalping, let captive women go free, did not commit indiscriminate murder of peaceful families which is usual, and fought with almost scientific skill, using advance and rear guards, skirmish lines and field fortifications."[55] Nonetheless, although Miles promised Joseph that they could return to their Idaho reservation, Sherman ordered the 448 who surrendered with Joseph placed on part of the Quapaw reservation in Oklahoma.

The Nez Perce rebellion and flight inspired tribes elsewhere in the region. Around 700 Bannack, Paiute, and Umatilla revolted at the Fort Hall and Lemhi reservations in June 1878. General Crook explained why: "Hunger. Nothing but hunger."[56] Like most other reservation Indians, the Bannack and Paiute suffered cheating and food shortages from corrupt officials and sutlers. Howard swiftly mobilized over a thousand troops from various garrisons across the region to converge against and force the bands to surrender. In skirmishes, the Indians killed nine soldiers and thirty-one civilians while suffering seventy-eight dead. The army escorted the bands back to their respective reservations where officials failed to alleviate the harsh conditions that provoked the uprising.

The Ute tribe numbered around 4,000 members among seven bands.[57] In an 1868 treaty, they received sixteen million acres in western Colorado split between two agencies. Then, in 1873, the government forced them to sign a treaty that reduced their territory to twelve million acres. Coloradans had pressured the federal government to take the San Juan Cession after gold and silver was found on it. That done, Colorado's government then pressured Washington to seize all Ute land and move the tribe to Indian Territory.

Nathan Meeker, the White River Ute reservation agent, personified the corrupt, tyrannical, hateful Indian Bureau official. After being appointed in 1878, he withheld annuities and demanded that the Ute stop hunting, become farmers and ranchers, and convert to Christianity. That enraged the Ute and their chiefs Ute Jack and Colorow. Meeker sent a panicked appeal to the army for protection. The Utes learned that Major Thomas Thornburgh was leading 153 troops and 25 volunteers to the reservation. On September 29, warriors launched separate attacks. One killed Meeker and nine other civilians, and captured five women and children. The other ambushed Thornburgh's column, killing him and thirteen other troops, wounding twenty-three, and besieging the rest, while suffering twenty-three dead.

General Sherman had Colonels Wesley Merritt, Randall Mackenzie, and Edward Hatch converge on White River but sought negotiations by commissioners. Ute Chief Ouray had not approved the revolt and convinced the rebels to release the women and children. The commissioners demanded that the Utes yield twelve men to be charged with murder and rape. In an 1880 treaty, the White River Ute were moved to the four-million-acre Umcompahgre Ute reservation and the federal government took title to their land. None of those accused of crimes was ever apprehended.

***

Throughout the post-war years, the United States fought a chronic war against Apaches in the Southwest.[58] In 1865, Mescalero Apaches escaped from their bleak reservation at Bosque Redondo on the Pecos River and returned to their homeland in New Mexico's White Mountains. From that stronghold, they raided settlements, mines, ranches, and travelers in the surrounding region. Elsewhere the Chiricahua Apache in the upper Gila River region and the Western

Apache in the Mogollon region launched their own raids, as did other tribes like the Yavapai and Walapai.

The Apache and other tribes fought mercilessly, raping, murdering, and looting. At times civilians and soldiers retaliated just as mercilessly. The worst massacre was on April 30, 1871, when 148 Tucson civilians attacked a peaceful Apache village near Fort Grant, and murdered at least 86 people and kidnapped 29 children.[59] Captain William Brown's troops cornered around a hundred Yavapai in Skull Cave and slaughtered them with ricocheted shots on December 28, 1872.

As in other regions, the army strategy was to garrison forts that hemmed in hostile bands and became bases for campaigns against them. The Apache were such brilliant raiders that no more than several hundred and as few as several dozen raided and mostly evaded the 5,000 troops deployed across the Southwest. Nonetheless, the army claimed success. For instance, by one count in Arizona from 1866 to 1870, troops fought 137 skirmishes during which they killed 649 Indians while suffering 26 killed and 58 wounded.[60] It was a whack-a-mole war in which a hostile band would briefly agree to return to its reservation while others abandoned theirs to resume raiding. General Howard got Cochise and his Chiricahua to submit in 1872, as did General Crook with the Tonto Apache and Yavapai in 1873 and Indian Agent John Clum with the Chiracahua in 1876 and again in 1877. War chiefs Victorio and Natiotish died fighting, Juh rode his horse off a cliff to evade capture, and Chatto, Naiche, and Ulzana survived. Geronimo was the last holdout who fought from 1881 until his final surrender at Skeleton Canyon on September 4, 1886. Geronimo and his band were first incarcerated at Fort Marion, Florida, then transferred permanently to Fort Sill, Oklahoma.

With deep satisfaction and relief, General Sherman concluded in 1887 that "I regard the Indians as substantially eliminated from the problem of the army. There may be sporadic and temporary alarms, but such Indian wars as have hitherto disturbed the public peace . . . are not probable. The army has been a large factor in producing this result, but . . . occupation by industrious farmers and miners of land vacated by the aboringines have been largely instrumental to that end." Even more important was "the railroad which used to follow in the rear now goes forward . . . in the great battle for civilization with barbarism."[61] To that, General Phil Sheridan added the destruction of the buffalo herds and lauded the hunters for having "done more . . . to settle the vexed Indian question than the entire regular army has done in the last thirty years. They are destroying the Indians' commissary."[62]

***

With one tragic exception, peace if not harmony thereafter prevailed. Tribes increasingly defended their rights with lawyers rather than warriors. The Cherokee were the first tribe to do so. Chief Justice John Marshall and his colleagues unanimously voted twice to uphold their lawsuits but that failed to prevent Georgia's government from taking their land in that state and President Jackson from forcing them to cede nearly all the rest of their land for an Oklahoma reservation.

The Ponca were the second tribe to get a favorable legal ruling.[63] Their traditional home was the region around the Niobrara River's mouth on the Missouri River, guaranteed by an 1865 treaty. Then the federal government mistakenly transferred that land to the Sioux, the Ponca's enemy, in the 1868 Treaty of Fort Laramie. The Ponca protested but Washington transferred the tribe to an Oklahoma reservation in 1877. Homesick, Chief Standing Bear led some of his people north back toward their homeland in early 1878. They got as far as the Omaha reservation when General George Crook had troops prepare to escort them back to the Oklahoma reservation. Crook sympathized with their plight and arranged for a lawyer to file a habeas corpus petition on their behalf. The case appeared before Judge Elmer Dundy of the United States District Court in Omaha. On April 30, 1878, Dundy ruled in *Standing Bear versus Crook* that the chief and his followers be released because the government had no legal right to detain them.

Thomas Tibbles, the *Omaha Herald*'s editor, took up the Ponca's cause to promote Indian rights and organized a nationwide speaking tour for Standing Bear and Susette La Flesche, an articulate Omaha woman also known as Bright Eyes. Their greatest support came in Boston when Massachusetts Governor John Long and Mayor Frederick Prince formed the Boston Indian Citizens Committee to champion Indian rights. Interior Secretary Carl Schurz spearheaded those who denied Indian rights and fought to prevent Standing Bear versus Crook from reaching the Supreme Court, fearing it would uphold Dundy's ruling. Nonetheless, Congress appropriated $165,000 to compensate the Ponca.

***

A movement arose to alleviate the plight of Indians in the 1880s.[64] In 1879, Mary Bonney Amelia Quinton formed the Women's National Indian Association that petitioned Congress for redress of Indian grievances in 1880, and peaked in the late-1880s with 98 branches in 28 states and 56 missions to alleviate reservation conditions. Herbert Welsh and Henry Pancoast founded the Indian Rights Association with the same goals at Philadelphia in 1882. A group of humanitarians led by Quaker Albert Smiley founded "Friends of the Indian" at the Mohonk Mountain resort in the lower Hudson River valley in 1883. They sought to liberate Indians from cultures they believed enslaved them in poverty and ignorance. Thomas Bland and Alfred Meacham founded the publication *Council Fire and Arbitrator* to promote Indian rights in 1878. Bland formed the National Indian Defense Association in 1885.

Humanitarians seek to overcome tragedies of poverty and injustice. At times, their good intentions can have unintended bad consequences. The slogan of most reform groups was "kill the Indian, free the man." They pressured the Indian Bureau to issue a directive in 1883 that forbad Indians from practicing their traditional religion. That directive blatantly violated the Constitution's First Amendment whereby "Congress shall make no law respecting an establishment of religion, or prohibiting the free exercise thereof." In the 1885 Indian Appropriation Act, Congress asserted the federal government's power over all tribal government, laws, and policies. The Supreme Court upheld that power in its ruling for *United States versus Kagama* in 1886.

That "kill the Indian, save the man" ideology culminated in the 1887 Dawes Severalty or General Allotment Act, largely drafted by Henry Dawes who chaired the Senate Indian Affairs Committee. The Dawes Act privatized communal reservation lands and set up schools to Americanize Indian children. Reservations were split into quarter sections for family heads and eighth sections for single people over 18 years old. The Dawes Act resulted in the tribes losing two-thirds of their reservation lands from 155,632,312 acres in 1881 to 77,865,373 acres in 1900 and 47 million by 1934. It also devastated tribal cultures. Teachers forced boarding school children to abandon their traditional dress, customs, and languages, and severely punished them for any infractions. The prototype for those schools was the Carlisle Indian Industrial School in Carlisle, Pennsylvania, founded in 1879 by Captain Richard Pratt who fought in the Civil War and Indian wars. By 1900, there were twenty-five off-reservation schools with Carlisle's the largest with a thousand students and eighty-one boarding schools on reservations.[65] Lakota Luther Standing Bear recalled his boarding school experience: "I gave up many things dear to the heart of a little Indian boy . . . Our accustomed dress was taken and replaced with clothing that felt cumbersome and awkward . . . We longed to go barefoot . . . Of course, our hair was cut . . . Instead of translating our names into English . . . we were just John, Henry, or Maggie . . . we had been forbidden to speak our mother tongue . . . robbing the Indian, but America of a rich heritage. The language of a people is part of their heritage."[66]

Indian schools proliferated during the twentieth century before being shut down in the late 1960s. The total number of government schools from 1819 to 1969 was 417 in 37 states and territories with over 190,000 total students. Many children lost more than their culture. At least 973 children died, mostly from disease, and were buried at 74 sites. Countless others suffered beatings and rapes.[67]

***

Two prophets rose among the Paiutes along Walker River in Nevada and their teachings eventually spread to other tribes. In 1870, Wodziwob began preaching the rejection of American beliefs, clothing, weapons, and equipment; reembrace of traditional dress, customs, and beliefs; and the Ghost Dance to commune with their ancestors. During the 1880s, Wovoka championed those same ideas through five-day ceremonies of dancing and meditating for eventual salvation reunited with their ancestors to live in happiness forever.

Sioux warriors Short Bull and Kicking Bear adopted Wovoka's teachings except for his pacifism, and instead wore "ghost shirts" that they believed deflected bullets.[68] In 1890, the Ghost Dance spread through the Sioux nation, most fervently among the Pine Ridge Oglalas and Rosebud Brules, while Sitting Bull was among the chiefs who embraced it. In early November, Daniel Royer, Pine Ridge's agent, asked for the army to send troops to suppress what he believed was an incipient rebellion.

The dispatch of troops, including the 7th Cavalry, to Pine Ridge, provoked the revolt they were supposed to deter. The attempt by Indian police to arrest Sitting Bull resulted in a shootout in which Sitting Bull and seven of his people along with eight police died on December 15. The Miniconjou and Hunkpapa bands led by Big Foot, Hump, and Spotted Elk fled the reservation on December 23. The 7th Cavalry's advanced guard under Major Samuel Whitside caught up at Wounded Knee on December 28, and he convinced them to return to the reservation. Colonel James Forsyth arrived with the rest of the regiment on December 29. Forsyth ordered the Sioux to surrender their firearms. A warrior's rifle discharged when a soldier grasped it. That prompted warriors and soldiers to open fire on each other. When the firing stopped eighty-two Sioux men, forty-four women, and eighteen children were dead and scores were wounded along with twenty-five soldiers dead and thirty-nine wounded. The battle of Wounded Knee was the last in the Indian wars that began on America's frontier 283 years earlier at Jamestown, the first settlement in 1607.

Chapter 8

DEVELOPERS AND OUTLAWS

"Boys, I believe I have found a gold mine." (James Marshall)

"Rainfall follows the plough." (Charles Wilbur)

"I just kept looking him in the eye as I walked toward him. And when he started talking to me I was pretty sure I had him. I tried to talk in as pretty a voice as I could manage and told him to throw his gun in the road. He did and that's all there was to it." (Wyatt Earp)

America's victorious war with Mexico and conquest of the Southwest soon reaped enormous wealth. In January 1848, James Marshall was in charge of building a sawmill on John Sutter's vast ranch in California's Sierra Mountain foothills. On January 25, Marshall plucked something glittering in the water, examined it, and gleefully declared, "Boys, I believe I have found a gold mine."[1] Although Sutter tried to keep the find quiet, word spread rapidly that there was gold in California's foothills. That inspired the frenzied "Gold Rush" of 1849 when 100,000 people reached California either overland or by ship via Panama or Nicaragua. California's population skyrocketed from 14,000 in 1848 to 223,856 in 1852.[2]

Few, however, got rich from panning gold from streams or digging it from the earth. Mine owners who struck seams certainly did if they could hold their stakes against rivals who challenged them with lawsuits and sometimes firearms. The best way to make money was to supply miners with all the provisions and tools they needed. A handful of entrepreneurs reaped fortunes from the Gold Rush, mostly from their headquarters in San Francisco. Most others failed at mining but found other livelihoods.

Historian Patricia Limerick called California's Gold Rush "the most important event in the history of the American West" for interrelated reasons.[3] Miners rapidly decimated and expelled local tribes, often blatantly violating existing treaties. They established towns, laws, and courts dependent on other regions for food and other vital supplies, thus economically and politically knitting together often far-flung territories. Hydraulic mining soon displaced placer mining with devastating results as miners fired water cannons with the pressure of 125 pounds per inch to blast away the soil of mountains into rivers. California's assembly passed the 1850 Foreign Miner's Tax that imposed a $16 monthly fee on foreign miners that American miners did not have to pay. That pressured foreigners to sell their claims to Americans.

When the gold strike occurred, California had a military governor, Colonel Richard Mason, who declared that the federal government owned any gold or minerals in trust for the American people. Forty-Niners scornfully ignored that declaration and increasingly called for a state government to resolve conflicting land claims and establish private property rights. Atop that, they sought a constitutional government to combat soaring numbers of murders, armed robberies, and scams. For instance, murders rates in San Francisco from 1840 to 1856 were six times worse per person than the city during the late 1990s, while those in the mining town of Sonora were fifty times worse than the nation's rate in the late 1990s. Vigilante groups in San Francisco and ever more towns fought crime with "necktie parties" whereby they caught suspects and after a swift judgement publicly hanged them as a warning to others.[4]

General Bennet Riley replaced Mason as governor on April 12, 1849, and took steps toward civilian government.[5] On June 3, he approved a fifteen-man legislative assembly that a group of ambitious and concerned San Franciscans had established on March 3. That assembly voted to convene a constitutional convention of forty-eight delegates at Monterey in October. The delegates drafted a constitution that enshrined private property for women and men alike, outlawed slavery, and denied citizenship to blacks, Chinese, and Indians and forbad them from testifying against whites in court. The convention issued the constitution and declared California a state on October 12, 1849. Riley called for an election on November 12 for voters to decide whether to ratify the constitution and who would be their assemblymen, governor, lieutenant governor, and two congressional representatives. Voters overwhelmingly approved the constitution by 12,061 to 811, elected Peter Burnett governor, and filled the other posts. On December 15, the assembly convened in San Jose and elected John Fremont and William Gwin senators to Congress. The next step was to send California's senators, representatives, and constitution to Washington for Congress's approval.

Getting Congress to approve California statehood was difficult. Slavocrats were opposed because they feared free states would outnumber slave states. Senator Henry Clay of Kentucky offered an initial compromise bill that Senator Stephen Douglass modified so that it passed both houses. The 1850 Compromise admitted California as a free state; let settlers in Utah and New Mexico decide whether to allow slavery; limited Texas to its present border; had Texas surrender its claim to land west to the Rio Grande in New Mexico in return for which the United States assumed its $10 million debt; strengthened the Fugitive Slave Law to require local authorities to cooperate with those pursuing escaped slaves; and for Washington City, abolished the slave trade while slavery remained legal.

***

Congress tried to accelerate eventual settlement of other territories by authorizing the Corps of Topographical Engineers to launch expeditions to survey possible railroad routes across the West.[6] Captain William Warner led a company east over the Sierras to the Humboldt River and back by a different route in 1849. Captain Howard Stansbury explored the Platte River route to the Great Basin from 1849 into 1850. In 1853, Isaac Stevens zigzagged west between the 47th and 49th Parallels after coming up the Missouri River by steamboat and met Captain George McClellan coming west from Puget Sound. In 1853, Captain John Gunnison followed the 38th Parallel into the Sevier River valley where a Paiute war party killed him and seven of his eleven men. Lieutenant Amiel Whipple followed the 35th Parallel from Fort Smith to Los Angeles in 1853 and 1854. Lieutenant John Parke explored the 32nd Parallel westward in 1854. Those surveys identified far more impossible than possible routes. The expedition reports were eventually published in eleven volumes. War Secretary Jefferson Davis, a Mississippi plantation owner, advocated the southern route.

For now, politics and money stymied building any route. Chicago, St. Louis, Memphis, and New Orleans were potential terminuses, each with networks of lines eastward sharing the benefits. Clusters of senators and congressmen from those four east-west swaths demanded a transcontinental railroad for themselves and denied one to their rivals. Atop that, a transcontinental railroad on any route would be enormously expensive. Only massive federal subsidies in land grants and low-interest loans could entice railroad executives into building a line.

***

Among the many ways that Washington developed the West was contracting supply and mail delivery to private companies. The War Department awarded the partnership of William Russell, Alexander Majors, and William Waddell the contract to supply all the western forts in 1854. By 1858, Russell, Majors, and Waddell had 4,000 men operating 3,500 wagons and 40,000 mules, horses, and oxen. Each wagon train had twenty-five wagons with each carrying three tons of goods, pulled by twelve oxen, and guided by a bullwhacker with a 12ft whip.[7]

The United States Post Office contracted a series of mail carriers further west on diverse routes. The first was from St. Louis to Salt Lake City in 1851. The second spanned the continent to California with John Butterfield's Overland Mail Company in 1857. That second route was an "oxbow" that ran 2,796 miles with 141 stations along with way from Tipton, Missouri, the railroad's terminus, southwest to El Paso, west to Yuma, Arizona, across the Mohave Desert to Los Angeles and north to San Francisco. Passengers paid $200 for a ticket and extra for food on that grueling 22-day journey. The Overland Mail Company made money on that route only because it annually received a $600,000 federal subsidy.

Russell, Majors, and Waddell received a federal contract for his Central Overland California and Pikes Peak Express Company, or Pony Express, to run 1,966 miles from St. Joseph, Missouri to Sacramento, California. The Pony Express began on April 3, 1860, with 120 riders galloping from 35 to 70 miles between 115 relay stations; a bag of mail could reach the end in ten days. Only the rich could afford to pay the $10 an ounce charge. Nonetheless, the Pony Express steadily lost money. The Pacific Telegraph Company and California State Telegraph linked Kansas City and Sacramento to establish the Overland Telegraph Company on October 24, 1861. Two days later the Pony Express finished its last run. That dragged Russell, Majors, and Waddell down into bankruptcy on March 21, 1862.

Meanwhile, Wells, Fargo, and Company amassed ever more profits largely from the private sector. In March 1852, Henry Wells and William Fargo founded their company in San Francisco with the goal of establishing a network of banks and stagecoach lines across California and eventually back east. By 1860, Wells Fargo had 147 offices that made most of their money trading and transporting gold. Ben Holladay filled that void with his own company before the American Express Company bought him and Butterfield out, and consolidated the West's mail routes with its subsidiary Wells Fargo Company in 1866.

***

An old political party with a new name emerged in time to run candidates for the 1854 midterm election and would field a presidential candidate for the 1856 election. The Republican Party was the latest incarnation of the Federalist Party that espoused Hamiltonism. Alexander Hamilton had advocated a muscular, problem-solving federal government that worked with the private sector to develop the economy with a central bank that stabilized and expanded the financial system; infrastructure like roads, bridges, and canals; tariffs that protected "infant industries" from foreign rivals; diplomacy that opened foreign markets to American products; incentives to encourage entrepreneurs, innovators, and inventors; public schools to nurture young minds; and an army and navy strong enough to deter foreign threats and protect America's swelling economic and strategic interests around the world. For Hamilton, the Constitution implicitly empowered the federal government to do anything that it did not explicitly forbid. The framers wanted a political system flexible and creative enough for future generations to wield to seize opportunities, and crush threats both foreign and domestic.

The Federalist Party was nationally viable only during the 1790s during the administrations of George Washington and John Adams. As Treasury Secretary from September 1789 to July 1795, Hamilton got Congress to enact most of his agenda, including the First Bank of the United States. The result was to transform a vicious cycle of high inflation, unemployment, poverty, and debt along with low growth, exports, entrepreneurship, and innovation into a virtuous cycle of high growth, innovation, exports, and an expanding middle class. But the Federalist Party suffered from Hamilton's failure to develop a grass-roots organization that mobilized voters and the 1798 Alien and Sedition Acts that violated civil liberties.

Thomas Jefferson and his Democratic-Republican Party won the 1800 election and dominated politics until 1832. Jeffersonians espoused a weak national government, state's rights, and slavery's expansion. By the 1820s, the party shed "Republican" to be the Democratic Party. The Democrats blundered badly by abolishing the United States Bank in 1811 and getting into the disastrous war with Britain in 1812. But they advanced American power and wealth with the Louisiana Purchase in 1803, Lewis and Clark expedition in 1804, a Second Bank of the United States in 1817, acquisition of East and West Florida in 1819, and the Monroe Doctrine asserting a sphere of influence over the Western Hemisphere in 1823.

For two generations, Hamiltonians lacked a party to promote their views. Then, in 1832, a group of Hamiltonians led by Senators Henry

Clay of Missouri and Daniel Webster of Massachusetts formed the Whig Party. During the next two decades, the Whigs competed with Democrats to control Congress and won presidencies under William Henry Harrison, Zachery Taylor, and Millard Filmore. The Whigs failed to prevent Democratic President Andrew Jackson from eliminating the Second Bank of the United States in 1836. The Whig Party dissolved in 1852 as factions broke away to form parties around specific issues like the Free Soil, American, and Liberty Parties that respectively espoused homesteading, immigration restrictions, and slavery's abolition.

The Kansas-Nebraska Act inspired the latest Hamiltonian avatar. On July 6, a convention of Hamiltonians at Jackson, Michigan announced the Republican Party's birth and called on like-minded others across the nation to establish their own branches. The Hamiltonian agenda was updated to include federal support for a trans-continental railroad, homestead act to encourage settlement of western territories, and colleges that developed teachers, scientific farming, and innovation.

The Republican Party nominated John Fremont as their presidential candidate for the 1856 election. In a three-man race, Fremont came in second with 33.1 percent of the vote and 117 electors to winner Democrat James Buchannan's 45.3 percent and 174 electors and Whig Millard Fillmore's 21.5 percent and 8 electors. The Republican and Whig candidates committed fratricide since their respective party platforms were essentially the same Hamiltonian agenda.

In the 1860 election, it was the Democratic Party that committed fratricide with its southern wing slavocrat candidate John Breckinridge getting 18.1 percent and 72 electors and its northern wing Stephen Douglas 29.5 percent and 12 electors, while Constitutional Union candidate John Bell got 12.6 percent and 39 electors, and Republican candidate Abraham Lincoln won with 39.8 percent and 180 electors. The secession of the southern states stripped Congress of most Democrats and left the Republican Party with overwhelming majorities in the Senate and House of Representatives.

President Lincoln worked closely with Senate and House Republican leaders not just to expand the army and navy to crush the rebellion but also to enact a Hamiltonian agenda that developed the economy. Through a series of laws including the National Banking Acts of 1863 and 1865, and the Internal Revenue Act of 1864, the Republicans reestablished a stable financial system of chartered national banks with reserve requirements, a national paper currency called the Greenback, and revenues through an income tax and bonds.

Lincoln and the Republican-dominated Congress boosted the West's economic development by selling cheaply and outright giving away federal lands to states, homesteaders, and railroads. Eventually, Washington distributed 521,000,000 acres including 181,000,000 to the railroads, 140,000,000 to the states, 100,000,000 in Land Office sales, and 100,000,000 in Indian Lands taken and sold.[8]

Two laws encouraged settlers to head west. The 1862 Homestead Act granted 160 acres of land to any man or woman 21 years or older who filed a claim, paid a $10 fee, and worked the land for five years. Or they could buy the land for $1.25 an acre after living on it for six months. The 1862 Morrill Land-Grant Act gave each state 30,000 acres of western land for each of its senators and representatives to sell to finance public education. That 140,000 acres distributed among and sold by the states helped establish state colleges. Later laws elaborated those two initial efforts. The 1873 Timber Culture Act doubled the amount of land to 320 acres if the homesteader planted and nurtured 40 acres of forest for ten years. The 1877 Desert Land Act granted 640 acres of land in arid regions if the farmer irrigated it within three years. The 1878 Timber and Stone Act let settlers buy non-farm land for $2.50 an acre. Those laws that let people more easily acquire public lands more than doubled the amount of farm acreage. The 1894 Carey Act granted each western state a million acres of federal lands to sell to finance dam and irrigation projects. By 1910, that Act encouraged the irrigation of 288,553 acres across the West.[9]

The results of those laws were spectacular. Only 119,000 of 1,500,000 farmers lived west of the Mississippi in 1850.[10] From 1607 to 1870, the amount of farm acreage expanded to 189,000,000 acres then soared to 225,000,000 acres by 1900. From 1862 to 1890, around 2,000,000 people settled on 372,659 farms established by the Homestead Act and its supplements.[11]

Technologies made farming less onerous. In 1867, Cyrus McCormick invented the self-rake reaper that scythed wheat and deposited it to the side for easy bundling. Great Plains sod was denser than sod back east. Traditional plows like John Deere's 1837 steel model could not turn western sods because soil packed on the blade. In 1868, James Oliver invented an iron plough with a moldboard treated so that it cut through sod without clogging. That let farmers plow deeper which drew more moisture toward the surface. Drills and windmills let farmers tap aquifers deep in the earth. Automatic binders and power threshers made those tasks much easier. Turkey Red or Durum wheat was developed on the Russian steppes and was perfect for similar climate and soil conditions on America's Great Plains. Silos, invented in 1875, gave farmers large places to store their harvests. Joseph Dekalb, an Illinois farmer, invented and patented barbed wire in 1874 and partnered with the Washburn and Moen Manufacturing Company to mass produce it in 1876. The price dropped from $20 for a hundred pounds in 1876 to $4 in 1890. Farmers began fencing their land to protect their crops, keep their own livestock and bar alien livestock. Gradually but steadily the "open range" got fenced in. Production soared as the number of work hours to produce a hundred bushels of wheat fell from 233 to 108 and of corn from 276 to 135 between 1840 and 1900. Traditionally a farmer could plant and harvest no more than seven and a half acres of wheat by hand but by 1890, he could manage 135 acres.[12]

8.1 Comparison of Man and Machine Crop Productivity Per Acre 1890[13]

	Time Worked		Labor Cost	
Crop	Hand	Machine	Hand	Machine
Wheat	61 hours	3 hours	$3.55	$0.66
Corn	39 hours	15 hours	$3.62	$1.51
Oats	66 hours	7 hours	$3.73	$1.07
Loose Hay	21 hours	4 hours	$1.75	$0.42
Baled Hay	35 hours	12 hours	$3.06	$1.29

Nonetheless, farm conditions were tough. People who settled the Great Plains had to live without access to wood for construction or stoves. They constructed sod houses of cut bricks usually 1ft by 2ft. The experience was unpleasant, with dust and insects nearly incessant. Only about half of the homesteaders ended up owning their land or keeping it once they got the title. Most people had to borrow money to pay for all the equipment they needed to start a farm and lost their land if they failed to pay what they owed. Storms could destroy and plagues of grasshoppers could devour a crop in an hour or so. Rainfall dwindled the further west one went across the plains. Countless settlers believed Charles Wilbur, a Nebraska booster, who insisted that "rainfall follows the plough" or the very act of tilling and sowing a field will attract rain that flourishes crops. That, of course, was false, as victims of that belief eventually discovered. The 1870s were relatively wet years as were the 1880s until 1886 when a drought hit much of the Great Plains and persisted until 1896.

Railroads were the economy's growth engine for most of the nineteenth century much as shipbuilding was for the eighteenth century and automobiles were for most of the twentieth century. America's first railroad was the three-mile Quincy Granite Railroad in Massachusetts in 1826. That inspired entrepreneurs elsewhere to form railroad companies that states incorporated. The growth was spectacular, to 762 miles by 1834 and 33,860 miles by 1864. Although a dense network of railroads bound the nation east of the Mississippi, few operated westward. In 1859, the Hannibal and St. Joseph Railroad linked those two towns alongside respectively the Mississippi and Missouri Rivers. The Missouri Pacific Railroad linked St. Louis and Kansas City in 1865. The Chicago and North Western Railroad reached the Mississippi River in 1855 and Council Bluffs, Iowa in 1867. The Chicago, Rock Island, and Pacific Railroad reached Council Bluffs in 1869.

Abraham Lincoln initiated a key act in the West's development when he signed the Pacific Railroad Act on July 1, 1862.[14] The act subsidized a transcontinental railroad by allocating a 400-foot right-of-way, ten alternative sections for each mile of track, and loans of $16,000 for each flatland mile, $32,000 for each foothill mile, and $48,000 for each mountain mile in 30-year bonds with 6 percent interest. When that failed to attract enough investors, in 1864 Congress amended the law to double the land grant and raise the number of shares of $100 par to $1 million worth.

The secession of the southern states and their war against the United States made the Transcontinental Railroad Act possible. By rebelling, the southern states abandoned possible routes from Memphis and New Orleans, which they could not afford to subsidize. Meanwhile, since 1857 engineer Theodore Judah had lobbied Congress for a route from Sacramento to Omaha. In 1859, California's legislature resolved to support a transcontinental railroad. By 1862, majorities in Congress backed the proposal by 35 to 5 in the Senate and 104 to 21 in the House of Representatives.

The Union Pacific and the Central Pacific built toward each other from their respective terminals of Omaha and Sacramento. "Big four" investors Leland Stanford, Mark Hopkins, Collis Huntington, and Charles Crocker, founded the Central Pacific on June 28, 1861, with Stanford president, Huntington vice president, Hopkins treasurer, Crocker a director, and Theodore Judah chief engineer. Stanford was elected California's governor in September 1861. The Union Pacific was founded on September 2, 1862, eventually with John Dix as president, Thomas Durant as vice president, and Colonel Grenville Dodge as chief engineer.

Congress granted the Union Pacific and Central Pacific respectively 19,100,000 and 7,300,000 acres; 125,000,000 acres of land to all western railroads just from 1862 to 1872; and 223,000,000 total acres granted by federal and state governments to railroads, of which the corporations later forfeited 35,000,000 acres for failing to develop them.[15] The Union Pacific raised an additional $11 million and $30 million through respective sales of its stocks and bonds. The Central Pacific bribed enough legislators to win a $1,659,000 loan from California.

The Central Pacific laid its first track on October 26, 1863, but made slow progress through the Sierra Mountains with 20 miles in 1864, 20 in 1865, 30 in 1866, and 46 in 1867, before reaching the Great Basin and laying the rest of the line in 1868 and 1869. The Union Pacific laid its first track on July 10, 1864, and steadily built westward year after year. The Central Pacific and Union Pacific linked at Promontory Point, Utah on May 10, 1869.

The total number of miles appropriately was 1,776 with the Central Pacific and Union Pacific respectively contributing 690 and 1,686. The soaring Sierra Nevada Mountains were the worst obstacle. The slopes were so steep that they could not be graded, only tunneled by blasting with black powder. The highest respective points for the Central Pacific and Union Pacific were 7,042ft in the Sierras and 8,242ft in Wyoming's Black Hills.

Immigrants supplied most labor for each railroad, Irish for the Union Pacific and Chinese for the Central Pacific. Mormons graded much of the Union Pacific section through Utah Territory. Both the Chinese and Irish organized strikes for better pay and fewer hours. The exact number of men who died building the railroad will never be known but accidents, disease, brawls, and Indians killed hundreds. Accompanying the Union Pacific was "Hell on Wheels," a movable makeshift village of prostitutes, barkeepers, and gamblers.

Three railroads initially competed for a route across the southern West from the Mississippi to the Pacific, the Atlantic and the Pacific, the Texas and the Pacific, and the Buffalo, Bayou, and Colorado. Each suffered bankruptcy and investors consolidated the remnants into the Southern Pacific Railroad. The Southern Pacific finished its transcontinental railroad to Los Angeles in 1881 but high charges for passengers and freight failed to stir the economy. The 1887 arrival of a second transcontinental line by the Atchison, Topeka, and Santa Fe Railroad produced a rivalry that drove down prices for passengers and freight by 75 percent and stimulated an economic boom for Los Angeles and the region. The Northern Pacific Road received 40,000,000 acres and in 1893 completed the link between Saint Paul and Seattle. By 1890, four transcontinental lines traversed the West and total rail mileage west of the Mississippi River reached 72,473. In 1893, the three largest railroads were the Union Pacific with 8,148 miles of track and $427,000,000 capitalization, the Northern Pacific with 5,216 miles and $370,000,000, and the Great Northern with 3,682 miles and $147,000,000.[16]

Financial scandals rode the rails. The Central Pacific's Big Four owners became notorious for their venality and corruption. The Union Pacific's directors were even worse. In 1864, they formed Credit Mobilier ostensibly to raise money for the Union Pacific. Instead, they used Credit Mobilier as a pyramid scheme with initial lavish payoffs for themselves that sent stocks soaring that attracted ever more investors until eventually the greed turned to terror that the stocks were grossly overvalued and then the frenzied selling began.

Jay Cooke wrangled the opportunity to sell $100 million worth of bonds to finance the Northern Pacific in 1869. Cooke's pyramid scheme eventually collapsed in September 1873 and that triggered a "Panic" that devastated the stock market and plunged the economy into a prolonged depression. The Northern Pacific along with countless other companies suffered bankruptcy. Jay Gould got rich peddling similar swindles for the Missouri Pacific in the 1880s, although not with as disastrous results.

Railroad companies attempted to coordinate their operations, standards, and prices with the Omaha Pool in 1870, the Southwestern Rate Association in 1876, and the Western Trunk Lines Association, the Transcontinental Traffic Association, and Pacific Coast Association all in 1883. The railroads wielded their oligopoly power to keep freight and passenger prices high. The stranglehold that the Central Pacific had over California's economy provoked critics to call it the "Octopus" and Frank Norris to write a damning novel about its machinations with that title that appeared in 1902.

Railroads colluded not just on prices but also on wages. They pushed down daily pay for brakemen from $2.50 to $1.75 for 12-hour shifts from 1866 to 1876 then imposed a 10 percent pay cut in 1877. That provoked a nation-wide railroad strike. Around a hundred people died in riots at various factories and stations in St. Louis, Kansas City, Omaha, and Ogden, Utah over two weeks. President Rutherford Hays sent in troops to break the strike. Congress passed the 1890 Sherman Anti-Trust Act to provide Washington the legal means to break up monopolies and oligopolies. Almost every state and territory enacted laws to regulate railroad rates and services. The trouble was that railroads bribed enough politicians and bureaucrats to water down or suspend any strict regulations.

8.2 Distribution of Labor Force in the United States by Percentages[17]

Regions	Agriculture	Mining	Forestry	Manufacturing	Services
1870					
United States	51.48	1.49	0.26	21.14	25.41
Plains	61.63	0.50	0.26	14.91	22.67
Southwest	73.67	0.31	0.16	7.04	18.80
Mountains	33.59	29.54	0.84	12.94	26.07
Far West	25.73	18.04	1.63	18.20	36.00
1890					
United States	40.62	1.97	0.54	24.30	32.31
Plains	51.47	1.29	0.33	16.42	30.35
Southwest	63.94	1.14	0.30	9.11	25.45
Mountains	26.53	12.71	1.18	19.99	38.57
Far West	28.85	4.44	2.30	22.55	41.32
1910					
United States	32.46	2.53	0.45	27.92	36.46
Plains	40.85	1.82	0.29	19.99	37.01
Southwest	57.67	1.77	0.36	12.37	27.78
Mountains	29.93	8.47	0.67	20.48	40.43
Far West	20.10	2.84	2.04	26.95	47.6

***

Rail travel was unpleasant for the first couple of decades, with hard wooden seats crammed with passengers. Then, in 1867, George Pullman unveiled at his Chicago factory the Pullman Passenger Car with soft seats, rugs, plenty of leg-room, polished wood, and brass decorations; the Pullman Sleeper Car with luxurious private rooms, a toilet at the end, and an attendant; and the Pullman Dining Car with table cloths, silverware, good food and wines, a decorated ceiling, and even a piano. Of course, those "first class" cars were reserved for those wealthy enough to afford a seat or berth.

California's 1849 gold rush was the first of a dozen or so west of the Mississippi. The next big strike came in May 1859 when a prospector found gold in Clear Creek near Pike's Peak on the Rocky Mountain's Front Range in Colorado. That inspired "Fifty-Niners" to head for that region. Within a year, the census found 34,277 people including 1,586 women living in Colorado, mostly in Denver and mining towns. There were strikes in Virginia City, Nevada in 1859, the Clearwater and Salmon Rivers in Idaho in 1861, Bannack and Virginia City in Montana in 1862, the Dakota Black Hills in 1875, Leadville, Colorado in 1877, Tombstone, Arizona in 1877, and Coeur d'Alene, Idaho in 1883.

Each rush followed the same pattern.[18] After a strike, the first prospectors used pans and cradles to separate gold from other rocks and soil from streams. Mining companies soon squeezed out prospectors by buying or stealing their claims. They used hydraulic hoses to wash away alluvial deposits into streams but that could not penetrate solid rock where most gold was embedded. For that "hardrock" or "quartz" mining replaced "placer mining." Boring through rock took powerful drills and dynamite along with picks, shovels, and pushcarts on rails to remove the debris then mills to smash the ore and lots of mercury to split gold from other minerals. Railroads provided a cost-effective means of getting ore to refineries and from there to markets.

Indian Agent Edward Stevenson explained mining's devastating effects: "The Indians . . . are wretchedly poor" because "nearly all the game has been driven from the mining region . . . by the thousands of our people who now occupy the once quiet home of these children of the forest. The rivers or tributaries . . . formerly were clear as crystal and abounded with the finest salmon and other fish . . . But the miners have turned the streams . . . so thick with mud . . . with the soil from a thousand hills."[19]

Meanwhile, hastily-built towns rose as merchants, builders, laborers, ranchers, farmers, gamblers, prostitutes, and thieves followed miners. Leadville, Colorado was a typical silver-mine boomtown that in 1879 numbered 188 gambling dens, 120 saloons, 19 beer halls, and four churches.[20] Vast amounts of money changed hands leaving a few spectacularly rich, most with enough to get by, and some impoverished. Bust followed boom when miners exhausted the available minerals. People rushed out, often to the next mineral strike leaving a ghost town behind.

A vicious cultural, political, economic, and ecological cycle determined booms and busts. John Opie explained that dynamic: "The history of boomtowns is invariably an environmental history . . . Natural resources . . . create a momentum for rapid localized development. This almost always means the invasion of a human population far beyond local capacity to support. The results are not only spoilation of the land, but also community pollution, waste, crowding, violence, and other human hardships. These developments are often justified as an extension of historic American individualism, freedom of opportunity, the entrepreneurial spirit, and acquisition of wealth."[21]

Washington stimulated the mining industry with several policies. The 1866 Mining Act modified by the 1872 Mining Act let miners claim land for $2.50 to $5.00 an acre depending on the mineral up to 160 acres in perpetuity by annually investing $100 on the grant. The 1873 Coal Lands Act dispensed lands for $10 to $20 an acre depending on its location. In 1879, Congress established the United States Geological Survey that helped miners find minerals. With Salt Lake City as his base, Ferdinand Hayden led annual expeditions to map swaths of surrounding regions from 1868 to 1872. An army exploring expedition led by Colonel George Custer discovered gold in the Black Hills in 1874. The influx of thousands of people founded Deadwood in 1875 and provoked an Indian war in 1876.

The United States paid Russia $7.2 million for Alaska in 1867. Although critics derided that deal as "Seward's Folly" for Secretary of State William Seward who cut it, the Senate ratified the treaty. Alaska eventually would yield not just enormous wealth in gold, lumber, furs, fish, and oil but a priceless strategic position in the northeast Pacific Ocean that helped the United States defeat the Japanese during World War II and the Soviet Union during the Cold War.

***

Perhaps 30 million bison grazed the Great Plains in 1800. Within eight decades, hunters and diseases wiped out nearly all of them.[22] The demand for buffalo robes by fur companies encouraged tribes to slaughter more bison than they normally would year after year. Diseases were secondary killers, anthrax, tuberculosis, and brucellosis spread by domestic cattle atop the plains in the early nineteenth century.

After the Civil War, ever more American hunters joined the slaughter; a skilled hunter could kill as many as a hundred buffalo a day and 3,000 in a year. On the southern plains alone, American and Indian hunters killed 4,374,000 and 1,215,000 bison, respectively, from 1874 to 1876.[23] Dodge City became the bison robe center for the southern plains after the Atchison, Topeka, and Santa Fe Railroad arrived in September 1872. Within three months, the railroad shipped east 43,029 robes and 1,436,290 pounds of meat.[24]

Frank Mayer was a typical bison hunter. He invested $2,000 to outfit himself with a wagon, horses, rifles, ammunition, skinning knives, and other needs. He marveled at the chance to make a lot of money: "Just think! There were 20,000,000 buffalo, each worth at least $3. At the very outside cartridges cost 25 cents each, so every time I fired one I got my investment back twelve times over. I could kill a hundred a day."[25] The result was enormous waste as skinners could not keep pace with killers. The flesh, skins, bones, organs, horns, and hoofs that Indians utilized, instead mostly rotted. By 1889, hunters had slaughtered virtually every bison except "200 in Yellowstone National Park, 25 in the panhandle of Texas, 20 in Colorado, 26 in southern Wyoming, ten in Montana, and four in the Dakota Territory" along with "550 in the wilds of Canada and 256 that were in captivity, which brought the total population of buffalo in North America . . . to a mere 1,091."[26]

Army leaders recognized that destroying the herds provided a strategic benefit. As Colonel Richard Dodge advocated in 1867, "kill every buffalo you can, every buffalo dead is an Indian gone." In 1875, General Philip Sheridan reckoned that buffalo hunters "have done in the last two years, and will do more in the next year, to settle the vexed Indian question than the entire army has done in the last thirty years. They are destroying the Indians' commissary."[27] The decimation of the buffalo devastated the plains tribes. Plenty Crows, a Crow warrior, mournfully explained that "when the buffalo went away the hearts of my people fell to the ground, and they could not life them up again. After this, nothing happened. There was little singing everywhere."[28]

***

The decimation of bison facilitated the cattle industry's growth. Around 5 million cattle grazed in Texas when the Civil War ended. Most of those cattle roamed free and were Longhorns, a cross between Spanish criollo and English longhorn breeds. Longhorn meat was tough, stringy, and cheap. Nonetheless, a steer that sold for $10 in Texas could fetch $35 at Sedalia, Missouri, the nearest railhead. An enterprising man or partners could reap a fortune employing cowboys to gather, brand, and drive a cattle herd north to that railhead.

The trouble was that Texas cattle carried a tick-borne fever that they had developed an immunity against. That disease afflicted northern cattle that had no immunity, causing them to waste away and die. Northern cattlemen soon recognized that Texas cattle affected their herds and got their state assemblies to ban them. Missouri was the first to bar Texas cattle from their farmlands in 1851 followed by Kansas in 1867.

The restrictions forced Texas cattlemen to drive their herds north to central Kansas on the plains west of a quarantine line where there were no farms to towns along the Kansas Pacific Railroad that established a stockyard and depot at Abilene in 1867 and Ellsworth in 1868 and reached Denver in 1869. The rival Atchison, Topeka, and Santa Fe Railroad extended to Wichita and Dodge City in 1872.[29]

Jesse Chisholm inaugurated cattle drives from Texas to Indian Territory in today's Oklahoma during the 1850s. After the Civil War, other Texas ranchers followed his "Chisholm Trail" eventually to Kansas towns. Partners Charles Goodnight and Oliver Loving had a huge ranch near Palo Duro Canyon and from 1866 drove herds to New Mexico and Colorado along what was called the Goodnight and Loving Trail. Word of their success inspired emulators. Cattle drives peaked in 1871 when 630,000 reached Kansas railheads. The cattle drive era was short-lived. Ranchers in the northern plains sent their cattle to eastern markets from the nearest railheads in their territories. In 1873, the Missouri, Kansas, and Texas Railroad reached Texas, giving Texan ranchers closer railheads that led to Kansas City. Nonetheless, cowboys drove as many as ten million cattle and a million horses north from Texas to various towns in various states from the mid-1860s to the mid-1890s.[30]

Gustavus Swift revolutionized the meat industry when he invented the refrigerated railroad car in 1882. Meatpacking plants on railroad lines could ship beef throughout the rail network. Beef prices fell 40 percent from 1883 to 1889. Chicago became the nation's meatpacking center with Swift, Armour, Hammond, and Morris the largest firms and its Union Stockyard the nation's largest by daily processing 21,000 cattle. Omaha, Fort Worth, Denver, and Kansas City became regional meatpacking centers.

That encouraged entrepreneurs to invest their money in cattle ranches. Richard King's ranch in south Texas was and remains America's largest with 825,000 acres. John Chisum owned a ranch in the Pecos River valley and drove cattle to Santa Fe and Fort Sumner. John Iliff founded Colorado's cattle industry. He opened a general store in Denver shortly after the Gold Rush began in 1859. He started buying worn out cattle from emigrants and grazed them on a ranch on the high plains. Within half a dozen years, he had 35,000 head. He got rich after winning a contract to supply the Union Pacific with cattle that he drove north to Cheyenne. Theodore Roosevelt bought a ranch on the Little Missouri River in 1883 and poured around $80,000 into it until the winter of 1886 and 1887 wiped out most of his herd. Attracted by visions of high profits and Wild West adventures, British entrepreneurs invested $45 million in American cattle ranches from 1882 to 1886. The Scottish Swan Land and Cattle Company acquired around 600,000 acres of rangeland in western Nebraska and eastern Wyoming. The Scottish Espuela Company owned the 500,000-acre

Spur Ranch in central Texas. By one count from "1800 to 1900, the total number of incorporated cattle companies in Montana reached 181; in Wyoming, 188; in Colorado, 324. And the aggregate capitalization for these states came to more than $27 million for Montana, more than $94 million for Wyoming, and more than $102 million for Colorado."[31]

Cattlemen formed Stock Grower Associations as oligopolies that kept cattle prices high and wages low, while claiming all "maverick" unbranded cattle as their own, intimidating independent ranchers, blacklisting cowboys who complained about bad pay, and catching and hanging rustlers. Stock Grower Associations got the Colorado and Kansas state assemblies to pass laws banning Texas cattle in 1885. The Supreme Court struck down those laws as an unconstitutional restraint on trade. They also lobbied Congress for a law that let ranchers lease and fence public lands for their herds. Many illegally appropriated public lands. President Grover Cleveland issued an executive order banning barbed wire on federal lands in 1885. Congress passed a law forbidding foreign investors from buying territory for cattle ranches in 1887.

The Johnson Country War from 1889 to 1892 pitted Wyoming's Stock Growers Association against independent, small-scale ranchers. The Association hired gunmen to terrorize the independents into selling out and leaving. They first murdered alleged rustlers James Avrell and Ella Watson. That appeared to curb rustling for a while but gradually the big stockowners suffered more losses. In April 1892, they hired and transported a force of twenty-four Texas gunmen to Johnson County, and gave them a list of enemies to execute. The gunmen killed Nate Champion at his ranch but were besieged by around 200 local small-scale ranchers and businessmen. The gunmen surrendered and returned to Texas.

Being a cowboy was not a glamorous profession. A trail-boss earned $125 and cowboys $30 to $40 a month herding, branding, and birthing cattle in often extreme temperatures from zero to a hundred degrees. On the ranch cowboys lived in a bunkhouse and on the trail they slept in a tent or under the stars depending on the weather. When riding herd, the most dangerous place was "point" or the front where the toughest bulls usually massed, followed by the flanks and rear. The most experienced cowboys rode point and the least experienced the rear where laggards were more easily managed. The worst part of riding the rear was having to wear a bandana to block all the dust stirred by the plodding herd. The most perilous time was a stampede, usually provoked by lightning and thunder. Cowboys had to gallop to the front of the herd beside the leaders and try to curl them into a wide circle until the cattle slowed and finally stopped. Of the 35,000 men

Mandan O-Keepa Ceremony, George Catlin. (Wikimedia Commons)

Bartering for a Bride, Alfred Miller. (Wikimedia Commons)

The Silenced War Whoop, Charles Schreyvogel. (Wikimedia Commons)

Last of the Buffalo, Albert Bierstadt. (National Gallery of Art)

John Sontag wounded by posse at battle of Stone Corral, California, 1893. (Wikimedia Commons)

Texas oil boom. (Wikimedia Commons)

The Great Depression, Dorothea Lange. (Wikimedia Commons)

Hoover Dam, 1941, Ansel Adams. (Wikimedia Commons)

Phoenix pollution. (KTAR News)

Las Vegas.

who joined cattle drives from 1866 to 1895, 63 percent were white, 25 percent were black, and 12 percent were Mexican.[32]

The cattle industry eventually self-destructed. Anyone could freely graze livestock on public lands. Ranchers competed to graze as many cattle on as much land as possible. The result was overgrazing as cattle destroyed the grasses that sustained them. When cattle first appeared on the plains, five acres of grassland could support one; by the 1880s, a cow needed 50 acres to survive. By 1885, the 20,000,000 cattle grazing the Great Plains nearly numbered the bison they had replaced. Deep freezes and flood-producing thaws decimated most herds on the northern plains in the winter of 1886 and 1887. The next spring, ranchers rounded up their surviving cattle and rushed them to market. That caused the supply to exceed demand and the price to drop to $1 a hundredweight compared to $9.35 in 1882, the peak year.

***

The logging industry reaped enormous profits from Washington's policy of giving away public lands. During the late nineteenth century, the logging industry soared in production to meet soaring demand for railroad ties, telegraph, telephone, and electric wire poles, building lumber, furniture boards, and firewood.[33] Corporations constructed railroad spurs deep into primal forests to extract logs that power saws and steam donkeys more easily cut. By 1914, forests in Washington, Oregon, and California produced 40 percent of the nation's lumber. Of that, Frederick Weyerhaeuser's corporation co-owned with the Northern Pacific Railroad half of Washington's forest and one-quarter of Oregon's.[34] Weyerhaeuser and other logging and railroad corporations reaped vast fortunes by clearcutting forests. That destroyed not just trees but entire ecosystems of soils and waters that once teemed with plants and animals.

8.3 Lumber Production by Major Political Subdivisions
(in million board feet)[35]

Year	California	Oregon	Washington	British Columbia
1849	5,000	16,852	4,080	n.a.
1859	196,000	41,169	77,125	1,750
1869	353,842	75,193	128,743	25,000
1879	326,340	177,171	160,176	50,000
1889	528,554	444,565	1.061,560	67,612
1899	737,760	734,181	1,428,205	252,580

Crime was a problem in most mining, cattle, and logging towns. Of course, all things are relative including criminality. Murders, robberies, and rapes varied considerably among western towns then and today. Indeed, western towns may have been less dangerous than modern cities. A comparison of crime in California's mining town of Bodie from 1877 to 1883 with eastern cities in 1980 found 84 robberies per 100,000 to 1,140 in New York, 996 in Miami, 628 in Los Angeles, 521 in San Francisco-Oakland, 347 in Atlanta, 294 in Chicago, and 245 for the entire United States. However, western mining towns were deadlier than eastern cities, possibly because nearly everyone was openly armed and most resisted rather than acquiesced to robberies. Bodie and Aurora California had murder rates of 116 and 64 per 100,000 compared to Miami with 32.7, Las Vegas with 23.4, Los Angeles with 23.3, New York with 21.0, Chicago with 14.5, Atlanta with 14.4, and San Francisco-Oakland with 11.7.[36]

One powerful force that exacerbated violence was the West's "code" of "stand your ground, don't back down, die before you run."[37] Ideally, that stance preserved one's honor, life, and property by deterring or, if need be, killing those intent on doing harm. In practice, that code probably provoked more killings than it prevented. Actually, that code was not born in the West but on the first frontiers in Jamestown and Plymouth, from which it developed over the following centuries. A man's honor meant never turning the other cheek to aggressors. Dueling was considered a proper way to settle disputes over honor even if most colonies and later states outlawed the practice. On the anarchic frontier, each man's ability and will to defend himself along with his self-reliance and enterprise became core American values. The men who led America's war for independence and drafted its Declaration of Independence and Constitution believed in natural laws and rights with self-defense the ultimate right and any means to that end justified. Julian Ralph, a journalist who wrote fourteen books, captured the pathology permeating most men in the typical frontier boomtown: "Men without the restraint of law, indifferent to public opinion, and unburdened by families, drink whenever they feel like it, wherever they have the money to pay for it, and whenever there is nothing to do . . . Bad manners follow, profanity becomes a matter of course . . . Excitability and nervousness . . . and then to correct this state of things the pistol comes into play."[38]

Historian Bill O'Neal recorded 587 gunfights among 255 gunfighters across the West.[39] He counted only confirmed, not alleged kills for men in two or more gunfights. Texas was the most prone to gunfights with

160 followed by Kansas and New Mexico with 70 each, Arizona with 60, and Oklahoma with 50. Most gunfighters were born and died in the West, with the most common boyhoods in Texas and Missouri. Two of three gunfighters died violently either in a gunfight, hanging, or suicide. One fascinating finding is the gap between Hollywood and history. Despite their depiction in movies as prolific killers, Wyatt Earp and the Sundance Kid apparently never gunned down anyone and Jesse James only one. As for the top ten primary occupations, there were 110 lawmen, 75 cowboys, 54 ranchers, 46 farmers, 45 rustlers, 35 hired gunmen, 34 soldiers, 26 bandits, 24 gamblers, and 22 laborers then further down the list 14 train robbers, 8 bank robbers, and 3 bounty hunters.[40]

8.4 Statistics for the Fourteen Most Prolific or Best-Known Gunfighters[41]

Rank and Name	Killings	Gunfights	Possible Killings or Assists
1. Jim Miller	12	14	1
2. Wes Hardin	11	19	1
3. Bill Longley	11	12	2
4. Harvey Logan	9	11	0
5. Wild Bill Hickock	7	8	1
10. Billy the Kid	4	16	5
14. Clay Allison	4	4	0
17. Cole Younger	3	7	2
19. Doc Holliday	2	8	2
20. Pat Garrett	2	6	2
26. Jesse James	1	9	3
28. Bat Masterson	1	3	0
32. Wyatt Earp	0	5	5
33. Sundance Kid	0	4	0

Accuracy, not speed, was essential to winning a gunfight. A coolheaded gunfighter who carefully aimed his pistol at his enemy's chest and squeezed the trigger was more likely to walk away than the hothead who tossed off all six shots in his enemy's direction. The best way to end up on Boot Hill was to fire a pistol by fanning it or slapping the trigger.

Some gunfights occurred because of wars between rival factions. The 1878 Lincoln County War pitted established businessmen Lawrence Murphy, James Dolan, John Riley, and their riders against newcomer businessmen John Tunstall, Alexander McSween, and their riders who called themselves regulators.[42] Among the regulators was William Bonney, nicknamed Billy the Kid. Over the next four years, gunfights resulted in fifteen killed and eleven wounded in the Murphy faction, and eight killed and twelve wounded in the Tunstall faction. Sheriff Pat Garret killed Billy the Kid in July 1881. In Tombstone, Arizona and surrounding Cochise County, business conflict was entangled in political conflict, with Democrat Sheriff Johnny Behan, Ike and Billy Clanton, Tom and Frank McLaury, and gunfighters like Billy Claiborne, "Curley Bill" Brocius, Johnny Ringo, and others against Republican John Clum, the mayor and editor of the *Tombstone Epitaph*, brothers Wyatt, Virgil, and Morgan Earp, John "Doc" Holliday, and other gunfighters.[43] Each side accused the other of corruption, cattle-rustling, stagecoach robberies, and other crimes. That feud climaxed on October 28, 1881, with the thirty-second gunfight at the O.K. Corral pitting the three Earps and Holliday against the Clantons, McLaurys, and Claiborne, in which bullets killed the McLaurys and Billy Clanton and wounded Morgan, Virgil, and Doc. In the following months, the Clanton faction killed Morgan and wounded Virgil, while Wyatt, Holliday, and other gunslingers eventually killed several of the Clanton gang.

Outlaw gangs often outgunned the town and county sheriffs and United States marshals.[44] The best lawmen offset that hard power disadvantage with soft psychological power. Wyatt Earp explained how he peacefully subdued one dangerous outlaw: "I just kept looking him in the eye as I walked toward him. And when he started talking to me I was pretty sure I had him. I tried to talk in as pretty a voice as I could manage and told him to throw his gun in the road. He did and that's all there was to it."[45]

Lawlessness often provoked vigilantism or the "right" of people to impose their own sense of justice against alleged criminals when either a formal judicial system does not exist, or will likely let the accused off or lightly punished. Across the West, vigilantes lynched hundreds of men and occasionally women accused of rustling, robbery, arson, rape, and murder. Here again, vigilantism was not a product of the West but of America's earliest frontier settlements. The line between a formal court and a lynch mob often blurred. During the Salem witch hysteria in 1692, the Massachusetts Court arrested hundreds of alleged witches and executed twenty of them. Elsewhere, vigilantism in the

South exceeded the West in the number of lynchings with mostly blacks targeted.

At least 210 vigilante groups operated west of the Mississippi from 1849 to 1902, and they executed 527 alleged criminals, usually by hanging. Most groups numbered between 100 and 300 members. The largest vigilante group was in San Francisco with around 8,000 members in 1856. Prominent political leaders served on the steering committees of some groups including senators Leland Stanford of California, Wilbur Sanders of Montana, and William McConnell of Idaho, and governors Leland Sanford of California, John Osborne and Fennimore Chatterton of Wyoming, Miquel Otero and George Curry of New Mexico. Most people backed the groups because they cut not just crime but court and incarceration costs.[46]

As in the South, at times western vigilantes lynched people innocent of any crime but whose businesses threatened local monopolies and oligopolies. Historian Richard Brown counted forty-two such "wars" from the early 1850s through 1919.[47] For example, the Southern Pacific Railroad's Big Four owners—Leland Stanford, Mark Hopkins, Charles Crocker, and Collis Huntington—ordered their gunmen to threaten violence against landowners who refused to sell their property. On May 11, 1880, a shootout between railroad gunmen and settlers resulted in two of the former and five of the latter killed.

***

Anglo-Americans discriminated against Hispanics, Asians, and blacks. They exploited the cheap labor of each group while denying them equal political, economic, social, and legal standing. Only white men could vote, sit on juries, run for public office, and serve as judges, lawmen, and assemblymen. Vigilantes often intimidated and sometimes murdered minorities that tried to assert their rights. Nonetheless, some Hispanics, blacks, and Asians managed to become wealthy despite the discrimination.

The 1848 Treaty of Guadeloupe Hidalgo transferred the Southwest Territory from Mexico to the United States. Around 100,000 Hispanics lived in that territory. They suffered discrimination by the Americans who conquered their territory, took their land on flimsy legal grounds, and imposed territorial and later state laws that denied them civil rights. Dispossessing Hispanics of their lands by unscrupulous Americans was quite easy. Most Hispanic people had lived for generations on land where an official title had disappeared or never existed. Slick lawyers could simply sue those who inhabited the desired lands.

Most Hispanics could not afford the fees, interest rates, and fines, nor understood English and the new laws in that language designed to deprive them.

Congress passed the 1851 Land Law that established a Land Claims Commission to determine who owned what in the newly acquired territories from Mexico. The Santa Fe Ring was a group of lawyers, politicians, and businessmen led by Thomas Catron who sought to take over the old Spanish land grants within New Mexico Territory in the late 1860s and early 1870s. Their worst fraud was bribing Land Commissioner James Williamson to expand the Maxwell Land Grant from 97,000 to 2,000,000 acres.

Countless African Americans joined the westward movement although few did so willingly. Most went as slaves and most of them to Texas. In 1836, of 30,000 American immigrants to Texas, around 5,000 were black and largely slaves. Many blacks, mostly newly liberated slaves, sought refuge in the West after the Civil War. Kansas was the most popular destiny because abolitionists had founded it. By 1880, 15,000 "Exodusters" or former southern blacks had settled forty towns in Kansas. The most prominent leader among them was Benjamin "Pap" Singleton who founded three settlements with the largest, Nicodemus, Kansas in 1877. Blacks numbered one of four cowboys on cattle drives from Texas. Many of them hung up their spurs in a Kansas black community.

Although most black westerners are lost to history, a few well known African Americans freely headed west in search of fortune and adventure. Jim Rose, Jim Beckwourth, and Moses "Black" Harris were famous Mountain Men. Bass Reeves was a United States Marshall in Oklahoma. Nat Love was a famed cowboy and later rodeo star. The 9th and 10th Colored Cavalry were first-rate regiments during late nineteenth century Indians wars while the 24th and 25th Colored Infantry played supporting roles.

Western state and territorial governments discouraged and some outright banned black immigrants. Oregon forbad blacks from residing in the state and that stayed on the books until 1926. The assemblies of California and Nevada passed laws forbidding miscegenation between blacks and whites, and did not repeal them until 1948 and 1959, respectively. Oregon and California did not ratify the Fifteenth Amendment until 1950 and 1962, respectively.

One courageous woman not only challenged a discriminatory rule actually forced its repeal. On April 17, 1863, a San Francisco streetcar conductor ejected Charlotte Brown because she was black. She sued the Omnibus Company for $200 in damages. The court awarded her a nickel, the fare. Three days later, she was ejected from a streetcar. She sued for $3,000 in damages. A jury awarded her $500 on January 17, 1865. A streetcar driver ejected her for the third time and she filed her latest suit. The Omnibus Company rescinded its rule forbidding black passengers.[48]

Around 150 Black Coloradans led by William Hardin and assisted by Frederick Douglass's sons Frederick and Lewis petitioned Congress not to approve the territory's statehood unless its constitution guaranteed the right to vote. Senator Charles Sumner of Massachusetts championed their cause. That struggle lasted from 1864 to January 1867, when Congress passed the Colorado Territorial Act that enfranchised black men. That helped propel a national movement for black male voting rights that culminated with the Fifteenth Amendment's ratification on February 3, 1870.

Chinese laborers were crucial for the success of the Central Pacific Railroad by supplying eight out of ten of its workers. Of 103,465 Chinese living in the United States in 1880, 75,132 were in California.[49] The 1882 Chinese Exclusion Act forbad any Chinese immigration for a decade. Congress renewed that law for another decade in 1892 and made it permanent in 1902. Initially the law slowed but did not stop Chinese from immigrating to the United States. The number of Chinese reached 107,488 in 1890, declined to 85,202 in 1920, then rose to 106,334 in 1940.

Chinese immigrants suffered chronic racism and sporadic violence. California's Supreme Court ruled in *People versus Hall* (1854) that Chinese had no rights and freed George Hall and two other men who had been convicted of murdering a Chinese man. Anti-Chinese riots in Los Angeles resulted in eighteen killed in 1871. White vigilantes murdered ten Chinese miners at Log Cabin Bar, Oregon in 1887. The worst massacre was 28 Chinese and the expulsion of 500 others at Rock Springs, Wyoming on September 2, 1885, after the Union Pacific Railroad fired its white workers and replaced them with lower-paid Chinese.

Prostitutes were another marginalized group. "Soiled Doves," as they were called in the West, were often among the first women to reach a frontier town, especially if cattle, mines, or logs was the key commodity.[50] They ranged in status, refinement, and price from madams running high-class brothels to wretched women beckoning from fetid alleys. Many drowned their sorrows with alcohol or numbed them with opium.

Religion was yet another source of conflict in the West. Mennonites and Hutterites, like the Amish, were Christian sects that tried to emulate the communalism and pacificism of Jesus and the early church. Mennonites founded Marion, Kansas. Unlike the Amish and Mennonites, Hutterites do use modern dress and machinery. They suffered discrimination by mainstream Christian sects.

Mormons numbered over 100,000 in 350 communities in Utah Territory in 1880. That Mormon stronghold irritated most Congressmen and presidents. Mainstream Christians tended to consider Mormonism a heretical faith, especially its practice of polygamy. They were appalled to learn that Mormon leader Brigham Young had twenty-seven wives and fathered at least fifty-six children. In 1879, the Supreme Court ruled in *United States versus Reynolds* that the Constitution guarantees freedom of religious belief but not necessarily of religious practice, opening the way for laws against polygamy. Congress passed the Edmunds Act that forbade polygamists from voting in 1882, and the Edmunds-Tucker Act that forbade any Mormon Church institution from owning more than $50,000 worth of assets. In 1887, Congress passed a law that rescinded the Mormon Church's corporation, nationalized its property, and disenfranchised Mormon women. That forced President Wilford Woodruff of the Mormon Church to announce that henceforth the religion and its followers would obey federal laws and end polygamy. The Mormon Church did not officially abolish polygamy until 1890. Congress approved Utah's application as a state in 1896.

***

The prevailing government policy and social ethic toward western lands was to exploit them for profit as quickly and extensively as possible. During the late nineteenth century, a diametrically-opposed policy and ethic appeared. Groups and publications pressured Washington and the state houses to conserve resources and preserve lands like the Appalachian Mountain Club from 1876, the Audubon Society from 1886, the Boone and Crockett Club from 1887, and the Sierra Club from 1892. Theodore Roosevelt and George Grinnell founded the Boone and Crocket Club ostensibly as a hunting club but also to pressure the federal and state governments to end clearcutting and begin to restore forests. Magazines appeared like *American Sportsman* in 1871, *Forest and Stream* in 1874, *Field and Stream* in 1874, and *American Angler* in 1881 that advocated conservation and preservation not just to benefit hunters and fishermen but for all Americans. Three individuals were especially influential.

George Perkins Marsh was a brilliant lawyer, congressman, diplomat, and historian who issued a dire warning to Americans about their future grounded on his study of humanity's past. In his 1864 book *Man and Nature,* he explained how different civilizations rose and fell according how well or poorly they exploited the natural world. He then surveyed the destruction that Americans had inflicted on the natural world that sustained them. He called on Americans moderately to conserve rather than waste natural resources so that future generations could also enjoy them.

Frederick Olmsted was a landscape architect renowned for designing New York's Central Park and Brooklyn's Prospect Park. He also advocated the conservation of natural resources and the preservation of regions with exceptional beauty. He spent three years in California managing the Rancho Las Mariposa Gold Mine that ultimately failed. During that time, he visited Yosemite Valley and the Mariposa Big Tree Grove, was stunned by their magnificence, and issued a report to Congress calling for their preservation. On June 30, 1864, President Lincoln and Congress found time within the Civil War to pass the Yosemite Act that transferred Yosemite Valley and the Mariposa Sequoia Grove to California as a state park. He argued that it was in America's national interest to preserve these and other regions of sublime beauty. Visiting parks could alleviate an array of emotional ailments aggravated by industrialization and urbanization: "The want of such occasional recreation where men and women are habitually pressed by their business or household cares often results in a class of disorders the characteristic quality of which is mental disability, sometimes taking the severe forms of softening of the brain, paralysis, palsy, monomania, or insanity, but more frequently of mental and nervous excitability, moroseness, melancholy or irascibility, incapacitating the subject for the proper exercise of the intellectual and moral forces."[51]

John Wesley Powell was a one-armed Civil War veteran who studied and taught science before and after the war. He was also a natural leader, organizer, and lobbyist. In 1867, he secured financial support from an array of colleges, the Smithsonian Institute, and the federal government to organize and lead an expedition that geologically surveyed Colorado. In 1869, he wielded his lobbying skills to get backing for a descent of the Green and Colorado Rivers. He had four 21-foot boats built with thick oak hulls. He gathered nine volunteers and spent weeks training them in rowing and survival skills on the Green River. They embarked at Green River City on May 24. They swiftly passed through a series of spectacular canyons, shooting rapids and finding calm water and sandy beaches to spend nights. They reached the Colorado River on July 17. Three men grew so discouraged they walked out. Paiutes killed them on the canyon rim. On August 30, Powell and his six remaining men reached the confluence of the Colorado and Virgin Rivers where they met three Mormons and an Indian fishing. They had spent three months and six days running the river between one American settlement and another.

In clear, precise prose, Powell wrote up his findings into "Explorations of the Colorado River of the West" (1875), "Report on the Geology of the Eastern Portion of the Unita Mountains" (1876), "Introduction to the Study of Indian Languages" (1877), and "Report on the Lands of the Arid Region of the United States" (1878). In his fourth report, he concluded that the Homestead Act's 160-acre limit was inadequate for the West where scarce rainfall and grass, and poor soil meant farms and ranches had to be much larger and needed irrigation to be viable. He recommended 800 acres for irrigated farms and 2,560 acres for livestock ranches. That provoked a backlash by cattle barons who feared competing with small-scale ranchers for grass and water. They made enough payoffs to throttle any laws designed to realize Powell's recommendations.

The greatest preservation victory was the creation of Yellowstone National Park. Henry Washburne, Montana's surveyor general, led a survey expedition that explored the Yellowstone plateau in 1870. Two members, Nathaniel Langford, and Cornelius Hedges, conceived the idea of preserving the region as a national park. Langford wrote two articles with sketches describing Yellowstone's geysers and stunning landscapes for *Scribner's Monthly*. Hedges wrote similar articles for Montana newspapers. Montana Territorial Governor Thomas Meagher embraced the idea. Those endorsements inspired Congress to appropriate $40,000 for a Geological Survey of the region led by Ferdinand Hayden in 1871. Accompanying Hayden were painter Thomas Moran and photographer William Jackson whose images when published fascinated the public. Hayden advised Congress to preserve Yellowstone and later called for public support for "a law setting it apart as a great public park for all time to come."[52] Among those who sought the creation of Yellowstone National Park was Jay Cooke, president of the Northern Pacific Railroad, who could profit by running a spur there for tourists. Senator Samuel Pomeroy of Kansas and Congressman William Kelly of Philadelphia were the Yellowstone Park Bill's chief sponsors. The debate began on December 18, 1871, the Senate approved by voice vote and the House of Representatives by 115 to 65 votes on February 27, and President Ulysses Grant signed the Yellowstone Park bill into law on March 1, 1872.

***

Congress established the territories of Colorado, Dakota, and Nevada in 1861 and Arizona and Idaho in 1863, Montana in 1864, and Wyoming in 1868, and the states of Kansas in 1861, Nevada in 1864, Nebraska in 1867, Colorado in 1876, and Washington, Idaho, Wyoming, North Dakota, South Dakota, and Montana in 1890. That culminated with the transformation of Indian Territory into Oklahoma.

Oklahoma's 1889 land rush perhaps best illustrated the frontier's end. The name Oklahoma comes from two Choctaw words, *okla* or people and *humma* or red. Oklahoma was a good name for that territory when it was reserved for Indians. The 1887 Dawes Act forced tribes to distribute land among members then sell the leftovers. Nowhere in the West did the federal government give away more land quicker than in Oklahoma. By April 22, 1889, Washington had taken and surveyed two million acres of former Indian lands for setters and deployed the cavalry to try to prevent anyone from sneaking in early. At noon, bugle calls around the border signaled the time for 50,000 impatiently waiting people to surge into the territory and grab some of that land for themselves. Within days all the lots of designated towns like Guthrie, the initial capital, Oklahoma City, Norman, and Kingfisher were taken, rude shelters erected, and businesses thriving. The Land Office recorded 1,920,000 acres claimed by "boomers" in 1889 alone with millions more taken in the following years.

Congress gave away the land before appointing a territorial government. The result was anarchy and sporadic violence as gangs fought to seize the best land for crops, pastures, or towns. Congress tried to remedy that by passing the Oklahoma Organic Act that formed a territorial government on May 2, 1890. The federal government imposed more land takeaways from the tribes and gave them away to settlers including 900,000 acres from the Sauk, Fox, and Potawatomi in September 1891, 3,000,000 acres from the Cheyenne and Arapaho in April 1892, and 6,000,000 acres from the Cherokee in September 1893. Land rushes followed each cession with the largest 100,000 settlers charging into the Cherokee Strip below the Kansas border.

***

Rising numbers of Americans sought to see what was left of the "Wild West" and enjoyed enough wealth and leisure time to do so.[53] That inspired publishers to produce guidebooks for the West that in turn encouraged tourists to set forth. The best seller was George Crofutt's *Transcontinental Tourist's Guide* first published in 1872 with eventually 350,000 sold.

Entrepreneurs established luxury resorts at mineral springs or seaside settings across the West. Among the first was Manitou Springs founded by William Palmer, the president of the Denver and Rio Grande Railroad that reached Colorado Springs in 1871. He enticed investors for a nearby European-style resort community he eventually called Manitou Springs and advertised as a luxury health resort where people could purge their ails in the mineral springs and genteel society. Other entrepreneurs developed their own adjacent facilities like the Cheyenne Mountain County Club, Colorado Springs Opera House, Broadmoor Casino, and Antlers Hotel. Elsewhere in Colorado, Walter Devereaux, a mining engineer, got rich after discovering and exploiting coal seams at Glenwood Springs. After the Denver and Rio Grande reached Glenwood in 1887, he began developing the Hotel Colorado and Natatorium as a luxury spa that opened in 1893. Meanwhile, to encourage rich residents he founded the Glenwood Polo and Racing Association in 1890.

California boasted its own grand hotels in the late nineteenth century. Charles Crocker, president of the Southern Pacific Railroad, developed the luxurious Hotel Del Monte at Monterey, California in 1880. Elisha Babcock and Hampton Story opened the seaside Hotel Coronado at San Diego in 1888. Another was the Raymond Hotel in Pasadena in 1886.

Fred Harvey built seventeen Southwest style hotels near rail stations at cities and towns across the West from 1896 to 1920. Among the more stunning was the Alvarado Hotel in Albuquerque and the Castaneda Hotel in Las Vegas, New Mexico. In 1902, he established an Indian department within Fred Harvey Company to employ Indian artists to sell their work to tourists. He hired and trained hundreds of "Harvey Girls," young, single, personable women dressed in uniform black dresses to serve customers and clean rooms. Many married and settled in western towns.[54]

Some railroad companies that neared or reached national parks built elaborate hotels there with western-style architecture and furnishings. The Northern Pacific built the 151-room Mammoth Hotel near Yellowstone Park's northwest entrance in 1883. From there, tourists could take a five-day camping trip around the park. The Northern Pacific hired investor Henry Child and architect Robert Reamer to develop the luxurious rustic Old Faithful Hotel of peeled logs with a soaring five-story lobby overlooking Old Faithful Geyser in Yellowstone that opened in 1904. They built the Canyon Hotel with a similar style overlooking Yellowstone Canyon in 1913. The Santa Fe

Railroad hired Fred Harvey and architect Charles Whittesley to design and build the El Tovar with a southwest style and adjacent Hopi House for sales of Indian arts and crafts overlooking the Grand Canyon in 1905. The Great Northern Railroad tapped architect Thomas McMahon to build 172-room Glacier Park Lodge in Glacier National Park in 1913. More than a century later tourists marvel at the stunning architecture and pay high prices for the rooms.

Chapter 9

ARTISTS AND WRITERS

> I see over my own continent the Pacific railroad surmounting every barrier.
> I see continental trains of cars winding along the Platte carrying freight and passengers.
> I hear the locomotives rushing and roaring, and the shrill steam-whistle.
> I hear the echoes reverberate through the grandest scenery in the world.
> I cross the Laramie plains, I note the rock in grotesque shapes, the buttes . . .
> Tying the Eastern to the Western Sea. The road between Europe and Asia.
> (Walt Whitman)

America's Centennial Exposition in Philadelphia was a giant coming of age celebration for the nation's vast array of feats over the preceding 100 years since independence. Nearly a million Americans and foreigners visited the Exposition over its half-year existence. They marveled at the array of machines in Agricultural Hall and Machinery Hall that animated an ongoing industrial revolution of mass factory production, mass transportation through an expanding network of railroads and canals, and mass communication through the telegraph and cheap newspapers. That revolution had a dark side. Huge corporations dominated the economy as monopolies or oligopolies in steel, railroads, and coal. In what would be called the Gilded Age, a few people got fabulously rich, the middle class expanded, and poverty afflicted millions of Americans. Air and water pollution choked cities and millions of people, sickening countless and killing many. Corruption worsened in Washington, the state houses, and swelling cities. Yet, despite these problems, most Americans had reason to be optimistic. The Civil War had ended 11 years earlier with the rebellion crushed, slavery abolished, and America reunified.

Then amidst the celebration in Philadelphia came stunning news of the slaughter of Colonel George Custer and 268 of his troops by Indian warriors at the Little Bighorn. Custer was a flamboyant leader who led from the front and won nearly every battle he fought against Confederate cavalry during the Civil War. Most people imagined that he would be just as victorious against Indians out West. Yet then and since Custer had as many detractors as fans. He symbolized American manhood for those who adored him and American imperialism and racism for those who despised him. Regardless, that military defeat reminded Americans that the West at once presented danger, opportunity, and, for artists and writers, inspiration.[1]

Indeed, what was called "Custer's Last Stand" inspired numerous artists, writers, and, in the twentieth century, filmmakers to render their versions. Best-known was Cassily Adams's 1888 painting of a buckskinned grim-faced Custer with sword in one hand and pistol in the other about to be overwhelmed with his few remaining troops by converging Sioux. Eventually 150,000 copies of a lithograph version were printed with almost every saloon featuring one above the bar.

The West intrigued plenty of other artists during this era. Of all the paintings, few depict the exhilaration of Manifest Destiny better than Emanuel Leutze's "Westward the Course of Empire Takes Its Way" (1862) inside the United States Capitol; Leutze's best-known painting is "Washington Crossing the Delaware" (1848). Then there is John Gast's crude but popular "Westward Ho (American Progress)" (1872) of a giant goddess with a white gown drifting above a prairie landscape covered with folks afoot and in wagons heading west; the painting's symbolic value far exceeds its artistic value.

The Texas Independence War and Mexican War inspired three artists. Texan artist William Huddle depicted the state's history through works like "Dawn at the Alamo" (1883) and "Surrender of Santa Anna" (1886). James Walker was a New York trained painter who accompanied General Winfield Scott's 1847 campaign that captured Mexico City. His "Battle of Chapultepec" (1858) was his best painting of that war. He returned to New York where he specialized in paintings with military themes. He went to California in 1870 and painted scenes of that state until his death in 1889. Among his best-known images was "Roping a Wild Grizzly" (1877). Journalist George Kendall and painter Carl Nebel also followed Scott's campaign and later in New York produced the *War between the United States and*

Mexico, Illustrated (1851), with the former's text and the latter's twelve color lithographs of war scenes.

George Bingham depicted frontier promise with "Daniel Boone Leading Settlers through Cumberland Gap" (1851), frontier danger with "The Concealed Enemy" (1846), and frontier fulfillment with "The Jolly Flatboatmen" (1846), "Shooting for the Beef" (1850), "County Election" (1851), "Stump Speaking" (1854), and "Verdict of the People" (1854). His best of the West was "Traders Descending the Missouri" (1845) of a grizzled older man in the stern paddling and glaring at the viewer, his half-Indian son leaning dreamily on their fur pack, and a bear cub chained in the bow as they glide in a pirogue down a tranquil river with a hazy luminous background.

John Stanley studied art with renowned teacher James Bowman and was inspired to paint western scenes after visiting George Catlin's Indian Gallery in New York. In 1841, he traveled to Fort Gibson to paint Indians from the "Civilized Tribes" that had settled in that region. He accompanied Colonel Stephen Kearney's expedition from Fort Leavenworth to Santa Fe then on to San Diego in 1846. In 1847, he journeyed to Oregon and eventually sailed back to New York. In 1850, he opened Stanley's North American Indian Galley with 135 paintings in New York. Like Catlin, he tried and failed to get the federal government to purchase his collection. He loaned most of his paintings to the Smithsonian Institute but, tragically, a fire destroyed nearly all of them in 1865. Among his best surviving works are "Oregon City on the Willamette River" (1852) and "Blackfeet Card Players" (1869).

The separate sojourns of three artists on the Great Plains inspired them later to paint scenes of hunters, pioneers, and Indians. Among their best were William Ranney's "Prairie Burial" (1848), "The Trapper's Last Shot" (1850), "The Scouting Party" (1851), "Advice on the Prairie" (1853), and "The Old Scout's Tale" (1853); Arthur Tait's " "Looking for the Trail" (1851), "The Trapper's Defense" (1860), and "Buffalo Hunters" (1862); and Carl Wimar's "Captive Charger" (1854), "Attack on an Immigrant Train" (1856), and "The Buffalo Dance" (1861).

Three artists spent years in California. William Jewett studied at New York's Academy of Design, then in 1850 moved to San Francisco, opened a studio, and mostly painted portraits of prominent Californians. Painter Charles Nahl passed several decades in California and his best works included "Miners in the Sierras" (1852), "Sacramento Indian" (1867), and "Sunday Morning at the Mines" (1872). Carl Hahn's most dramatic painting was "Looking Down Yosemite Valley from Glacier Point" (1874).

Three artists sought to capture the West's grandeur. The best was Albert Bierstadt who first saw the West as a member of Colonel Frederick Lander's 1859 expedition to map the Overland Trail. He next went West in 1863 and this time stayed, mostly in San Francisco. His most dramatic landscapes include: "Thunderstorm in the Rocky Mountains" (1859), "Valley of Yosemite" (1864), "The Rocky Mountains—Landers Peak" (1863), "Storm in the Rockies—Mount Rosalie" (1866), "Domes of the Yellowstone" (1867), "Sunset in Yosemite Valley" (1868), and "Seal Rocks, Farallon Islands" (1873), with his most iconic, "Emigrants Crossing the Plains" (1867), "Among the Sierra Nevada Mountains of California" (1868), and "Last of the Buffalo" (1889). Bierstadt's romantic style and transcendental themes emulated those of Frederick Church. Thomas Moran also spent years exploring and painting the West. His best works include the stunning "Grand Canyon of the Yellowstone" (1872), "The Castle Geyser, Yellowstone National Park" (1873), "Chasm of the Colorado" (1874), and hallucinogenic "The Mirage" (1879) of a trapping party riding through a vast glimmering mirage before towering, jagged rose-colored cliffs and an azure sky. Thomas Hill created his own splendid series of Sierra vistas like "Yosemite Valley from Below Sentinel Dome" (1876).

As for sculpture, Horatio Greenough's "The Rescue" depicted a frontiersman subduing a tomahawk-wielding warrior who threatened his wife and baby behind him. Greenough completed the sculpture for the Capitol in 1850, it was installed in 1854 and remained there until its removal for storage in 1959. The era's most evocative sculpture was Ferdinand Pettrich's marble "The Dying Tecumseh" (1856) that commemorated the brilliant Shawnee Indian leader who had valiantly resisted America's expansion. Much like ancient Romans viewing "The Dying Gaul," Americans could at once romanticize a valiant enemy while feeling pride and relief that ultimately their superior civilization had prevailed.

***

Photography emerged as a fine art during this time. A stereoscope was a device that produced a double photographic image that appeared three-dimensional. The first versions were large and unwieldy. In 1859, Oliver Wendell Holmes, later a Civil War veteran and Supreme Court justice, invented an inexpensive handheld stereoscope that Americans could purchase along with photographs. That in turn encouraged photographers to take appealing images often of distant, exotic places across America, especially the West.

Carleton Watkins, Timothy O'Sullivan, William Henry Jackson, Andrew Russell, and Eadweard Muybridge created hundreds of images of the West. Of them, perhaps most iconic was Russell's "Driving of the Golden Spike, Promontory, Utah, May 10, 1869" of the transcontinental railroad's completion and O'Sullivan's "Ancient Ruins in Canyon de Chelly" (1873). Two collections helped preserve part of the West. Watkins' 1862 photos of Yosemite Valley inspired Congress to grant Yosemite Valley to California as a state park. The Geological Survey issued Watkins' twenty-eight photos of Yosemite as a book in 1868. Jackson's 1871 photos of Yellowstone as a member of Ferdinand Hayden's expedition influenced the congressional vote to create Yellowstone National Park in 1872.

San Francisco was the best-documented western city through photos. George Fardon's *San Francisco Album: Photographs of the Most Beautiful Views and Public Buildings* (1856) provided remarkable images of that city. Eadweard Muybridge produced a thirteen-shot panorama of the city in 1877. Among the more prolific producers of western images was the Lawrence and Houseworth Company of San Francisco with their shots of Yosemite Valley, the Sequoias, San Francisco City and Bay, and 135 images of the Central Pacific Railroad's stations, trains, tunnels, and scenery. The railroad images sold so well that Alfred Hart in Sacramento and Charles Savage in Salt Lake City set up their own studios for similar photos, and the Union Pacific hired Andrew Russell as its official photographer. The Union Pacific published Russell's collection with commentary by Samuel Hayden, who directed the Geographical Survey in a book titled *The Great West Illustrated* in 1868. Those increasingly familiar images encouraged investors in both railroads and later countless passengers after they were completed.

Yosemite Valley inspired the most landscape photographers, of whom Josiah Whitney produced a *Yosemite Book* (1869) of essays and photos. Not all photos were elegiac. Arundell Hull's "Long Steve Hanged at Laramie by Vigilantes" (1868), William Bell's "Sergeant Frederick Wesleyan Killed by Cheyenne at Fort Wallace" (1870, and Laton Huffman's "Taking the Monster's Robe—Skinning Buffalo" (1882) depicted the aftermath of violence. Bell's image is gruesome with Wesleyan's naked, mutilated body riddled with arrows.

***

Most of America's best authors of the nineteenth century—Nathaniel Hawthorne, Herman Melville, Edgar Allen Poe, Henry James—did not use the West for their stories. However, in their respective greatest novels, Hawthorne did set his *The Scarlet Letter* (1850) on New England's frontier while Melville set *Moby Dick* (1851) on the wilderness of vast oceans.

Three authors crossed the continent to California and began their writing careers there. Bret Harte arrived in 1853 and after a dozen years of pursuing various careers including merchant and teacher, he turned to writing. He edited the magazine *Overland Monthly* from 1868 to 1871, and penned popular short stories like "Luck of the Mining Camp" (1868), and "The Tennessee Partner" (1868), and "The Outcasts of Poker Flat" (1869). Mark Twain spent time in Virginia City, Nevada, and later San Francisco. He first achieved literary fame with publications of short stories like "The Celebrated Jumping Frog of Calaveras County" in 1865. His 1871 book *Roughing It* is a hilarious account of his journey west in 1862 to escape the Civil War and seek his fortune. Ambrose Bierce stayed east to fight in the Civil War and later his best fiction reflected the horrors and absurdities he experienced. After the war, he moved to San Francisco and mostly wrote as a journalist and essayist for newspapers like the *San Francisco Examiner, Argonaut, Overland Monthly,* and *California.* His *Nuggets and Dust Planned Out in California* (1873) was his most western story collection. He was a brilliant wit, best known for his *Cynic's Word Book* (1906), also called *The Devil's Dictionary.*

Pulp fiction proliferated throughout the era thanks to technologies that made publishing steadily cheaper and a swelling, literate, middle class. Irwin and Erastus Beadle began printing "dime novels" with 35,000 to 70,000 words in 1860, swiftly emulated by dozens of other publishers. By the time the Beadle brothers shut their presses permanently in 1898, they had churned out 3,158 titles and millions of copies.[2] Two pulp authors were noteworthy, although not for their style or profundity. John Rollin Ridge, part Cherokee, was the first Indian to have a novel published, *The Life and Adventures of Joaquin Murietta, the Celebrated California Bandit* (1854). Most prolific of pulp writers was Edward Judson with his pen name Ned Buntline. He celebrated "Buffalo Bill" Cody as the "King of the Border Men." Being a household name certainly eased Cody's initial challenge of finding financial backers for his Wild West Show. There were no significant poets of the West during these decades. Walt Whitman did write an ode to America and its transcontinental railroad in his poem "Passage to India" (1871) with an excerpt as this chapter's epigram.

The discipline of history became "professional" in late nineteenth-century America. Historians sought to ground their work in primary sources and analyze them as dispassionately and objectively as possible. Two focused on the West, especially California.

Hubert Howe Bancroft was an amateur historian who was inspired to write about California and the West after arriving in San Francisco to manage a business in 1852. He and a team of assistants collected, collated, and analyzed primary sources on the West, then wrote thirty-nine volumes of history with just Bancroft's name on the covers. Although the writing is dry, the analysis is usually solid, and ever since historians have treasured them.

Josiah Royce was the first native Californian to write about the state's history. He was born in Grass Valley in the Sierra foothills, raised in San Francisco, got an undergraduate degree at the University of California at Berkeley and a doctorate at Johns Hopkins, then taught philosophy at Harvard University for 34 years. He was a prolific author with most of his books on philosophy. His only prominent history was *California: A Study of American Character, from the Conquest in 1846 to the Second Vigilance Committee in San Francisco* (1886). For that, his key interview was with an aging John Fremont and his wife Jessie who opened up to the amiable young man. Royce offered this damning revisionist assessment: "General Fremont was simply not the conqueror of California. All that he did . . . was of no effect except to alienate the people."[3] As a historian, Royce sought to understand the key decisions of leaders as shaped by psychological, social, political, economic, cultural, and natural forces that they could neither fully understand or control. He viewed the frontier as pathological with its violence and anarchy, transformed by hardworking, good-hearted people who developed farms, businesses, churches, and governments. He conveyed this theme in his novel *Feud of Oakville Creek: A Novel of California Life* (1887).

A number of first-rate memoirs appeared during these decades including Francis Parkman's *Oregon Trail* (1849), Hector Garrard's *Wah-to-Yah and the Taos Trail* (1850), Philip St. George Cooke's *Scenes and Adventures in the Army, or the Romance of Military Life* (1857), D.W.H. Davis's *El Gringo, or New Mexico and Its People* (1857), Mark Twain's *Roughing It* (1871), Clarence King's *Mountaineering in the Sierra Nevada* (1872), and George Custer's *My Life on the Plains* (1872). Two wives of controversial generals produced entertaining if idealized accounts of their lives, Elizabeth "Libbie" Custer's *Boots and Saddles* (1885), *Tenting on the Plains* (1889), and *Following the Guidon* (1890), and Jessie Benton Fremont's *Souvenirs of My Life* (1887), *Far West Sketches* (1890), and *Origins of the Fremont Expedition* (1891).

Two writers wrote on the plight of Indians. Helen Hunt Jackson first visited southern California in 1871 and moved there permanently in 1881. She was twice married. Disease killed her first husband, Captain Edward Hunt, and her sons. Her second husband was William Jackson, a rich banker who encouraged her to write. She was a poet who was inspired to champion Indian rights after hearing lectures by Ponca Chief Standing Bear and Omaha woman Bright Eyes in Boston in 1879. She protested America's treatment of Indians in her *Century of Dishonor* (1881) and her novel *Ramona* (1884) about California's Indians. Her writings contributed to the movement to alleviate conditions on reservations that culminated with the 1887 Dawes Act. One prominent Indian author emerged in late nineteenth century America. Sarah Winnemucca wrote about the experiences of herself and her people in *Life Among the Paiutes: Their Wrongs and Claims* (1883).

PART IV: THE MODERN AMERICAN WEST 1891–1980

Chapter 10

BOOMERS AND BUSTERS

> "I stand tonight facing west on what was once the last frontier. From the lands that stretch 3000 miles behind me, the pioneers of old gave up their safety, their comfort, and sometimes their lives to build a new world here in the West . . . But the problems are not all solved and the battles are not all won, and we stand today on the edge of a new frontier." (John Kennedy)

> "In our mad rush to dam every river, chop down every tree, utilize all resources to the ultimate limit . . . we might . . . destroy the very things that have made life in America worth cherishing and defending." (Sigurd Olsen)

Symbolically, the modern West began with the Census Bureau's announcement that America's frontier disappeared by 1890 and ended with Ronald Reagan's inauguration as president on January 20, 1981.[1] During those decades, the West transformed economically and politically from a backwater into a powerhouse.

Economically, President Franklin Roosevelt's New Deal and World War II programs, investments, and subsidies from 1935 to 1945 were revolutionary. Influxes of people and industries morphed towns into cities and cities into sprawling megacities. An increasingly diversified economy steadily reduced the West's boom and bust economy dependent on extracting natural resources that were refined elsewhere

Politically the change was insidious rather than dramatic. The last four states of the lower forty-eight emerged, Utah in 1896, Oklahoma in 1907, and New Mexico and Arizona in 1912. Ideologically, conservatives and liberals struggled constantly over whether government should favor big business or small businesses, owners or workers, developers or conservationists and preservationists. In those days, the Republican and Democratic Parties had liberal and conservative wings. From the late nineteenth century through the mid-twentieth century, liberalism often had the edge in its endless tug-of-war with conservatism in the West. For instance, among the states and territories, Wyoming granted women the right to vote in 1868, Montana elected Jennette Rankin as the first women to the House of Representatives in 1917, and Wyoming elected Nellie Ross the first woman governor in 1924. The West was also the scene of the most violent and radical labor organization, the socialist International Workers of the World (IWW). However, most battles over the West's fate were fought in Washington rather than the state or, until 1912, territorial capitals. A series of presidents and congresses regulated or outright protected ever more western landscapes from mining, logging, grazing, and homesteading by imposing national forests, parks, and wildernesses, and protected ever more people from pollution with clean air and water standards.

Yet gradually conservatives became more powerful. Ironically, many people became more conservative as their wealth expanded thanks to all those government programs. Blue-collar workers whose ancestors might have supported liberal causes in the late nineteenth and twentieth century's first half increasingly backed conservative causes, including tax cuts that almost exclusively favored the rich and cuts in government services that benefited themselves. Those political shifts in the West and other regions culminated with Reagan's 1980 election to the presidency. By then the Democratic Party was mostly liberal and the Republican Party mostly conservative.

***

The 1890 Census counted 6,451,000 people in seventeen states and territories that were so dispersed that the frontier no longer meaningfully existed. The five largest cities were San Francisco with 298,000 people, Denver with 197,000, Los Angeles with 50,000, Salt Lake City with 45,000, and Seattle with 43,000. That West was then America's most progressive region. Among the West's most prominent liberals from 1890 to 1920 were Republican senators Hiram Johnson of California and William Borah of Idaho, William U'Ren of Oregon's House of Representatives, and Governor Peter Norbeck of South Dakota.

Most farmers of that era backed progressive policies. They did so because they faced worsening prices for their crops. Washington's giveaway of hundreds of millions of acres of land to farmers combined with dozens of inventions that increased farm productivity led to huge crop surpluses that exceeded demand. In comparing average prices between the years 1870–3 and 1894–7, wheat fell from $106.70

to $63.30 a bushel, corn from $43.10 to $29.70 a bushel, and cotton from $15.10 to $5.80 a pound. Meanwhile the cost of shipping goods by rail rose as one journeyed west, although prices did steadily drop everywhere. From 1873 to 1897, the price per ton for the Pennsylvania Railroad east of Chicago fell from $1.26 to $0.56, for the Burlington Railroad west from Chicago to the Missouri River from $1.61 to $0.75, and for the Burlington Railroad west of the Missouri from $4.50 to $1.28. Companies built and operated grain elevators that monopolized regions and charged high prices. An oligopoly of eleven companies dominated Chicago's grain elevators.[2]

Those chronic problems caused most farms to pile up debt, many to fail, and ever more farmers to organize to pressure the federal, state, and local governments for aid. Oliver Kelley, a former Department of Agriculture commissioner, formed with seven other farmers the Grange or Patrons of Husbandry at Fredonia, New York in 1867. The Grange was dedicated to mutual support among members and lobbying government to keep prices for shipping and storing grain low. The founders inspired other chapters to form across the country. In 1873, those groups united in a convention to establish the National Grange. By 1874, 1,500,000 people were members. Many chapters bought and operated their own processing plants and grain elevators. The Grange's most important political victory was getting Illinois's government to cap grain elevator prices in 1871. After being fined for violating that law, the Munn and Scott Company sued, arguing that the law was unconstitutional for taking their profit without due process. In *Munn versus Illinois* (1877), the Supreme Court justices ruled by seven to two that the Illinois law was constitutional because it protected the public good.

Inspired by that progressive ruling, a New York Grange chapter formed the National Farmers' Alliance as a more explicitly political lobby group in 1877. The Farmers' Alliance became the Populist or People's Party in 1892 during a convention with 1,500 delegates at Omaha on July 4. For that year's election, the Populist Party adopted its Omaha Program, largely written by Ignatius Donnelly, that advocated a silver currency; nationalization of the railroads, and set, cheap freight charges; nationalization of the telephone and telegraph lines, and set, cheap charges; collectives for storing crops to maintain stable and high prices; income taxes on the rich; direct election of senators; referendums, recalls, and initiatives; and single-term presidents. The Populists nominated James Weaver as their presidential candidate. As a third party candidate, Weaver did quite well by winning 8.5 percent of the vote and five states, all in the West—Idaho, Nevada, Colorado, Kansas, and North Dakota. In Colorado, Populist Party candidate Davis Waite won the governorship.[3]

William Jennings Bryan, a congressman from Nebraska from 1891 to 1895, adopted Populist Party goals to win the Democratic Party's nomination for the 1896, 1900, and 1908 elections, and lost each time. His core issue was abandoning the gold standard and embracing silver money. Gold was relatively scarce and thus kept its value while silver's supply steadily expanded, leading its value to fall. Bryan and other Populists favored inflation because it reduced the real value of debts, thus benefiting debtors and hurting lenders. They ignored the reality that inflated prices for goods and services diminished buying power and thus income.

The proliferation of newspapers helped fuel interest in politics. Newspapers boomed in the late nineteenth century with cheap ink and paper, cutting-edge printing machines, and a mass, literate public. Many were called "the yellow press" for their increasingly tawdry stories and even "fake news" that boosted sales. New York City alone had half a dozen dailies sited within a block of each other near City Hall. Of them the rivalry between William Randolph Hearst's *New York Journal* and Joseph Pulitzer's *New York World* was especially fierce. They instructed their journalists to do anything for a scoop, and rewarded them generously when they succeeded. Sensational stories, true or not, sold big. Their sensationalistic stories over Spain's brutality in Cuba provoked outrage among the public and politicians that made the subsequent Spanish-American War in 1898 nearly inevitable.

Women first entered national politics in the West. Fourteen of the twenty states that let women vote before the 1920 constitutional amendment were in the West, including Wyoming in 1869, Utah in 1870, Colorado in 1893, Idaho in 1896, Washington in 1910, California in 1911, Arizona, Oregon, Arizona, and Kansas in 1912, Montana and Nevada in 1914, North Dakota and Nebraska in 1917, and South Dakota and Oklahoma in 1918. The motivations for each state assembly to let women vote varied. With a ratio of five men to one women, Wyoming's bachelors hoped to entice potential brides with an enlightened policy. That partly explained votes favoring women's suffrage in other states with skewed ratios between the sexes. Utah's lawmakers sought to reinforce polygamy with overwhelming numbers of voters to uphold it against any challengers. The first female mayor was Mary Howard of Kanab, Utah in 1912, and first big city mayor was Bertha Landes of Seattle in 1926. Jennette Rankin was the first female member of the House of Representatives, elected in 1915. Marian "Ma" Ferguson and Nellie Tayloe Rose won the respective governorships of Texas and Wyoming in 1925.

***

Conservationists and preservationists recognize that humanity's well-being depends on nature; overexploiting, wasting, and polluting nature ultimately harms humanity. However, they differ in their values, goals, and priorities. Conservationists are essentially materialists and utilitarians who want to exploit water, soil, forest, and wildlife only at levels that allow them to replenish themselves.[4] Preservationists revel in nature's aesthetic and spiritual beauty and seek to preserve as much of the natural world as possible. More than anyone, Gifford Pinchot and John Muir developed those respective outlooks and battled each other for supremacy.[5]

Gifford Pinchot, the Forest Service chief, exemplified the conservationist materialist, utilitarian outlook: "Conservation does mean provision for the future, but it means also . . . the right of the present generation to the fullest necessary use of all the resources with which this country is so abundantly blessed . . . The first principle of conservation is development . . . The first duty of the human race is to control the earth it lives upon . . . The natural resources must be developed and preserved for the benefit of the many, not merely for the profit of the few . . . The outgrowth of conservation, the inevitable result, is national efficiency."[6]

John Muir was among America's greatest leaders for wilderness preservation.[7] He was born in Scotland and immigrated to Wisconsin with his family when he was 11. He trained to be a mechanic, invented several devices, and studied at the University of Wisconsin for two years. An eye accident that almost destroyed his sight prompted him to rethink his life. After recovering, he embraced Transcendentalism and began a journal in which he developed his own version. He embarked on a thousand-mile hike to the Gulf of Mexico to explore the country. He headed West to San Francisco, arriving in March 1868, then on to the Sierra Mountains where he explored. In 1871, he met Ralph Emerson during his publicized visit to Yosemite Valley. Muir impressed Emerson who encouraged him to publish his writings as essays in national magazines. Muir's first key writing was "God's First Temples: How Shall We Preserve Our Forests?" for the *Sacramento Record-Union* in February 1876. He had a mystic's mind that saw the interdependence of all things and nature's sublimity: "When we try to pick out anything by itself, we find it hitched to everything else in the universe. The whole wilderness in unity and interrelation is alive and familiar . . . the very stones seem talkative, sympathetic, brotherly. No particle is ever waste or worn out but eternally flowing from use to use."[8]

Robert Johnson, *Century* magazine's editor, published two essays by Muir that advocated transforming Yosemite Valley and its surrounding region into a national park. Inspired, Johnson pressured leading senators and representatives to do so. Both houses of Congress passed the Yosemite National Park Act on October 1, 1890, and President Benjamin Harrison signed it the next day.

Muir and a group of fellow preservationists established the Sierra Club on June 4, 1892.[9] The Sierra Club is dedicated to promoting the enjoyment of wilderness and lobbying the federal, state, and local governments to protect as much of the natural world as possible. Muir explained why that was vital: "Thousands of tried, nerve-shaken, over-civilized people are beginning to find out that going to the mountains is going home; that wildness is a necessity, and that mountain parks and reservations are useful not only as fountains of timber and irrigating rivers, but as fountains of life." He scorned the "temple destroyers, devotees of ravaging commercialism" who "have a perfect contempt for Nature, and, instead of lifting their eyes to the God of the mountains, lift them to the Almighty Dollar." He condemned a proposal to dam the Hetch Hetchy River in Yosemite National Park to provide drinking water for San Francisco: "Dam Hetch Hetchy! As well dam for water-tanks the people's cathedrals and churches, for no holier temple has ever been consecrated by the heart of man."[10]

Saving and restoring the nation's forests from massive clearcutting became more imperative as they diminished. The Department of Agriculture assigned Franklin Hough to assess the nation's forests in 1876. Such an enormous mission took Hough two years. In 1878, he presented his "Report upon Forestry" that revealed widespread clearcutting, soil erosion, and siltation of rivers and streams. Harvard biology professor Charles Sargent conducted his own study with similar dismal findings. The Department of Agriculture formed a Division of Forestry and named German forester Bernard Fernow its first chief from 1886 to 1889. The trouble was that his division could merely survey what was left of forests on federal lands and propose reforms but was not empowered to protect them from rapacious logging corporations or replant them.

The decisive turning point came on March 3, 1891, when Congress passed the General Revision Act, also called the Forest Preserve Act, that authorized presidents to establish national forests on federal lands. Presidents Benjamin Harrison, Grover Cleveland, and William McKinley respectively set aside 16 million, 21 million, and 9 million forest acres, mostly in the West.

McKinley appointed Gifford Pinchot to head the Forest Service in 1898. Pinchot was the best man in America for that position. He studied botany and geology at Yale, then attended the forestry school in Nancy, France. He managed the forest surrounding the Vanderbilt Estate in North Carolina, and served on the National Academy of Sciences' National Forest Commission in 1896. He expanded the Forest Service from eleven employees and a $28,520 budget in 1898 to 150 employees and a $150,000 budget in 1902. He asserted a policy of sustained forestry that imposed limits on cutting forests so that they replenished themselves, and planting trees where forests had been clearcut. He got those goals codified in the 1897 Forest Management Act that required the government to pursue policies that ensured "a continuous supply of lumber for the use and necessities of citizens of the United States." Bernard Fernow, who preceded Pinchot as forestry chief, explained the policy as stark utilitarianism: "the principal object of the forest has nothing to do with beauty or pleasure. It is not, except incidentally, an object of aesthetics, but an object of economics."[11]

***

Theodore Roosevelt was the most western of America's presidents although he only lived there a few years.[12] He first visited the West to hunt bison on the northern plains in 1883. He was then a New York State assemblyman. He suffered the death of both his mother and wife from disease on February 14, 1884. After finishing his term as assemblyman, he went to the Little Missouri River, bought a ranch, and over the next three years invested over $80,000 in cattle. Although westerners initially dismissed him as an eastern dude, he steadily won their respect by his hard work, toughness, and leadership. He knocked out a bully in a saloon. When two men stole his rowboat, he pursued in another boat with two of his men, caught them at gunpoint, and had them incarcerated. When a neighboring cattle baron threatened him, he rode alone to his house and got him to apologize. He started a cattle association among the region's ranchers. The severe winter of 1886 into 1887 wiped out his herd and he returned east to a career as a federal civil service commissioner, New York City police commissioner, assistant secretary of the navy, lieutenant colonel of the 1st Volunteer "Rough Rider" cavalry regiment during the Spanish-American War, vice president under William McKinley, and president after McKinley's assassination.

Roosevelt reveled in wild nature: "There are no words that can tell of the hidden spirit of the wilderness, that can reveal its mystery, its melancholy, and its charm. There is delight in the hardy life of the open, in long rides, rifle in hand, in the fight with dangerous game." He sought to transform the way Americans perceived and used natural resources. He worried that Americans were growing too soft, complacent, and conformist. He called on Americans to lead a "strenuous life" to invigorate themselves and the nation. He explained why: "As our civilization grows older and more complex we need a greater and not a less development of the fundamental frontier virtues."[13]

No president promoted both the conservation and preservation of America's land more than Roosevelt. During his White House years from 1901 to 1909, he led the establishment of 5 national parks, 18 national monuments, 20 dam and irrigation projects, 55 wildlife preserves, and 137 national forests; commissions on public lands, inland waterways, farming, and national conservation; and expanded the national forests from 43 million to 194 million acres, with almost of all that across the West. He formed a Public Lands Commission to review all public land laws and their effect on the nation's development in 1903. He got Congress to pass the 1905 Transfer Act that shifted National Forests from the Interior Department to the Agriculture Department and established the Forestry Bureau to manage them. He reappointed Gifford Pinchot, a professional forester, to head the Forestry Bureau. He got Congress to pass the 1906 Antiquities or Lacey Act that empowered the president to designate federal lands with "historic landmarks, historic and prehistoric structures, and other objects of historic or scientific interests" as National Monuments.

The 1902 National Reclamation or Newlands Act established the Reclamation Service, renamed the Bureau of Land Reclamation in 1923, to create systems of dams, irrigation, and piped water in sixteen western states. Sales of federal lands would fund those projects. Roosevelt appointed Frederick Newell to head the Reclamation Service. The Reclamation Act eventually transformed the West. The first two projects—the Salt River in Arizona and Truckee River in California—were relatively modest but thereafter the projects steadily expanded in scale.

Roosevelt's conservation crusade culminated with his White House conference from May 13 to 15, 1908, when a thousand prominent political, scientific, business, and leaders, including all the state governors attended. In his address, he advocated conservation as vital for guarding the nation's security, prosperity, and well-being because "the natural resources of our country are in danger of exhaustion if we permit the old wasteful methods of exploiting them longer to continue."

He attributed America's economic growth to "the rapid development, and . . . the rapid destruction of our natural resources." He noted the irony that: "Our position in the world has been obtained by the extent and thoroughness of the control we have achieved over nature; but we are more, and not less, dependent upon what she furnishes than at any previous time of our history." He called "the wise use of all of our natural resources . . . is the great material question of today." Doing so demanded a reversal of self-destructive attitudes and policies: "In the past we have admitted the right of the individual to injure the future of the Republic for his own present profit. In fact, there has been a good deal of demand for unrestricted individualism, for the right of the individual to injure the future of us all for his own temporary and immediate profit. The time has come for a change. As a people we have the right and duty . . . of obeying the moral law, of requiring and doing justice, to protect ourselves and our children against the wasteful development of our natural resources."[14]

Roosevelt resolved a crisis with Japan over discrimination against Japanese immigrants in San Francisco. Japanese immigration to the United States rose steadily after Congress passed the 1882 Chinese Exclusion Act. Japanese came for the same reasons as Chinese had earlier. Poverty pushed them and demand for their labor pulled them to farm fields and construction sites. And they endured the same racist attitudes and acts. Many Americans accused Japanese of undercutting their businesses with cheap prices for goods and services by keeping low living standards. San Francisco Mayor James Phelan segregated white and Asian school children in 1906. Japan's government protested. California laws forbad Japanese and Chinese from owning land. Los Angeles segregated public swimming pools and gold courses.

Tokyo condemned that array of racist policies. In 1907, Roosevelt arranged a "gentlemen's agreement" whereby Tokyo capped its immigrants while Washington accepted those with family members already in the United States. Japanese men got around the restriction with a loophole by marrying "picture brides" who could come live with them in America. Another vital loophole was the Fourteenth Amendment whereby any one born in the United States was automatically an American citizen. Japanese parents bought land and registered it in their American-born childrens' names.

Roosevelt did not run for a third term, but instead supported his then close friend William Taft as the Republican candidate for the 1908 election. Taft won but as president fired Pinchot as Forest Service chief and favored corporate over conservation and preservation interests. Roosevelt and other reformers established the Progressive Party for the 1912 election. As a third party candidate, Roosevelt won 23.2 percent of the vote and 88 Electoral College votes, behind Democrat Woodrow Wilson's 41.8 percent but well above Republican William Howard Taft's 23.2 percent and Socialist Eugene Debs' 6.0 percent. Progressive Party victories included Hiram Johnson for California's governorship, and Senate seats for William Borah of Utah, Francis Newlands of Nevada, and George Norris of Nebraska.

***

Across the West, reliable and abundant water for households, businesses, and agriculture was an increasingly contentious issue as the population expanded, especially in southern California. Three men—a newspaper publisher, an engineer, and a mayor turned speculator—transformed Los Angeles from a small city into a megapolis in the early twentieth century. Abundant water was critical to that metamorphosis. Harrison Otis was a journalist and newspaper editor who moved to Los Angeles to edit the *Los Angeles Times* in 1882 and took over the newspaper in 1886. At that time, the city's population was only 12,500. Until his death in 1917, he ceaselessly boosted Los Angeles by encouraging migrants and investors, especially those who built railroads, dams, and canals. He formed the Colorado River Company with his son-in-law Harry Chandler to build a canal from that river to Los Angeles. By 1900, the city's population had expanded to 100,000.

William Mulholland was an engineer charged with establishing the Los Angeles Department of Power and Water. He found a source of water for Los Angeles in Owens Valley, 233 miles away east of the Sierra Mountains.[15] He partnered with Fred Eaton, the mayor from 1898 to 1900, to buy up 100,000 acres of land in adjacent San Fernando Valley where a reservoir would hold the water conveyed from Owens Valley. Otis and Chandler became major investors in the San Fernando Mission Land Company. Otis promoted the project through the *Los Angeles Times* while Chandler and Eaton won over key political allies. In 1907, all twenty-five members of Los Angeles's city council voted for $25 million in bonds to finance a project that dammed the Owens River and built the 223-mile long canal with 53 tunnels accompanied by 120 miles of railroad, 170 miles of power lines, 270 miles of telephone line, and 500 miles of road linking the reservoir to Los Angeles.[16] The project was completed and the water began flowing on November 5, 1913. Most of the water irrigated crops in San Fernando Valley on land owned by Mulholland, Otis, Chandler, and their cronies. Acreage soared from 3,000 acres in 1913 to 75,000 in 1918. Those crops fed Los Angeles's swelling population that reached 577,000 in 1920.

Owen Valley's fate provided a cautionary tale for water development. The water dropped 8,000ft and provided a steady flow until Los Angeles's population exceeded the supply. The reservoir steadily dried up and wind blew toxic dust through Owen's Valley, sickening and driving away residents. Local radicals waged a guerilla war against the canal by dynamiting sections of it. Los Angeles's government sent a hundred policemen and detectives to restore order and protect the canal. As demand surpassed supply, the city extended the canal to Mono Lake 60 miles north of Owens Valley and acquired canals linking Los Angeles and the Colorado River. Los Angeles had another source of water in the 11.4 billion gallon reservoir behind the Saint Francis Dam in San Francisquito valley north of the city. In 1928, that dam collapsed and the cascade wiped out towns and ranches downstream, and drowned over 450 people.

***

Mining experienced a production renaissance from new technologies like cyanide and oil flotations at the turn of the century. That let miners exploit ore from previously discarded tailings and extract ore with gold, silver, or copper as little as one percent. The most productive mining towns included Tonopah and Goldfields, Nevada, Cripple Creek, Colorado, Coeur d'Alene, Idaho, Mercur, Utah, Homestead, South Dakota, Bisbee, Arizona, and Butte, Montana.

Mining made owners rich, gave miners steady incomes while the seams lasted, and enriched consumers with countless products directly or indirectly derived from refined minerals. Yet mining devastated nature. Mines caused deforestation as they consumed enormous amounts of wood for support. The Comstock Lodge alone took 600 million feet of timber as braces and 2 million to fire forges.[17] Mines poisoned waters that people depended on for drinking and irrigation. Mineral refiners belched poisonous clouds into the air and eventually people's lungs, crops, and water.

Mining victims gradually began demanding compensation. The first legal victory came in 1884 when the Ninth Circuit Court of Appeal ruled in *Woodruff versus North Bloomfield et al* that a mining company in California's Central Valley had to pay damages to local farmers for damage to their water and soil. The ruling's broader effect was to empower the government to regulate the discharge of mine wastewater in rivers that provided irrigation and drinking water. The question then was whether Washington would do so. Congress responded by shifting that duty. The 1893 Calminetti Act let states regulate mines on federal lands within their borders. It would be nearly a century before Congress began passing laws that regulated mining.

Mining was the most dangerous occupation.[18] Annually during the 1870s out West, various accidents like cave-ins and explosions killed one of eighty miners and crippled one of thirty.[19] Atop that, mine-owners often cut wages and raised work hours. To alleviate those harsh conditions, the Western Federation of Miners (WFM), founded in 1893, organized strikes at Leadville in 1894, Telluride in 1901, Cripple Creek in 1903 and 1904, and Ludlow in 1914. In 1916, it renamed itself the International Union of Mine, Mill, and Smelter Workers (IUMMSW). Some WFM strikes resulted in violence. Mine owners at Cripple Creek, Colorado, provoked a conflict with miners when they extended the workday from eight to nine hours without a pay raise. During the Cripple Creek strike, a union worker set off a bomb that murdered thirteen non-union workers on June 6, 1904. Governor James Peabody declared martial law and dispatched the National Guard to restore order. The National Guard rounded up 1,562 workers, authorities interrogated them, and the governor had 238 banished from the state. During the WFM's Ludlow strike, seventy-four people died, with the most on April 20, 1914, with the "massacre" in which bullets killed ten men and a child while thirteen women and children suffocated to death hiding beneath a tent that caught fire.

The International Workers of the World (IWW), founded in 1905 and dedicated to a communist revolution, provoked even worse violence.[20] Scores of people died in battles between the IWW and local authorities or in IWW terrorist attacks over the next dozen years. The IWW's leader Big Bill Hayward died non-violently and is buried at the Kremlin in Moscow along with communist journalist John Reed and not far from Vladimir Lenin. Joe Hill, the IWW's unofficial poet laureate, was found guilty of murder and executed in 1915. The IWW strike in Wheatland, California resulted in five deaths and a hundred arrests on August 3, 1914. During the IWW's Centralia, Washington strike in 1919, five members died in a battle with American Legionnaires on November 11.

The IWW either directly committed or indirectly encouraged terrorism. Harrison Otis, who owned the *Los Angeles Times,* rejected any unionization of his workers. On October 1, 1910, two militants and brothers, John and James McNamara, detonated a bomb that murdered twenty-one people at the *Los Angeles Times* building. Police caught the McNamaras who admitted their guilt. A bomb exploded on

Market Street in downtown San Francisco during a Preparedness Day parade on July 22, 1916, killing ten people and wounding forty more. Police arrested anarchists Tom Mooney and Warren Billings, who were convicted and respectively received death and life imprisonment penalties.

The IWW led a copper miner strike in Bisbee, Arizona in 1917. Sheriff Harry Wheeler put out a call for armed volunteers to help him restore order. Over 2,000 appeared. Wheeler and his men rounded up 1,200 IWW strikers, packed them in sealed railway cars, and left them in the desert. Soldiers at a nearby camp opened the doors and released the men who otherwise would likely have suffocated to death from the heat and lack of oxygen.

Among Washington's most disastrous policies were the 1872 Mine Act and 1873 Coal Lands Act that gave away vast amounts of public lands to miners for miniscule fees. President Roosevelt tried and failed to rescind those laws. In 1906, he did designate 66,000,000 acres protected from takeover by private interests and forced some coal companies to return lands that they had fraudulently claimed. President Taft withdrew 3,000,000 more acres from coal company acquisition. President Woodrow Wilson signed the 1920 Lands Leasing Act that henceforth let the Interior Secretary issue two-year leases up to 2,560 acres to corporations to prospect and twenty-year leases if they struck ore, coal, or ore; corporations had to pay a 5 percent annual royalty on oil production and $0.05 to $0.15 for a ton of coal depending on location. The practical effect was continuing to enrich corporations with no significant compensation to the American people who owned those lands.

***

Meanwhile, the United States faced foreign threats. During the 1910s, Mexico collapsed into civil war. Francisco "Pancho" Villa and his rebel army controlled much of northern Mexico as Conventionalists opposed to Constitutionalists headed by President Venustiano Carranza in Mexico City. On March 9, 1916, he led a raid against Columbus, New Mexico in which his men killed ten civilians and eight soldiers and wounded fifteen soldiers. The American troops killed sixty-seven of Villa's men and captured seven. President Woodrow Wilson ordered General John Pershing to lead 6,000 troops into Mexico to destroy Villa and his army. Pershing was an Indian war veteran who was nicknamed "Black Jack" because he once commanded the black 9th Cavalry Regiment. Over the next eleven months, Pershing's expedition fought a series of skirmishes during which it suffered 65 dead, 67 wounded, 24 captured, and three missing while inflicting 168 dead, 155 wounded, and 19 captured on Conventionalists and 82 dead and 51 wounded on Constitutionalists.[21]

Wilson recalled Pershing and his troops on February 7, 1917, as war with Germany appeared increasingly likely. The legacy of America's defeat of Mexico during their war from 1846 to 1848 and purchase of the Southwest from Mexico contributed to Wilson's decision to ask Congress for a war declaration against Germany.

Europe's great powers had been at war since August 1914, with Britain, France, Belgium, Italy, and Russia fighting Germany, Austria, and Turkey. British intelligence intercepted a telegram from German Foreign Minister Arthur Zimmerman to Germany's ambassador in Mexico in January 1917, instructing him to encourage Mexico to war against the United States in return for which Germany would help Mexico regain lands lost to the United States with the 1848 Treaty of Guadeloupe-Hidalgo. The German government did so hoping to bog down the United States in a war against its neighbor as Berlin was about to resume submarine warfare against any ships, including American vessels, steaming with war supplies to its enemies.

Wilson was outraged when he received a copy of Zimmermann's message from Britain, as was the American people when he released it to the press in February. German submarines sank three American ships in March. On April 2, Wilson asked Congress for a war declaration; the Senate voted 82 to 6 in favor on April 4 and the House of Representatives 373 to 50 in favor on April 6.

The Wilson administration eventually mobilized and sent two million troops to France, which proved decisive in breaking the stalemate and defeating Germany. The fighting ended on November 11, 1918. Meanwhile, America's economy expanded with government orders for war goods. Europeans sold off most of their investments in the United States and borrowed billions of dollars from American banks. The United States emerged from World War I as the world's financial and manufacturing powerhouse. That victory came at an enormous cost of 116,708 American dead and 117,466 wounded. Yet those losses were a fraction of the 15 to 22 million soldiers and civilians who died during the war. Wilson failed to get the Senate to ratify the Versailles Treaty that committed the United States to joining a future League of Nations dedicated to international peace. That failure was among the many causes of an even worse world war that erupted a generation later that the United States eventually joined.

World War I affected the West in two vital ways. The demand for food and minerals sharply boosted the West's economy. Of the couple hundred thousand or so westerner volunteers and conscripts, thousands were buried in France and many thousands more came back maimed in body or spirit to their families and communities.

***

Majorities voted for three conservative Republicans dedicated to minimal federal government in the White House from 1921 to 1933. The first two presidents, Warren Harding and Calvin Coolidge, presided over steady economic growth known as the "Roaring Twenties."

The automobile industry was the American economy's growth engine through most of the twentieth century, much like railroads for the nineteenth century and shipbuilding for the eighteenth century. Germans invented the automobile based on a gas-driven internal combustion engine in 1886. An American mechanic built the first car in the United States in 1893. Scores of other entrepreneurs began their own automobile companies. Henry Ford revolutionized the industry with assembly-line mass production of the reliable Model-T in 1908. The price steadily dropped from $850 in 1908 to $300 in 1920. Other automobile producers emulated his production techniques and mass-produced their own popular versions. By 1920, there were 7,500,000 cars and trucks on America's roads, up from 8,000 motor vehicles in 1900.

Automobile associations arose to lobby the federal, state, and local government for paved roads and safety regulations for building and operating vehicles. The National League for Good Roads led that way after its establishment in 1892. Washington and state governments gradually established bureaucracies to deal with those issues. From 1905, the federal Office of Public Roads slowly acquired more regulatory and building powers. In 1912, Congress appropriated $500,000 to improve roads for mail carriers. The American Association of State Highway Officials formed in 1914.

Pressure rose on Washington for a federal road system. Carl Fisher, an Indianapolis entrepreneur, led the way by establishing the transcontinental Lincoln Highway from Times Square in New York City to Lincoln Park in San Francisco in 1913.[22] That route would not be completely paved for a couple of decades. The 1916 Federal Road Act appropriated $75 million to aid state governments with transportation departments to pave roads. A 1921 amendment required states to establish state highway systems that Washington would aid. In 1925, the American Association of State Highway Officials asked Washington for a federal highway system that integrated state systems. The federal government established the Joint Board of Interstate Highways that began designating, numbering, and aiding construction of routes. As for numbers, east-west and north-south routes were respectively even and odd.

Route 66 is America's most beloved twentieth-century national road.[23] In 1926, Cyrus Avery, a Tulsa entrepreneur, conceived the 2,400-mile Route 66 to link Chicago and Los Angeles with his home city around mid-way. The Joint Board officially designated Route 66 on November 11, 1926. That road was not fully paved until 1938.

The state and federal road systems economically boosted each region, especially the isolated, sparsely populated West. Trucks conveyed crops, livestock, and minerals to distant markets at a fraction of previous costs. Cars swiftly carried rural shoppers to nearby towns when the need or desire arose rather than weekly, often day-long round-trip journeys by horse-drawn wagons. Civic organizations swelled with members. Buses gathered farm and ranch kids for schools in town and conveyed passengers between towns, cities, states, and coasts. As trucks and buses conveyed more cargo and passengers, trains lost that business and steadily declined in income, frequency, and service.

An expanding middle class with cars and annual vacations caused a tourism boom, especially across the West at remote national parks and historic sites where neighboring towns profited. For instance, the number of annual visitors to Yosemite rose from 199,000 in 1910 to 920,000 in 1920 to 2,775,000 in 1930.[24] Congress aided that tourism boom with the 1916 National Park Act that established the National Park System with farsighted Stephen Mather its first superintendent, and new national parks Glacier in 1910, Rocky Mountain in 1915, Zion in 1919, and Bryce in 1929.[25]

The oil and automobile industries developed rapidly together during the early twentieth century. Lucky strikes and deeper wells produced soaring amounts of petroleum refined into gasoline to fuel soaring numbers of automobiles produced with increasingly sophisticated assembly line techniques that reduced costs. Ever more oil appeared west of the Mississippi River. The West produced 9 percent of the nation's oil in 1900 and 72 percent in 1911 with most coming from California, Texas, and Oklahoma.[26] The transformation began when a rig at Spindletop Field near Beaumont, Texas struck a geyser in January 1901. John Rockefeller's Standard Oil monopoly controlled 90 percent of the nation's oil until 1911 when an anti-trust suit broke up that corporation into separate businesses.

The Teapot Dome scandal of the 1920s provoked the latest round in the perennial debate over the fate of natural resources on public lands.[27] President Harding transferred control over naval oil reserves from the Navy Department to the Interior Department in 1921. Interior Secretary Albert Fall then leased three naval oil reserves at Teapot Dome in Wyoming and Elk Hill and Buena Vista in California to two oil magnates, Henry Sinclair of Sinclair Oil Corporation and Edward Doheny of Pan American Petroleum and Transport Company at below market rates without any competitive bids in 1922. A congressional investigation revealed that Fall had received a $100,000 no-interest "loan" from Doheny and $404,000 in additional gifts from Sinclair and Doheny. Congress returned the naval oil reserves to the Navy Department in 1927. A jury convicted Fall of felony bribery charges in 1929.

***

Agribusiness experienced a productivity revolution during the early twentieth century. Tractors, fertilizers, herbicides, and pesticides made it easier to plow and harvest more crops. The hours to nurture an acre of crops fell from 58 hours in 1830 to three in 1930.[28] Congress accelerated that productivity revolution with more laws that eased the ability of families and businesses to own or exploit federal lands like the 1909 Enlarged Homestead Act that increased free acreage from 160 to 320 and the 1919 Stock Raising Homestead Act that increased free acreage to 640.

Farm income rose steadily in the twentieth century's first two decades. With crop prices indexed at 100 in 1899, they reached 189.2 by 1910 then nearly doubled during World War I when Europeans demanded ever more food and other crops to meet the demand of their armies and their reduced farm production. Typically bust followed boom. Farm income declined steadily from the height of $17,600,000,000 in 1919 to $6,900,000,000 in 1931.[29] A complex of reasons caused that. Ever more farmers used tractors, pesticides, and herbicides to increase production while European farms returned to full productivity after World War I. Rising supply and falling demand in foreign markets caused commodity prices to fall. Farmers reacted by growing more crops that further swelled supplies and so cut prices. The number of trucks on American farms skyrocketed from 25,000 in 1915 to 1,490,000 in 1945. Farmers had more land to farm because cars and trucks replaced wagons and buggies drawn by horses. Pastures along with hay and oat crops were transformed into croplands that fed humans. Most farmers borrowed money to pay for the tractors, other equipment, pesticides, and fertilizers that produced more crops. Falling income made servicing that debt increasingly difficult and for many impossible. Bank foreclosures on farm rose steadily. The farm population peaked at 31,393,000 in 1920 then dropped to 30,2216,000 in 1940.[30]

To alleviate that vicious cycle of worsening problems, progressives in Congress devised the McNary-Haugen Farm Relief Act that empowered the federal government to maintain commodity prices at their average level from 1910 to 1914 by establishing an agency that bought surplus crops, stored them, and sold them to foreign countries. Business interests pressured President Coolidge to veto versions of that bill in 1927 and 1928.

Irrigation water was critical to agribusiness in the West. Commerce Department Secretary Herbert Hoover negotiated the Colorado River Pact with seven states split between Upper Basin Wyoming, Colorado, New Mexico, and Utah, and Lower Basin Nevada, Arizona, and California in 1922.[31] The Bureau of Reclamation estimated that the river's annual flow was 17.5 million acre feet; that proved to be a gross overestimation with the actual figure about two-thirds of that. Mexico eventually demanded a set share of the river. The 1944 Treaty for Utilization of the Waters of the Rio Grande, Colorado, and Tijuana Rivers empowered the International Boundary and Water Commission to ensure that each country received constant shares of those three rivers. For the Colorado, Washington annually allocated Mexico 1.5 million acre feet.

***

Racism persisted across much of the West for much of the twentieth century. The revival of thc white supremacist organization the Ku Klux Klan spearheaded racism during the 1920s. The Klan emerged in the former southern rebel states during Reconstruction to terrorize newly liberated blacks who sought to vote, run for office, and run businesses that competed with whites. The 1872 Ku Klux Klan Act empowered the federal government to repress that terrorist organization. Federal marshals, prosecutors, and troops succeeded in doing so by the mid-1870s. The Klan revived during the 1910s as a backlash against blacks across the south and Catholic, Jewish, and Asian immigrants in cities and rural regions. The Klan was especially powerful in several western states, Texas, Oklahoma, and Oregon.

The worst race riot occurred in Tulsa, Oklahoma on May 31 and June 1, 1921.[32] On the morning of May 31, Sarah Page, a 17-year-old elevator operator, accused Dick Rowland, a 19-year-old black man, of sexually assaulting her. After the police arrested Rowland, around seventy-five black men from Greenwood District, a prosperous black neighborhood, armed themselves, packed into cars, and drove to the police station where Rowland was held. When a police officer tried to take a pistol from one of the men, it discharged. The blacks opened fire and police returned fire. Ten whites and two blacks died in the firefight. The blacks returned to Greenwood District. That night and the following day, a mob of hundreds of whites attacked Greenwood to loot and burn 1,356 homes and 191 businesses causing $1.5 million of real estate and $750,000 of private property damage, killed at least 24 blacks, injured at least 183, and forced thousands to flee, according to the Oklahoma Department of Vital Statistics. Death estimates by other investigators ranged from 75 to 300.

Foreigners, especially Asians, Latin Americans, and Africans, were another racist target. The 1921 National Origins Act and its tougher 1924 version imposed quotas on immigrants by national origin with the largest numbers given Europeans and miniscule numbers other regions around the world. Two foreign residents sued to become citizens and the Supreme Court decided their cases. In *Takeo Ozawa versus the United States* (1922), the Supreme Court ruled that Ozawa, who was born in Japan but had been an American resident since 1894, was ineligible because the 1906 Naturalization Act limited citizenship to "free white persons" or persons of African nativity or persons of African descent. In *United States versus Bhagat Sigh Thind* (1923), Thind argued that with his northern India origins he had Indo-Aryan ancestry and so was a Caucasian. The Court ruled that a "common sense definition" of white person denied that Thind was a white and thus eligible.

***

America's Great Depression began with the stock market's collapse in October 1929. Throughout the late 1920s, the gap widened between stock prices and the value of the companies they represented, driven by speculative greed. The frenzied buying turned to frenzied selling when speculators feared the market would plummet, which became a self-fulfilling prophecy. President Herbert Hoover exacerbated the Great Depression first by actually cutting the federal budget to reduce the national debt then by signing the 1930 Smoot-Hawley Act that raised tariffs on imports 50 percent, which devastated world trade when foreign countries retaliated. The only significant step Hoover and Congress took to alleviate the economy was establishing the Reconstruction Finance Corporation (RFC) that provided low interest loans to businesses.

Prolonged drought and farmer practices of plowing virtually all earth on one's land produced the "Dust Bowl," devastating wind storms that blew away much of the southern Great Plains soil during the 1930s.[33] The worst years were 1934 with twenty-two regional storms, 1935 with forty, 1937 with sixty-eight, and 1938 with seventy-two. The Dust Bowl's epicenter was the Texas and Oklahoma panhandles and southwest Kansas. By 1938, around 250,000 square miles of once productive soil had blown away leaving wasteland behind. Winds carried the soil across the nation and inflicted brownouts in cities as far as Washington and New York. "Okie" was the derogatory term for the 750,000 desperate people who fled the Dust Bowl to California and other regions where most lived in squalid squatter camps and performed menial jobs like picking fruit to survive. Dorothea Lange's photos and John Steinbeck's novel *The Grapes of Wrath* (1939) brilliantly conveyed the demoralization, poverty, and hunger those refugees suffered.

10.1 American Gross National Product: Depression, New Deal, and World War II[34]

Year	Nominal GDP (trillions)	Real GDP (trillions)	Real Percentage Change
1929	$0.105	$1.109	
1930	$0.092	$1.015	-8.5
1931	$0.077	$0.950	-6.4
1932	$0.060	$0.828	-12.9
1933	$0.057	$0.817	-1.2
1934	$0.067	$0.906	10.8
1935	$0.074	$0.986	8.9
1936	$0.085	$1.113	12.9
1937	$0.093	$1.170	5.1
1938	$0.087	$1.132	-3.3
1939	$0.093	$1.222	8.0
1940	$0.103	$1.330	8.8
1941	$0.129	$1.566	17.7
1942	$0.166	$1.862	18.9
1943	$0.203	$2.178	17.0
1944	$0.224	$2.352	28.0
1945	$0.228	$2.329	-1.0

Democratic candidate Franklin Roosevelt crushed Hoover in the 1932 election with 57.4 percent of the vote and 472 electors to 39.6 percent and 59 electors. Democrats won majorities in Congress, with 58 to 37 Republican and one Farmer-Labor Party Senate seats, and 313 to 117 Republican and five Farmer-Labor House of Representatives seats. Roosevelt was an open-minded pragmatist, a Hamiltonian. He explained the "New Deal" outlook: "We can no longer escape into virgin territory; we must master our environment . . . We have been compelled by stark necessity to unlearn the too comfortable superstition that the American soil was mystically blessed with every kind of immunity to grave economic maladjustments, and that the American spirit of individualism—all alone and unhelped by the cooperative efforts of government—could withstand and repel every form of economic disarrangement or crisis."[35]

His policies to fight first the Great Depression then the Second World War transformed America, especially the West.[36] No region economically benefited more from the array of government programs than the West, which received $7,582,434,000 from an array of New Deal programs from 1933 to 1939.[37] Historian Gerald Nash explained those revolutionary changes: "It transformed a colonial economy based on the exploitation of raw materials into a diversified economy that included industrial and technological components. It spawned another significant population boom and brought unprecedented expansion to most western cities. It greatly diversified the ethnic and racial composition of the West . . . It opened up new opportunities for Native Americans at the same time it created new problems for them. In addition, it unveiled new directions for science in the West and served to quicken and deepen the cultural life of the region."[38]

The Civilian Conservation Corps (CCC) was among the most successful New Deal programs. Men joined to receive a monthly salary, live in barracks or tents, and eat three daily meals in return for restoring eroded soils, replanting clearcut forests, building hiking trails, improving flood control, and fighting fires. Eventually 2 million men participated in the CCC that gave them meaningful work, discipline, training, and dignity in return for repairing America's severely damaged natural heritage. The West accounted for the lion's share of CCC projects and camps.

Roosevelt launched a series of programs to alleviate the plight of farmers, especially in the hard-pressed West.[39] The 1933 Agricultural Adjustment Act established the Agricultural Adjustment Administration (AAA) that bought and stored surplus crops to maintain steady prices. The Farm Security Administration, Farm

Credit Administration, and Resettlement Administration provided an array of aid to the needy. Roosevelt formed a Great Plains Drought Committee and the Committee on the Future of the Great Plains to study the crises and propose solutions. The Interior Department established the Soil Erosion Service to help farmers conserve their soil in 1933 and renamed it the Soil Conservation Service in 1935. The 1936 Soil Conservation and Domestic Allotment Act set up programs that taught farmers to contour and terrace farm. Meanwhile, the Forest Service eventually planted 200 million trees to stabilize and replenish soil destroyed by the Dust Bowl.

As for livestock, the Drought Relief Service bought 8,000,000 cattle from June 1934 to January 1935, disposed the sick and fattened the rest then sold them to meatpackers. The 1934 Taylor Grazing Act attempted to restore federal lands devastated by overgrazing by ranchers. Henceforth, ranchers who wanted to graze their livestock on public land had to get permits and pay fees for each animal. The Grazing Service designated 142 million acres of public lands for grazing, determined the carrying capacity of each ecosystem, and limited livestock on each to sustain the grass.[40]

Several dam projects initiated decades earlier were completed during the 1930s. Many were engineering marvels. Construction on Hoover Dam began on November 13, 1932, and ended on March 23, 1935; Hoover Dam is 1,255ft wide, 726ft high, 660ft thick at the base and 45ft thick at the top, and is composed of 66 million tons of concrete.[41] Fort Peck Dam was a 3.7-mile long earthen dam on the upper Missouri River. The Bureau of Reclamation also finished Bonneville Dam on the Columbia River in 1937 and Grand Coulee Dam on the Missouri River in 1941. Dams on rivers flowing into the Pacific devastated the salmon that swam up those rivers to breed. The Fish and Wildlife Service established fisheries to breed and release salmon and other species that dams had destroyed.

Roosevelt ended the series of Homestead Acts in 1935 by proclaiming protection for the remaining 165.7 million acres and imposing "sustained-yield" standards for exploiting renewable natural resources on federal lands. Henceforth, businesses could only cut trees, graze cattle, or divert water to the extent that those resources naturally replenished themselves. That provoked howls from lumber, ranching, and farm interests.

Four other programs were especially effective in developing the economy and alleviating poverty. The 1933 Works Progress Act established the Works Progress Administration (WPA) and Public Works Administration (PWA) that funded local projects like post offices, administrative buildings, bridges, roads, and other infrastructure. The 1933 National Industry Recovery Act permitted workers to form unions. In 1935, the pragmatist American Federation of Labor (AFL) and socialist Congress of Industrial Organizations (CIO) joined to form the AFL-CIO. The 1935 Social Security Act established the Social Security Administration to provide pensions to retired and disabled people.

***

Roosevelt was also committed to alleviating conditions for Indians.[42] Their plight legally reached a nadir in 1902 when the Supreme Court ruled in *Lone Wolf v. Hitchcock* that Congress had "plenary" or absolute powers over Indian policy and could even void treaties between Washington and the tribes. Indian Bureau directives in 1883, 1921, and 1922 prevented Indians from freely following their traditional religions including such practices as the Sun Dance, potlatch, and even dancing. The Indian Bureau outlawed the American Indian Church that used the hallucinogen peyote as a sacrament.

Thereafter Indians won a series of political and legal victories that eventually granted them equal rights with other Americans. The first victory came in *Winters v. the United States* (1908) when the Supreme Court for the first time affirmed that reservations had water rights. Washington conferred citizenship on Indians in 1924. Yet Indians still lacked full control over their reservations or spirituality.

John Collier was determined to change that.[43] He came to deeply appreciate Indian spirituality after spending time with the Pueblo Indians in 1920. He protested government restrictions on Indian spiritual practices, arguing that they violated the Constitution's protection of religious freedom. He summarized his views in his 1924 pamphlet "The Indian and Religious Freedom" published by the American Indian Defense Association. For a dozen years, Collier was an articulate impassioned voice crying in the political wilderness. Then, in 1933, Roosevelt appointed him Indian Bureau commissioner. In 1934, Collier issued the pamphlet "Indian Religious Freedom and Indian Culture" that called for liberating Indians from existing restrictions, including mandatory Christian classes in government Indian schools. That inspired majorities in Congress to pass the 1934 Indian Reorganization Act. That law halted the privatization of Indian lands, gave greater authority to tribal councils, and provided tribes with grants and low interest loans to promote economic development. Each tribe could freely choose whether to follow the

Indian Reorganization Act. By then, many people had accepted privatization and Christianity. The result was that 181 tribes with 129,750 people accepted and 77 tribes with 86,365 people rejected that law.[44] The 1935 Indian Arts and Crafts Act freed Indians to market their goods beyond reservations. The 1936 Oklahoma Indian Welfare Act alleviated poverty for that state's tribes. Collier steadily closed Indian boarding schools while increasing the number of day schools on reservations. He also expanded reservation lands from 47 million to 56 million acres.

***

During World War II, Washington achieved full employment with federal contracts for munitions, equipment, weapons, provisions, uniforms, and other vital war supplies along with building and manning scores of military bases. Those policies pumped money, jobs, and infrastructure into every region and was especially welcomed in poorer regions. The West received the lion's share, over $70 billion from 1941 to 1945.[45]

California received 12 percent of all government procurement dollars and war spending accounted for 45 percent of the state's economy for the war years. San Francisco Bay, Long Beach, and San Diego hosted the region's most shipyards, factories, warehouses, and oil depots. Southern California's aircraft industry alone employed 243,000 workers at its peak production in 1943. Throughout the war, Washington procured $7,093,370 worth of aircraft production from Los Angeles. Another $4.7 billion went to shipyards with complexes in San Francisco Bay and Long Beach near Los Angeles employing 280,000 workers in 1943.[46]

The Defense Plant Corporation (DPC), a Reconstruction Finance Corporation (RFC) subsidiary, worked with private businesses to establish or transform factories for war production. That program created entire industries that the private sector could not do alone by providing 96 percent of the money for new rubber plants, 90 percent for magnesium plants, 71 percent for aircraft plants, and 58 percent for aluminum plants. The DPC underwrote fourteen of the fifteen largest aircraft plants west of the Mississippi River. In all, the DPC spent $1,853,634,000 building 344 factories across the West. The Metals Reserve Corporation was another RFC subsidiary that boosted the West's economy by buying $275,000,000 worth of its minerals.[47] Three of the $2 billion Manhattan Project's four vital facilities to build atomic weapons were in the West, at Los Alamos, New Mexico, Hanford, Washington, and Livermore, California while the fourth was at Oak Ridge, Tennessee. Washington developed both the natural and synthetic rubber industries. The Agriculture Department bought the rights and property of the only private American producer of natural rubber, the International Rubber Company. The Forestry Department planted 45,000 acres of rubber trees. Meanwhile, the federal Rubber Reserve Corporation built twenty-three factories mostly on the West Coast or in Texas.[48] Industrial complexes consumed enormous amounts of electricity. During the previous two decades, Washington's Bureau of Land Reclamation and Army Corps of Engineers developed a series of dams that generated hydroelectricity. For instance, Bonneville Dam and Grand Coulee Dam on the Columbia River supplied the hydroelectric power that fueled Boeing Corporation factories in Seattle and the Hanford nuclear energy plant on the Columbia. The Roosevelt White House worried that the array of programs was creating business oligopolies. In June 1942, the administration got Congress to establish the Smaller War Plants Corporation to nurture factories that supplied critical niche products.

Even Hollywood got into the act. The Office of War Information worked with the movie industry to produce dramatic and documentary films that boosted morale and support for the war, a critical source of soft psychological power. The 80 million Americans who weekly went to the movies were a huge audience. Producer Walter Wanger explained that, "American film is our most important weapon as no other country has developed its film industry to compete with ours. The problem of enlightenment of the masses is the greatest visual educational factor accepted by the masses."[49]

Washington also underwrote long-term research and education. The Office of Scientific Research and Development (OSRD) distributed $99 million among western universities. For instance, Washington subsidies, guidance, and contracts helped California's Institute of Technology and the University of California at Berkely establish respectively the Jet Propulsion Laboratory and the Radiation Laboratory. The 1944 General Infantry (GI) bill provided veterans with money for higher education, unemployment, and housing.

10.2 Major War Supply Contracts and War Facilities, 1940–5 in dollars[50]

Supply Contracts, June 1940–September 1945			Facilities, June 1940–June 1945	
State	Combat Supply	Other Supply	Industrial	Military
Arizona	94,854,000	31,115,000	100,592,000	134,116,000
California	14,255,117,000	2,195,524,000	1,013,778,000	1,511,447,000
Colorado	244,634,000	116,920,000	170,350,000	174,479,000
Idaho	12,049,000	6,421,000	17,049,000	101,992,000
Montana	12,966,000	15,081,000	12,956,000	41,106,000
Nevada	1,521,000	32,402,000	151,542,000	88,050,000
New Mexico	11,133,000	9,356,000	13,325,000	101,506,000
North Dakota	1,582,000	5,938,000	120,000	1,572,000
Oregon	1,629,809,000	182,829,000	100,603,000	163,842,000
South Dakota	201,000	4,584,000	150,000	65,908,000
Texas	3,749,561,000	2,224,979,000	1,166,836,000	837,582,000
Utah	79,136,000	34,345,000	284,394,000	153,097,000
Washington	3,408,305,000	379,331,000	341,058,000	327,949,000
Wyoming	12,770,000	68,419,000	25,535,000	23,431,000

Eventually 14,000,000 Americans served in the armed forces during World War II. That depleted work forces in industry and agriculture. Washington alleviated those shortages with women of all races, Hispanics, African Americans, and foreign laborers. A poster of "Rosey the Riveter," a female factory worker confidently raising her fist, became a national icon. The Bracero Program jointly overseen by the Agriculture Department's Farm Security Administration and the Department of Justice's Immigration and Naturalization Bureau employed 309,538 foreign workers, including 219,000 Mexicans, at farms and other industries on half-year renewable contracts; the government paid transportation costs and required employers to provide minimal pay, health, and housing benefits for the workers. Nearly a million blacks, mostly from the South, emigrated to western states, especially California, to work in defense industries; 340,000 blacks moved to Los Angeles and 125,000 to San Francisco and Oakland.[51]

The populations of both Pacific and Mountain western states expanded during the war, the former significantly from 9,824,000 to 13,060,000, and the latter slightly from 4,172,000 to 4,237,000. The Pacific state's population soared 38.9 percent compared to a national average of 8.7 percent. San Diego's population increased 147 percent from 1941 to 1945.[52] Among the Mountain states, New Mexico, Arizona, Utah, Nevada gained people while Montana, Idaho, Wyoming, and Colorado lost them. The Office of War Mobilization and Economic Stabilization, Coordinator of Defense Housing Agency, and War Manpower Commission helped find housing for all those migrants.

10.3 Population Changes in Western States, 1940–5[53]

Division and State	1940	1945
Mountain States	4,172,000	4,237,000
Montana	556,000	463,000
Idaho	524,000	509,000
Wyoming	250,000	244,000
Colorado	1,133,000	1,118,000
New Mexico	534,000	539,000
Arizona	509,000	602,000
Utah	554,000	612,000
Nevada	112,000	148,000
Pacific	9,824,000	13,060,000
Washington	1,751,000	2,274,000
Oregon	1,100,000	1,294,000
California	6,982,000	9,491,000

During the war, 21,767 Indians served in the armed forces and 40,000 worked in industries or agriculture. The most celebrated Indian contribution to the war was the 500 or so radio "code talkers" who mostly spoke Navajo but also Comanche and Lakota that the enemy never understood. Two Indians won Congressional Medals of Honor and 71 others earned Air Medals. Ira Hayes, a Pima, was among the Marines that raised the flag on Iwo Jima's Mount Suribachi. General Clarence Tinker, an Osage, was the highest-ranking Indian.

Those contributions to the war effort encouraged Indians to organize politically. Delegates from around thirty tribes met at the National Congress of American Indians in Denver from November 15 to 18,

1944. They dedicated the National Congress of American Indians "to enlighten the public toward a better understanding of the Indian race; to preserve Indian cultural values; to seek an equitable adjustment of tribal affairs, to secure and to preserve rights under Indian treaties with the United States."[54]

Ethnic and racial discrimination and even violence marred the war years. The worst violence in the West erupted in Los Angeles. Hispanic gang members in Los Angeles wore baggy "zoot suits" and called themselves "*pachucos*," although the term originated with El Paso gangs. In August 1942, a murder by one gang member of another gang's member provoked a police crackdown that rounded up over 300 suspects. Fights erupted between gangs and military personnel on leave in April, May, and from June 3 to 13, 1943. Fortunately, no one was killed or seriously injured and property damage was limited. What was dubbed the "zoot suit riots" revealed chronic underlying prejudices and tensions.[55]

The federal government committed its worst violation of a group's constitutional rights against Japanese-Americans during World War II. Japanese-Americans numbered 126,947 on the mainland United States, 157,905 in Hawaii, and 263 in Alaska, or 285,115 altogether in 1940. Japanese Americans distinguished themselves between first (Issei) and second (Nisei) generations. Most were Nisei born in the United States and so American citizens while over 100,000 were Issei who remained alien residents. In the months after Japan's attack on Pearl Harbor, the FBI arrested around 1,500 alien Japanese residents on suspicion of espionage and interned them under custody of the Immigration and Naturalization Service (INS).[56]

President Roosevelt issued Executive Order 9066 empowering the army to designate "military areas" and remove from them "any or all persons" considered a security threat on February 18, 1942.[57] On March 2, General John Dewitt, who commanded the Western Defense Command headquartered at San Francisco, declared two military zones that included California, Oregon, Washington, and Arizona, and informed Japanese Americans that they would have to leave those states or else be interned. To enforce those zones, Roosevelt established the War Relocation Authority on March 18. About 5,000 Japanese Americans migrated from those regions to other states. On March 24, Dewitt issued the first of 108 internment orders over the next five months to intern Japanese communities that was completed by August. Eventually 120,313 Japanese-Americans suffered internment, including 111,236 from the West Coast, 1,118 from Hawaii, and 1,735 from elsewhere. They were split among ten camps, of which most were former Civilian Conservation Corps (CCC) facilities at remote western sites.

That policy was extremely popular. An American Institute of Public Opinion survey found that 93 percent of Americans approved and 1 percent opposed interning Japanese alien residents and 59 percent approved and 39 percent opposed interning Japanese American citizens.[58] Meanwhile, Congress repealed the 1882 Chinese Exclusionary Act in 1943, legalized the existing Chinese population in the United States and let others become residents.

The internment policy had a contradiction and a violation. The order did not affect Japanese-Americans in Hawaii, certainly far more vulnerable for possible espionage and sabotage. Under international law, a government can intern alien residents of an enemy country but not one's own citizens. By interning American citizens, the Roosevelt administration grossly violated their constitutional rights. The Supreme Court issued two crucial rulings on December 18, 1943. In *Korematsu versus United States*, the justices unanimously ruled that interning foreign Japanese residents was constitutional under the due process principle. In *Ex Parte Endo*, they unanimously ruled that citizens could not be held without charges. That let Japanese American citizens leave the camps although resident aliens still had to stay. Until then the only way to leave the camps was for men to enlist in a special regiment established for Japanese Americans, the 442nd. Eventually over 14,000 men served in the 442nd which fought in Italy and received the most combat awards of any American unit, twenty-one Medals of Honor and eight unit presidential citations. Eventually Japanese Americans found justice, although far too little far too late. The Ninth Circuit Court of Appeals ruled in 1987 that the United States had illegally interned Japanese-American citizens during World War II. In 1988, Congress passed the Civil Liberties Act that apologized for the illegal internment of Japanese-American citizens and paid compensation to the survivors or their heirs.

***

America's economy and population "boomed" after the war for a generation until 1973. Wartime shortages and full employment led to unprecedented savings that people spent on consumer goods or invested in businesses. Fourteen million men and women took off their uniforms to get jobs or go to college, and get married. The pent-up demand for sex and children was just as profound, leading to the "baby boom" generation. Low priced loans for automobiles and homes spread suburbs around cities. The Cold War with the Soviet Union and communist movements worldwide also fueled economic growth by continued federal spending for the military industrial complex. American policies that aided the reconstruction of Western Europe and Japan transformed them from mass poverty, destruction, and despair vulnerable to a communist revolution to mass prosperity that demanded American goods and services. All those forces combined to propel a virtuous economic cycle of rising spending, investments, incomes, education levels, construction, productivity, exports, imports, population, more spending, and so on. Soaring populations and sprawling suburbs had a dark side with worsening smog, traffic jams, "ticky tacky houses," and ugly strip malls.

That boom enriched the West more than other regions, especially "sunbelt" cities where factories, workers, and retirees moved for less expensive lifestyles.[59] In 1980, the Southwest boasted five of the top ten largest metropolises that included Los Angeles, Houston, Dallas, San Diego, and Phoenix. California led America's postwar baby boom and suburbanization. The state's population swelled from 6,907,000 in 1940 to 23,667,764 in 1980, with nearly eight of ten people living in the two largest metropolitan areas Los Angeles with 12,738,000 and San Francisco with 5,809,000. Neighboring Arizona also boomed with its two largest cities, Phoenix and Tucson, respectively soaring from 65,000 to 1,422,000 and from 36,818 to 453,000 between 1940 and 1980. Water from three sources sustained that growth, Hoover Dam on the Colorado, the Central Arizona Project of dam complexes on the Gila and Salt Rivers, and aquifers across the state. Electricity from hydroelectric dams and coal-fired power plants fueled the air conditioners that made those cities livable during scorching summers. Suburban sprawl and pollution afflicted Phoenix and Tucson like other western cities.

The most astonishing transformation was that of Las Vegas, Nevada, just five hours by car from Los Angeles. Los Vegas's population rocketed from 8,422 in 1940 to 438,000 in 1980. The entrepreneurship of flamboyant characters like Howard Hughes, Bugsy Siegel, and Steve Wynn boosted that expansion. Mobster Siegel revolutionized the gambling industry by investing in the Golden Nugget and Frontier Club casinos and the Flamingo Hotel on Sunset Strip from 1942 to 1946; rival gangsters had Siegel murdered at the Flamingo in 1947.

Postwar affluence and the baby boom led ever more Americans to enjoy a couple of weeks annual vacation. Many increasingly passed those weeks on the road with the West's stunning landscapes, national parks, and historic sites among favorites. Symbolically if not substantively, the 2,448-mile Route 66 from Chicago to Los Angeles was America's best-known road after World War II. In 1946, that road got two big boosts. Songwriter Bobby Troup celebrated it with his 1946 "Got My Kicks from Route 66" and Jack Rittenhouse wrote the first guidebook for Route 66. From 1947, the Main Street of America Highway Association promoted Route 66.

The 1956 Federal Aid Highway Act established the National System of Interstate and Defense Highways paid by a tax on gasoline, tires, motor oil, buses, and trucks funneled into the Federal Highway Trust Fund. The interstate system boosted the national economy often at the expense of towns that did not receive a nearby exit. Of the regions, the West benefited most as superhighways linked its swelling cities with the rest of the nation. Alas, for nostalgia-lovers an expressway eventually overrode nearly all of Route 66.

All along, Cold War programs stimulated the national economy, nowhere more than at factories, research institutions, and military bases across the West. A major expansion of spending came after the Soviet Union beat the United States into space by launching its Sputnik satellite in 1957. That provoked fears that the Soviets had surpassed Americans in scientific expertise. The Eisenhower administration and Congress responded with the 1958 National Defense Education Act that helped sponsor and fund scientific research and education at universities, corporations, and research institutes with the West enjoying the lion's share.

***

Washington passed two conservation laws that especially affected the West. In 1946, Congress established the Bureau of Land Management for all public lands that were not part of the National Park system. The 1960 Multiple Use-Sustained Yield Act required the Forest Service to restrict logging to a rate that let forests replenish themselves to keep the same tree supply.

A Cassandra warned of mostly hidden dangers lurking in ever more cities and landscapes across America. Rachel Carson was a scientist and environmentalist whose 1962 book *Silent Spring* exposed how the unregulated discharge of pesticides, herbicides, fertilizers, and other often carcinogenic chemicals devastated species and posed a worsening threat to humanity. She explained that: "we have put poisonous and biologically potent chemicals indiscriminately in the hands of persons largely or wholly ignorant of their potentials for harm. We have subjected enormous numbers of people to contact with theses poisons, without their consent and often without their knowledge . . .

This is an era of specialists, each of whom sees his own problems and is unaware of or intolerant of the larger frame in which it fits. It is also an era dominated by industry, in which the right to make a dollar at whatever cost is seldom challenged."[60]

***

John Kennedy briefly served as president from his inauguration on January 20, 1961 until his assassination on November 22, 1963. His lasting achievements were more symbolic than substantive. He delivered some brilliantly written speeches with western themes and allusions that expressed ideal versions of America's history, culture, and future. In July 1960, during his acceptance speech for the presidential nomination at the Democratic Party convention in Los Angles, he offered these inspiring words: "I stand tonight facing west on what was once the last frontier. From the lands that stretch 3000 miles behind me, the pioneers of old gave up their safety, their comfort, and sometimes their lives to build a new world here in the West . . . But the problems are not all solved and the battles are not all won, and we stand today on the edge of a new frontier—the frontier of the 1960s, a frontier of unknown opportunities and paths, a frontier of unfulfilled hope and threats."[61] In a 1963 speech, he eloquently explained the paradoxical relationship between Americans and the natural world they depend on for their prosperity: "The history of America is, more than most nations, the history of man confronted by nature . . . It has been the story of a rich and varied natural heritage shaping American institutions and American values, and it has been equally the story of Americans seizing, using, squandering, and, belatedly, protecting and developing that heritage." He called on Americans to "expand the concept of conservation to meet the imperious problems of the new age . . . in order to recover the relationship between man and nature and to make sure that the national estate we pass on to our multiplying descendants is green and flourishing."[62]

Lyndon Johnson actually fulfilled many of Kennedy's promises after replacing him in the White House. Johnson was the most genuine western-born president. He grew up on a hardscrabble farm in the Texas Hill Country and later developed his own ranch. He graduated from teacher's college, was a high school teacher, then won election to the House of Representatives in 1937, the Senate in 1948, became Majority Whip in 1951, Majority Leader in 1954, and vice president in 1960. He was a brilliant politician on both the election circuit and backroom dealmaking. He was a fervent believer in Roosevelt's New

Deal whose programs helped transform the Texas Hill Country from poverty to prosperity with paved roads, electricity, and irrigation. He dedicated his administration to achieving a Great Society in America that eliminated poverty and racism, and provided equal opportunity for people to better themselves through education and entrepreneurship, and to live longer, heathier lives.

During the 1964 election, two western-born candidates faced off for the first and so far only time. Johnson's opponent was Republican Party candidate Barry Goldwater, a senator from Arizona since 1952 and fiercely opposed to the array of "Big Government" New Deal and Great Society programs and policies. Johnson decisively trounced Goldwater with 61.9 percent of the vote and 486 electors to 38.5 percent and 52 electors. Johnson won every western state except Goldwater's Arizona and five Deep South states. That stunning result appeared to make the West as liberal as most of the rest of the country. Yet Goldwater exemplified the conservatism budding across the West and the growing economic and political power of "sunbelt states" that would blossom within a generation.

The excesses of Johnson's Great Society programs and commitment to an expanding war in Indochina were major reasons for the West's political transformation. Many Americans condemned the welfare and affirmative action programs as worsening joblessness, crime, poverty, neglected children, reverse discrimination, taxes, and national debt. In Indochina, over 58,000 Americans died and hundreds of thousands were wounded in a war that the United States ultimately lost. Race riots and anti-war protests plagued Washington and scores of other cities.

The Civil Rights movement sought to overturn laws and policies that discriminated against blacks. In the West, Texas and Oklahoma had especially egregious Jim Crow laws that limited the rights of blacks to attend good schools, live in white neighborhoods, and vote and run for public office. Congress passed and Johnson signed three laws that eliminated racial discrimination at the federal level, the 1964 Civil Rights Law, the 1965 Voting Rights Law, and the 1968 Housing Rights Law. Most states enacted similar laws. That legal revolution helped stimulate a cultural evolution of growing toleration among racial, ethnic, and religious groups.

Yet violence and riots accompanied the Civil Rights Movement. Countless black neighborhoods in inner cities across the nation were locked into vicious cycles of mass poverty, joblessness, crime, corrupt and inept officials, empty buildings, bad public schools and other services, and brain drain of the brightest and most ambitious individuals. Tensions between residents and police were hair triggered. Watts was and remains a mostly black Los Angeles district trapped in that vicious cycle. A police arrest of a drunk black driver led to riots that left thirty-four people dead, hundreds of stores looted and burned, and $40 million worth of damage from August 11 to 16, 1965. The Black Panthers were the most powerful radical black group dedicated to armed insurrection against the United States. Huey Newton, Bobby Seale, and Eldridge Cleaver founded the Black Panthers in Oakland, California in 1966, and they rapidly established branches in inner cities across the country. Scores of police, Black Panthers, and people caught in crossfires died in shootings.

American Indians had their own civil rights movement with moderate and radical wings.[63] That activism grew exponentially after World War II. The National Congress of American Indians (NCAI) formed during a conference of a hundred delegates from forty tribes at Denver in 1944. Pan-Indian groups eventually included the National Tribal Chairmen's Association, National Indian Youth Council, Native American Rights Fund, Council of Energy Resource Tribes, National Indian Youth Council, Society of American Indians, National Congress of American Indians, National Indian Education Association, and American Indian Movement.

Their pressure resulted in some key reforms. Under the 1946 Indian Claims Commission Act, the United States established an Indian Claims Commission to hear cases of treaty violations by tribes. From 1953 to 1978, tribes submitted 852 suits that were consolidated into 370 petitions split among 617 dockets of which they won 58 percent by the time the Commission dissolved in 1978. The reward was usually money that eventually totaled $818 million rather than land.[64] The 1968 Indian Civil Rights Act explicitly granted them full constitutional rights. The 1975 Indian Self-Determination and Education Assistance Act and the 1976 Indian Health Care Improvement Act respectively increased funding for schools and clinics. The Supreme Court acknowledged the inherent limited sovereignty of Indian tribes in *United States versus Wheeler* (1978).

Inspired by black radicals, Indian radicals called for "Red Power." In 1968, a group of ex-convict Sioux and Chippewas including most prominently Dennis Banks, Russell Means, and Leonard Peltier formed the American Indian Movement (AIM). Two hundred AIM activists occupied Alcatraz Island on November 20, 1969, and offered to buy it for $24-worth of trinkets; they held Alcatraz until federal marshals arrested and removed them on June 11, 1971. During a mass protest against "the Trail of Broken Treaties" in Washington in 1972, a group of AIM activists overran and ransacked the Bureau of Indian Affairs. AIM took over Wounded Knee on the Pine Ridge reservation on February 27, 1973, and killed two FBI agents. A collection of FBI agents, BIA agents, and federal marshals converged to surround the compound. The siege lasted 71 days until the radicals surrendered on May 8, 1973. Peltier was convicted of murder.

A key element of the American Indian Movement was for Indians to have pride in being themselves. Russell Means was among those who despised the term "Native American" concocted by academics as the latest imposition: "we were colonized as American Indians and we will gain our freedom as American Indians."[65] With time, many radicals became moderates. For instance, Crow Dog, a Sioux and Native American Church leader, initially backed the radicals but later sought healing by inviting all Americans to annual Sun Dances.

The Hopi tribe's council of religious leaders sent President Nixon an extraordinary letter in 1970 that explained their traditional relationship with nature and how Americans had devastated that: "We are granted our stewardship by virtue of our instruction as to the meaning of Nature, Peace, and Harmony as spoken to our People by . . . the Great Spirit . . . The white man, through his insensitivity to the way of Nature, has desecrated the face of Mother Earth . . . The white man's desire for material possessions and power has blinded him to the pain he has caused Mother Earth." They invited the president "and all spiritual leaders everywhere to meet with us and discuss the welfare of mankind so that Peace, Unity, and Brotherhood will become part of all men everywhere."[66]

A portion of Hispanic Americans also embraced political activism. Cesar Chavez established and led the United Farm Workers that demanded higher wages, health care, and reduced work hours for those who labored in crop fields. The United Farm Workers conducted a series of strikes and boycotts to pressure federal and states governments to enact those policies. The Chicano movement emphasized ethnic pride and succeeded in pressuring ever more universities to adopt Chicano Studies departments.

***

During Johnson's tenure, one issue above all affected the West. Preservationists scored their greatest victory when Johnson signed the Wilderness Protection Act on September 3, 1964. That Act immediately designated 54 regions and 9.1 million acres as wilderness accessible only to people on foot or horse and closed to any commercial exploitation. Since then the system has expanded to 757 wildernesses with 109.5 million total acres in 44 states and Puerto Rico. That was the triumph of visionaries who for decades literally cried in the wilderness but eventually formed choruses that overwhelmed opponents.[67]

Aldo Leopold was a Forest Service biologist who culled predators. Watching the light die in a cougar's eyes that he mortally wounded provoked an epiphany. He realized that cougars had as much biological right to exist as humans, and that predators are a natural and healthy part of any ecosystem of countless interdependent species. Humans have an ethical and self-interested duty to sustain rather than destroy nature. Those insights are the core of his "Land Ethic" that he elaborated through his *Sand County Almanac* (1949). He explained "Land Ethic" as an extension of traditional ethics that "rest upon a single premise: that the individual is a member of a community of interdependent parts. His instincts prompt him to compete for his place in that community, but his ethics prompt him also to cooperate (perhaps in order that there may be a place to compete for). The land ethic simply enlarges the boundaries of the community to include soils, waters, plants, and animals, or collectively, the land . . . In short, a land ethic changes the role of Homo Sapiens from conqueror of the land community to plain member and citizen of it. It implies respect for his fellow-members, and also respect for the community."[68] He advocated designated wildernesses as regions that could "absorb a two-weeks' pack trip" free of all commercial or mechanized activity.[69] A breakthrough came when Forest Service Chief William Greeley agreed to designate and protect a stretch of the Gila National Forest as wilderness in 1926.

Robert Marshall grew up in New York City dreaming of being a frontiersmen like his heroes Meriwether Lewis and William Clark. Like Leopold, he was a biologist who worked for the Forest Service and advocated wilderness protection. His 1933 *National Plan for American Forestry* included a system of designated wildernesses. On January 21, 1935, he led the founding of the Wilderness Society as a lobby group; the monthly magazine *Living Wilderness* presented essays and photos of potential wildernesses. When asked how many wildernesses America should have, he replied, "how many Brahms symphonies do we need?"[70] Tragically, heart attacks killed Marshall and Leopold before their dream became reality.

The Wilderness Society led by Howard Zahniser allied with the Sierra Club led by David Brower to oppose dams that would destroy the Colorado River's Glen Canyon and the Green River's Echo Canyon during the early 1950s. They testified at congressional hearings, wrote articles for popular magazines like *Life, Reader's Digest, Newsweek,* and *Collier's* and their groups distributed pamphlets with titles like "Will

You DAM the Scenic Wild Canyons of Our National Park System?" Brower explained that: "the wilderness we now have is all we will ever have" or just 2 percent of the country. Other articulate advocates joined their crusade. Backcountry guide and nature writer Sigurd Olsen asked Americans if "in our mad rush to dam every river, chop down every tree, utilize all resources to the ultimate limit . . . we might . . . destroy the very things that have made life in America worth cherishing and defending?"[71] Wallace Stegner, a novelist and essayist, argued that: "Something will have gone out of us as a people if we ever let the remaining wilderness be destroyed . . . if we drive the last remaining wild species into zoos or to extinction; if we pollute the last clear air and dirty the last clean streams and push our paved roads through the last of the silence . . . For an American, insofar as he is new and different at all, is a civilized man who has renewed himself in the wild . . . Save a piece of country like that intact, and it does not matter . . . that only a few people will go into it. That is precisely its value."[72]

Eventually in 1956, politicians cut a deal whereby the Bureau of Reclamation would dam Glen Canyon and spare Echo Canyon as Dinosaur National Monument. Brower and Eliot Porter rafted Glen Canyon and published their respective thoughts and photos in *The Place No One Knew: Glen Canyon on the Colorado* (1963).

The alliance conducted a survey of federal public lands and identified 160 potential wildernesses. Zahniser drafted the Wilderness Act and found Senate and House sponsors. The process began in June 1957 and ended May 1964, during which there were nine prolonged hearings, 6,000 pages of testimony, and the bill was rewritten or resubmitted sixty-six times.[73] The issue split the country with preservationists pitted against conservationists and materialists. The mining, oil, lumber, and agribusiness industries did everything possible to throttle the bill. Nonetheless, the final votes were overwhelmingly in favor, with 73 to 12 in the Senate on April 10, and 373 to one on July 30, 1964.

That victory further boosted the environmental movement's numbers and political clout. Membership swelled in all the major groups including the Sierra Club, Wilderness Society, Nature Conservancy, Audubon Society, and Friends of the Earth. They spiked a proposed dam in the Grand Canyon with united lobbying of Congress and advertisements with highlights like "Should we also flood the Sistine Chapel so Tourists Can Get Nearer the Ceiling?" They succeeded in getting Congress to pass the National Wild and Scenic Rivers Act, modeled on the Wilderness Act, that Johnson signed on October 3, 1968.

***

Yet another man born in the West won the presidency in 1968, although few people including himself thought of him as a westerner. Richard Nixon grew up in Yorba Linda, a small California town between Los Angeles and San Diego. He served in the naval reserves during World War II, got a law degree from Duke University then won a House seat in 1946, a Senate seat in 1950, and served as Eisenhower's vice president from 1953 to 1961, He was the Republican Party's presidential candidate but lost to Kennedy by a narrow margin in the 1961 election. In 1968, he beat Democratic Party candidate Hubert Humphrey and American Party candidate George Wallace with 43.4 percent of the vote and 301 electors to 42.7 percent and 191 electors and 13.5 percent and 46 electors.

Ideologically Nixon was a center-right candidate between Humphrey at center-left and Wallace at far right. He was a pragmatic problem-solver and a conservationist who recognized that sustainable development and public health were vital American interests. To those ends, he signed into law the National Environmental Policy Act (1969), Coal Mine Health and Safety Act (1969), Environmental Protection Agency Act (1970), Clean Air Act (1970), Environmental Quality Improvement Act (1970), Federal Water Pollution Control Act (1970), Occupational Health and Safety Act (1970), Clean Water Act (1972), Consumer Product Safety Act (1972), and Endangered Species Act (1973). Three new institutions emerged to help administer partly or fully these laws, the Environmental Protection Agency (EPA), Council on Environmental Quality (CEQ), and Occupational Health and Safety Administration (OSHA).

The National Environmental Policy Act expressed these American values: "The Congress recognizing the profound impact of man's activity on the interrelations of all components of the national environment, particularly the profound influences of population growth, high density urbanization, industrial expansion, resource exploitation, and new and expanding technological advances, and recognizing further the critical importance of restoring and maintaining environmental quality to the overall welfare and development of man, declares . . . the continuing policy of the Federal Government" to act as a trustee for each generation and "ensure for all Americans safe, healthful, productive, and aesthetically and culturally pleasing surroundings," to "attain the widest range of beneficial uses of the environment without degradation," to "preserve important historic, cultural, and natural aspects of our national heritage."[74] To help fulfill those goals any construction project required an environmental impact study to be approved before it could proceed.

The Council on Environmental Quality issued a 1970 report that captured the political dynamic that promoted pollution and stymied any attempts to fight it: "Public decisions, like private decisions, suffer from the inadequate balancing of short-run economic choices against long-term environmental protection. There is a nearly irresistible pressure on local government to develop local land in order to increase jobs and extend the tax base—even if the land is valuable open space or an irreplaceable marsh. The problem is amplified by the proliferation of agencies, all completing narrowly, without consideration of broader and often common goals. The development that generates economic benefits in a town upstream may create pollution and loss of recreation in a town downstream."[75]

During the late 1960s, preservationism became a mass movement led by organizations like the Sierra Club, Audubon Society, Wilderness Society, Friends of the Earth, and Nature Conservancy. Yet it was an individual, ecologist John McConnell, who perhaps did more to promote that mass movement. During a UNESCO conference at San Francisco in 1969, he proposed an international teach-in on environmental issues. That inspired Wisconsin Senator Gaylord Nelson to propose a congressional resolution for an Earth Day celebration for April 22, 1970, and after winning approval, he got Denis Hayes appointed the National Coordinator. More than million people across the United States gathered to learn about the issues and demand policies that alleviated problems. That in turn pressured Nixon and Congress to pass that array of conservation programs.

***

America's economic interdependence with the world usually benefited consumers with inexpensive products from overseas and hurt producers who could not compete. During the late 1960s and throughout the 1970s and 1980s, foreign rivals, especially from Japan, dumped cheaper, often better-made products in the United States and elsewhere around the world that devastated American industries like television, automobiles, steel, and shipbuilding.

Then in October 1973, two international oil alliances—the dozen-member Organization for Petroleum Exporting Countries (OPEC) and six-member Organization for Arab Petroleum Exporting Countries (OAPEC)—inflicted devastating blows to the global economy by quadrupling oil prices, nationalizing foreign-owned corporations in their countries, cutting production, and for several months cutting off exports to the United States. Their excuse for doing so was retaliation against Israel backed by the United States during the Yom Kippur War against Egypt and Syria. The result was a decade of stagflation—low growth and high prices—for the United States and the rest of the world.

Those chronic problems caused politicians to shelve most proposed policies that mostly affected the West. During his four years as president from 1977 to 1981, Jimmy Carter lost more such fights than he won. One victory was the 1978 Indian Religious Freedom Act that committed the federal government to upholding the right of Indians to worship freely and protect their sacred sites. He enraged most westerners when he proposed cutting $5 billion from eighteen western hydraulic projects. The outcry forced him to restore all but four of the cuts. Carter rekindled western rage when he proposed an MX ballistic missile system with hundreds of silos across much of Nevada and Utah. Politicians from those states and elsewhere protested the financial cost for the nation and environmental devastation that system would inflict. He shelved that plan. He infuriated the fossil fuels industry with consumption taxes and alternative energy subsidies.

Carter's greatest conservation achievement affected not the West but Alaska when he signed the Alaska National Interests Act into law on December 2, 1980. The act preserved in Alaska "nationally significant natural, scenic, historic, archeological, geological, scientific, wilderness, cultural, recreational, and wildlife values." In all, Washington protected 104 million acres or 28 percent of Alaska's land area, including 56 million acres of wilderness. That was an extraordinary victory given the array of logging, mining, and oil corporations that fought the bill every step of the way. Spearheading the bill was the Alaska Coalition of 1,500 national, state, and local environmental organizations led by the Sierra Club, Wilderness Society, National Audubon Society, Friends of the Earth, and National Parks and Conservation Society. The votes in Congress were 268 to 157 in the House of Representatives and 78 to 14 in the Senate. Nonetheless, corporate interests still won plenty of concessions. The federal government owned 99 percent of Alaska's land when it became a state in 1959, but transferred lands to the state government and today owns only 61 percent. Although only one percent of Alaska is privately owned, corporations can exploit the natural resources of the nearly 70 percent of the state that is unprotected. In learning of the Alaska Act's passage, Edward Abby wrote: "I may never in my life get to Alaska but I am grateful that it is there. We need the possibility of escape as surely as we need hope."[76]

Abby's sentiment expressed the outlook of conservationists and preservationists alike but infuriated conservatives. Those who championed the unregulated exploitation of public lands, especially across the West, would soon capture the White House.

Chapter 11

ARTISTS AND WRITERS

"It was a hard land, and it bred hard men to hard ways." (Louis L'Amour)

"The only equality I recognize is being equal to the situation." (The Virginian)

"You're either on the bus or off the bus." (Ken Kesey)

Wonderful paintings and sculptures, novels and poems, films and plays, and other arts from 1890 to 1980 depicted the traditional and modern West.[1] And then there were works that may have lacked artistry but attracted countless enthusiastic viewers and readers.

William "Buffalo Bill" Cody was a former Pony Express rider, bison hunter, and army scout before he turned showman.[2] He promoted a nostalgic, heroic version of the West through his increasingly elaborate Wild West Show that he inaugurated at North Platte, Nebraska in 1882 and moved to Omaha in 1883. The show was such a hit that he embarked on annual tours around America and parts of Europe until 1916. Each show's climax reenacted Custer's Last Stand with "real Indians." Indeed, Sitting Bull was among the stars in 1885. Another star was Annie Oakley, an expert markswoman. In London, Queen Victoria attended the show during her Silver Jubilee in 1887. Buffalo Bill had many emulators. By one count, there were 116 Wild West Shows between 1883 and 1957.[3]

Rodeos or formal contests among cowboys for their riding and roping skills before paying audiences also became increasingly popular in the late nineteenth and early twentieth centuries.[4] The first known rodeo was at Deer Trail, Colorado in 1869. The first known rodeo to offer prizes was at Prescott, Arizona in 1888. The first city to sponsor an annual rodeo was Cheyenne, Wyoming with its Frontier Days from 1898. Madison Square Garden in New York City annually hosted the World Championship Rodeo from 1926 to 1959. The Rodeo Cowboys Association formed in 1945. Women got into the act with the Girls Rodeo Association founded in 1949, the Women's Professional Rodeo Association (WPRA) in 1982, and the Professional Women's Rodeo Association (PWRA) in 1987. Gay cowboys organized their first rodeo at Reno in 1975 and established the International Gay Rodeo Association (IGRA) in 1985.

***

During the modern West's first two decades, no artist exceeded Frederick Remington in the range and quality of his works. He spent years in the West as a rancher, artist, and journalist, and brilliantly conveyed cavalrymen, warriors, outlaws, and cowboys through paintings and bronze sculptures. He was as prolific as he was brilliant with "2,750 paintings and drawings, twenty-five bronzes, eight books, a novel, a play, and countless magazine articles."[5] Scores of his illustrations appeared in magazines like *Harper's Monthly*, *Century*, and *Outing*, and in books by his friends Owen Wister, Theodore Roosevelt, and Libbie Custer. Among his most iconic paintings were "Dash for the Timber" (1889), "Fight for the Water Hole" (1903), "Cavalry Charge on the Southern Plains" (1907), "Downing the Night Leader" (1907), "Stampede" (1908), and "Unknown Explorers" (1908), and sculptures "The Bronco Buster" (1895) and "The Mountain Man" (1903). He wrote short stories and novels including *Pony Tracks* (1895), *Crooked Trails* (1898), *Men with the Bark On* (1900), and *John Ermine of the Yellowstone* (1902). The rapidly modernizing West eventually ruined his romantic vision. He wrote his wife in 1900 that he would "never come west again. It is all brick buildings—derby hats and blue overhauls—it spoils my early illusions—and they are my capital."[6]

Like Remington, Charles Russell headed West inspired by the romantic vision, but stayed there the rest of his life, mostly in Great Falls, Montana. His paintings were as dazzling as Remington's with an even brighter palette. Among his greatest were "Last of His Race" (1899), "Bronc to Breakfast" (1908), "In Without Knocking" (1909), and "Carson's Men" (1913).

Four other artists produced enduring works. Henry Farny's most iconic painting was "The Song of the Talking Wire" (1904) of snowy plains and an Indian wrapped in a buffalo robe leaning against a telegraph pole, his head bent toward the mysterious clicks emanating from the wire. Charles Schreyvogel specialized in dramatic battle scenes like "My Bunkie" (1889), "How Kota!" (1901), "Custer's Demand" (1903), and "Rescue at Summit Springs" (1907).

During the early twentieth century, the art of brilliant illustrator Newell Convers "N.C." Wythe adorned many books and covers of magazines like the *Saturday Evening Post, Harper's, Century, Western World,* and *Collier's.* Among his most striking western themes were "Hahn Pulled his Gun" (1906) and "Wild Bill Hickok at Cards" (1916). Of all the art works that depicted the West from 1890 to 1920, among the most iconic was James Fraser's bronze "End of the Trail" (1898) of a mounted Indian slumped forward with a spear pointed downward atop a drooping horse.

Two American defeats—the Alamo and Little Bighorn—inspired many painters. For the Alamo, the best-known images were Henry McArdle's "Dawn at the Alamo" (1905) and Robert Onderdonk's "Fall of the Alamo" (1903). For the Little Bighorn, Otto Becker's "Custer's Last Stand" (1890) was the most dramatic and popular image with hundreds of lithograph copies decorating saloons across the country. Other versions included William De La Montagne Cary's "Battle on the Little Bighorn" (1876), John Mulvaney's "Custer's Last Rally" (1881), and Frederick Paxon's "Custer's Last Stand" (1899).

Three photographers specialized in western scenes. Edward Curtis dedicated his life to preserving as many possible images, sounds, and stories of Indians. By one count between 1900 and 1930, he "visited 80 tribes, took more than 40,000 photographs, made over 10,000 recordings of Indian songs and stories . . . and wrote twenty volumes of texts to accompany a series of magnificent portfolios that added up to five hundred sepia masterworks in the art of photography."[7] Of his photos, most iconic is "Canyon de Chelly, Navajos" (1904). Two other photographers produced memorable images. Arnold Genthe photographed the aftermath of San Francisco's earthquake with the most stunning image being his "View of Burning City from Russian Hill" (1906). George Fiske's "Kitty Tasch and Friend on Glacier Point" (1890) depicted two daredevil women in Victorian dress doing the cancan on a narrow granite ledge thousands of feet above Yosemite Valley.

The development of national park lodges with their rustic western style and Harvey hotels with their mission revival style inspired furniture makers to design appropriate furnishings for each. A. J. Forbes created the first mission-style furniture as contemporary versions of traditional Spanish colonial furniture in 1894, and it soon became popular for Southwest-style homes and businesses. Forbes was influenced by the rustic elegant style of furniture and furnishings called Craftsman that Gustav Stickley developed and promoted with the monthly *Craftsman* magazine. Frank Lloyd Wright invented the Prairie or organic style of architecture and taught it first at Taliesin

East near Spring Green, Wisconsin from 1911 then at Taliesin West near Phoenix in 1937.

***

Frederick Jackson Turner may be the most influential American historian. His 1893 essay, "The Significance of the Frontier on American History" provoked an intellectual watershed for debating, understanding, and writing about the West.[8] He argued that the "true point of view in the history is not the Atlantic coast, it is the Great West. Even the slavery struggle . . . occupies its important place in American history because of its relation to western expansion." He emphasized how natural, social, economic, and political forces constrain and channel human beliefs and behavior. The hard, collective work of individuals in different professions shapes history much more than leaders who often struggle to comprehend and manipulate those forces. American history was progressive, thanks to the frontier where people developed democratic institutions and principles. This celebrated passage captures his outlook: "Stand at the Cumberland Gap and watch the procession of civilization, marching single file—the buffalo following the trail to the salt springs, the Indian, the fur-trader and hunter, the cattle-raiser, the pioneer farmer—and the frontier has passed by. Stand at South Pass in the Rockies a century later and see the same procession with wider intervals between."[9] He worried that the nation might stagnate with the frontier's disappearance and called on Americans to develop new metaphorical frontiers in thought, science, and philanthropy.

Turner got his doctorate from Johns Hopkins University in 1890 then taught at the University of Wisconsin from 1890 to 1910 and Harvard University from 1910 to 1922. He was profound but not prolific, more a philosopher of history than a historian and with ideas conveyed more through essays than books. He received a Pulitzer Prize for his collection of essays called *The Frontier in American History* (1920).

In contrast, Theodore Roosevelt was a prolific author who somehow squeezed enough time between a series of political posts from New York assemblyman to American president and a family life with six kids to write over thirty books. Among them was his *Winning of the West* series with the first two volumes published in 1889, the third in 1894, and the fourth in 1896. He shared Turner's view that the frontier forged American values of enterprise, individualism, exceptionalism, and democracy. Yet, Roosevelt was a traditional historian who center-staged heroic leaders in the frontier's transformation into civilization.

He called for Americans to be heroic by adopting a "strenuous life" of physical, mental, and moral development that enriched everyone.

Frederick Paxon replaced Turner at the University of Wisconsin and propounded his views of the American West and frontier. Historian Richard Etulain reckons that Paxon, by mentoring over 200 master and doctorate students, was "perhaps the most significant teacher and writer of frontier history in the first half of the twentieth century."[10] His key books were *The Last American Frontier* (1913) and Pulitzer Prize-winning *History of the American Frontier* (1924).

Scholarly journals that specialized in the West and its regions appeared in the 1920s and 1930s but few lasted long. Most prominent were *Texas Review*, renamed *Southwest Review* when its headquarters shifted from Austin to Dallas, *The Midland* in Iowa, *The Frontier* in Montana, *Prairie Schooner* in Nebraska, *Folk-Say* in Oklahoma, and the *New Mexico Quarterly*. Boosters and historians founded the Santa Fe Trail and Boone's Lick Association in 1911 and the National Old Trails Road Association in 1912.

A number of memoirs celebrated the West and helped boost the conservation and preservation movements. John Muir wrote elegiac accounts of his wilderness experiences in the Sierra Mountains and elsewhere including *The Mountains of California* (1894), *Our National Parks* (1901), and *The Yosemite* (1912). Adolphe Bandelier mostly depicted the Southwest in his *A New Mexico David and Goliath and Other Stories and Sketches of the Southwest* (1891), *A Tramp Across the Continent* (1892), and *The Land of Poco Tiempo* (1893). John Van Dyck was not as popular but was nearly as profound with his nature books *The Desert* (1901), *The Mountains* (1916), and *The Grand Canyon of the Colorado* (1920). Mary Austin's *Land of Little Rain* (1902) celebrated the austere, complex ecology of California's desert, and *Land of Lost Borders* (1909) and *Land of Journeys' Ending* (1924) the Southwest. Three Indians produced moving books grounded on their experiences, Omaha Francis LaFlesche with *The Middle Five: Indian Boys at School* (1900); Santee Sioux Charles Eastman with *Indian Boyhood* (1902) and *From the Deep Woods to Civilization: Chapters in the Autobiography of an Indian* (1916); and Lakota Sioux Black Elk with *Black Elk Speaks* (1932) transcribed by John Neihardt.

Two female writers achieved fame during this era. Mary Hallock Foote wrote the most novels set in the West. She was born into a middle-class family in the lower Hudson River valley, and attended the Female Collegiate Academy in Poughkeepsie and the Cooper Union Institute of Design in New York. In 1876, she married engineer Arthur Foote and thereafter they lived in western mining towns in California,

Idaho, and Colorado. She wove her experiences and observations into her novels *The Horse-led Claim* (1883), *The Chosen Valley* (1892), *Coeur d'Alene* (1894), *The Prodigal* (1900), and *The Ground Swell* (1919), and wrote two historical novels of earlier times, *The Royal Americans* (1910) and *The Picked Company* (1912). She illustrated her novels and stories that appeared in magazines like *Century* and *Scribner's*. Wallace Stegner based his novel *Angle of Repose* on her life. Willa Cather is the most acclaimed female novelist who set many of her early stories in the West. Her childhood on Nebraska's frontier inspired her novel *O Pioneers* (1913) and her imagination her later novels *My Antonia* (1918) and *Death Comes to the Archbishop* (1927) based on the life of Archbishop Jean-Baptiste Lamy of Santa Fe. She spent most of her later life far from the West in New York City's Greenwich Village.

Four male writers set many of their novels in the contemporary West. Hamlin Garland was an Iowan whose novels of rural agrarian unrest included *Main Travelled Roads* (1891) and *Rose of Dutcher's Cooley* (1895); he revealed how that high grass prairie region shaped his own development in his autobiography *A Son of the Middle Border* (1917). Frank Norris was Chicago-born but as a young man moved first to Oakland then San Francisco. He exposed the machinations of San Francisco politics in his novel *McTeague* (1899) and the railroad monopoly in *The Octopus* (1901). Peritonitis killed him and his promising literary career in 1902. Jack London was born in San Francisco, left home in his late teens to hobo around the West, did odd jobs for income, spent over a year in Alaska, eventually married and bought a home near Sonoma, California and along the way wrote essays, short stories, and novels. He is best known for his novels set on Alaska's frontier like *Call of the Wild* (1903) and *White Fang* (1906), but he also wrote two novels inspired by his Sonoma experiences, *Valley of the Moon* (1913) and *Little Lady of the Big House* (1916). His core theme was how men and beasts struggle to survive against dangerous and indifferent natural forces. In its own category is Frank Baum's novel *The Wonderful Wizard of Oz* (1900) written mostly for teenage readers. The novel begins with Dorothy at her Kansas farm before a tornado whisks her to a mythical land "over the rainbow."

As for short stories, although Stephen Crane is best known for his *Red Band of Courage* (1895) set in the Civil War, he wrote several short stories that depicted the West of which "The Bride Comes to Yellow Sky" (1898) is best known. Charles Lummis gathered and published collections of Southwest legends that included *Spanish Pioneers* (1893), *Pueblo Indian Folk Stories* (1894), *The King of the Broncos and Other Stories of New Mexico* (1897).

Four very different yet powerful poets found inspiration in the West for many of their poems. Robinson Jeffers set many of his poems in California, especially the coast where he lived near Carmel, including his collection *Californians* (1916). In Santa Fe, Alice Corbin Henderson founded and edited the journal *Poetry*. Her collection *Red Earth* (1920) of poems about New Mexico was critically acclaimed. John Neihardt was Nebraska's Poet Laureate for such works that glorified history like *Song of Hugh Glass* (1915), *Song of the Indian Wars* (1925), and *Song of Jed Smith* (1941). Thomas Ferril sought to debunk western myths in many of his poems including *High Passage* (1926) and *Westering* (1934).

***

American writers created their nation's best-known literary genre during the early twentieth century when the "western" emerged with cowboys, outlaws, and lawmen as protagonists.[11] No matter what side of the law he was on, that character was courageous, stoic, taciturn, enterprising, independent, skilled at riding, shooting, fist-fighting, and surviving, and displaying such virtues as protecting innocent folks in danger and helping those in need. Western heroes exemplified an ideal image of American manhood, one that most men wished they could emulate and instead lived vicariously. The West is at once a place of possible refuge and death, but above all freedom from one's past failures and freedom to realize one's dreams. Westerns may be the most existential of literary genres as death stalks everyone and can claim anyone any time. The West is a violent Darwinian world in which one must either kill or be killed. As for women, most are secondary characters for the hero to rescue and love. Women are usually resilient and adventurous but tend to restrain and refine the hero, which is why he is so wary of them. A series of varying harsh or beautiful landscapes act as characters by providing the hero with opportunities or challenges.

The quality of westerns then and since varied considerably. Pulp and literary writers use words for different purposes. Pulp fiction employs cliched characters, stories, settings, and themes for readers who crave their comforting familiarity. Max Brand, Ernest Haycox, Luke Short, Clarence Mulford, Bertha Bower, and Eugene Rhodes were among the more prolific and better pulp writers. Mulford developed the cowboy character Hopalong Cassidy in six novels. Literary writers strive to create characters, stories, settings, and themes vividly distinct from those of other writers in search of readers searching for inspiring originality. Two early western authors, whose stories are more literary than pulp, are Owen Wister and Zane Grey.

Owen Wister was born into a wealthy Philadelphia family and went to Harvard where he became friends with Theodore Roosevelt. Like Roosevelt, Wister went West as a young men to heal emotional and physical ailments. His novel *The Virginian: A Horseman of the Plains* (1902) tells the tale of a ranch foreman who is a gentleman to the ladies, a dead shot against outlaws, and an upholder of duty and honor exemplified by his principles, "A man's gotta do what he's gotta do," "The only equality I recognize is being equal to the situation," and "Let the best man win, whoever he is." His fiancé, schoolteacher Molly Stark Wood, gives him the choice to fight bully Trampas or marry her. Although he kills Trampas in a shootout, she forgives and marries him.

Zane Grey usually topped best-seller fiction lists from 1912 to 1928. Like Wister, Grey was an easterner inspired by the West. Among the more popular of his fifty-six westerns were *Last of the Plainsmen* (1908), *Heritage of the Desert* (1910), *Riders of the Purple Sage* (1912), *Light of the Western Stars* (1914), *The Desert of Wheat* (1919), *Wanderer of the Wasteland* (1923), and *The Vanishing American* (1925). In two of his novels, he explored controversial groups. Within a year of its publication, there were a million sales of *Riders of the Purple Sage* with its heroic cowboy character Lassiter torn between his love for Jane Withersteen and skepticism for her Mormon religion. In his *The Desert of Wheat*, Grey pitted heroic all-American farmers against Godless communist Wobblies amidst the national "Red Scare."

***

The West and westerns inspired many filmmakers.[12] Director Edwin Porter's *The Great Train Robbery* appeared in 1903, inaugurating the "western" film genre. In 1912, Thomas Ince established the Bison 101 Ranch in the Santa Monica Mountains and there produced a number of westerns including *Custer's Last Fight* (1912), *Hell's Hinges* (1916), and *Wagon Tracks* (1919). David Wark "D.W." Griffith directed *Ramona* (1910) based on Helen Hunt Jackson's novel, *The Battle of Elderbush Gulch* (1913), *Squaw Man* (1913), and *The Spoilers* (1914). The silent era's most popular cowboy stars were Bronco Billy Anderson, Tom Mix, William Carey, and William Hart. Hart also directed westerns with *Tumbleweeds* (1925) considered his best. The most notable westerns during the 1920s were James Cruze's *The Covered Wagon* (1923), Irving Willat's *North of 36* (1924), John Ford's *The Iron Horse* (1924), and George Seitz's *The Vanishing American* (1925) along with Hart's *Tumbleweeds*. In a theatrical class of his own was Will Rogers, part-Cherokee, cowboy and humorist who appeared in fifty silent and twenty-one talkie movies, and had a stage act doing rope tricks as he gently satirized powerful politicians, businessmen, and mobsters, and wrote newspaper essays.

***

Taos was the first western town to become an artist colony. That began in 1898 when the wagon of painters Ernest Blumenschein and Bert Phillips busted a wheel and as it was repaired they marveled at the scenery. They decided to stay, started painting, and invited artist friends to join them. Gradually others trickled in, found cheap studios, painted, and reveled in each other's company and the region. Joseph Henry Sharp founded the Taos Society of Artists in 1915 that eventually included Blumenschein, Philips, Irving Couse, Oscar Berninghaus, Victor Higgins, Martin Hemmings, Catherine Carter Critcher, Herbert Dunton, and Walter Ufer. Their talents varied but none rose to the level of Remington or Russell. Of their paintings, perhaps the most spectacular was Ufer's "Where the Desert Meets the Mountain" (1922). Painters who sojourned in Taos or Santa Fe from their New York City studios included Robert Henri, Marsden Hartley, John Marin, John Sloan, and Georgia O'Keefe.

Mabel Dodge Luhan established the most elaborate and enduring Taos salon.[13] Her father was a rich Buffalo banker whose wealth she inherited at a young age. She lived in Florence, Italy from 1905 to 1912, and New York City from 1912 to 1917 during which time she attracted artists, writers, thinkers, and Bohemians to her Greenwich Village brownstone. She visited Taos in 1917, was smitten, and moved there. At that time, she was married to artist Maurice Sterne. She began an affair with Tony Luhan, a Taos Pueblo headman, divorced Sterne, and married Luhan.

She bought a 150-year old three-room adobe house on 12 acres between the town's limits and the Taos Pueblo reservation and expanded it with a three-story center and one-story wings with rooms facing the Sangre de Christo Mountains. She hosted and inspired an astonishing array of creators including: "writers Mary Austin, Myron Brinig, Witter Bynner, Willa Cather, Harvey Ferguson, Aldous Huxley, Spud Johnson, D.H. Lawrence, Oliver La Farge, Jean Toomer, and Frank Waters; painters, sculptors, and photographers Ansel Adams, Dorothy Brett, Andrew Dasburg, Miriam DeWitt, Maynard Dixon, Nicolai Fechin, Laura Gilpin, Marsden Hartley, Ernest Knee, Ward Lockwood, John Marin, Georgia O'Keefe, Agnes Pelton, Ida Rauh,

Arnold Ronnebeck, Maurice Sterne, Paul Strand, Rebecca Strand, Cady Wells, and Edward Weston; musicians Carlos Chavez, Dane Rudyar, and Leopold Stokowski; theater designer Robert Edmond Jones and dance choreographer Martha Graham; social theorists, anthropologists, and folklorists John Collier, Carl Jung, Jaime de Argulo, Elsie Clews Parsons, and Ella Young."[14] Luhan was more than just the queen bee of that continually morphing ensemble. She wrote *Edge of the Taos Desert* (1917), *Winter in Taos* (1935), and *Taos and Its Artists* (1947), and dabbled in painting and poetry. She was controversial, often deliberately. Most townspeople, Taos Indians, and even her own guests deplored her domineering, loud, manipulative demeanor.

***

Georgia O'Keefe is the best-known modern artist inspired by the American West. She was born at Sun Prairie, Wisconsin, and studied art at Chicago's Art Institute and New York's Art Students League. She first experienced the high plains as an art teacher at the West Texas Normal College in Canyon, near Palo Douro Canyon from 1912 to 1914 before teaching at the University of Virginia in 1915. In Charlottesville, without her knowledge a friend sent her portfolio to Alfred Stieglitz, a photographer whose Gallery 291 on Fifth Avenue just north of Washington Square displayed both European and American modern art. He encouraged her to come to New York. Although stunned by his invitation, she accepted and moved there in 1916. He not only helped develop her career but divorced his wife to marry her.[15] She was a renowned artist when Mabel Dodge Luhan invited her to Taos for an extended visit in 1929. O'Keefe was enchanted and returned annually for a month or two each summer before permanently living there from 1949. She eventually moved into an adobe mansion at Abiquiu with a nearby studio at Ghost Ranch. Her more iconic paintings include: "Taos Pueblo" (1929), "Black Cross with Red Sky" (1929), "Rancho Church" (1930), "Cow's Skull" (1931), "From the Faraway Nearby" (1937), "Grey Hills" (1941), "Red Hills and Bones" (1941), "Pelvis with Pedernal" (1943), "Pedernal with Shadows and the Moon" (1943), "Patio Door with Green Leaf" (1956), "White Patio with Red Door" (1960), "Sky Above White Clouds I" (1962), and "Sky Above White Clouds IV" (1965)

During the 1930s and 1940s, three artists provided realist versions of the West. Carl Rungus is best known for his wildlife paintings. Among Maynard Dixon's most powerful works were "Earth Knower" (1932), "Open Range" (1942), and "Desert Southwest" (1944). Wilhelm

Koerner's paintings illustrated history books by John Lafarge and Bernard De Voto and several Zane Grey novels. His illustrations accompanied more than forty western stories that appeared in the *Saturday Evening Post* from 1930 to 1935. Most iconic was his *Madonna of the Prairie* (1922) of an angelic pioneer woman before a Conestoga wagon whose arch appears like a halo.

Five painters labeled regionalists emerged in the Great Depression. Thomas Hart Benton was a Missouri native famed for such sensual, tawdry, flowing paintings of the West like "Boomtown" (1928), "Cattle Loading, West Texas" (1930), "Cradling Wheat" (1938), "Threshing Wheat" (1939), "The Hailstorm" (1940), and "July Hay" (1943), and murals like "America Today" (1930–1), "Arts of Life in America" (1933), and "Social History of Missouri" (1935–6). Iowan Grant Wood is best known for his "American Gothic" (1930) of a stoic, joyless Iowa farm couple; other prominent works with western themes included "Arbor Day" (1932),"Death on Ridge Road" (1934), "Dinner for Threshers" (1934), and "Spring in Town" (1940). Kansan John Curry's most acclaimed paintings included "Baptism in Kansas" (1928), "Tornado over Kansas" (1929), "Hogs Killing a Rattlesnake" (1930), and "Line Storm" (1934). Alexandre Hogue was Missouri-born but immigrated to Texas where he painted his "Erosion Series" like "Dust Bowl" (1933), "Drought Survivors" (1936), "Mother Earth Laid Bare" (1938), and "The Crucified Land" (1939). New Mexican Paul Hurd's better noted paintings included "Rancheria" (1938), "Dry River" (1938), "Rio Hondo" (1941), and "The Gate and Beyond" (1950). Texan Jerry Bywaters' "Ranch Hand and Pony" (1938) and "Oilfield Girls" (1940) were among his best.

Photographers provided brilliant images of the West. Paul Strand was part of Alfred Stieglitz's society in New York. Stieglitz advocated a painterly style of photography that Strand initially embraced and later rejected for a more precise style exemplified by his "Landscape with Cross, New Mexico" (1932) and "Church, Buttress, Rancho de Taos" (1932). Dorothea Lange is most famous for her stark images of impoverished westerners struggling to survive the Dust Bowl like "The Great Blow of 1934" (1934), "Tent City, Tulare, California" (1936), and "Migrant Madonna" (1936). Among Arthur Rothstein's most striking were "A Bank that Failed" (1935), "Fleeing a Dust Storm, Cimarron County, Oklahoma" (1936), and "Stock Watering Hall Almost Covered by Erosion" (1936). Many of Edward Weston's photos were sensual, nearly surreal images of parts of beautiful women, shells, driftwood, and scenes like "Ovens, Taos Pueblo" (1933). Laura Gilpin produced two books of photos of New Mexico's landscapes and Indian peoples,

The Rio Grande, River of Destiny (1939) and *The Pueblos* (1941). Ansel Adams produced the grandest photos of the West with his "Moonrise, Hernandez, New Mexico" most iconic. He founded the Group f/64 dedicated to deep focus photography, the photo magazine Aperture, and the Center for Creative Photography at the University of Arizona, and produced eight books with essays and hundreds of his photos and an autobiography.[16]

During the mid-twentieth century, visionaries created three monumental works that depicted the West. Sculptor Gutzon Borglum designed, directed, and helped carve 60ft-high faces of Presidents George Washington, Thomas Jefferson, Abraham Lincoln, and Theodore Roosevelt from a granite cliff on Mount Rushmore in the Black Hills. The project began in 1927, finished in 1941, and cost nearly $1 million. In 1940, Korcak Ziolkowksi began blasting and jackhammering a 641ft long and 563ft high sculpture of Crazy Horse out of a granite outcropping 17 miles away, after receiving a commission from Sioux Chief Henry Standing Bear. Ziolkowksi died in 1982 but his foundation has continued his work. More than eight decades later, only a rough image of the Sioux chief's face and his pointing arm has emerged. Above the Mississippi River at St. Louis, the stainless steel 630ft tall "Gateway to the West" arch was constructed from 1963 to 1965 for $13 million from a design by Eono Saarinen.

***

During the interwar years, numerous authors set their novels in the West. Ole Rolvaag's trilogy *Giants in the Earth* (1927), *Peder Victorius* (1929), and *Their Father's God* (1931) explored the life of Scandinavian immigrants on the northern plains. Harvey Fergusson's novels, *The Blood of the Conquerors* (1921), *Wolf Song* (1927), *In Those Days* (1929), and *The Conquest of Don Pedro* (1954) take place in the Southwest. H.L. Davis's Pulitzer Prize-winning *Honey in the Horn* (1935) depicted frontier Oregon in the early twentieth century. Vardis Fisher mostly depicted rural Idaho in his novels *In Tragic Life* (1932), *Passions Spin the Plot* (1934), *We Are the Betrayed* (1935), *No Villain Need Be* (1936), and *Mountain Man* (1965). The best of Frederick Manfred's five-novel Buckskin Man Tales was *Lord Grizzly* (1954) about mountain man Hugh Glass's near-fatal bear fight, abandonment by his comrades, and epic journey of recovery and vengeance. The others included *Riders of Judgment* (1957), *Conquering Horse* (1959), *Scarlet Plume* (1964), and *King of Spades* (1965). Mari Sandoz was a Nebraska native who wrote vivid histories like *Old Jules* (1935), *Crazy Horse* (1942), and *Cheyenne Autumn*

(1953), and novels like *Slogum House* (1937), *Winter Thunder* (1954), *The Horse Catcher* (1957), and *The Story Catcher* (1962). Frank Waters wrote some intriguing novels including *The Wild Earth's Nobility* (1935), *Below Grass Roots* (1937), and *The Dust within the Rock* (1940), and brilliantly explored Indian perspectives in *People of the Valley* (1941) and *The Man Who Killed the Deer* (1942). Walter Clark is best known for his *The Oxbow Incident* (1940) about a lynching but his *Track of the Cat* (1949) depicted just as dark a vision of the West. Laura Ingalls Wilder also tapped into her western childhood to write a series of novels for girls like *Little House in the Big Woods* (1932), *Little House on the Prairie* (1935), and *Little Town on the Prairie* (1941). Two Indian writers emerged in the 1920s. Okanogan Cristal McLeod Galler, pen-named Mourning Dove, was the first Indian women with to publish a novel, *Co-ge-we-a* (1927). Cree D'Arcy McNickle tapped his dual-culture experiences including boarding school for *The Surrounded* (1936).

John Steinbeck set many of his novels in the then contemporary West of the mid-twentieth century. His Pulitzer Prize-winning *The Grapes of Wrath* (1939) depicted the plight of the Joad family that abandoned their farm engulfed by the Dust Bowl and immigrated to California where they were exploited farm laborers. His other novels with western mostly Californian settings and themes included *Tortilla Flats* (1935), *Of Mice and Men* (1937), *The Red Pony* (1938), *Cannery Row* (1945), and *East of Eden* (1952).

***

During the mid-twentieth century, influential historians of the West emerged who combined excellent scholarship, analysis, and writing. The greatest was Bernard DeVoto who wrote over forty histories and novels including Pulitzer Prize-winning *Across the Wide Missouri* (1947) and National Book Award-winning *The Course of Empire* (1942). Others included Herbert Bolton and his *The Spanish Borderlands* (1921); Walter Prescott Webb and his *Great Plains* (1931); John Howard and his Pulitzer Prize-winning *Montana: High, Wide, and Handsome* (1943); James Malin and his *The Grassland of North America* (1947); Henry Nash Smith and his *Virgin Land: The American West as Symbol and Myth* (1950); Dale Morgan and his *Jedediah Smith and the Opening of the West* (1953); Wallace Stegner and his *Beyond the Hundredth Meridian: John Wesley Powell and the Second Opening of the West* (1954); David Lavender and his *Bent's Fort* (1954); Gerald Nash and his *American West in the Twentieth Century* (1973); and Frederick Merk and his *History of the Westward Movement* (1978). The most comprehensive if not poetic account was

Ray Billington's *Westward Expansion*, published in 1949 and updated by Martin Ridge in 1982, that became the standard textbook for countless Western History college courses.[17] *Westward Expansion* offered a revised version of Turner's theme that finessed most criticisms. Two authors presented controversial revisionist views of American Indians, Dee Brown with his *Bury My Heart at Wounded Knee: An Indian History of the American West* (1970) and Vine Deloria with *Custer Died for Your Sins: An Indian Manifesto* (1969), *God Is Red: A Native View of Religion* (1972), and *Red Earth, White Lies: Native Americans and the Myth of Scientific Fact* (1995). Scholars founded the Western History Association in 1961 and its journal, the *Western History Quarterly*, in 1970, and the Western Literary Association and its journal *Western American Literature* in 1965.

Beyond academia, a number of non-fiction books appeared that challenged traditional ways of looking at the West and the rest of America. Aldo Leopold's *A Sand County Almanac* (1949) called for a "land ethic" that made preserving nature central to humanity. Rachel Carson's *Silent Spring* (1962) revealed the devastating effects of chemical fertilizers, pesticides, and herbicides on animal and human life. Edward Abbey's *Desert Solitaire: A Season in the Wilderness* (1968) celebrated the sensual and spiritual joys of living within rather than from nature. Ivan Doig's *This House of Sky: Landscapes of a Western Mind* (1978) was a thought-provoking memoir that delved into what being a westerner can mean.

Arguably, Wallace Stegner was the greatest writer about the West. In his fourteen novels, fifty-eight short stories, two histories, two biographies, five collections of essays, and memoir history, he wrote mostly about the twentieth century West inspired by his own experiences. He received fourteen literary awards. His most acclaimed books were the novels *Big Rock Candy Mountain* (1943), *Wolf Willow* (1962), Pulitzer Prize-winning *Angle of Repose* (1971), and National Book Award-winning *The Spectator Bird* (1977), and the biography *Beyond the Hundredth Meridian: John Wesley Powell and the Second Opening of the West* (1954). He was born in Lake Mills, Iowa but eventually lived in twenty-eight states and Canada. He taught at the University of Wisconsin, Harvard University, and Stanford University where he founded and directed the Creative Writing Program.

Louis L'Amour was the bestselling author of eighty-five novels with millions of copies and over 400 short stories from 1950 to his death in 1988. Among his most acclaimed novels were *Hondo* (1953), *Heller with a Gun* (1955), *Sacket* (1961), *High Lonesome* (1962), *The Lonesome Gods* (1983), *Jubal Sackett* (1985), and *The Last of the Breed* (1986). His favorite place to write was a corner room at the Strater Hotel in

Durango, Colorado, where daily he typed a dozen or so pages until he finished his latest novel. Literary critic Jane Thompkins extolled his writing: "L'Amour puts you inside the hero's shirt, makes you taste what he tastes, feel what he feels. Most of the sensations the hero has are not pleasurable: he is hot, tired, dirty, and thirsty much of the time; his muscles aching."[18] Perhaps one L'Amour line best personifies the western, this one from *Heller with a Gun*: "It was a hard land, and it bred hard men to hard ways."[19] L'Amour was as tough, adventurous, and enterprising as any of his characters. He grew up on the North Dakota plains, left at age 15 to seek his fortune, worked as a seaman, lumberjack, miner, circus elephant handler, tank-destroyer commander during World War II, and boxer who won fifty-one of fifty-nine fights.[20]

Two other early postwar writers produced first-rate westerns, although neither approached L'Amour's output. A.B. Guthrie best novels included *The Big Sky* (1947), Pulitzer Prize-winning *The Way West* (1949), *These Thousand Hills* (1956), *The Last Valley* (1975), and *Fair Land, Fair Land* (1982). Jack Schaefer's *Shane* (1949) was a classic western in theme and terse writing, later made into a classic western film. His other acclaimed westerns include *The Canyon* (1953), *Old Ramon* (1961), *Incident on the Trail* (1962), and *Monte Walsh* (1963).

For the first time, the number of literary writers penning novels on the contemporary West approached those of the traditional West. Edna Ferber's *Giant* (1952) depicted conflict between a rich rancher and a wildcat oilman in Texas. Ken Kesey set his *One Flew Over the Cuckoo's Nest* (1962) in an Oregon insane asylum and *Sometimes a Great Notion* (1964) in the Northwest's logging industry. Joan Didion presented bleak visions of the modern West of soulless suburbs, strip malls, congested highways, smoggy skies, and empty lives in her *Run River* (1963) and *Play It as It Lays* (1970) along with her collections of essays. John Nichols set his *Milagro Beanfield War* (1974) of class, ethnic, and cultural conflicts in contemporary northern New Mexico. Edward Abbey's novel *The Monkey Wrench Gang* (1975) concerned a group of environmentalists that committed "ecotage" against developers that were destroying wilderness. Tony Hillerman wrote a bestselling series of murder mystery novels set in the Southwest, most with Navajo detectives Joe Leaphorn and Jim Chee the heroes. Some authors specialized in short shorties like Jack Schaefer's *Tales from the West* (1961), Norman Maclean's *A River Runs through It and Other Stories* (1976), and Annie Proulx's "Brokeback Mountain" (1997), which broke new ground by depicting gay cowboys, and "The Governors of Wyoming" (1999). As for theater, Sam Shepard's *Operation Sidewinder* (1970), *Buried Child* (1978), and *True West* (1980) explore the contemporary West.

Beatnik writers mostly depicted urban life. The characters of Jack Kerouac's *On the Road* (1957) traversed the modern West between San Francisco and New York with prolonged stays in Denver, usually Colfax Avenue's tenements and honky tonks. Alan Ginsberg's most famous book *Howl and Other Poems* (1956) and Lawrence Ferlinghetti's *Coney Island of the Mind* (1958) are mostly set in or inspired by San Francisco.

Few writers have matched prolific Larry McMurtry's mastery of prose and storytelling for novels set in both the wild and recent West like *Horseman, Pass By* (1961), *Leaving Cheyenne* (1963), *The Last Picture Show* (1966), Pulitzer Prize-winning *Lonesome Dove* (1985), *Texasville* (1987), *Anything for Billy* (1988), *Streets of Laredo* (1993), and *Comanche Moon* (1997), to name some of the more acclaimed. He spent most of his life writing and running a bookstore in Archer City, Texas, where he died in 2021. Terry Johnston was as prolific if not as profound; his thirty-one novels on the frontier West included nine on the fur trade and three on Custer, of which *Carry the Wind* (1982), *Borderland* (1983), and *One-Eyed Dream* (1988) are among his most popular.

Several Indian writers appeared in the postwar era. Kiowa Scott Momaday was a novelist, poet, playwright, and essayist whose prolific works included Pulitzer Prize-winning *House Made of Dawn* (1968) and *The Way to Rainy Mountain* (1969). Laguna Pueblo Leslie Marmon Silko's most acclaimed novel was *Ceremony* (1977). Blackfoot James Welch was a novelist, poet, and essayist whose *Winter in the Blood* (1974), *The Death of Jim Loney* (1979), and *Fools Crow* (1986) received the most accolades. Asian American writers mostly set their stories in the contemporary Far West, including Carlos Bulosan's *America Is in the Heart* (1946) about Filipino-Americans, John Okada's *No-No Boy* (1957) about Japanese Americans, and Maxine Hong Kingston's *The Woman Warrior* (1976) and Amy Tang's *Joy Luck Club* (1989) about Chinese Americans.

The contemporary West inspired several poets for some of their work. Most of Zen Buddhist Gary Snyder's poems are centered in nature, especially the Sierra Mountain foothills near his commune in collections like *The Back Country* (1957), *Turtle Island* (1974), and *Ax Handles* (1983). William Stafford explored the contemporary West through collections like *West of Your City* (1960), *Traveling through the Dark* (1962), *Allegiances* (1970), and *A Glass Face in the Rain* (1982). Prominent Indian poets included Muskogee (Creek) Joy Harjo, Navajo Luci Tapahonso, and O'Oldham Ofelia Zepeda. Elko, Nevada hosted the first cowboy poetry gathering in 1985. Among the more popular cowboy poets were Omar Barker and Paul Zarzyski.

***

The quality of artists who depicted either the traditional or modern West in the postwar era fell short of previous generations. Many of Edward Hopper's paintings depicted the new West of affluence and travel, although the characters were silent and remote from each other, absorbed in their separate worlds. Among his best were "Western Motel" (1957) and "People in the Sun" (1960). A group of men who had ranching experience and painted western themes established the Cowboy Artists of America in 1965. The best realist illustrators of western cowboys, Indians, and troopers included Frank McCarthy, Howard Terpening, Tom Lovell, and John Clymer. Harry Jackson produced larger-than-life sculptures with "Sacagawea" (1980) and "John Wayne" (1984) among the more acclaimed.

Several Indian artists achieved fame in postwar America. Dorothy Dunn was an artist and teacher who founded the Studio School at the Santa Fe Indian School in 1932 and for 30 years taught there. The Institute of American Indian Art superseded the Studio School when it was established in 1962. Among the most famous graduates was Chiricahua Apache Allan Capron Houser (Haozous) for his drawings and sculptures. San Ildefonso Maria Martinez was renowned for her shiny black pottery. Navajo Rudolph Carl (R.C.) Gorman was most renowned for his stylized depictions of Navajo women in traditional dress. Two artists were controversial for their expressionist style and satires of their subjects, Luiseno Fritz Scholder for paintings like "The American Indian" (1970) and "Custer" (1970), and Kiowa Thomas "T.C." Cannon's "Village with a Bomb" (1972) and "Two Guns Arikara" (1973).

Numerous Hispanic artists found inspiration in their traditional culture. Judith Baca supervised a lengthening mural called "The Great Wall of Los Angeles" that began in 1967, and was acclaimed for her paintings "Las Tres Marias" (1976) and "Uprising of the Mujeres" (1979), and mural "Guadeloupe" (1990). Other notable paintings included Yolanda Lopez's "Portrait of the Artist as the Virgin of Guadeloupe" (1978) and Ester Hernandez's "Sun Mad" (1982).

Several artists sculpted or decorated landscapes called "Earthworks." Robert Smithson composed "Spiral Jetty" (1969–70) by curling 6,650 tons of stones into Great Salt Lake. Michael Heizer bulldozed 240,000 tons of earth to create his "Double Negative" (1969–70). Walter de Maria pounded 400 stainless steel poles into a grid in New Mexico's desert and called it "Lightening Field" (1970–7). Christo Javaceff used fabric to drape landscapes. His greatest installation in the West was his "Running Fence," an 18ft high white nylon wall that meandered 24½ miles through a stretch of Marin and Sonoma Counties north of

San Francisco Bay from 1972 to 1976. Most ambitious of all is Heizer's "City" in Garden Valley in the desert 160 miles north of Las Vegas. He began the project of abstractly carved hills and ridges in 1972. Half a century and $40 million later he was far from finishing his vision.

San Francisco spawned two counterculture movements. The Beatniks were a small community of writers, artists, and musicians that gradually came together in the late 1940s and slowly expanded in the 1950s. They celebrated freedom of expression best expressed by Jazz music. They had communities in both New York's Greenwich Village and San Francisco's North Beach with their cafes, bookstores, and then inexpensive housing. Novelist Jack Kerouac and poets Alan Ginsberg and Lawrence Ferlinghetti, who owned the City of Lights Bookstore, were the greatest Beatnik authors. The Hippies were a mass youth movement that celebrated freedom of lifestyle, love, and creativity, communalism, and mind-expanding drugs like marijuana, LSD, magic mushrooms, and peyote. Folk and Rock music was as vital to Hippies as Jazz was to Beatniks. San Francisco's Haight Asbury district of quaint Victorian homes became the Hippie movement's epicenter. Bands like the Jefferson Airplane and Grateful Dead lived in the neighborhood. Hippies had mass human Be Ins and Love Ins in nearby Panhandle Park.

Ken Kesey, author of *One Flew Over the Cuckoo's Nest,* formed the "Merry Prankster" commune at La Honda, California dedicated to free love, LSD, and creativity in 1964. Transient members included the Grateful Dead and the Hells Angels. Kesey and his followers converted a school bus into a rolling home, painted it psychedelically, and with rock music blaring from loudspeakers toured America. Tom Wolfe brilliantly conveyed the antics of Kesey and his rolling community in his *Electric Cool Aid Acid Test* (1968); authoritarianism lurked beneath the seeming anarchy as Kesey warned dissidents, "You're either on the bus or off the bus."

Santa Fe eventually surpassed Taos as an art center. The city was easily reached by train, and had a larger population and better accommodations than remote Taos 60 miles north. In 1909, farsighted state assemblymen established the Museum of New Mexico with the Palace of the Governors the centerpiece. Edgar Hewitt, the Museum of New Mexico's director, sought to revive traditional Indian arts and crafts while boosting the economy with all the tourists they could attract. In 1922, he did so by inaugurating the Southwest Indian Fair and Industrial Arts and Craft Exhibition, and encouraging Pueblo artists to participate. He offered free admission to anyone wearing traditional dress. Santa Fe's Indian and western art markets steadily expanded from the 1960s. The Institute of American Indian Art and its Museum of Contemporary Indian Arts, founded in 1962, accelerated the expression of Indian artists.

Taos, however, retained its title as a Bohemian refuge. Millicent Rogers was a talented, charismatic New York City woman who came to Taos and established an artist colony. She was born into an oil rich family, became a model and socialite, married and divorced three husbands, and sojourned for years in Europe. In 1947, she moved to Taos, bought an adobe, and began collecting Indian art and designed southwest style jewelry. The most prominent members of her salon were writers Frank Waters and Oliver La Farge. She died in 1953. Her son Paul Peralta-Ramos established the Millicent Rogers Museum in 1956.

During the late 1960s, hippies overran Taos, established communes, and often clashed with the conservative Hispanic population that resented their unconventional behavior and condescending attitudes. By 1969, Hippies and natives numbered 2,000 and 3,500 of the populations of Taos and 3,314 and 14,000 of Taos County.[21] Dennis Hopper was an actor, painter, photographer, moviemaker, and poet who, with Peter Fonda and Jack Nicolson, filmed the nihilistic biker movie *Easy Rider* around Taos in 1969. He bought the Mabel Dodge Luhan estate from her daughter and periodically lived there until 1978. Hopper made his "Mud Palace" the scene of drug and sex orgies. He sold the property to George and Kitty Otero who transformed it into Las Palomas de Taos, a spiritual and wellness center.

***

Westerners carried music with them, even those who never sang or played a hymn or ballad. For most frontier folks a musician with a fiddle or banjo was rare good fortune. With his violin, Reuben Fields revived the spirits of the Lewis and Clark expedition during evenings after exhausting days pulling by rope the keelboat up swift water or portaging the dugouts and all the equipment around rapids. As towns developed, saloonkeepers, brothel madams, and church deacons ordered pianos for their establishments. With time, westerners sang songs about themselves that either they or easterners composed.

The first records were Howard "Jack" Thorp's *Songs of the Cowboys* in 1908 and John Lomax's *Cowboy Songs and Other Frontier Ballads* in 1910. The Cowboy music genre, soon called Country and Western, took off with "talkie" movies in 1928, with both ballads and symphonic soundtracks increasingly growing popular across the nation and eventually around the world. Popular Hollywood crooners included Gene Autrey, Tex Ritter, and Roy Rogers. During the 1930s and 1940s, the most popular Country and Western stars were Bob Wills and the Texas Cowboys and Hank Williams. Woody Guthrie expanded the genre to include folk songs that depicted the dark side of contemporary West and America, especially his *Dust Bowl Ballads*. Guthrie deeply influenced Bob Dylan whose most western-themed album was *John Wesley Hardin* (1968). Buffy Sainte Marie, a Cree, gave a bleak Indian perspective with songs like "Now That the Buffalo's Gone" and "My Country 'Tis of Thy People Dying." During the 1970s, a Country version of Rock music emerged led by performers like the Outlaws, New Riders of the Purple Sage, Pure Prairie League, Crazy Horse, and Cowboy Junkies. Among Neil Young's most popular albums were western-themed *After the Gold Rush* (1970) and *Heart of Gold* (1972) along with his song "Cowgirl in the Sand." Western themes inspired two of Bruce Springsteen's best albums, *Badlands* (1978) and *Nebraska* (1982).

***

The inauguration of "talkie" movies with *The Jazz Singer* in 1928 enhanced the viewer's experience of dialogue and acting. The first talkie western was *In Old Arizona* (1929) which earned five Oscar nominations and won Best Actor for Warner Baxter who played the Cisco Kid. Among the best westerns of the 1930s were *Billy the Kid* and *The Big Trail* in 1930, *Squaw Man* and *Cimarron* in 1931, *The Plainsman* in 1937, and *Union Pacific, Dodge City, Jesse James,* and *Frontier Marshal* in 1939. The Golden Age of westerns lasted from 1945 to 1960 when Hollywood annually produced around seventy-five or one of four movies. Classic westerns that combined fine direction, acting, stories, and reinterpretations of familiar themes included: Gary Cooper in *High Noon* (1952), Alan Ladd in *Shane* (1953), William Wilder's *The Big Country* (1958) starring Gregory Peck, Howard Hawk's *Red River* (1948) and *Rio Bravo* (1959), John Sturges's *The Magnificent Seven* (1960), and *How the West Was Won* (1962) with parts directed by John Ford, Henry Hattaway, and George Marshall. Leading western actors were Gary Cooper, Jimmy Stewart, Randolph Scott, Henry Fonda, Burt Lancaster, Kirk Douglas, and John Wayne.

Director John Ford presented an elegiac if mythical version of the West. He directed John Wayne in *Stagecoach* (1939), *Red River* (1948), *Fort Apache* (1948), *She Wore a Yellow Ribbon* (1949), *Rio Grande* (1950) and *The Searchers* (1956).[22] Of those, *The Searchers* presents the bleakest vision as Wayne's character seeks to rescue or kill his niece kidnapped and violated by Comanches. He presented a mostly mythical view of Wyatt Earp and the OK Corral in his *My Darling Clementine* (1942) with Henry Fonda in the starring role. His *The Man Who Shot Liberty Valance* (1962) subverts the western myth with the cynical newspaper editor proclaiming, "This is the West, sir. When you have to choose between history and legend, print the legend. And so I've done." Ford's last film, *Cheyenne Autumn* (1964), treated Indians sympathetically.

During the 1950s, no one shaped the West's pop-cultural image more than Walt Disney through film, television, and a theme park. In 1955, he opened Disney Land in Anaheim, a Los Angeles suburb. The park's sections include Frontierland, Tomorrowland, Main Street, Adventureland, and Fantasyland. His movies received fifty-nine Academy Award nominations, of which twenty-two won. Among them was not his most popular western, *Davy Crockett, King of the Wild Frontier* (1955). That and all his other products presented idealistic versions of their subjects.

During the 1960s, ever more revisionist westerns appeared that questioned traditional notions of heroism, good guys and bad guys, and history itself. Clint Eastward played cynical, violent, amoral characters in *A Fistful of Dollars* (1964), *For a Few Dollars More* (1965), *The Good, the Bad, and the Ugly* (1966), *High Plains Drifter* (1973), and *The Outlaw Josey Wales* (1976). Others included *The Oxbow Incident* (1943), *Johnny Guitar* (1954), *The Professionals* (1966), *Once Upon a Time in the West* (1968), *Butch Cassidy and the Sundance Kid* (1969), Robert Altman's *McCabe and Mrs. Miller* (1971), Sam Peckinpah's *Ride the High Country* (1961), *The Wild Bunch* (1969), and *Pat Garret and Billy the Kid* (1973), Marlon Brando and Jack Nicolson in *Missouri Breaks* (1976), and Michael Cimino's *Heaven's Gate* (1980). The most realistic depiction of Indian warfare was Robert Aldrich's *Ulzana's Raid* (1972) starring Burt Lancaster.

Meanwhile, John Wayne's movies persisted in depicting versions of the traditional hero in *The Alamo* (1960), which he directed as well as starred as Davy Crockett, *True Grit* (1969), *The Cowboys* (1972), and *The Shootist* (1976). Strangely, the colorful life of the Mountain Men has inspired only four good films during this era, *Big Sky* (1952), *A Man Called Horse* (1969), *Jeremiah Johnson* (1972), and *The Mountain Men* (1980). Films notably sympathetic to Indians included *Fort Apache* (1948), *Broken Arrow* (1950), *Cheyenne Autumn* (1964), *A Man Called Horse* (1970), *Little Big Man* (1970), *Soldier Blue* (1970), and *Buffalo Bill and the Indians, or Sitting Bull's History Lesson* (1976). Dustin Hoffman played a Zelig-like character born white but adopted by Indians in

Little Big Man (1970). Elliott Silverstein's *The Ballad of Cat Ballou* (1965) and Mel Brooks's *Blazing Saddles* (1974) lampooned westerns.

Some excellent films explored the contemporary West, including *Bad Day at Black Rock* (1955), *Giant* (1956), *The Misfits* (1962), *Lonely Are the Brave* (1962), *Hud* (1963), *Bonnie and Clyde* (1967), *Easy Rider* (1969), *The Last Picture Show* (1971), and *One Flew Over the Cuckoo's Nest* (1976). Of those no film better depicted ranch life along with conflicts between rich and poor, westerners and easterners, cowboys and oilmen, men and women, older and younger generations, Caucasians and Hispanics, and the traditional and modern West than *Giant*. *Easy Rider* reversed the western as the nihilistic bikers headed east from Los Angeles with their drug money and were gratuitously murdered in Florida. Milos Forman's *One Flew Over the Cuckoo's Nest* was based on Ken Kesey's novel set in an insane asylum and starred Jack Nicolson as Randall McMurphy, the freedom-loving nonconformist determined to break free.

Pulp movies were to film as pulp fiction was to literature. Hollywood churned out a stunning 2,000 low-budget B-Western flics from 1935 to 1954 alone. Most cost a week and a few thousand dollars to make and made money as double features when half of Americans weekly went to the pictures. Television eventually ended the B-Westerns.[23]

The first westerns appeared on television in 1955. Three years later, eight of the top ten most popular television shows were westerns, of which *Gunsmoke* enjoyed the most viewers and lasted the longest, twenty seasons from 1955 to 1975. Television westerns peaked in 1958 with eighteen new shows and westerns ranking seven of the top ten and twelve of the top twenty-five shows. The volume peaked in 1959 with forty-seven broadcast during prime time.[24] During the 1960s, *Death Valley Days*, *Bonanza*, *Rawhide*, *Wagon Train*, *Maverick*, *Big Valley*, *The Wild Wild West*, and *The High Chaparral* were among the most watched. Clint Eastwood was among the rare television actors who made the leap to the "big screen." He first acquired fame as the moody cowboy Rowdy Yates on *Rawhide*. Then there were the *Death Valley Days* accounts of true western tales told on the radio from 1930 to 1945, and on television from 1952 to 1970 with each episode narrated by a host, including Ronald Reagan from 1964 to 1966. By 1980, traditional westerns disappeared from television, killed off by post-Vietnam skepticism and irony about American history along with the soaring popularity of morality tales set into outer space with *Star Trek* and other science fiction shows.

PART V: THE POST-MODERN AMERICAN WEST SINCE 1981

Chapter 12

REDS AND BLUES

"I don't recognize the United States government as even existing." (Clive Bundy)

"We're simply trying to eliminate them. Our goal is to destroy environmentalism once and for all." (Ron Arnold)

"Those crazies in Montana who say . . . kill AFT agents because the U.N.'s going to take over—well, they're beginning to have a case." (Dick Morris)

The modern West began with the frontier's end in 1890 and ended with Ronald Reagan's election to the White House in 1980. During that time, the West transformed from a political and economic sideshow dependent on the East into a dynamic, diversified economic and political powerhouse. Like the rest of the country, the postmodern West's economy has a relatively expanding service sector and diminishing manufacturing, mining, and agribusiness sectors for both wealth and jobs; and a widening wealth gap between the rich elite and the middle class and poor. The globalization and automation of production combined with trickledown economic policies largely caused that transformation. Postmodern American society is increasingly multicultural and skeptical or outright scornful of traditional notions of American identity, history, and culture. Those economic and cultural changes at once shape and are shaped by politics, with liberal Democrats championing postmodern values and conservative Republicans championing traditional American values.[1]

The distinction between "blue" liberal Democrats and "red" conservative Republicans began with the 2000 election. Tim Russert, an NBC journalist renowned for his tough but civil questioning, originated the political color code. That inspired other networks along with newspapers to embrace the red-blue divide along with three other colors, with pink center-right, light blue center-left, and purple solid center. Eventually another political color emerged, black, the color for anarchist and nihilist terrorists.

A color-code map of the United States by congressional districts reveals those in cities and college towns as blue islands in red rural seas. That stark contrast obscures the spectrum of views within each district. Every individual's political identity is shaped by a unique mix of class, race, ethnicity, religion, gender, population density, education, and personal experiences whose relative importance usually changes over one's life. Generally speaking, liberal Democrats tend to be better educated, white collar workers, black, Hispanic, and Asian, urban, and female while conservative Republicans tend to be less educated, blue collar workers, white, rural, and male although plenty of each profile espouses the opposite and the suburbs are a tossup.

In the West as in other regions, shifting demographics leads to shifting political outlooks and thus outcomes. The West's congressional color code has changed from 1980 through today. As the West's cities expanded from native migrants and foreign immigrants, liberal democratic voters grew in numbers and power. Populations diversified with Asian, Latin, American, Caribbean, and African immigrants far more numerous than European immigrants. As crime, congestion, home prices, taxes, and homelessness rose in California, hundreds of thousands left that state for better lifestyles in interior western cities. In 1980, the West Coast states of California, Oregon, and Washington leaned blue and the interior western states leaned red. In the 1992 election, Bill Clinton and George H.W. Bush split the West, with the Democrat winning eight states with 96 electoral votes and the Republican eleven states with 81 electoral votes. By 2020, demographic changes rendered New Mexico, Colorado, Nevada, and Arizona light blue, and West Coast California, Oregon, and Washington bright blue while the other western states stayed red or pink.

So far, three postmodern West residents won the presidency, all conservative Republicans. Ronald Reagan served from 1981 to 1989, George H.W. Bush senior from 1989 to 1993, and George W. Bush junior from 2001 to 2009. None were born there. As young men Reagan and Bush senior moved to the West to develop careers, the former from Illinois to be an actor in Hollywood, California, the latter from Connecticut to be an oil corporation executive in Midland, Texas. Bush took his family with him and Bush junior grew up in Midland and is the most western of the three with a Texas twang, former chewing tobacco habit, and good ole boy demeanor. As president each followed a Republican agenda of trickle-down tax cuts, expanded military spending, and attempts to cut business regulations and giveaway public lands.

Women steadily won more public offices across the nation, with the West boasting some of the most prominent. California has elected more women to high office than any other state. Barbara Boxer was a congresswoman from 1983 to 1993 and a senator from 1993 to 2017. Diane Feinstein was San Francisco's mayor from 1978 to 1988 and a United States senator from 1992 to the present. Nancy Pelosi is a congresswoman representing her San Francisco district from 1983 to the present, and was speaker of the House from 2019 to 2023. Democrats Patricia Schroeder served in the House of Representatives from 1973 to 1997, and Barbara Jourdan was elected the first black member of the House of Representatives from her Houston, Texas district, and served from 1973 to 1979. Among Republicans, Dixy Ray Lee and Kay Orr were the respective governors of Washington from 1977 to 1981 and Nebraska from 1987 to 1981; Patience Sewell Latting, Kathy Whitmire, and Annette Straus were the respective mayors of Oklahoma City from 1971 to 1983, Houston from 1982 to 1992, and Dallas from 1987 to 1991; and Nancy Kassebaum was elected a senator from Kansas in 1978 and served until 1997. Sandra Day O'Connor, the first female supreme court justice was an Arizonan.

Westerners increasingly voted for minority candidates. Hispanics Henry Cisneros and Frederico Pena respectively won the mayorships of San Antonio and Denver, and Bill Richardson won New Mexico's governorship. Japanese-Americans Samuel Hayakawa was a senator from California from 1977 to 1983, Robert Matsui was a congressman from 1979 to 2005, and David Mineta was San Jose's mayor from 1967 to 1975 then a congressman from 1975 to 1995. Chinese American David Wu was a congressman from 1999 to 2011 from Portland. In 2020, black members of the House of Representatives from the West included Democrats Maxine Water, Barbara Lee, and Karen Bass of California, Eddie Johnson, Al Green, Sheila Lee, and Colin Alfred from Texas, Jose Neguse from Colorado, and Marilyn Strickland from Washington, and Republican Burgess Owen from Utah.

***

As for the other "Red America," American Indians have made significant economic progress, although they trail in some areas.[2] Of the 574 federally recognized tribes, nine of ten reservations are located in the West. Indians numbered 6,790,000 or 2.09 percent of the population in 2020. In 2019, their average income was $42,825, higher than blacks with $41,935 but behind Hispanics with $51,811 and whites with $68,785. Indian unemployment was 6.1 percent, the same as blacks but worse than Hispanics with 4.3 percent and whites with 3.3. percent. Slightly more than half of Indians or 50.8 percent owned their homes, a higher rate than Hispanics or blacks but behind whites with 72.3 percent. Indians lagged in higher education with only 15.0 percent holding a bachelor's degree compared to 16.4 percent of Hispanics, 26.6 percent of blacks, and 33.5 percent of whites. As for residence, around seven of ten Indians live in urban areas while 26 percent live on reservations.[3]

Ever more tribes economically benefited from opening casinos on their reservations. The Florida Seminole tribe led the way in 1979 when the council agreed that a casino could earn desperately-needed revenues to address an array of socioeconomic problems among themselves. They acted on their right as an autonomous political entity to establish a casino. The idea worked. Their casino made plenty of money to alleviate incomes, education, and infrastructure. One by one other tribes founded their own casinos, usually with similar results. Congress tried to regulate Indian casinos with the 1988 Indian Gaming Regulatory Act that established three categories of casinos and required tribes to negotiate with their state government before establishing one. In 2021, 243 tribes in 29 states had casinos with a combined revenue of $39 billion.[4]

Indians have also achieved some national political posts. So far, Cheyenne Ben Nighthorse Campbell won the highest political post, that of senator from Colorado in 1992 and served until 2005. President Joe Biden named Deb Haaland, a Laguna Pueblo and congresswoman, to be the first Indian Interior Department secretary in 2020. In 2022, four Indians were members of the House of Representatives, Republicans Chickasaw Tom Cole of Oklahoma, Cherokee Markwayne Mullin of Oklahoma, and Cherokee Yvette Herrell of Minnesota, and Democrat Ho Chunk Sharice Davids of Kansas.

Nonetheless, each tribe faces varying challenges. Human nature and politics plague Indian tribes like all other groups. Greed and fear can shape tribal policies. Corrupt politicians and bureaucrats palm bribes to turn a blind eye or turn over control of lucrative contracts to corporations. Many reservations suffer the disastrous effects of unregulated mining, overgrazing, and water wastage. The core dilemma for Indians is reviving their shattered traditions and reconciling them with modern American life.

Indian identity is entangled in the legal question of whether being Indian is primarily a political or racial category. Most tribes require official enrolled members to be at least 25 percent genetically Indian, yet maintain that they are primarily political entities. The *Brackeen versus Haaland* case tested that question. Non-Indians Chad and Jennifer Brackeen sued to keep custody of a baby boy with a Navajo mother and Cherokee father, and adopt his sister after a court transferred his custody to an Indian relative of the children. Their suit was backed by the states of Texas, Louisiana, and Indiana against Interior Secretary Haaland and five tribes including the Navajo and Cherokee. The 1978 Indian Child Welfare Act required judges in custody battles to place Indian foster children with extended family members or tribal members if possible. Around one of three Indian children placed in foster care end up with non-Indian parents. In 2018, Texas's Supreme Court struck down the law as unconstitutional for promoting racial discrimination and violating the child's best interests for adoptive parents. The Supreme Court heard the case in November 2022 and issued a ruling on June 15, 2023. By 7 to 2, they upheld the Indian Child Welfare Act and required the Brackeens to turn over the boy to his Indian relatives.[5]

Some tribes are struggling to get Washington to fulfill treaty duties centuries after they were signed. For instance, under the 1835 Treaty of New Echota, the Cherokee sold their lands in the Smokey Mountains for land in Oklahoma and a non-voting delegate in Congress. They got the land but not the delegate. There are 430,000 Cherokee, just 150,000 fewer than Wyoming's 584,309 people, who as members of a state enjoy not just a voting representative but also two senators. In 2019, the Cherokee nation designated Kimberly Teechee as their representative but Congress did not accept her and the Supreme Court did not rule on whether it should.[6]

***

On behalf of the American people, the federal government owns 27.1 percent or 615,311,596 of the nation's 2,271,343,360 acres. Twelve western states account for 92 percent of those federal lands. That includes 80.1 percent of Nevada, 63.1 percent of Utah, 61.9 percent of Idaho, 52.3 percent of Oregon, 46.7 percent of Wyoming, 45.4 percent of California, 38.9 percent of Arizona, 36.2 percent of Colorado, 31.7 percent of New Mexico, 29.0 percent of Montana, and 28.6 percent of Washington. Then there is a sharp drop for the remaining western states with federal lands accounting for only 6.5 percent of South Dakota, 5.3 percent of North Dakota, 3.8 percent of Oklahoma, 2.3 percent of Texas, 1.5 percent of Nebraska, and 1.4 percent of Kansas.[7]

Although the West's economy steadily diversifies, its dependence on Washington persists. Federal programs boost the West's prosperity with hundreds of billions of annual subsidies like military bases, national research institutes, government contracts for products along with grazing, logging, and mining on federal lands, and farm subsidies. Western realities increasingly refute western myths. Ironically, no region has a larger share of people living in metropolitan areas. Nonetheless, politically the rural West has power beyond its sparse and often declining numbers of inhabitants. Economically the West is split between dynamic and troubled sectors. Innovative technology centers include Microsoft's campus near Seattle, Washington; Silicon Valley around San Jose, California; Little Silicon Valley around Austin, Texas; Hewlett-Packard's campus at Boise, Idaho; Honeywell and Sperry in Albuquerque. Meanwhile, farmers and ranchers suffer an array of related challenges including rising production costs and diminishing prices for their products.

***

Ironically the very success of federal programs that helped develop the economy, cut water and air pollution, finance higher education, and thus expand wealth and opportunities eventually provoked a swelling movement that opposed those very policies. Many people want to believe that their successes depended solely on their own efforts. Conservatives exploited that yearning by championing the message that "big government" actually impeded development that only self-reliance and free markets created.

Nowhere across the nation was that message more popular than in the West. In reality, the West took three times more federal money via an array of workfare programs than it paid in revenues. Yet most westerners tended to deny that reality, preferring to cling to their regional mythology of self-made, self-reliant individuals. Thomas Frank explored those phenomena in his 2005 book *What's the Matter With Kansas?*.[8]

The "Sagebrush Rebellion" is the ongoing efforts by many westerners to privatize federal lands and deregulate the economy, including eliminating laws that protect nature.[9] Although Sagebrushers eventually called themselves the "Wise Use Movement," that was a false advertisement. They want to return the West to the lawless Darwinian survival of the fittest time when might made right.

The Sagebrush Rebellion erupted in the late 1970s. California led the way when two California conservative political activists—Howard

Jarvis and Paul Gann—got enough signatures to place on the 1978 ballot Proposition 13, the People's Initiative to Limit Property Taxation to no more than 2 percent. Voters approved Proposition 13 by 53 percent to 47 percent. Then in 1979, Nevada conservative leaders demanded that the federal government privatize its lands that comprised 80 percent of the state. Senator Orin Hatch of Utah promoted a bill whereby Washington transferred 544,000,000 acres to thirteen western states.

Ronald Reagan embraced the Sagebrush Rebellion as part of the conservative Republican coalition that won him the White House in 1980. He crushed sitting president Jimmy Carter with 50.8 percent of the vote and 489 electors to 41.1 percent and 49 electors; independent candidate John Anderson won 6.6 percent of the vote. Reagan won every western state. His previous elected positions included president of the Screen Actors Guild from 1947 to 1952 and 1959 to 1960, and California's governor from 1967 to 1975.

In countless minds, Reagan was an iconic westerner because of his rugged good looks, amiable demeanor, cowboy movie roles, and California ranch where he cleared brush and rode his horse. People confused the celluloid Reagan with the real one and believed he was as heroic as the characters he portrayed. In reality, Reagan was no hero; he spent World War II making B-movies and propaganda films in Hollywood. That myth was especially egregious when he competed against George H.W. Bush for the Republican Party's nomination. Bush was a genuine hero, a combat pilot who flew 58 missions in the Pacific, was shot down, and earned the Distinguished Flying Cross. Yet Reagan's campaign derided Bush as a "wimp" and promoted Reagan as the all-American hero.[10]

As president, Reagan was determined to enact the Sagebrush agenda of transferring as many federal lands as possible to the states or exploitation by corporations. Spearheading that crusade were Interior Secretary James Watt, Environmental Protection Agency (EPA) Director Anne Gorsuch, and Bureau of Land Management (BLM) Director Robert Buford. Each purged professionals and packed vacancies with people from the industries they were supposed to regulate, cut the number of lawsuits against business that violated the law, and eliminated or weakened regulations that protected public lands and reduced air and water pollution.

Those policies delighted all and enriched many Sagebrushers but enraged countless other Americans. In 1983, over a million Americans and 125 Indian tribes signed a petition demanding that Watt resign; Reagan reluctantly had Watt do so on October 9, 1983. Congress found Gorsuch in contempt and she resigned on March 3, 1983. Congress also found Rita Lavelle, the EPA Waste Management director, in contempt; a jury found her guilty of perjury and a judge sentenced her to five years' probation, a $10,000 fine, and six months in prison. Eventually justice caught up to Watt. On January 2, 1996, he was indicted on eighteen counts of felony perjury and obstruction of justice for influence peddling. Watt got off easy, a plea bargain to a misdemeanor of withholding documents, five years' probation, a $5,000 fine, and 500 hours of community service.

The Reagan administration's scandals darkened the Sagebrusher image so they changed their brand name to the Wise Use Movement. The American Freedom Institute, a subsidiary of Reverend Sun Myung Moon's Unification Church, underwrote the first "Wise Use" conference at Reno in 1988. The keynote speaker was Ron Arnold who issued a twenty-five point blueprint to privatize all public lands, maximize corporate welfare, minimize taxes and regulations, and eliminate all New Deal, Great Society, and civil right programs. Arnold revealed the rage, hatred, and violence that animates many in the Wise Use Movement: "We're out to kill the fuckers. We're simply trying to eliminate them. Our goal is to destroy environmentalism once and for all."[11]

Wise Users argue that you can have jobs or nature, not both, economic development or environmental protection, not both. They attack the federal government programs that transformed the West from an economic backwater into mass prosperity. They claim to be "strict constructivists" when interpreting the Constitution unless the framers' "original intent" actually opposed their position. They insist that under their "unitary executive theory," Congress can never empower a bureaucracy to draw and enforce economic, social, and environmental regulations, it can only do so itself. They "prove" their cases with "junk science" and "fuzzy math" along with an array of specious conspiracy theories. Among their targets are the National Science Foundation, the National Academy of Sciences, the American Association for the Advancement of Science, and the International Panel on Climate Change. They mask the true nature of their movement with Trojan Horse names like the National Wetlands Coalition, Healthy Forests Coalition, Alliance for Climate Change and the Environment, Environmental Conservation Organization, Global Climate Coalition, and Wildlife Legislative Fund. A favorite tactic is launching "Strategic Lawsuits against Public Participation" (SLAPP) against environmental groups that protest their pollution and destruction of nature policies.

Powerful organizations back the Sagebrush Rebellion, Wise Use Movement, and related conservative causes with financial, legal, and intellectual aid. Among the West's most powerful interest groups are the Cattleman's Association, American Farm Bureau Federation,

National Rifle Association, American Petroleum Institute, American Mining Congress, Coal Association, Blue Ribbon Coalition, National Association of Manufacturers, Alliance for America, People for the West, Inholders Association, Western States Public Lands Coalition, American Forest Resource Alliance, Western States Public Lands Coalition, and Forest Products Association along with thousands of corporations and companies. Think tanks include the Heritage Foundation, Cato Institute, American Enterprise Institute, and First Liberty Institute. Litigious corporations include the Washington Legal Foundation, Pacific Legal Foundation, Rocky Mountain States Legal Foundation, and Federalist Society.

Conservative causes have no end of enthusiastic financial donors. None have been more generous, wide-ranging, and effective than those of brothers David and Charles Koch. In 1971, David Koch founded at Colorado Springs the Libertarian Party to abolish all economic, social, health, and environmental regulations and agencies. Charles Koch founded the libertarian Cato Institute in Washington in 1977. Joseph Coors of the Coors Beer fortune was another key financier. Coors established the Rocky Mountain Legal Foundation headed by James Watt. Agribusiness behemoths like Archer Daniels Midland, Cargill, Monsanto, and Conagra are heavy contributors to Wise Use lobby groups and politicians.

Mass media supporters include the newspapers *The Wall Street Journal* and *Washington Times;* cable television networks Fox News with such stars as Bill O'Reilly, Sean Hannity, Tucker Carlson, and Laura Ingraham from 1996, Breitbart News from 2007, and Newsmax from 2014; and what supporters call "talk radio" and critics call "rant radio" or "hate radio" with the king Rush Limbaugh who broadcasted from 1988 to 2021.

Seemingly inspired by God's command in Genesis to "multiply and subdue the earth," evangelicals enthusiastically back the Wise Use Movement. The most powerful groups included Jerry Falwell's Moral Majority in the 1980s and Ralph Reed's Christian Coalition in the 1990s, sects like Oral Roberts's Evangelistic Association from 1947 and University in Tulsa from 1963, James Dobson's Focus on the Family in Denver from 1975, and Bill McCartney's Promise Keepers in Colorado Springs from 1991.

***

The overlapping Sovereign Citizen and Posse Comitatus movements figuratively if not literally wave the black flag. They share the Wise Use Movement's goal of privatizing public lands, but are anarchists that seek to destroy the federal and state governments. They believe each individual is free to decide which laws to follow and which to ignore. They recognize no government beyond the county level which they seek to control. Their first takeover was Catron County, New Mexico in 1990. Most critically, many of them believe that violence and even mass murder is a justified means to their ends.

Ted Kaczynski, nicknamed the Unabomber, was a brilliant mathematician with a bachelor's degree from Harvard and a masters and doctorate from the University of Michigan who taught at the University of California at Berkely. Then, in 1971, he resigned and moved to a small cabin near Lincoln, Montana. He was obsessed with the destructive nature of many high technology products and hated the people who devised them. From 1978 to 1995, he sent package bombs to scientists and engineers that killed three people and injured twenty-three others. After learning he was the Unabomber, his brother informed the FBI who arrested him in 1996. In 1998, a jury found Kaczynski guilty of murder and other felonies, and the judge sentenced him to eight consecutive life sentences in a federal prison.

Randy Weaver was a militia and Sagebrush activist who lived with his family on Ruby Ridge in Boundary County Idaho. In 1988, he ran for sheriff with the promise that he would not enforce any gun control or public land protection laws. He sold illegal guns and refused to pay income taxes. Learning of his crimes, the Bureau of Alcohol, Tobacco, and Firearms (ATF) had an undercover agent try to buy an illegal gun from him. Although Weaver sold him two sawed off shotguns in October 1989, the ATF did not indict him until December 1990 and arrest him until January 17, 1991. Judge Stephen Ayers, a Reagan appointee and sage brusher, released him without bail. Weaver refused to appear for his February 1991 trial and repeatedly told the press that he and his family "will not obey your lawless government."[12] Weaver became a Sagebrush hero, celebrated by right-wing media and political leaders.

Fearing a violent confrontation, the federal government hesitated to uphold the law for a year and a half, thus undermining the rule of law not just in Idaho but across the nation. Finally, prosecutors decided to act. On August 21, 1992, six federal marshals surrounded Weaver's house. When the dogs started barking, Weaver, his 14-year-old son Sam, and friend Kevin Harris advanced with guns to investigate. An agent shot a dog dashing toward him. The agents then called on Weaver to surrender. The three Sagebrushers opened fire, killing one agent and wounding another. The four agents returned fire and killed

Sam Weaver. The agents then retreated with their wounded colleague and called for support.

The FBI's elite Hostage Rescue Team took over. A hundred FBI agents backed by twenty-six Idaho guardsmen surrounded the compound on August 22. When Weaver appeared armed at the door, an FBI agent fired a shot that grazed his arm and killed his wife Vicki, standing behind him. The FBI tried to starve Weaver and his family out. On August 26, they let Lieutenant Colonel James "Bo" Gritz, a far right wing hero, act as intermediary. Gritz convinced Harris to surrender on August 30 and Weaver on August 31, and gave each a Nazi salute as they did so.

The trial was just as controversial as the shootings and siege. The defense lawyer for Weaver and Harris tried to put the federal government on trial for murder. The prosecution countered by charging Weaver and Harris with an array of felonies including murder and felonious assault. A sympathetic jury acquitted Harris and Weaver of those serious charges, and merely found Weaver guilty of not appearing at his earlier trial date. Weaver was fined $10,000 and sentenced to eighteen months in prison. Later he and his two daughters won a wrongful death suit whereby the federal government paid him $10,000 and his daughters $1 million each.[13]

Branch Davidians are on offshoot of Seventh Day Adventists. In 1955, Victor Houteff founded the group around the belief that Jesus's Second Coming was imminent. Davidians were still waiting in 1959 when Houteff's widow, Florence, announced that Jesus would soon visit Texas. Nearly nine hundred followers moved to Mount Carmel, near Waco, where they hoped to greet the Messiah's return before being whisked off to heaven.

And there the dwindling congregation waited until 1990, when David Koresh joined them. Koresh revitalized the movement with his mix of millennium and anti-government messages. The Davidians amassed a huge weapons stockpile for Armageddon. Rumors of this arsenal were confirmed in May 1992, when a United Parcel Service shipment broke open and grenades clattered on the ground. Fortunately, none exploded. The terrified deliveryman notified the sheriff who in turn informed the AFT. An investigation revealed that Koresh and other Davidians were selling and buying illegal weapons.[14]

The AFT acquired search warrants and scheduled a raid on the compound for February 28, 1993. The result was a disaster. As seventy AFT agents converged, the Davidians opened fire, killing four and wounding several agents. The AFT returned fire, wounding Koresh and his father-in-law, and killing several others including a woman nursing her baby.

The same FBI Hostage Rescue Team that conducted the Ruby Ridge siege took over the Davidian standoff. The siege lasted fifty-one days. During the third week, the FBI was able to coax out twenty-two children accompanied by two women. On April 19, 1993, the FBI finally tried to flush out the Davidians by pumping tear gas into the building. Determined to die as martyrs, Koresh and his followers started fires around the compound. Eighty Branch Davidians died, including twenty-one children, in the inferno. Amidst the charred ruins, investigators found 292 firearms, 46 of which were illegal, along with scores of hand grenades.

Thus did David Koresh and his followers become the far right's latest martyrs. Supporters shrilly claimed that it was the federal government rather than the Davidians that caused the fires and killed those people. Tens of thousands of Linda Thompson's video titled "Waco—The Big Lie" and "Waco II: The Big Lie Continues" not only promoted this rightist myth but a spectrum of other conspiracy theories including that President Bill Clinton was a murderer, drug kingpin, and Soviet agent. Sagebrush extremists everywhere were more determined than ever to attack the federal government.

Among the tens of thousands who vowed to avenge Ruby Ridge and Waco, Timothy McVeigh and a tight group of co-conspirators realized this vision.[15] On April 19, 1995, they exploded a truck bomb outside Oklahoma City's federal Alfred P. Murrah Building that destroyed $1 billion in property and 168 lives, including 19 children, and wounded over 800 other people.

For McVeigh it was a very short step from fantasizing to actually committing mass murder. In April 1991, he tried and failed to join the Green Berets—not surprisingly, he flunked the psychological test. Enraged, he quit the army. Without military discipline to hold together his troubled psyche, he drifted deeper into hate-filled obsessions. But his formal planning to destroy the federal government began only after the Waco infernal.

Shortly after the Oklahoma City explosion, the FBI and other agencies launched a massive manhunt and offered a $2 million reward for information leading to the arrest of the terrorists. It was McVeigh's stupidity rather than sleuthing that cracked the case. McVeigh's hatred of government was so dogmatic that he refused to license his automobile. A trooper pulled him over 80 minutes after the explosion. McVeigh might have gotten away with a ticket had the trooper not noticed a 9mm pistol badly concealed in his jacket. The trooper arrested him on charges of carrying a concealed weapon and driving without a license plate or license. Two other stupidities made McVeigh a prime suspect. He left behind in the patrol car a business card with the note that he needed five more dynamite sticks. A later search of his car uncovered notes that linked him with the bombing. A final blunder revealed one of his conspirators. McVeigh listed James Nichols, the brother of his partner Terry Nichols, as his next of kin in the police report.

Yet, despite all those amateurish mistakes, McVeigh became the extreme right's "hero." Although that mass murder appalled most Americans, the number and ranks of militia groups swelled in the months following the explosion from 224, with 45 openly neo-Nazi, in 39 states to 859 in 1996. In 1997, courts sentenced McVeigh to death, Nichols to life imprisonment, and Michael Fortier, who assisted them and knew of the pending attack, to twelve years.[16] McVeigh was killed by lethal injection at the federal prison in Terre Haute, Indian on June 11, 2001. Shortly before his death, he was asked if he felt sorry for the 19 children along with the 151 adults he murdered. McVeigh replied, "I have no sympathy for them" and dismissed them as "collateral damage."[17]

President Bill Clinton gave a typically moving eulogy for the Oklahoma City dead and spoke out against hate: "We hear so many loud and angry voices in America today who leave the impression . . . that violence is acceptable. Some of us have not discharged our responsibilities. It is time we all stood up and spoke against that kind of reckless speech and behavior."[18] But Clinton and other moderates backed off from explicitly noting the connection between rightist rhetoric and terrorism. Right-wing politicians and media immediately attacked Clinton for his judicious words.

Among the most powerful Sagebrushers were Montana's militia groups that convinced most of that state's legislators to pass a bill rendering federal agents subject to arrest for kidnapping, trespassing, and theft if they arrested someone without the local sheriff's permission. Governor Marc Racicot vetoed the bill. The Montana Freemen exemplified right-wing anarchism. They tried to enrich and empower themselves by practicing such rightist theories as "debt-money" and "common law" by issuing their own money, lawsuits, bounties, subpoenas, courts, and judgments. In January 1993, three dozen Freemen took over the Garfield County courthouse, declared their own government, then dispersed without being arrested. Although banks foreclosed on Freemen property, the police were either too afraid or sympathetic to evict the heavily armed squatters. In November and December 1995, grand juries charged a dozen Freemen with varied felonies including kidnapping, fraud, threatening public officials, criminal syndicalism, grand larceny, and armed robbery. Although the FBI had investigated the Freemen for months, they simply backed state and local police in surrounding the Freemen ranch and demanding surrender in December 1995. Still smarting from criticism of how they handled the Ruby Ridge and Waco sieges, the FBI did not try to force the Freemen to give up even though their own operations cost $300,000 a day. After an 81-day standoff, the Freemen surrendered on March 25, 1996.[19]

Barack Obama's election as the first black president in 2008 enraged the far right. Governor Rick Perry reacted to his presidency by declaring his hope that Texas seceded from the United States. The number of so-called "patriot" groups soared from 149 in 2008 to 512 in 2009 and 1,274 in 2011. Of those groups, 127 were explicitly militia groups. Whatever the category, many groups openly called for vandalism, beatings, and outright murder of liberal politicians.[20] Not just leaders of self-styled "patriot" groups but even some Republican politicians openly advocated violence to advance their agenda. Former Minnesota governor Tim Pawlenty told a cheering group that they should "take a nine-iron and smash the window out of big government in this country." Dick Morris, a Republican political advisor, stated on Fox News that, "Those crazies in Montana who say . . . kill AFT agents because the U.N.'s going to take over—well, they're beginning to have a case."[21]

The Bundy gang in southeast Oregon and northeast Nevada became an anarchist icon.[22] Clive Bundy was a rancher who swelled his wealth by running cattle on public lands without paying for the privilege. By 2016, he owed the federal government and American taxpayers over $1 million in fees. His excuse for breaking the law was the same as countless other anarchists: "I don't recognize the United States government as even existing."[23] The threats of Bundy, his sons, and their supporters to die fighting any attempt by the federal or state governments to enforce the law against them intimidated officials from doing so. Not content with his victory, his sons, Ammon and Ryan Bundy, and twenty-four other militants invaded and took over the Malheur National Wildlife Refuge headquarters on January 2, 2016. The FBI finally acted by mobilizing agents and surrounding the refuge. The anarchists bulldozed barriers around the building, broke into safes and stole money, computers, and cameras, and trashed the property. The Bundy gang surrendered after a 41-day standoff during which one of them was killed and another wounded in a shootout when they tried to evade a police roadblock. Although courts found twenty-six of twenty-seven gang members guilty on an array of charges, the Bundy brothers and five other defendants escaped justice on the central accusation "conspiracy." Anarchists across the nation cheered the jury's not-guilty verdict on October 29, 2016.

Not just far-right groups committed terrorism. Two radical leftist organizations wielded "ecoterrorism" to protect nature. Earth First! led by Dave Forman and the Earth Liberation Front (ELF), founded respectively in 1980 and 1992, were the most prominent groups that sought to realize the slogan "No Compromise in Defense of Mother Earth!" Edward Abbey's 1975 novel *The Monkeywrench Gang* provided radicals the justifications and nonviolent strategies to throw "monkey wrenches" into the gears of industrial society. For instance, driving 10in nails into ancient trees in old growth forests and announcing that "spiking" would deter loggers from chainsawing them. Pouring chloride into a bulldozer's gas tank will wreck the engine. An Earth First! pamphlet described monkeywrenching as safe, easy, fun, and effective "in stopping timber cutting, road building, overgrazing, oil and gas exploration, mining, dam building, powerline construction, off-road-vehicle use, trapping, trapping, ski area development and other forms of destruction of the wilderness." It also emphasized that Monkeywrenching was non-violent, not organized, individual, targeted, and timely.[24] Both organizations have a dozen or so chapters in different countries.

***

Anarchists have a political agenda that they fight to realize; they may commit terrorist acts to their ends but not suicide attacks. Nihilists murder for the sake of murder and usually expect to be killed doing so. The most horrific are mass murders of children. From 1979 to 2022, there were 1,924 shootings at schools from kindergarten through high school, during which 637 people died and 1,734 were injured. Two of the worst occurred in the West. On April 20, 1999, twelfth graders Eric Harris and Dylan Klebold murdered twelve students and one teacher, and wounded twenty others at Columbine High School in Littleton, Colorado. On May 24, 2022, former student Salvador Ramos murdered nineteen students and two teachers, and wounded seventeen others at Robb Elementary School in Uvalde, Texas.[25]

With each massacre, liberals and conservatives renewed their debate over what to do. Liberals called for assault weapon bans and other restrictions on owning firearms and ammunition. Conservatives argued that any restrictions on firearms violates the Constitution's Second Amendment that reads: "A well-regulated militia, being necessary for the security of a free state, the right of the people to keep and bear arms shall not be infringed." Conservatives interpret that to allow unrestricted gun ownership so that Americans can rebel against a tyrannical government. Liberals explain that the amendment only permits gun ownership for government regulated militia group members who protect the federal and state governments that are empowered to regulate what kind of firearms can be owned and who can own them. The middle position is that the founders believed in natural law whose fundamental right is self-preservation, and thus they would back an individual's right to arm himself for self-defense, while reserving government's right to regulate what arms are appropriate.[26]

***

During the 2016 election, Republican candidate Donald Trump won the Electoral College with 304 to 277 for Democratic candidate Hilary Clinton, although Clinton won more popular votes, 65,853,514 or 48.1 percent to Trump's 62,984,828 or 46.1 percent. As president, Trump enacted the Republican agenda of trickle-down tax cuts, boosts in military spending, business deregulation, replacement of professional civil servants with ideologues, and giveaways of public land to corporations. His first interior secretary, Ryan Zinke, resigned on January 2, 2019, after investigations revealed he had accepted tens of thousands of dollars' worth of gifts possibly in exchange for political favors. Trump sparked controversy for denouncing America's allies, embracing America's adversaries like Russia's Vladimir Putin and North Korea's Kim Jong-un, imposing a ban on Muslim immigrants, withdrawing the United States from the 2015 international agreement that prevented Iran from developing nuclear weapons and the 2016 Global Warming Accord, and making racist, sexist, and vulgar comments. The *Washington Post* fact-checked Trump's written and spoken words during his four years as president and counted 30,573 "false or misleading statements."[27]

Trump faced accusations of having committed felonies and even treason. Special Counsel Robert Mueller led a two-year investigation of Trump's ties to Russia during his 2016 election campaign, and found that Russia had massively interfered to promote Trump, attack Clinton, and discredit American democracy along with ten examples of Trump's obstruction of justice, but not enough convictable evidence of Trump's collusion with the Kremlin. Congress first impeached Trump in January 2020, but the Senate fell short of convicting him of abuse of power by 52 to 48 and obstruction of Congress by 53 to 47.

Trump's supporters adored him with cult-like devotion whose zealotry grew with his lies, bullying, cheating, bluster, and boasting along with soaring evidence that he was guilty of an array of felonies.

Trump devotees tended to be white working class, rural, former military people without college degrees and with hobbies like gun collecting, hunting, and Nascar. Many had suffered stagnant or declining incomes for decades that they bitterly blamed on globalization, the Organization for Petroleum Exporting Countries (OPEC), the North American Free Trade Agreement (NAFTA), legal and illegal immigrants, and reverse racism from affirmation action. They believe they are victims and martyrs, project their worst flaws onto hated others, and acclaim Trump as their savior. Among Trump's supporters were such extreme militant groups as the Proud Boys, Oath Keepers, and Q-Anon.

Trumpians argue that the Black Lives Matter (BLM), animated by Critical Race Theory, is radical, racist, and violent. They cite BLM riots in dozens of cities in 2020, when mobs fought police and looted and burned businesses and public buildings, and inflicted nineteen deaths, hundreds of injuries, and from $1 billion to $2 billion in damages. The most destructive riots were in New York, Minneapolis, and especially Seattle and Portland where BLM, Antifa, and other radical groups captured districts then battled police for months. They condemn Critical Race Theory for being as odious a philosophy as Marxism. Like Marxism, Critical Racists divide all of humanity into two antagonistic groups but based on race rather than class in which a minority of whites, every one of whom is racist, systemically suppresses and exploits everyone else who are virtuous people of color and who are justified in using any means to liberate themselves and win reparations.[28]

During the 2020 election, Democrat candidate Joe Biden decisively beat Trump by 81,283,501 votes or 51.3 percent and 306 electors to 74,223,975 votes or 46.8 percent and 232 electors. The West split between them with majorities of voters in California, Oregon, Washington, Nevada, Arizona, New Mexico, and Colorado for Biden, and those of Idaho, Montana, South Dakota, North Dakota, Wyoming, Kansas, and Texas for Trump. Two of Nebraska's electors backed Trump and one Biden.

Trump refused to concede defeat and instead claimed, with no evidence, that the election had been stolen from him by massive ballot stuffing at the polls. He urged his supporters to mass in Washington on January 6, 2021, the day Vice President Mike Pence and Congress would certify the election results. Around 20,000 Trumpians appeared that day. In an hour-long harangue on the White House lawn, Trump called on them "to fight like hell or you're not going to have a country anymore," and told them to march to the Capitol where he would join them. Around 2,000 Trumpians invaded the Capitol to prevent Pence and members of the House of Representatives and Senate from certifying Biden's election as president. Eventually police expelled the rioters after they inflicted $2.7 million in damage to the Capitol and severely injured 138 police officers, of whom four later committed suicide. Most of the rioters eventually faced justice. By November 6, 2024, the U.S. Attorney for the District of Columbia had charged 1,561 insurgents various felonies and misdemeanors, and so far had convicted 1,028.[29]

Meanwhile, Trump escaped justice for the insurrection and an array of other criminal charges. The House of Representatives voted to impeach Trump for inciting insurrection but the Senate acquitted him with a 57 to 43 vote, ten votes short of the 67 or two-thirds necessary for conviction on January 13. Nancy Pelosi, the House of Representative's majority leader, authorized creation of a "Select Committee to Investigate the January 6 Attack on the Capitol" with seven Democrats and two Republicans, including Liz Cheney of Wyoming and former Vice President Dick Cheney's daughter. By December 2022, the committee had interviewed over 1,000 witnesses, compiled over a million pages of evidence, issued a thousand-page report, and submitted its findings to the Justice Department. Attorney General Merrick Garland assigned Jack Smith to head the January 6 investigation and another investigation of Trump's illegal retention of thousands of official documents, many top secret. Meanwhile, public prosecutors in New York City and Fulton Country, Georgia indicted Trump on an array of charges. In 2024, Trump faced ninety-one felony criminal counts from the four courts. His lawyers, Trump appointed judges, and the Supreme Court's six right wing justices managed to delay indefinitely three of the four cases. However, the New York City court's jury found him guilty of thirty-four felonies. But he will not serve a day in prison for them.

***

President Biden struggled to reverse Trump's destructive policies. He selected people with impeccable character to serve in his administration and the federal courts; got Congress to enact bills that boosted middle class incomes, economic infrastructure, and green energy technologies; restored good relations between the United States and the European Union (EU) and North Atlantic Treaty Organization (NATO); recommitted the United States to the 2016 Global Warming Accord; and led international efforts to provide military aid to Ukraine and cut trade with Russia after its invasion of Ukraine on February 24, 2022. One failure was preventing illegal immigration as over 1.8 million entered the United States in 2022 alone. Nonetheless, during the 2022 mid-term election, the Democratic Party managed to pick up a Senate seat and limited its losses in the House of Representatives to 221 Republicans and 213 Democrats.

One national monument's fate exemplified the blue-red tug-of-war over the West. President Obama designated Bear Ears National Monument of 1,351,849 acres in southern Utah on December 26, 2016. President Trump slashed Bear Ears 85 percent to 201,876 acres and opened it to gas and oil production. The Hopi, Zuni, Navajo, and Ute tribes sued the Trump administration for effectively destroying Bear Ears National Monument. President Biden restored the original acreage and required the Bureau of Land Management to "meaningfully engage" with the region's tribes to ensure that policies "affecting the monument reflect the expertise and traditional and historical knowledge of interested tribal nations and peoples."[30]

Biden designated 450,000 acres of the Mohave Desert's Spirit Mountain region a protected area on December 2, 2022. That designation established a wildlife corridor embracing the Mohave National Preserve, Castle Mountain Monument, Sloan Canyon, and Lake Meade Recreation Area. However, he did not grant that area the strict legal protection of a national monument because he wanted the possibly of wind turbines and solar panels to be installed on parts of it. He made his announcement before a summit of Indian chiefs at the White House, telling them that: "I'm grateful to so many of you that have led the fight to protect it. There's so much more that we're going to do to protect tribal lands."[31]

The blue-red tug-of-war naturally extends to the federal institutions that manage public lands and enforce pollution laws. Of those, the Environmental Protection Agency (EPA) provokes the worst Conservative rage and attempts to neuter its powers. Republican Presidents Ronald Reagan, George W. Bush, and Donald Trump appointed as directors ideologues who purged as many professionals as possible and replaced them with fellow believers in privatizing as much public land as possible. The Supreme Court's six conservatives stripped the EPA of its power to establish and enforce anti-pollution regulations in *West Virginia versus the Environmental Protection Agency* (2022), insisting that only Congress could set regulations. In doing so, they ignored the 1970 and 1990 Clean Air Acts whereby Congress explicitly empowered the federal government to do exactly that. Experts, not politicians, are best capable of understanding problems, proposing solutions, and enforcing compliance. The immediate issue was a lawsuit by West Virginia's government on behalf of fossil fuel producers everywhere to prevent EPA from enacting regulations that cutback carbon dioxide emissions. The result was to gut Washington's ability to cut global warming pollution and enforce a range of other anti-pollution, conservation, and preservation laws.

***

The 2024 presidential election initially was a rematch of Biden versus Trump. Biden did so poorly in their one debate that ever more Democratic Party leaders pressured him to withdraw from the race. He did so on July 21, but endorsed Vice President Kamala Harris to succeed him rather than let the upcoming Democratic Party convention decide among multiple candidates. The contrast between Trump and Harris was stunning in their respective campaigns and one debate. Trump's speeches were demagogic streams of invective, boasts, lies, and insults. Harris projected a joyful, centrist message of pragmatic problem-solving and national unity. Trump was impeached twice as president and found guilty for committing thirty-four felonies. Harris was a former public prosecutor and California's attorney general. Trump promised as president to eviscerate the federal civil service, especially legal, intelligence, and scientific experts, and fill those posts with his loyalists. Harris promised to uphold the law.

Trump trounced Harris by 2.3 million votes, winning 49.8 percent of the total and 312 electoral votes to her 48.3 percent and 221. Among western states, Trump won Idaho, Montana, Wyoming, North Dakota, South Dakota, Utah, Nevada, two of Nebraska's three districts, Kansas, Oklahoma, Texas, and Arizona, while Harris won California, Oregon, Washington, Colorado, New Mexico, and Nebraska's Omaha district. In Congress, Republicans retained control of the House and retook the Senate. Back in the White House, Trump realized the Sagebrush-Anarchist agenda for the West by eviscerating the federal workforce, laws, rules, and mores; pardoning the 1,500 or so indicted or convicted January 6 rioters; and opening protected federal lands to mining and other exploitive corporations. Atop that he devastated American democracy, wealth, power, prestige, and security by refusing to comply with court orders; initiating a global trade war and recession by imposing tariffs from 10 percent to 125 percent on other countries; siding with Russian President Vladimir Putin in trying to conquer as much of Ukraine as he can; denigrating NATO and the European Union; and withdrawing from the Global Warming Treaty. The Supreme Court's six right-wing justices contributed to this anti-democratic revolution with numerous rulings, most critically *Trump versus United States* (2024) that immunized Trump for any laws he broke during his "official duties" as president; *Citizens United versus FEC* (2010) that allowed unlimited spending in elections; *West Virginia versus EPA* (2022) that limited the government's power to regulate air pollution; and *Macdonnell versus United States* (2015) that essentially legalized corruption. These court rulings of course undermine democracy not just across the West, but across America.

Chapter 13

FIRES AND WATERS

> "The rancher (with a few honorable exceptions) is a man who strings barbed wire all over the range; drills and bulldozes stock ponds; drives off elk and antelope and bighorn sheep; poisons coyotes and prairie dogs; shoots eagles, bears, and cougars on sight; supplants the native grasses with tumbleweed, snakeweed, poverty weed, cowshit, ant hills, mud, dust, and flies. And then he leans back and grins at the TV cameras and talks about how much he loves the American West." (Edward Abby)

An ecosystem is a biological community of organisms interacting with each other and their physical environment in which all animals and plants nourish each other. No ecosystem is isolated; all are more or less interdependent. There are countless ecosystems on earth which itself is one giant ecosystem. Each ecosystem has a carrying capacity of different types of organisms and numbers for each in dynamic equilibrium with one another. The overpopulation of one or more organisms can destroy that equilibrium and thus the ecosystem by consuming far more of its food sources than can naturally replenish themselves.

Humanity has exceeded the earth's carrying capacity. The number of people and their production, consumption, and pollution soars increasingly beyond the earth's ability to sustain them. The result is a vicious cycle of related environmental catastrophes including ozone layer depletion, deforestation, desertification, biocide, and global warming.

During the mid-1980s, climatologists found overwhelming evidence that the earth was rapidly warming because of the carbon dioxide and other chemicals spewed into the atmosphere during the industrial revolution and population explosion of recent centuries. In 1988, the United Nations responded to those dire findings by establishing the International Panel on Climate Change (IPCC) of 2,500 climatologists to compile and analyze data with supercomputers on global warming's causes and effects from around the world, and periodically issue reports. The IPCC issued six reports through 2022, each with a more sophisticated analysis and alarming conclusion. Global warming will cause sea levels to rise from melting glaciers, inundating the current homes and work places of hundreds of millions of people living near sea level; hurricanes to become more powerful and destructive as they absorb energy and moisture from warmer waters; droughts to last longer; crops to stunt or wither from higher temperatures; forest fires to be more frequent and catastrophic; ever more of the earth to be uninhabitable; starvation, disease, and desperation to afflict ever more of humanity; and the collapse of increasing numbers of governments, economies, and societies into anarchy, violence, and mass death and refugees.

Global warming is inflicting worsening damage to the United States. From 2011 to 2021, 90 percent of American counties suffered such severe damage from storms, flooding, fires, and droughts that the federal government declared them disaster zones and provided them aid. During that decade, 700 counties endured five or more disasters, and 29 states had at least one annual disaster while five states had 20 disasters. California alone received twenty-five federal disaster designations and $2.5 billion in federal aid.[1] In 2023, Phoenix suffered thirty-one straight days of temperatures above 110 degrees. Overall, global warming has inflicted more catastrophes on the American West than on other regions.

***

Ecologically, Americans severely damaged parts of the West long before global warming's devastating effects became evident. Among the frontier's negative legacies is the mindset of exploiting lands for all they are worth then abandoning them when profits dwindle. The result is the decimation of wildlife, grasslands, forests, water, and soil. Pests and fires destroy ever more swaths of forest leaving them browned or blackened. Half a million abandoned mines leech carcinogenic toxins into streams and aquifers, winds whip radioactive dust from thousands of uranium waste mounds into people's lungs; cancer rates climb. Of the nation's 1,303 Superfund Sites for priority federal pollution cleanup, California had 97, Colorado 19, Idaho 6, Kansas 12, Montana 16, Nebraska 15, Nevada 1, New Mexico 15, Oregon 13, North Dakota 0, South Dakota 2, Texas 51, Utah 15, Washington 51, and Wyoming 2.[2] There are radioactive wastelands like Hanford,

Washington and Rocky Flats, Colorado. Hanford alone has 54 million gallons of radioactive water that is slowly seeping through the ground toward the Columbia River six miles away; cleanup costs are at least $528 billion but federal and state officials are deadlocked over how to clean up and pay for the deadly mess.[3] Alien plant and animal species devastate native plants and animals along with forests, grasslands, rivers, and lakes, with cheatgrass, knapweed, spruce amphids, white pine blister rust, band elm bark beetles, golden algae, and Russian thistle that becomes tumbleweeds after it dies especially destructive. It is often said that people are loving the national parks to death.[4] Traffic jams and pollution foul ever more parks. Campers and backpackers must reserve sites sometimes months ahead. Depending on the season, All Terrain Vehicles (ATVs) and snowmobiles roar across and degrade swaths of public lands.

Sprawl, congestion, and smog steadily engulf the mega-metropolitan West of Los Angeles, San Diego, Phoenix, Tucson, Denver, Kansas City, Salt Lake City, Las Vegas, Oklahoma City, Dallas-Fort Worth, Houston, and Seattle. Home and rental prices soar there and in mid-sized cities like Boulder, Bozeman, Missoula, Cheyenne, Santa Fe, Reno, and Portland along with resort towns across the West. Workers cannot afford to live near where they work. That harms the economy, as businesses cannot attract the laborers that sustain them. Local government suffered too as they lacked enough teachers, police, and firefighters.

***

During the twentieth century, nothing developed the West more than the Bureau of Reclamation and the Army Corps of Engineers. founded a century apart in 1802 and 1902.[5] Rivalry between those bureaucracies literally dammed and, critics argue, figuratively damned America during the twentieth century. Sites steadily dwindled in cost-benefit economic viability but that did not inhibit the Corps or Bureau from racing to get congressional authorization to plug them. The result was a revolutionary transformation of the West's economic, political, social, and cultural essence from pastoral to hydraulic. Previously rugged individuals and groups struggled to survive and thrive across the West. Thereafter every westerners' livelihood has more or less depended on massive systems of dams, reservoirs, irrigation, and aqueducts that provide networks of hydroelectric power and water to distant cities, towns, and farms. That transformed the West from a poor, sparsely populated region into an increasingly urbanized, suburbanized, and prosperous one during the twentieth century. The hydraulic West lets cities, crop fields, and pastures sprawl across deserts, soaks countless lawns and golf courses, and fills countless bathtubs and backyard pools.

Spectacular behemoth dams like Hoover, Bonneville, and Coulee are well known, but nearly all of the 50,000 dams plugging western streams are much smaller. Nonetheless, each is an engineering and political triumph. Among the most astonishing are the Colorado-Big Thompson, Frying Pan-Arkansas, and San Juan-Chama projects that bore tunnels through mountains to carry water from one side to the other.

Yet that success is built literally and figuratively on dust. The West is an "Oasis Civilization" with soaring households and businesses hooked on dwindling water supplied by snow packs, rivers, reservoirs, and aquifers. For instance, Phoenix and the rest of Maricopa County alone daily use more than 2.2 billion gallons of water, twice that of New York City but with half the population.[6] Federal, state, and local governments have overallocated rivers and aquifers. The once mighty Arkansas River with its swift current and quicksands so treacherous to cross is now either dried up or little more than an irrigation ditch for a couple hundred miles across the high plains. Water is rapidly disappearing from years of drought, overuse, waste, and abuse. Dams are silting up. Irrigation water is salinating crop fields and livestock pastures thus diminishing yields. Dropping reservoir levels cut water and electricity as more people demand more crops, livestock, water, and energy. The West is experiencing its worst drought since 800 AD according to tree rings. Global warming steadily cuts annual snowfall in the mountains, which means less spring runoff.

Annual floods are a natural part of most river ecosystems. Dams halt inundations, which is good for people living in flood plains downstream but bad for nature. Floodwaters carry soil away from some places and spread it elsewhere, and they gouge new channels and abandon older ones. The natural result is usually more diverse vegetation and wildlife. Water in reservoirs behind dams is usually too warm for river fish, which lake fish replace.

The same human demand, abuse, and waste also steadily diminishes aquifers across the nation but most direly across the West. The Ogallala Aquifer extends 174,000 square miles beneath parts of eight Great Plains states—Texas, Oklahoma, New Mexico, Colorado, Kansas, Wyoming, Nebraska, and South Dakota.[7] The aquifer originally had over 5 billion acre feet of water in rock strata 100 to 400ft beneath the earth's surface. In the late 1940s, the development of center-pivot irrigation pumps made large-scale agribusiness on the high plains viable by drawing 800 gallons of water a minute from the Ogallala aquifer. From an airplane, the summer ground appears covered with green circles of 133 acres of wheat, corn, or other crops with the pivot in the center and its arm a quarter mile long. Those "wheels of fortune" enriched agribusiness corporations that consume 90 percent of the water and contribute 20 percent of the region's economy. The trouble is that annually farmers drain as much as 5ft while nature restores an inch. The aquifer's average level has dropped 300ft and the deeper the level the worse the cost in bringing it to the surface. Many towns on the high plains flourished for several decades then steadily dwindled in population as the aquifer diminished beneath them.

The Colorado River is supposed to supply water to 40 million people and 5.5 million acres of farm and ranch land in seven western states along with millions of people in Mexico.[8] The seven states are split between the Upper Basin of Wyoming, Colorado, Utah, and New Mexico, and the Lower Basin of California, Arizona, and Nevada. The Colorado River watershed and its reservoirs are rapidly dwindling from drought and overuse. Most of that water comes from two reservoirs, Lake Mead and Lake Powell, respectively behind Hoover Dam and Glen Canyon Dam. In 2022, Lake Mead was only 27 percent full, its lowest level since Hoover Dam was finished and the reservoir began filling in 1937. Eventually that dropping level will endanger not just water supplies but also hydroelectric power. Yet mostly inaction prevails in each of the seven state capitals and hundreds of city halls. Camille Touton, the Bureau of Reclamation commissioner, complained that: "States collectively have not identified and adopted actions of significant magnitude that would stabilize the system."[9] In June 2023, the Interior Department negotiated a deal with the lower states to cut 2.3 million acre feet over the next three years. Yet, even if the states somehow engineer those cuts, they will slow not stop let alone reverse the decline.[10]

The United States legally owes Mexico enough water for 2.3 million people and 500,000 acres of croplands.[11] The Colorado River now rarely flows into the Gulf of Mexico but dries up a score or so miles from the ocean. The United States delivers Mexico by canal its share of 1.5 million acres feet of the Colorado under the 1944 Treaty for Utilization of the Waters of the Rio Grande, Colorado, and Tiajuana Rivers.

The California State Water Project is a system of 21 dams and 700 miles of canals, pipelines, and tunnels that carry water from rivers in the northern region to households in San Francisco Bay, irrigated farm fields in the Central Valley, and households in southern California.

The system's most extraordinary segments are the stations that pump water through pipelines over 1,920-foot high Tehachapi Mountain Pass into the Los Angeles region. That water helped boost California's population from 15,717,204 in 1960 when the project began to 39,185,605 in 2022. Yet drought is diminishing that flow as the state's population rises and northern Californians increasingly resent sending water south when their own supply is literally evaporating.

Even when water is available, it may not be fit for drinking or crops. When water irrigates western landscapes it gathers cocktails of chemicals, especially salt, that often end up returning to a river where it is drawn again for irrigation further downstream. For instance, the Arkansas River has virtually no salt in its headwaters but reaches 2,020 parts per million just 120 miles downstream. Depending on the concentration, salt water diminishes and from 2,020 parts per million kills crops.[12] Salinity is minimal in the headwaters and fifteen hundred parts per million when the Colorado enters Mexico. Salination annually inflicts as much as $400 million in economic damage across the Colorado basin. The 1974 Colorado River Basin Control Act mitigated that with desalination projects, most vitally the plant at Yuma, Arizona. Desalination is very expensive and energy intensive. Yuma plant water costs $300 per acre-foot compared to $3.50 per acre-foot in the upper basin.[13] Historian Marc Reisner noted the irony that "Congress has chosen to . . . purify water at a cost exceeding $300 an acre-foot so that upriver irrigators can continue to grow surplus crops with federally subsidized water that costs them $3.50 an acre-foot."[14]

Great Salt Lake is steadily drying up with increasingly deadly results for wildlife and 2,500,000 people living nearby in the sprawling Salt Lake City metropolitan region. Salt Lake City's population soared after the government dammed and diverted water from the Bear, Weber, and Jordan Rivers flowing down from the Wasatch Mountain range north and east of the valley. A prolonged drought and rising demand for the waters that feed Great Salt Lake caused its surface area to plummet from 3,300 square miles to 1,000, and its salinity to nearly double from 9 percent to 17 percent from 1980 through today. At some point, the salt concentration will wipe out the briny shrimp and blow flies that 10 million migratory birds annually depend on for food. Winds whipping across the dry lakebed carry dust storms laden with arsenic and other deadly chemicals into the lungs of millions of people. The governments of Utah and Salt Lake City barely acknowledge that worsening catastrophe let alone take any decisive actions that might mitigate it.[15]

***

Fires across the West steadily become more frequent, hotter, larger, and destructive. The West, along with the rest of the world, is locked into a vicious cycle of global warming, drier forests and grasslands, more and worse mega fires that release more global warming chemicals into the atmosphere, and worse global warming. California experienced its ten worst fire seasons in the decade between 2012 and 2022. In southern California, Santa Anna winds blow powerfully from the Great Basin to dry and bake the region, often toppling electric transformers and power lines that spark fires.

The Forest Service faces a dilemma. Fire is a natural part of forests across the West. Sporadic fires sparked by lightening burn patches that often become meadows with more diverse plants and wildlife the following year. For decades, the policy was to suppress fires and maximize lumber production. The trouble was that led to denser forests with debris-filled floors. Increasingly, when a fire erupts, it rages rather than mildly crackles and burns as in a virgin forest with periodic natural fires. A natural western forest might have 60 trees per acre while a managed forest today has an average 1,089 trees per acre.[16] Global warming exacerbates forest fires because the prolonged drought and rising temperatures across the West have turned forests into tinderboxes that a spark can explode into conflagrations. The fires are so hot that they scorch the earth and prevent vegetation from regrowing there.

Recently, the Forest Service has tried to preempt conflagrations with over 4,500 annual prescribed burns. Although the Forest Service safely contains 99.84 percent of those burns, tragically some escape control. Two happened in May 2022 on the eastern slopes of New Mexico's Sangres de Cristo Mountains where eventually three months of fires destroyed 250,000 acres of forest and over 1,000 buildings, mostly homes.

The Forest Service cannot keep pace with the number of trees that insects and drought kill and become fuel for fires. In 2022, California alone had 140 million dead trees. Of 2.4 million dead trees just in Yosemite National Park, the Forest Service cleared only one percent. Yet even when a swath is cleared, the immediate cost exceeds the benefit. For instance, a contractor that thinned forest in Yosemite received $60 for 25 tons of material that cost $1,200 to $1,200 to cut, gather, and transport.[17]

Sequoias can live over 2,000 years, rise over 200ft, and have 20ft diameters. Logging destroyed most Sequoias in the late nineteenth and early twentieth centuries before they received National Forest Service protection. Fires threaten to destroy California's remaining

Sequoias. From 2015 to 2021, fires burned 85 percent of Sequoia forests compared to burning 25 percent over the previous century. Then in July 2022, fires partly burned 32 of 37 groves with 75,000 Sequoias left in 13,300 acres. To protect the survivors, the Forest Service cleared brush, wrapped trees in foil and fire retardant, and installed sprinkler systems that pump up to 20 gallons a minute around the base of each trees.[18]

Redwoods can live nearly as long and grow as tall as Sequoias, and are just as imperiled by fire and global warming. The remaining forests are close to the coast and rely on moisture from fog along with annual rains to thrive. Global warming prolongs and worsens droughts and diminishes fogs. Redwood forests are drying out and the giants are dying. The world's tallest tree is a redwood, Hyperion, which rises 379ft in a remote section of Redwood National Park in northern California. In addition to drought and fire, Hyperion is endangered by hikers who denude the surrounding foliage and compact the earth, and by climbers that spike their way up it to the top. Park rangers have closed off the area around Hyperion with $5,000 fines and six month prison terms for anyone caught approaching it. Hyperion is a symbol of both the immediate impact of too many visitors loving nature to death and the vicious cycle of ecological disasters unleashed by humanity's population and pollution explosion.[19]

The most devastated forest was underwater. Kelp forests along the Pacific coast are complex ecosystems in which scores of fish species and mammals like seals and sea otters feed, breed, and hide. A "blob" of warm water caused by global warming and propelled by the El Nino inversion destroyed 95 percent of the kelp forest along the northern California coast in 2014. Among the species nearly wiped out were starfish, already weakened by a wasting disease. Starfish eat sea urchins. With that predator gone, sea urchins proliferated across the ocean floor, blocking the ability of kelp to root and grow again.[20]

Literally and figuratively, hiking the 2,650-mile Pacific Crest Trail is among life's peak experiences. Every year a hundred or so finish the entire trail. Doing so demands not just enormous physical and emotional strength but planning. Before leaving, hikers send food packages to post offices along the way. Thru-hikers begin at the Mexican border in spring for the 700-mile leg through mostly desert until they reach the high Sierras as the snowpack melts. Hikers often need to wear crampons to get over the iciest stretches. They must reach the trail's north end at the Canadian border before snow buries the Cascade Mountains. Global warming renders that trek increasingly challenging. Annually snowpack and water sources diminish while forest fires devastate longer stretches of the trail.

***

Extinction threatens countless species across the West. For instance, monarch butterflies once numbered tens of millions. They migrate in western and eastern flyways to breed and eat along the way. The western flyway is from Washington to a forest in central Mexico, the eastern from Maine to Florida. Monarchs face oblivion as their numbers plummeted 99.9 percent from 1980 to 2022. Pesticides and herbicides, especially Glyphosate, a carcinogen used in Roundup is the worst cause of that population collapse by wiping out milkweed, the monarch's vital food source.[21]

The dams on rivers flowing into the Pacific Ocean that controlled flooding and provided hydroelectricity and water to regions and irrigation devastated salmon populations. Thirteen species of salmon and trout are endangered in the Columbia River watershed. Salmon swim up rivers to breed then swim down rivers and into the ocean to feed the rest of the year. Salmon were central to the sustenance and culture of Northwest Indians. Fifteen tribes signed treaties with Washington that guaranteed their ability to fish for salmon. For decades, those tribes fruitlessly lobbied Washington D.C. and their state governments to restore the salmon runs and thus their cultures. During the 2020s, the federal government will remove four dams on the lower Snake River. That project will cost as much as $27.2 billion to replace the hydroelectricity and water lost with the dams.[22]

The revival of grizzly bears and reintroduction of wolves are two rare preservation success stories. During the twentieth century, hunters shot grizzlies to extinction's brink and wolves to extinction in the West. In 1800, around 50,000 grizzlies lived across the West. By 1980, only around 500 grizzlies survived on 2 percent of their former range in the northern Rocky Mountains. Since then, hunting bans, expansion of protected territory, and reintroduction of non-aggressive females caused the population to expand to 1,200 by 2022. Wildlife experts released twenty-one Canadian wolves into Yellowstone National Park in March 1995 and eleven Mexican wolves in the Apache-Sitgreaves National Forest in 1998. By 2022, wolves numbered 1,600 in the northern Rockies and 200 in Arizona and New Mexico.

Wild horses and burros are among the West's more beloved icons. By the 1960s, they dwindled as ranchers rounded them up to sell to manufacturers who used the meat for dogfood, hoofs for glue, and skin for baseball covers. Congress enacted and President Nixon signed the 1971 Wild Free-Roaming Horse and Burro Act that protects them. In the decades since a new problem has arisen, overpopulation and overgrazing by those wild horses and burros that numbered around 65,000 and 18,000 by 2022. Conservationists want to cull those herds to sustainable levels but wild horse and burro-loving protective groups prevent that.

***

The reasons for the ecological problems plaguing the West are clear—a toxic mix of greed and creed. For nearly four centuries most Americans, especially westerners, measured progress by business profits and such symbols as landscapes encrusted with rotting tree-stumps, tall smokestacks belching pollution, dammed rivers, artificial lakes, feed lots crowded with thousands of cattle, and train engines pulling scores of cars heaped with coal. Those who did could cite the Bible to justify doing so. In Genesis 1.28, God issues this command to humanity: "Be fruitful and multiply and fill the earth and subdue it; and have dominion over . . . every living thing that moves upon the earth." Boosting that attitude was the Puritan conception of wilderness as Satan's abode filled with wild beasts and savage tribes that must be destroyed and the land transformed into productive farms and villages.

Oklahoma Republican Senator James Inhofe epitomized the mingled greed and creed of global warming deniers. He won election to the Senate in 1994 and was repeatedly reelected until he retired in 2023. Of the $10,746,604 he raised in donations for his 2014 and 2020 reelection campaigns, the most—$1,271,761—came from "Energy and Natural Resource" contributors followed by $974,899 of "Nonitemized."[23] On February 28, 2015, he gave a Senate speech in which he threw a snowball collected from a snowfall that day and cited that as evidence for denouncing the "hysteria of global warming" as a "hoax." Like countless ignorant people, he confused weather with climate. Astonishingly, he chaired the Senate Environmental Committee but wielded his power to invite and elicit testimonies mostly from deniers. Inhofe represented both the big business interests that helped underwrite his campaigns and the delusions of legions of people with minds corrupted by an extreme ideology at war against science.

***

Ironically, the region of the United States most dependent on Washington for its economic well-being most celebrates the mythology of rugged individualism. Historian Richard White captured the paradoxes and hypocrisies of that relationship and attitude: "The American West, more than any other section of the United States, is a creation, not so much of individual or local efforts, but of federal efforts. More than any region, the West has historically been a dependency of the federal government." Yet, that reality does not inspire gratitude, but instead provokes denial and resentment among most inhabitants: "Westerners usually regarded the federal government much as they would regard a particularly scratchy wool shirt in winter. It was all that was actually keeping them warm, but it still irritated them."[24]

The harsh reality of western development belies the romantic stereotypes. Edward Abbey captured the hypocrisy and narcissism of many westerners: "the rancher (with a few honorable exceptions) is a man who strings barbed wire all over the range; drills and bulldozes stock ponds; drives off elk and antelope and bighorn sheep; poisons coyotes and prairie dogs; shoots eagles, bears, and cougars on sight; supplants the native grasses with tumbleweed, snakeweed, poverty weed, cowshit, ant hills, mud, dust, and flies. And then he leans back and grins at the TV cameras and talks about how much he loves the American West."[25]

For the near future, although most Americans embrace varying conservation and preservation values, short-term big business corporate interests will prevail. The reason is simple. Corporations figuratively and literally outgun the organizations that promote conservation and preservation. Industries have "captured" many government institutions established to regulate them at the federal, state, and local level. For the federal government in Washington and field offices, lumber corporations dominate the Forest Service; coal, oil, and natural gas corporations the Bureau of Land Management; ranchers the Bureau of Grazing, and agribusiness corporations the Agriculture Department and Bureau of Reclamation. That corporate takeover also tends to prevail for most state government offices, especially across the West.

Corporations pollute because it is profitable. Convictions of polluters are rare and penalties are feeble. Corporations pay token amounts for their crimes, a mere tip from their vast profits. That emboldens rather than deters polluters. Corporation lawyers write the laws and regulations that politicians pass and bureaucrats implement. For instance, the 1872 Mining Act remains a politically impregnable giveaway of vast public wealth to private corporations despite calls and efforts by conservationists and preservations to reform or abolish it.

America is bitterly split between those who reject and those who embrace science as the basis for public policies, between those who champion corporate interests and those who champion human interests. Nowhere is that war between "red" and "blue" adherents more crucial or acrimonious than in the West.

Chapter 14

ARTISTS AND WRITERS

> "When I am photographing in clear-cuts . . . there is a sense of the world coming apart. But after I've been there long enough to get over the shock of the violence . . . I am discovering things . . . You can stand in the most hopeless place, and . . . you can experience moments that are right, that are whole." (Robert Adams)

The four greatest centers for western art are Santa Fe, Taos, Jackson Hole, and Scottsdale. Each town has hundreds of galleries and gift shops selling sublime paintings, sculptures, and crafts along with tourist kitsch. Santa Fe hosts the greatest number of galleries featuring western and Indian art with hundreds downtown and in other districts. The Santa Fe Institute was established in 1984 as a symposium for those dedicated to exploring and protecting wild places.

Marfa in west Texas is a mini art center. The town first acquired fame as the site where much of the 1956 film *Giant*, starring Elizabeth Taylor, Rock Hudson, and James Dean, was filmed. The crew stayed at the Hotel Paisano, a beautiful Spanish revival filled with mission style furnishings that opened in 1930. Then, in 1971, Donald Judd, a sculptor, entrepreneur, and visionary, settled in Marfa, enchanted by the town's charm, large inexpensive spaces for his sculptures, and the vast stark surrounding landscapes. Judd bought up 565 buildings on 340 acres, and established the Judd Foundation to sponsor his 100 or so aluminum abstract sculptures and help underwrite other artists. In 1986, Judd founded the Chianti Foundation to supplement the Judd Foundation. His promotions attracted scores of artists, writers, and entrepreneurs to Marfa. The most prominent artists included Claes Oldenburg, Coosje van Bruggen, Richard Long, Roni Horn, David Rabinowitz, Ilya Kabakov, and Ingolfur Arnarsson.[1]

The American West inspires countless contemporary artists. Two Indian artists produced remarkable and controversial works. Cannupa Hanska Luger is a leading contemporary artist who seeks to broaden the expression of American Indian art. His most famous work was "Every One," a black and white image of an woman composed from 4,000 fist-sized ceramic balls to commemorate the 4,000 Indian woman said to have disappeared from reservations. He used a variety of mediums like ceramics, canvas and paint, tires, metal, and paper. His Mandan, Arikara, Hidatsa, and Lakota ancestry is as mixed as his art.[2] With a style inspired by Andy Warhol, Luiseno Fritz Scholder painted many stereotypical Indians to expose and transcend the image in works like "Indian with Beer Can" (1967) and "Super Indian No. 2" (1972).

By far the funniest Indian artist is San Domingo Ricardo Cate whose cartoon strip "Without Reservations" has appeared in the *Santa Fe New Mexican* newspaper since 2005. His first collection, *Without Reservation: The Cartoons of Ricardo Cate,* appeared as a book in 2012. Typical of his humor was the scene with an Indian behind a desk informing a perplexed man in Renaissance clothing, "I am sorry Mr. Columbus, but your Discovery card application has been denied."

Likewise, the American West inspires countless photographers. Robert Adams captures the post-modern West with his bleak photos of tract house suburbs in the desert, clearcut or burned forests, and parched lakes. The rapacious hand of man is evident but the landscapes are mostly empty of people. He explained his vision: "When I am photographing in clear-cuts . . . there is a sense of the world coming apart. But after I've been there long enough to get over the shock of the violence . . . I am discovering things . . . You can stand in the most hopeless place, and . . . you can experience moments that are right, that are whole."[3]

***

An array of historians, journalists, novelists, and poets wrote about the post-modern West. Conceptually the most important was Patricia Nelson Limerick who with her *Legacy of Conquest: The Unbroken Past of the American West* (1987) was as influential as Frederick Jackson Turner in defining western history.[4] She updated the West's history to the latest headlines, argued that aggression, violence, exploitation, and racism characterized the entire history, and highlighted the tribulations and contributions of minorities and women that traditional historians downplayed or overlooked. Thereafter ever more scholars joined New History ranks and now dominate the field.

Two journalists won fame for exploring different dimensions of the West. Roger Welsch was a Great Plains folklorist, University of Nebraska professor, and essayist most famed for his "Postcards from Nebraska" series. He explained folklore's enduring and protean nature: "An individual may tell any story he wishes or knows, but a widely told and known narrative—folklore—is under constant pressure of communal memory, still fallible but with an internal mechanism of constancy and accuracy the popular or high culture story can never enjoy."[5] Lakota Tim Giago was a University of Nevada graduate who began writing a weekly column on Indian affairs for the Rapid City Journal in 1979, founded *Lakota Times* as the first independent newspaper devoted to a tribe's affairs in 1981, renamed it *Indian Country Today* with stories that spanned the nation in 1992, founded the *Lakota Journal* in 2000 and the *Native Sun News Today* in 2009. Meanwhile, he established the Native American Journalists' Association in 1984. He was a political activist whose most symbolic victory was getting South Dakota to rename its Pioneer Day, annually celebrated on Columbus Day, Native American Day.[6]

Outstanding memoirs include John Nichols' *The Last Beautiful Days of Autumn* (1982); William Kittredge's *Hole in the Sky: A Memoir* (1992), Kathleen Norris's *Dakota: A Spiritual Geography* (1993); Rick Bass's *Book of Yaak* (1996); and Terry Tempest Williams' *Refuge: An Unnatural History of Family and Place* (1991), *Desert Quartet* (1995), *Leap* (2001), and *Red: Passion and Patience in the Desert* (2001).

As for novelists, few rival Cormac McCarthy's bleak, violent version of the West in his *Blood Meridian, or the Evening Redness in the West* (1985); his Border Trilogy set in the recent West including *All the Pretty Horses* (1992), *The Crossing* (1994), and *Cities of the Plain* (1998); and *No Country for Old Men* (2005). Most of Barbara Kingsolver's novels are set in the modern West including *The Bean Tree* (1988), *Animal Dreams* (1990), and *Pigs in Heaven* (1993). Louise Erdrich tapped the Chippewa side of her heritage to write such best-selling novels as *Love Medicine* (1984), *The Beet Queen* (1986), and *Tracks* (1988) mostly set in the northern plains and Minnesota. Ivan Doig wrote thirteen novels mostly set in the West, including his trilogy *English Creek* (1984), *Dancing at the Rascal Fair* (1987), and *Ride with Me, Mariah Montana* (1990) following a Montana family from 1889 to 1989. Marilynne Robinson won a Pulitzer Prize for her *Gilead* (2004). Spokane-Coeur d'Alene Alexis Sherman's *Reservation Blues* (1995) and *Smoke Signals* (1998) are comic-tragic novels about Indians in contemporary America. Rick Bass explored life on mostly bleak plains in *Platte River* (1994) and *All the Land to Hold Us* (2013). Jim Harrison set many of his novels, novellas, and poems in his adopted state of Montana including *Legends of the Fall* (1979), *The Road Home* (1998), *True North* (2004), and *Great Leader* (2011).

Over the past half century, cowboy poetry has become increasingly popular. The number of annual poetry contests across the West has soared past a hundred. Baxter Black was among the most popular cowboy poets. Like many, he began composing verse to dismiss some of the tedium on the trail. Black rode the rodeo circuit when he was younger before entering the poetry circuit. He wrote a weekly column called "On the Edge of Common Sense" that appeared in over a hundred publications. His over thirty books of poetry and prose sold more than a million copies.[7]

***

Big screen films and television programs about the West dwindled but were usually first rate. Clint Eastwood wrote, directed, and starred in *Unforgiven* (1992) which won the Best Picture Oscar. Two films portrayed Indians sympathetically, *Dances with Wolves* (1990) and *Geronimo: An American Legend* (1993). Two quite good versions of the O.K. Corral appeared in *Tombstone* (1993) and *Wyatt Earp* (1994), with Earp respectively played by Kurt Russell and Kevin Costner, and Doc Holiday by Val Kilmer and Denis Quaid. *Open Range* (2003) starred Costner and Robert Duvall as grizzled cowboys on a last cattle drive and shootout before barbed wire fenced them out. *Meek's Cutoff* (2010) recounted the true tragic fate of a wagon train bound for California when its guide Stephen Meek got them lost in the Great Basin. A fine version of *True Grit* starring Jeff Bridges, Matt Damon, and Hailee Steinfeld appeared in 2010. Alejandro Iñárritu's *The Revenant* (2015) about Hugh Glass's mauling by a grizzly, abandonment by his comrades, and quest for vengeance was visually stunning although beset with many inaccuracies and improbabilities. Costner directed, partly wrote, and starred in two parts of *Horizon: An American Saga* (2024) of an array of pioneers who found and develop a frontier town. Six contemporary westerns were also celebrated, Ridley Scott's *Thelma and Louise* (1991) about two women on the run after one of them murdered a rapist; *Lone Star* (1996) about lawmen and outlaws in Texas; Ang Lee's *Brokeback Mountain* (2005) about two gay sheep rancher lovers; Joel and Ethan Cohen's *No Country for Old Men* (2007) about a psychopathic murderer and hitman after a man who ran off with a fortune in drug money; Jane Campion's *The Power of the Dog* (2021), a homoerotic story set on a Montana ranch in the 1920s; and *Killers of the Flower Moon* (2024) based on the true story of a white gang led by lawyer William Hale who murdered as many as twenty-four Osage landowners to gain title to their oil wealth.

Television westerns were just as scarce. The series *Lonesome Dove* based on Larry McMurtry's novel appeared to critical acclaim in 1989. *Dr. Quinn, Medicine Woman* featured Jane Seymour as a western town doctor that was a popular Saturday evening melodrama from 1993 to 1998. HBO produced *Deadwood* from 2004 to 2007, lauded for its writing, acting, and realism. Two award-winning series depicted the modern West. *Breaking Bad* ran from 2008 to 2013 with the main character played by Brian Cranston who is dying of cancer and manufactures methamphetamine to underwrite his habit and family in Albuquerque. The heroes of AMC's *Dark Winds* are two Navajo detectives, Joe Leaphorn and Jim Chee, who solve crimes that sometimes have supernatural elements; the series that began in 2022 is based on Tony Hillerman's novels. Hulu's *Reservation Dogs* is a comedy series about four Indian teenagers on an Oklahoma reservation that debuted in 2021.*The English* (2022) featured an Englishwoman who teams up with a Pawnee army scout to journey West to track down the murderers of her son. *American Primeval* (2025) explores the 1857 "war" between the United States government and the Mormons of Utah that climaxed with the Mountain Meadows massacre. The History Channel's series *Mountain Man* since 2012 has depicted tough, resourceful men and women mostly in the West living off the land, hunting, gathering, and surviving with traditional and modern skills and equipment. Ken Burns and Stephen Ives produced the eight-part PBS series *The West* (1996), and Burns *Lewis and Clark: The Journey of the Corps of Discovery* (1997).

The most popular series was *Yellowstone* that began in 2022 and was set in Montana with the Dutton family, headed by patriarch John played by Kevin Costner pitting their ranching interests against big corporations and a local Indian tribe that want to take over their land and government environmental policies that want to regulate their land. The Duttons wield Machiavellian and Social Darwinian values and tactics to keep what they have and take more, with members insisting that "There's no such thing as morality" and "Right and wrong are so far from this place, I don't think it factors in at all." After being elected governor, John Dutton shamelessly uses his power to enrich his family and allies.*Yellowstone* is especially popular in red states. It has two engaging prequels, *1883* and *1923*.[8]

***

As for Country and Western music, during the 1980s it shed its "Western" half and became pure "Country." Nonetheless, some artists kept exploring traditional and contemporary western themes in their music. Willie Nelson, Waylon Jennings, Johnny Cash, and Kris Kristofferson toured as the Highwaymen from 1985 to 1995. Other superstars with western tinged albums and songs included Garth Brooks, Clint Black, Dwight Yoakam, George Strait, Emmy Lou Harris, and Reba McIntire.

More than anyone, Willie Nelson exemplified the western singer-songwriter. He was born and bred in Texas, and retreats to his ranch in the Hill Country between tours. One journalist described Nelson as a "scrambler of categories" who was "down home and urbane, countercultural and traditional, a political progressive who occupies the loftiest perch in America's most conservative musical genre."[9] Certainly, with ninety-eight albums Nelson is the most prolific musician in any genre. Of them, his album *Red Headed Stranger* (1976) was the most western with its fifteen songs depicting the life of a frontier murderer and drifter who finally achieves redemption. In 1978, he and Jennings wrote the revisionist song "Mammas Don't Let Your Babies Grow Up to Be Cowboys."

Ken Burns and Dayton Duncan produced an outstanding eight-part PBS series on the history of Country music in 2019.[10] That history will continue to unroll for the near future, as Country music remains a popular genre in America and for countless fans elsewhere around the world.

Chapter 15

LEGACIES

> "Few people even know the true definition of the term, 'West'; and where is its location?
> Phantom-like it flies before us as we travel." (George Catlin)

> "I reckon I got to light out for the Territory ahead of the rest, because . . . she's going to . . . civilize me and I can't stand it. I been there before." (Huck Finn)

> "When the last red man has vanished from the earth, and the memory is only the shadow of a cloud moving across the prairie, these shores and forest will still hold the spirits of my people." (Duwamish Chief Sealth)

Painter George Catlin posed a question and expressed a paradox that has puzzled countless thoughtful Americans for four centuries: "Few people even know the true definition of the term, 'West'; and where is its location? Phantom-like it flies before us as we travel."[1]

So just what and where is the West today, and what and where has it been? The American West has many overlapping related versions. The biggest divide is the frontier and post-frontier West. The frontier West lasted from Jamestown's founding in 1607 to the battle of Wounded Knee in 1890 and was at once a direction, a process, and a state of mind. America's frontier West had three phases, pre-Mississippi from Jamestown to the Louisiana Purchase, 1607 to 1803; early Trans-Mississippi from Lewis and Clark to the Treaty of Hidalgo Guadeloupe, 1804 to 1848; and late Trans-Mississippi from the gold strike at Sutter's Mill to Wounded Knee, 1848 to 1890. Conquest and colonization was the process. Leading the way were hunters, explorers, traders, soldiers, and settlers.

As such, America's West and Frontier were essentially synonymous as long as the frontier lasted. Although the frontier officially ended when the 1890 Census Bureau said it no longer existed, the metaphor remains as vivid and popular as ever. Presidents and other leaders regularly evoke "frontier" to encourage Americans to embark on their latest challenging enterprises and adventures. President John Kennedy famously called his goals for the United States "a new frontier" and exhorted Americans to explore the frontier of space and put a man on the moon within a decade.

For over four centuries the American West has also been a morphing idea, a collage of symbolic images and slogans, a mythology mostly grounded on real people and events. For countless people, the West represented exhilarating liberty, beauty, and opportunity. Josiah Gregg spent nine years trading between Missouri and Mexico. In his memoir *Commerce of the Prairies*, he concluded: "I have striven in vain to reconcile myself to the even tenor of civilized life in the United States . . . I am almost ashamed to confess that scarcely a day passes without my experiencing a pang of regret that I am not now roving at large upon those western plains. Nor do I find my taste peculiar; for I have hardly known a man who has ever become familiar with the kind of life which I have led for so many years, that has not relinquished it with regret . . . The wild, unsettled, and independent life of the prairie-trader makes perfect freedom . . . He is in daily . . . exposure of his life and property, and in the habit of relying on his own arm and his own gun . . . [for] protection . . . He lives in no society which he must look up to or propitiate."[2]

Among the many traits that distinguish Americans from the rest of humanity is mobility, or the freedom to abandon one place for another hopefully better. The West symbolizes and realizes that. Countless people fled West to escape debts, crimes, family, neighbors, or failures. Mark Twain's *Huckleberry Finn* ends with Huck asserting: "I reckon I got to light out for the Territory ahead of the rest, because . . . she's going to . . . civilize me and I can't stand it. I been there before."[3] There are dissenters from that idea. Patrician Limerick disagrees that the West was a refuge to lose oneself from one's past: "The West was not where we escaped from each other, but where we all met."[4] Of course, both were possible and often fulfilled for countless of those who went there.

Then there is the West's mythology. Richard Slotkin devoted three vast, profound tomes to exploring that.[5] Myths are integral to humanity, at once reflecting and distorting how people see themselves and their world. Slotkin explained: "Myths are stories drawn from a society's history that have acquired through persistent usage the power of symbolizing that society's ideology and of dramatizing its moral consciousness—with all the complexities and contradictions that consciousness may contain."[6] People tend to simplify stories with each retelling, often boiling them down to key symbols, characters, and events. Those stories are vital for conveying that society's core values and how best to realize them along with its worst threats and how best to thwart them. History cannot be understood without the myths that inspire and shape the beliefs and acts of individuals and groups.

A bundle of related myths animate the West. Indeed, the West actually has two opposed mythologies, one traditional and centuries old, the other revisionist and recent. The West's traditional mythology is essentially a grander version of America's, that of adventurous, self-reliant, enterprising individuals who explored, settled, and developed the land while overcoming hardships, deprivation, and original peoples at once savage and noble whose descendants today enjoy America's array of freedoms and opportunities. Revisionist scholarly and popular writings, documentaries, and movies from the 1960s through today promoted an alternative mythological West characterized by conquest, injustice, racism, and the devastation of native peoples and ecosystems. The hero is as central to the traditional mythology as the villain is to the revisionist version. Old Western and New Western historians acknowledge the truths and inseparability of both versions while respectively emphasizing traditional or revisionist views in their writings and lectures. That mostly-good, mostly-bad dichotomy of Old versus New historians pervades every political, economic, sociological, and ecological dimension of the West.

Unquestionably, Americans believed themselves to be an exceptional, superior society from the first settlers. Massachusetts Governor John Winthrop expressed that view in a 1630 sermon in which he called the new American society "a city on a hill" to inspire all other peoples to admire, emulate, and join. Two and a half centuries later, Thomas Jefferson urged Americans to establish an "empire of liberty" across the continent that would elevate anyone within it. Two nineteenth-century concepts bolstered American exceptionalism and expansion. New York newspaper editor John O'Sullivan insisted that America's "manifest destiny" was to spread its superior civilization across the continent and beyond for the enlightenment and enrichment of all. "Social Darwinism" was the application by Herbert Spencer and other philosophers of Charles Darwin's notion of natural selection among different species that led to the evolution of more sophisticated species into a survival of the fittest struggle among human groups with those stronger naturally conquering and exploiting those weaker. That struggle was "progressive" because conquerors developed and asserted superior organizations, technologies, enterprises, values, and leadership against lesser peoples, thus uplifting their subjects along with themselves.

Americans asserted that mythology of exceptionalism to explain and justify their wars against and conquest of indigenous peoples. Indian wars erupted frequently from Jamestown's founding in 1607 to the last battle at Wounded Knee in 1890. Nearly every war resulted in the devastation of one or more tribes, the seizure of much of their lands, and the subjection of the survivors on reservations. Myths helped Americans morally justify and emotionally accept those wars, atrocities, and conquests. They saw themselves as a superior, civilized, enterprising, adventurous people bringing Christianity, law, private property, and morality to "savages." They martyrized themselves as the victims of Indian violence and mayhem, recounting horrific tortures that the "savages" inflicted on their captives. In doing so, they projected their own aggression, violence, exploitation, and atrocities onto a hated, feared enemy. For instance, Americans turned two disastrous, avoidable defeats—the Alamo and the Little Bighorn—into symbols of national greatness, each the equivalent of Thermopylae. The heroic frontiersman at the Alamo and troopers at the Little Bighorn died fighting to their last rounds to advance American civilization.

The West morphed from the nation's political, economic, and cultural sideshow into a region as dynamic and diverse as the East during the modern and post-modern eras. A series of federal programs like the 1862 Homestead Act, 1872 Mining Act, and 1902 Reclamation Act laid the groundwork that arrays of New Deal, World War II, and Cold War policies, programs, and subsidies realized. Throughout those decades, political tugs-of-war were incessant between liberals and conservatives, among materialists, conservationists, and preservationists, between nationalists and multiculturalists, between business owners and workers, between traditionalists and progressives, and other opponents whose relative power, victories, and defeats varied over time.

***

What is indisputable about the West is that zigzagging across it offers endless sublime and fascinating experiences. There is no better place to start that journey than at Gateway Arch's observation deck 630ft above the St. Louis landing. Gaze eastward and imagine a thousand miles to the Atlantic, first to Jamestown and then to Plymouth where the first two colonies began. Then pass through two centuries of American history to the Louisiana Purchase before gazing westward over the continent and two centuries of the West's history to the present. Next stop is the Museum of Western Expansion beneath the Arch. From there head west on Locust Street fourteen blocks to the Campbell House Museum. Robert Campbell was born in Ireland, came to America as a young man in 1821, spent a decade as a mountain man during which he made a fortune, then settled in St. Louis to invest in steamboats, railroads, hotels, and finance.[7] Then drive several miles to Bellefontaine Cemetery and seek the gravestones of Campbell, William Clark, Thomas Hart Benton, Benjamin Bonneville, Manuel Lisa, John O'Fallon, and Stephen Kearney.

Then cut loose across the West. There is poetry just in the names of the West's greatest national parks, Yellowstone and Glacier, Grand Canyon and Death Valley, Badlands and Tall Grass Prairie, Redwoods and Sequoia, Saguaro and Joshua Tree, along with the West's iconic animals that might be spotted, bison and wolves, cougars and coyotes, elk and moose, bald eagles and roadrunners, big horn sheep and mountain goats, diamondback rattlers and Gila monsters, wild horses and donkeys. One can canoe or raft mighty rivers like the Missouri, Columbia, and Colorado, and hike up 14,452ft Mount Whitney in the Sierras, 14,411ft Mount Rainier in the Cascades, and 7,232ft Black Elk Peak, formerly Harney Peak, in the Black Hills. Part of the visceral appeal of any wilderness adventure is the chance you might not make it back alive. You could drown shooting rapids, get mauled by a grizzly, poisoned by a rattlesnake, freeze, fry, or thirst to death, or lose your grip and plunge from a cliff into oblivion.

Along the way are evocative historic sites, of ancient Indian spiritual sites at Medicine Wheel and Painted Rock; Indian villages at Chaco Canyon and Taos Pueblo; the Lewis and Clark expedition at Fort Mandan and Fort Clatsop; the Great Plains' bison robe trade at Bent's Fort and Fort Union; army garrisons at Fort Laramie and Fort Robinson, Fort Davis and Fort Leavenworth; Indian War battles at the Little Bighorn and Big Hole; mining towns at Tombstone and Virginia City, Deadwood and Bisbee; and ghost towns at Bodie and Bannack.

The modern West has engineering marvels like Boulder Dam and Golden Gate Bridge; huge stone monuments like Mount Rushmore and Crazy Horse; iconic roads like Route 66 and Highway 1; meccas like Las Vegas and Salt Lake City; nuclear weapons development like Los Alamos and Hanford; military bases like Cheyenne Mountain and Camp Pendleton; western art towns like Taos and Scottsdale, Jackson Hole and Marfa; Indian museums in Sacramento and Cody; fur trade museums in Pinedale and Chadron; cowboy museums in Cody and Oklahoma City; railroad museums in Sacramento and Cheyenne; western art museums in Denver and Santa Fe; rodeos at Pendleton and

Cheyenne; New Age centers at Sedona and Big Sur; and alleged UFOs at Roswell and Area 51. There are still places to stay with a flavoring of the Old West reputedly with lingering spirits like the St. James Hotel in Cimmaron, New Mexico, the Occidental Hotel in Buffalo Wyoming, the Irma Hotel founded by Buffalo Bill in Cody, Wyoming, the Silver Queen in Virginia City, Nevada, and the Copper Queen in Bisbee, Arizona.

And finally, there are sites of great tragedy, slaughter at Sand Creek and Wounded Knee, Greenwood District in Tulsa and the Alfred P. Murrah Building in Oklahoma City; dispossession at Bosque Redondo and Manzanar; assassinations of John Kennedy at Hely Plaza and Robert Kennedy at the Ambassador Hotel; FBI shootouts with anarchists at Ruby Ridge and Waco; and shootings by nihilists of children at schools in Aurora and Uvalde.

***

The West is partly what we believe it is. Everyone harbors his or her own unique version of the West. More vitally, the West is what everyone who inhabited it did within it collectively or individually from the first band of humans through the present. The West is what we, and all those who came before us make or unmake, and do or not do with it. The West is all those vast majestic landscapes seemingly untouched by man. The West is also all those kitschy knick-knacks and tee shirts in countless gift shops. The West is all those lands devastated by clearcut forests, overgrazed grasslands, drained lakes and rivers, sprawling cities and farms, and poisoned air and water with cocktails of toxic often carcinogenic chemicals. The West is the American dream of freedom, reinvention, and fulfillment stretched across vast seemingly endless horizons.

ENDNOTES

Introduction

1 For overviews of different interpretations of the West, see: John Clark, ed., *The Frontier Challenge: Responses to the Trans-Mississippi West* (Lawrence: University Press of Kansas, 1971); Michael Malone, ed., *Historians and the American West* (Lincoln: University of Nebraska Press, 1983); Roger Nichols, ed., *American Frontier and Western Issues: A Historiographical Review* (New York: Greenwood Press, 1986); Clyde Milner, ed., *Major Problems in the History of the American West* (Lexington, Mass.: Heath, 1989); Gerald Nash, *Creating the West: Historical Interpretations, 1890-1990* (Albuquerque: University of New Mexico Press, 1991); Kenneth Etulain, ed., *Writing Western History: Essays on Major Western Historians* (Albuquerque: University of New Mexico Press, 1991); Donald Worster, *Rivers of Empire: Water, Aridity, and the Growth of the American West* (New York: Oxford University Press, 1992); Clyde Milner, Carol O'Connor, and Martha Sandweiss, eds, *The Oxford History of the American West* (New York: Oxford University Press, 1994); Dee Brown, *The American West* (New York: Touchstone, 1995); Clyde Milner, ed., *A New Significance: Re-envisioning the History of the American West* (New York: Oxford University Press, 1996); Dee Brown, *Bury My Heart at Wounded Knee: An Indian History of the American West* (New York: Holt, 2007); John Faragher and Robert Hine, *Frontiers: A Short History of the American West* (New Haven, Conn.: Yale University Press, 2008); Ned Blackhawk, *Violence over the Land: Indians and Empires in the Early American West* (Cambridge, Mass.: Harvard University Press, 2008); Anne F. Hyde, *Empires, Nations, and Families: A New History of the North American West* (New York: Ecco, 2012); William Wyckoff, *How to Read the American West: A Field Guide* (Seattle: University of Washington Press, 2014); Robert Hine and John Faragher, *The American West: A New Interpretative History* (New Haven, Conn.: Yale University Press, 2017); David Wrobel, *America's West: A History, 1890-1950* (New York: Cambridge University Press, 2017); H.W. Brands, *Dreams of El Dorado: A History of the American West* (New York: Basic Books, 2020); Sarah Deutsch and Richard Etulain, *Making a Modern U.S. West: The Contested Terrain of a Region and Its Borders, 1898-1940* (Lincoln: University of Nebraska Press, 2022); Brenden Rensink, *The North American West in the*

Twenty-First Century (Lincoln: University of Nebraska Press, 2022); Anne F. Hyde, *Born of Lakes and Plains: Mixed-Descent Peoples and the Making of the American West* (New York: W.W. Norton, 2023); Naoise Mae Sweeney, *The West: A New History in Fourteen Lives* (New York: Dutton, 2023).

2 Historians end the West as a region at the ocean and do not include Hawaii and other Pacific island possessions, nor do they include detached Alaska, although it is studied as a late frontier.

3 Patricia Nelson Limerick, *The Legacy of Conquest: The Unbroken Past of the American West* (New York: W.W. Norton, 1987), 90.

4 Paul Hutton, "From the Little Big Horn to Little Big Man: The Changing Image of the Western Hero in Popular Culture," *Western Historical Quarterly*, vol. 7, no. 1 (January 1976), 19, 19–45.

5 J. Hector St. John de Crevecoeur, *Letters from an American Farms and Sketches of Eighteenth Century America* (New York: Penguin Classics, 1986), 69–70.

6 Lewis Hyde, ed., *The Essays of Henry D. Thoreau* (New York: Farrar, Straus, and Giroux, 2002), 158.

7 T.K. Whipple, *Study Out the Land, Essays* (Berkeley: University of California Press, 1943), 65.

8 Milner, "Introduction,"*Oxford History of the American West*, 3.

9 Ray Billington and Martin Ridge, *Westward Expansion: A History of the American Frontier* (New York: Macmillan, 1982).

10 Earl Pomeroy, "Toward a Reorientation of Western History: Continuity and Environment,"*Mississippi Valley Historical Review*, vol. 41, no. 4 (March 1955), 579–600.

11 Earl Pomeroy, *The Territories and the United States, 1861-1890: Studies in Colonial Administration* (Philadelphia: University of Philadelphia Press, 1947).

12 Walter Nugent, "Frontiers and Empires in the Late Nineteenth Century,"*Western Historical Quarterly*, vol. 20, no 4 (November 1989), 394, 393–408.

13 Patricia Nelson Limerick, *The Legacy of Conquest: The Unbroken Past of the American West* (New York: W.W. Norton, 1987); Patricia Nelson Limerick, Clyde Milner, and Charles Rankin, eds, *Trails: Toward a New Western History* (Norman: University of Oklahoma Press, 1991).

For the most comprehensive, in-depth New Western history, see Richard White, *It's Your Misfortune and None of My Own: A New History of the American West* (Norman: University of Oklahoma Press, 1991). For other prominent versions, see: Jerome Steffen, *Comparative Frontiers: A Proposal for Studying the American West* (Norman: University of Oklahoma Press, 1980); Robert Hine, *The American West: An Interpretive History* (Boston: Little, Brown, 1984); Gerald Nash and Richard Etulain, eds, *The Twentieth Century West: Historical Interpretations* (Albuquerque: University of New Mexico Press, 1989); William Cronon, George Miles, and Jay Gitlin, eds, *Under an Open Sky: Rethinking America's Western Past* (New York: W.W. Norton, 1993); Clyde Milner, Carol O'Connor, and Martha Sandweiss, eds, *The Oxford History of the American West* (New York: Oxford University Press, 1994); Patricia Nelson Limerick, *Something in the Soil: Legacies and Reckoning in the New West* (New York: W.W. Norton, 2000); Robert Hine, John Faragher, and Jon Coleman, *The American West: A New Interpretive History* (New Haven, Conn.: Yale University Press, 2017).

14 Limerick, *Legacy of Conquest*, 26.

15 For American Indian / Native American / Indigenous American studies, see: Eduardo Duran and Bonnie Duran, *Native American Postcolonial Psychology* (Albany: State University of New York Press, 1995); Donald Fixico, *The American Indian Mind in a Linear World: American Indian Studies and Traditional Knowledge* (New York: Routledge, 2003); Devon Mihesuah, *Indigenous American Women: Decolonization, Empowerment, Activism* (Lincoln: University of Nebraska Press, 2003); Clara Sue Kidwell, *Native American Studies* (Lincoln: University of Nebraska Press, 2005); Sara Heitshu and Thomas Marshall, *Native American Studies: A Guide to Reference and Information Studies* (New York: Libraries Press, 2007); Roxanne Dunbar-Ortiz, *An Indigenous People's History of the United States* (New York: Beacon Press, 2015); Philip Deloria, *Playing Indian* (New Haven, Conn.: Yale University Press, 2022); Ned Blackhawk, *The Rediscovery of America: Native Peoples and the Unmaking of U.S. History* (New Haven, Conn.: Yale University Press, 2023); Kathleen DuVal, Native Nations: A Millenium in North America (New York: Random House, 2024).

For this book, Indian will most commonly be used to designate the first waves of people over thousands of years. Nearly all American Indians take pride in that identity. The academic term "native American" is problematic since anyone born in the United States can claim that identity. Kimberly Huyser, "Data and American Indian Identity," *Sage*, vol. 19, no. 3 (2020), 10–15.

16 Richard White, "Trashing the Trails," Limerick, Milner, and Rankin, *Trails*, 39.

17 Gerald Nash, *The American West Transformed: The Impact of the Second World War* (Bloomington: University of Indiana Press, 1985).

18 For examples of New West studies of race, gender, class, and labor, see: Margaret Jacobs, *White Mother to a Dark Race: Settler Colonialism, Maternalism, and the Removal of Indigenous Children in the American West and Australia, 1880-1940* (Lincoln: University of Nebraska Press, 2011); Laura Barraclough, *Charros: How Mexican Cowboys Are Remapping Race and American Identity* (Berkeley: University of California Press, 2014); Kerry Fine et al., *Weird Westerns: Race, Gender, Genre* (Lincoln: University of Nebraska Press, 2020); Shirley Boteler Mack, *Dreaming with the Ancestors: Black Seminole Women in Texas and Mexico* (Norman: University of Oklahoma Press, 2021).

19 Roderick Nash, *Wilderness and the American Mind* (New Haven, Conn.: Yale University Press, 1982), ix.

20 Alexis de Tocqueville, *Democracy in America* (Chicago: University of Chicago Press, 2000), 461.

21 White, *New History of the American West*, 616.

22 Michael Johnson, *New Westers: The West in Contemporary American Culture* (Lawrence: University Press of Kansas, 1996).

23 Nash, *Creating the West*, 200.

24 For overviews of symbolism and archetypes, see: Joseph Campbell, *The Hero with a Thousand Faces* (New York: MJF Books, 1949); Carl Jung, *Man and His Symbols* (New York: Dell Publishing, 1968); David Thelen, ed., *Memory and American History* (Bloomington: University of Indiana Press, 1990). For studies of the archetypal western hero, see: Kent Steckmesser, *The Western Hero in History and Legend* (Norman: University of Oklahoma Press, 1965); Paul Hutton, "From the Little Big Horn to Little Big Man: The Changing Image of the Western Hero in Popular Culture," *Western Historical Quarterly*, vol. 7, no. 1 (January 1976), 19–45; Frank Bergon and Zeese Papanikolas, eds, *Looking Far West: The Search for the American West in History, Myth, and Literature* (New York: American Library, 1978); Robert Morgan, *Lions of the West: Heroes and Villains of Westward Expansion* (New York: Shannon Ravenal Book, 2012); Hampton Sides, *Blood and Thunder: The Epic Story of Kit Carson and the Conquest of the American West* (New York: Anchor, 2005); David McCullough, *The Pioneers: The Heroic Story of the Settlers Who Brought the American Ideal West* (New York: Simon and Schuster, 2020). For European views of the American West, see: Ray Billington, *Land of Savagery, Land of Promise: The European Image of the American Frontier in the Nineteenth Century* (New York: W.W. Norton, 1981).

25 Carl Degler, "Why Historians Change their Minds," *Pacific Historical Review*, vol. 45, no. 2 (May 1976), 183, 167–84.

26 John Faragher, ed., *Rereading Frederick Jackson Turner* (New Haven, Conn.: Yale University Press, 1994), 18, 22.

Chapter 1: Regions and First Peoples

1 Jeffrey Goodman, *American Genesis: The American Indian and the Origins of Modern Man* (New York: Summit Books, 1981); Brian Fagan, *The Great Journey: The Peopling of Ancient America* (London: Thames and Hudson, 1987); Stuart Fidel, *The Prehistory of the Americas* (New York: Cambridge University Press, 1987); Joseph Greenburg, *Language in the Americas* (Stanford, Calif.: Stanford University Press, 1987); Alvin Josephy, ed., *America in 1492: The World of the Indian People before the Arrival of Columbus* (New York: Vintage, 1992); Charles Mann, *1491: New Revelations of the Americas before Columbus* (New York: Vintage, 2011); Michael Oberg and Peter Olsen-Harbich, *Native America: A History* (New York: Wiley-Blackwell, 2022).

2 Mann, *1491*, 158, 189, 190; Olive Patricia Dickason, *Canada's First Nations: A History of Founding Peoples from Earliest Times* (Norman: University of Oklahoma Press, 1992), 21, 23, 25; Ruth Gruhn, "Linguistic Evidence in Support of the Coastal Route of Earliest Entry into the New World,"*Man*, Volume 23, Number 2 (1988), 77–100.

3 James Mooney, *The Aboriginal Population of America North of Mexico* (Washington D.C.: Smithsonian Institute, 1928); Alfred Kroeber, "Native American Population,"*American Anthropologist*, vol. 36, no. 1 (January-March 1934), 1–25; William Devevan, ed., *The Native Population of the Americas in 1492* (Madison: University of Wisconsin Press, 1992).

4 Bertha Dutton, *American Indians of the Southwest* (Albuquerque: University of New Mexico Press, 1975).

5 Thomas Mails, *The People Called Apache* (New York: BDD Illustrated Books, 1993).

6 Walter Prescott Webb, *The Great Plains* (1931) (Lincoln: University of Nebraska Press, 1981); Brian Blouet and Frederick Luebke, eds, *The Great Plains: Environment and Culture* (Lincoln: University of Nebraska Press, 1979); Dan Flores, *The Natural West: The Environmental History of the Great Plains and Rocky Mountains* (New York: Oxford University Press, 2003); Dan Flores et al., *American Serengeti: The Last Big Animals of the Great Plains* (Lawrence: University Press of Kansas, 2016).

7 Thomas Mails, *The Mystic Warriors of the Plains* (New York: Barnes and Noble Books, 1991).

8 Ray Billington and Martin Ridge, *Westward Expansion: A History of the American Frontier* (New York: Macmillan, 1982), 355.

9 Karl Schlesier, ed., *Plains Indians, 500-1500: The Archeological Past of Historic Groups* (Norman: University of Oklahoma Press, 1994).

10 John Ewers, *Indian Life on the Upper Missouri* (Norman: University of Oklahoma Press, 1968), 9.

11 Anthony McGinnis, *Counting Coup and Cutting Horses: Intertribal Warfare on the Northern Plains, 1738-1889* (Evergreen, Colo.: Evergreen Press, 1990).

12 "Plenty Coups Mourns the Vanishing Buffalo, Recorded in 1950," Carolyn Merchant, ed., *Major Problems in American Environmental History* (New York: D.C. Heath, 1993), 302.

13 Royal Hassrick, *The Sioux* (Norman: University of Oklahoma Press, 1964).

14 T.R. Fehrenbach, *Comanches: The History of a People* (New York: Anchor Books, 2003); Pekka Hämäläinen, *The Comanche Empire* (New Haven, Conn.: Yale University Press, 2008).

15 Fehrenbach, *Comanches*, 76–81, 112, 108, 114, 100–04.

16 For the best overview, see: Ella Clark, *Indian Legends from the Northern Rockies* (Norman: University of Oklahoma Press, 1989).

17 Alvin Josephy, *Nez Perce Country* (Lincoln: University of Nebraska Press, 2007).

18 Virginia McConnell Simmons, *The Ute Indians of Utah, Colorado, and New Mexico* (Boulder: University Press of Colorado, 2001).

19 Steven Simms, *Ancient Peoples of the Great Basin and Colorado Plateau* (New York: Routledge, 2008).

20 Robert Ruby et al., *A Guide to the Indian Tribes of the Northwest* (Norman: University of Oklahoma Press, 2010).

21 Jon Daehnke, *Chinook Resilience: Heritage and Cultural Revitalization on the Lower Columbia River* (Seattle: University of Washington Press, 2017).

22 Damon Atkins and William Bauer, *We Are the Land: A History of Native California* (Berkeley: University of California Press, 2021).

23 Lynn Gamble, *The Chumash World at European Contact: Power, Trade, and Feasting among Complex Hunter-Gatherers* (Berkeley: University of California Press, 2017).

24 Alfred Crosby, *The Columbian Exchange: Biological and Cultural Consequences of 1492* (New York: Praeger, 2003).

25 Russell Thornton, *American Indians Holocaust and Survival: A Population History since 1492* (Norman: University of Oklahoma Press, 1987).

26 Roger Gottlieb, ed., *This Sacred Earth: Religion, Nature, Environment* (New York: Routledge, 1996), 132.

27 "An Indian Woman Deplores the Soreness of the Land, Recorded in 1925," Merchant, *Major Problems in American Environmental History*, 261.

Chapter 2: Conquistadors and Missionaries

1 J.H. Parry, *The Age of Reconnaissance: Discovery, Exploration, and Settlement, 1450-1650* (Berkeley: University of California Press, 1982); J.H. Parry, *The Spanish Seaborne Empire* (Berkeley: University of California Press, 1990).

2 Laurence Bergreen, *Columbus: The Four Voyages, 1492-1504* (New York: Penguin, 2012).

3 Robert Hine, John Faragher, and Jon Coleman, *The American West: A New Interpretive History* (New Haven, Conn.: Yale University Press, 2017), 12.

4 William Maltby, *The Rise and Fall of the Spanish Empire* (New York: Red Globe Press, 2008); Fernando Cervantes, *Conquistadores: A New History of Spanish Discovery and Conquest* (New York: Viking, 2021).

5 For the best overview of how European states conquered much of the world, see: Jared Diamond, *Guns, Germs, and Steel: The Fates of Human Societies* (New York: W.W. Norton, 1999).

6 Victoria Lyall and Teresita Romo, eds, *Traitor, Survivor, Icon: The Legacy of La Malinche* (New Haven, Conn.: Yale University Press, 2022).

7 Eugene Bolton, *Spanish Borderlands: A Chronicle of Florida and the Southwest* (New Haven, Conn.: Yale University Press, 1921); Peter

Gerhard, *The North Frontier of New Spain* (Princeton, N.J.: Princeton University Press, 1982); David Weber, ed., *New Spain's Far Northern Frontier: Essays on Spain in the American West, 1540-1821* (Albuquerque: University of New Mexico Press, 1979); John Bannon, *The Spanish Borderlands Frontier, 1513-1821* (Albuquerque: University of New Mexico Press, 1990); David Weber, *The Spanish Frontier in North America* (New Haven, Conn.: Yale University Press, 1992).

8 Alvar Nunez Cabeza de Vaca, *Chronicle of the Narvaez Expedition* (New York: Penguin, 2002).

9 Edward Spicer, *Cycles of Conquest: The Impact of Spain, Mexico, and the United States on the Indians of the Southwest, 1533-1960* (Tucson: University of Arizona Press, 1962); D.W. Meinig, *Southwest: Three Peoples in Geographical Change, 1600-1970* (New York: Oxford University Press, 1972); Thomas Hall, *Social Change in the Southwest, 1350-1880* (Lawrence: University Press of Kansas, 1989); Ramon Gutierrez, *When Jesus Came the Corn Mothers Went Away* (Palo Alto, Calif.: Stanford University Press, 1991).

10 Mann, *1491*, 146.

11 White, *New History of the American West*, 19; Gutierrez, *When Jesus Came*, xxviii.

12 Marilyn Fedewa, *Maria of Agreda: Mystical Lady in Blue* (Albuquerque: University of New Mexico Press, 2010).

13 Donald Chipman, *Spanish Texas, 1519-1821* (Austin: University of Texas Press, 1992).

14 Gutierrez, *When Jesus Came*, xix.

15 Andrew Knaut, *The Pueblo Revolt of 1680: Conquest and Resistance in Seventeenth Century New Mexico* (Norman: University of New Mexico Press, 1995); David Weber and Edward Countryman, *What Caused the Pueblo Revolt of 1680?* (New York: St. Martin's Press, 1999).

16 Elizabeth John, *Storms Brewed in Other Men's Worlds: The Confrontation of Indians, Spanish, and French in the Southwest, 1540-1795* (College Station: Texas A & M Press, 1975).

17 David Hackett Fischer, *Champlain's Dream: The European Founding of North America* (New York: Simon and Schuster, 2008).

18 Gutierrez, *When Jesus Came*, 153, 167, 180, 300; Hämäläinen, *The Comanche Empire*, 98.

19 White, *New History of the American West*, 33.

Chapter 3: Americans and Frontiers

1 Anne Lombard, *Colonial America: A History to 1763* (New York: Wiley Blackwell, 2011); Scott Weidensaul, *The First Frontier: The Forgotten History of Struggle, Savagery, and Endurance in Early America* (New York: Harper, 2012); Christian Koot, *Empire at the Periphery: British Colonists,*

Anglo-Dutch Trade, and the Development of the British Atlantic, 1621-1713 (New York: New York University Press, 2015); William Nester, *The Struggle for Power in Colonial America, 1607-1776* (New York: Lexington Books, 2019).

2 William Bradford, *Of Plymouth Plantation* (New York: Modern Library, 1981), 70.

3 Eric Dolin, *Fur, Fortune, and Empire: The Epic History of the Fur Trade in America* (New York: W.W. Norton, 2010), 107.

4 For overviews of colonial warfare, see: Howard Peckham, *The Colonial Wars, 1689-1762* (Chicago: University of Chicago Press, 1964); Douglas Leach, *Roots of Conflict: British Armed Forces and Colonial Americans, 1677-1763* (Chapel Hill: University of North Carolina Press, 1986); Ian Steele, *Warpaths: Invasions of North America* (New York: Oxford University Press, 1994); Scott Weidensaul, *The First Frontier: The Forgotten History of Struggle, Savagery, & Endurance in Early America* (New York: Houghton Mifflin, 2012); William Nester, *The Struggle for Power in Colonial America* (New York: Lexington Books, 2017).

5 For the most comprehensive and systematic overview, see: William Nester, *The Great Frontier War: Britain, France, and the Imperial Struggle for North America, 1607-1755* (Westport, Conn.: Praeger, 2000); William Nester, *The First Global War: Britain, France, and the Fate of North America, 1756-1775* (Westport, Conn.: Praeger, 2000). For French strategy in the last war, see: William Nester, *The French and Indian War and the Conquest of New France* (Norman: University of Oklahoma Press, 2014). See also: Fred Anderson, *The Crucible of War: The Seven Years' War and the Fate of Empire in British North America, 1754-1766* (New York: Vintage, 2001).

6 John Ross, *War on the Run: The Epic Story of Robert Rogers and the Conquest of America's First Frontier* (New York: Random House, 2009); Tim Todish, ed., *The Annotated and Illustrated Journals of Major Robert Rogers* (Fleischmanns, N.Y.: Purple Mountain Press, 2002); Tiffany Potter, ed., *Ponteach, or the Savages of America, a Tragedy* (Toronto: University of Toronto Press, 2010).

7 William Nester, *"Haughty Conquerors": Amherst and the Great Indian Uprising of 1763* (Westport, Conn.: Praeger, 2000).

8 John Faragher, *Daniel Boone: The Life and Legend of an American Pioneer* (New York: Henry Holt, 1992).

9 William Nester, *The Revolutionary Years, 1775-1789: The Art of American Power during the Early Republic* (Washington D.C. Potomac Books, 2011).

10 William Nester, *The Frontier War for American Independence* (Mechanicsburg, Penn.: Stackpole Books, 2004); William Nester, *George Rogers Clark: "I Glory in War"* (Norman: University of Oklahoma Press, 2012).

11 William Nester, *The Hamiltonian Vision, 1789-1800: The Art of American Power during the Early Republic* (Washington D.C.: Potomac Books, 2012);

William Nester, *The Jeffersonian Vision, 1801-1815: The Art of American Power during the Early Republic* (Washington D.C.: Potomac Books, 2013).

12 John Opie, *The Law of the Land: 200 Years of American Farmland Policy* (Lincoln: University of Nebraska Press, 1987).

13 Ray Billington and Martin Ridge, *Westward Expansion: A History of the American Frontier* (New York: Macmillan, 1982), 266.

14 Wiley Sword, *President Washington's Indian War: The Struggle for the Old Northwest, 1790-1795* (Norman: University of Oklahoma Press, 1985).

15 Eric Dolin, *Fur, Fortune, and Empire: The Epic History of the Fur Trade in America* (New York: W.W. Norton, 2010), 155.

16 Donald Jackson, *Thomas Jefferson and the Stony Mountains: Exploring the West from Monticello* (Norman: University of Oklahoma Press, 1993).

17 Adrienne Koch and William Peden, eds, *The Life and Selected Writings of Thomas Jefferson* (New York: Modern Library, 1998), 363.

18 Charles Cerami, *Jefferson's Great Gamble: The Remarkable Story of Jefferson, Napoleon, and the Men behind the Louisiana Purchase* (Naperville, Ill.: Sourcebook, 2003), 58.

19 Nester, *Jeffersonian Vision*, 38.

Chapter 4: Explorers and Traders

1 For the best overviews, see: Stephen Ambrose, *Undaunted Courage: Meriwether Lewis, Thomas Jefferson and the Opening of the West* (New York: Simon and Schuster, 1996). Gary Moulton, ed., *The Definitive Journals of Lewis & Clark*, 9 vols (Lincoln: University of Nebraska Press, 2002).

2 Thomas Jefferson Instructions to Meriwether Lewis, 1803, Clyde Milner, ed., *Major Problems in the History of the American West* (Lexington, Mass.: D.C. Heath, 1989), 132–6.

3 John Allen, *Passage through the Garden: Lewis and Clark and the Image of the American Northwest* (Urbana: University of Illinois Press, 1975); James Ronda, *Lewis and Clark among the Indians* (Lincoln: University of Nebraska Press, 1984).

4 William Goetzmann, *Army Exploration in the American West, 1803-1863* (New Haven, Conn.: Yale University Press, 1959); William Goetzmann, *Exploration and Empire: The Explorer and the Scientist in the Winning of the American West* (New York: Alfred Knopf, 1966).

5 For the best overviews, see: Hiram Crittenden, *The American Fur Trade of the Far West*, 2 vols (1935) (Lincoln: University of Nebraska Press, 1986); Bernard De Voto, *Across the Wide Missouri* (1947) (Boston: Houghton Mifflin, 1975); David Wishart, *The Fur Trade of the American West, 1807-1840* (Lincoln: University of Nebraska Press, 1992); Eric Dolin, *Fur, Fortune, and Empire: The Epic History of the Fur Trade in America* (New York: W.W. Norton, 2010).

6 William Swagerty, "Marriage and Rocky Mountain Trappers," Milner, *Major Problems in the History of the American West*, 181–97.

7 Richard Oglesby, *Manuel Lisa and the Opening of the Missouri Fur Trade* (Norman: University of Oklahoma Press, 1984).

8 Axel Madsen, *John Jacob Astor: America's First Millionaire* (New York: John Wiley, 2001).

9 James Ronda, *Astoria and Empire* (Lincoln: University of Nebraska Press, 1990).

10 David Dary, *The Santa Fe Trail: Its History, Legends, and Lore* (New York: Penguin, 2000); Stella M. Drumm, ed., *Down the Santa Fe Trail and into Mexico: The Diary of Susan Shelby Magoffin, 1846-1847* (Lincoln: University of Nebraska Press, 1982).

11 Matthew Harris and Jay Buckley, eds, *Zebulon Pike, Thomas Jefferson, and the Opening of the West* (New York: Oxford University Press, 2021).

12 Billington and Ridge, *Westward Expansion*, 330; Dary, *Santa Fe Trail*, 162.

13 William Lass, *A History of Steamboating on the Upper Missouri* (Lincoln: University of Nebraska Press, 1962).

14 "Stephen Long Expedition Report of a Frontier Barrier, 1821," in Milner, ed., *Major Problems in the History of the American West*, 142.

15 Richard Hofstadter, *The American Political Tradition* (New York: Alfred Knopf, 1948), 59.

16 William Nester, *The Age of Jackson and the Art of American Power, 1815-1848* (Washington D.C.: Potomac Books, 2013).

17 Richard Clokey, *William H. Ashley: Enterprise and Politics in the Trans-Mississippi West* (Norman: University of Oklahoma Press, 1990).

18 Fred Gowans, *Rocky Mountain Rendezvous: A History of the Fur Trade Rendezvous, 1825-1840* (Layton, Utah: Peregrine Books, 1985).

19 Dale Morgan, *Jedediah Smith and the Opening of the West* (Lincoln: University of Nebraska Press, 1964); George Brooks, ed., *The Southwest Expeditions of Jedediah Smith: His Personal Account of the Journey to California* (Lincoln: University of Nebraska Press, 1989); Harrison Dale, *The Explorations of William Ashley and Jedediah Smith, 1822-1829* (Lincoln: University of Nebraska Press, 1991).

20 John Reid, *Contested Empire: Peter Skene Ogden and the Snake River Expeditions* (Norman: University of Oklahoma Press, 2002).

21 Barton Barbour, *Fort Union and the Upper Missouri Fur Trade* (Norman: University of Oklahoma Press, 2001).

22 Madsen, *Astor*, 229.

23 "Speech of the 4 Bears, a Mandan Warrior to the Arrikarees and Mandan, 30th July 1837," in Milner, ed., *Major Problems in the History of the American West*, 48.

24 David Weber, *The Tao Trappers: The Fur Trade in the Far Southwest, 1540-1846* (Norman: University of Oklahoma Press, 1982).

25 Bill Gilbert, *Westering Man: The Life of Joseph Walker* (Norman: University of Oklahoma Press, 1989).

26 Stella Drumm, ed., *Down the Santa Fe Trail and into Mexico: The Diary of Susan Shelby Magoffin, 1846-1847* (Lincoln: University of Nebraska Press, 1982), 104, 114, 124.

27 Robert Berkhofer, *Salvation and the Savage: An Analysis of Protestant Missions and American Indian Response, 1787-1862* (Lexington: University Press of Kentucky, 2014).

28 Clifford Drury, *Marcus and Narcissa Whitman and the Opening of Old Oregon* (Glendale, Calif. A.H. Clark Publisher, 1973).

29 Martin Napersteck, *Sex and Manifest Destiny: The Urge that Drove Americans Westward* (Jefferson, N.C.: McFarland and Company, 2012), 197.

30 Leonard Arrington, *Great Basin Kingdom: An Economic History of the Latter Day Saints, 1830-1900* (Cambridge, Mass.: Harvard University Press, 1958); Nels Anderson, *Desert Saints: The Mormon Frontier in Utah* (Chicago: University of Chicago Press, 1969); Jan Shipps, *Mormonism: The Story of a New Religious Tradition* (Urbana: University of Illinois Press, 1985); Leonard Arrington and Davis Bitton, *The Mormon Experience: A History of the Latter-Day Saints* (Urbana: University of Illinois Press, 1992).

31 Paul Reeves and Ardis Parshall, eds, *Mormonism: A Historical Encyclopedia* (Santa Barbara, Calif.: ABC-CLIO, 2010), 93.

32 Leonard Arrington, *Brigham Young: American Moses* (Urbana: University of Illinois Press, 1986).

33 John Faragher, *Women and Men on the Overland Trail* (New Haven, Conn.: Yale University Press, 1979); John Unruh, *The Plains Across: The Overland Emigrants and the Trans-Mississippi West, 1840-1860* (Urbana: University of Illinois Press, 1982).

34 Unruh, *Plains Across*, 84–5.

35 Daniel Brown, *The Indifferent Stars Above: The Harrowing Saga of the Donner Party* (New York: Mariner Books, 2015); Unruh, *Plains Across*, 144, 113; Sally Denton, *American Massacre: The Tragedy at Mountain Meadows, September 1857* (New York: Vintage, 2004).

36 J.S. Holliday, *The World Rushed In: The California Gold Rush Experience* (New York: Touchstone, 1981), 120.

37 David Weber, *The Mexican Frontier, 1821-1846; The American Southwest* (Albuquerque: University of New Mexico Press, 1982), 206.

38 Richard Henry Dana, *Two Years Before the Mast: A Personal Narrative of Life at Sea* (1840) (New York: The Modern Library, 2001), 91, 93, 186–7.

Chapter 5: Warriors and Peacemakers

1 Shane Mountjoy, *Manifest Destiny: Westward Expansion* (New York: Chelsea House, 2009), 10.

2 Frederick Merk, *Manifest Destiny and Mission in American History: A Reinterpretation* (New York: Vintage, 1995); Anders Stephanson, *Manifest Destiny: American Expansionism and the Empire of Right* (New York: Hill and Wang, 1995); Thomas Hietala, *Manifest Destiny: American Exceptionalism and Empire* (Ithaca, N.Y.: Cornell University Press, 2002); David Maybury-Lewis, *Manifest Destinies and Indigenous Peoples* (Cambridge, Mass.: Harvard University Press, 2009); Shane Mountjoy, *Manifest Destiny: Westward Expansion* (New York: Chelsea House, 2009); Martin Napersteck, *Sex and Manifest Destiny: The Urge that Drove Americans Westward* (Jefferson, N.C.: McFarland and Company, 2012).

3 For the best overviews of all the wars, see: Spencer Tucker, ed., *The Encyclopedia of the North American Indian Wars, 1607-1890*, 2 vols (Santa Barbara, Calif.: ABC-CLIO, 2011).

For the best overviews of official federal relations with the tribes, see: Paul Prucha, *A Bibliographical Guide to the History of Indian-White Relations in the United States* (Chicago: University of Chicago Press, 1977); Paul Prucha, *The Great Father: The United States Government and the American Indians* (Lincoln: University of Nebraska Press, 1986); Robert Utley, *The Indian Frontier of the American West, 1846-1890* (Albuquerque: University of New Mexico Press, 1984); Philip Weeks, *"Farewell, My Nation": American Indians and the United States in the Nineteenth Century* (New York: John Wiley, 2016).

4 Peter Matthiessen, *Indian Country* (New York: Fontana, 1986), frontispiece.

5 Donald Jackson, *Thomas Jefferson and the Stony Mountains: Exploring the West from Monticello* (Norman: University of Oklahoma Press, 1993), 216–17.

6 "Chief Sharitarish Foretells the End of the Pawnee Way of Life, 1822," Albert Hurtado and Peter Iverson, eds, *Major Problems in American Indian History* (Lexington, Mass.: D.C. Heath, 1994), 237–8.

7 Nancy Isenberg, *Fallen Founder: The Life of Aaron Burr* (New York: Viking, 2007); Andro Linklater, *An Artist in Treason: The Extraordinary Double Life of General James Wilkinson* (New York: Walker Publishing Company, 2009).

8 Harris Warren, *The Sword Was Their Passport: A History of American Filibustering in the Mexican Revolution* (Baton Rouge: Louisiana State University Press, 1943).

9 Peter Cozens, *Tecumseh and the Prophet: The Heroic Struggle for America's Heartland* (New York: Vintage, 2021).

10 For the most in-depth overview, see Donald Hickey, *The War of 1812: A Forgotten Conflict* (Urbana: University of Illinois Press, 1990).

11 William Nester, *The Arikara War: The First Plains Indian War, 1823* (Missoula, Mont.: Mountain Press Publishing Company, 2001).

12 Ronald Satz, *American Indian Policy in the Jacksonian Era* (Norman: University of Oklahoma Press, 2002).

13 Tucker, ed., *The Encyclopedia of the North American Indian Wars,* 1:2011.

14 Billington and Ridge, *Westward Expansion,* 313.

15 Prucha, *Great Father,* 70.

16 Satz, *American Indian Policy in the Jacksonian Era,* 49.

17 "Cherokee Editor Elias Boudinot Opposes Removal, 1828," in Hurtado + and Iverson, eds, *Major Problems in American Indian History,* 210.

18 For the best book on Mexico's northern borderlands from 1821 to 1846, see: David Weber, *The Mexican Frontier, 1821-1946: The American Southwest Under Mexico* (Albuquerque: University of New Mexico Press, 1982).

19 Gregg Cantrell, *Stephen F. Austin: Empresario of Texas* (Austin: Texas State Historical Association, 2016).

20 Weber, *Mexican Frontier,* 80.

21 Ibid., 177.

22 Marshall De Bruhl, *Sword of San Jacinto: A Life of Sam Houston* (New York: Random House, 1993).

23 Jeff Long, *Duel of Eagles: The Mexican and U.S. Fight for the Alamo* (New York: William Morrow, 1990); Albert Nofi, *The Alamo and the Texas War of Independence: Heroes, Myths, and History* (New York: Da Capo Press, 2001).

24 Mark Derr, *The Frontiersman: The Real Life and Many Legends of Davy Crockett* (New York: Quill Books, 1993), 225.

25 Susan Prendergast Schoelwer, *Alamo Images: Changing Perceptions of a Texas Experience* (Dallas: Southern Methodist University Press, 1985); Jose Enrique de la Pena, *With Santa Anna in Texas: A Personal Narrative of the Revolution* (College Station: Texas A & M Press, 1997), 53.

26 Robert Utley, *Lone Star Justice: The First Century of the Texas Rangers* (New York: Berkely Book, 2002).

27 David Pletcher, *The Diplomacy of Annexation: Texas, Oregon, and the Mexican War* (Columbia: University of Missouri Press, 1973); Robert Merry, *A Country of Vast Designs: James K. Polk, the Mexican War, and the Conquest of the American Continent* (New York: Simon and Schuster, 2009).

28 John Eisenhower, *So Far From God: The U.S. War with Mexico, 1846-1848* (New York: Doubleday, 1989); Jack Bauer, *The Mexican War, 1846-1848* (Lincoln: University of Nebraska Press, 1992); Joseph Wheelan, *Invading Mexico: America's Continental Dream and the Mexican War, 1846-1848* (New York: Carroll & Graf Publishers, 2007).

29 Weber, *Mexican Frontier,* 195.

30 William Nester, *The Old West's First Power Couples: The Fremonts, the Custers, and Their Epic Quest for Manifest Destiny* (Tucson: Rio Nuevo Publishers, 2020).

31 Eisenhower, *So Far from God*, xviii, 369–70; Bauer, *Mexican War*, 397–8.

Chapter 6: Artists and Writers

1 Barbara Novak, *Nature and Culture: American Landscape and Painting, 1825-1875* (New York: Oxford University Press, 1995).

2 Lewis Hyde, ed., *The Essays of Henry D. Thoreau* (New York: North Point Press, 2002), 149, 162.

3 Dawn Glanz, *How the West Was Drawn: American Art and the Settling of the Frontier* (Ann Arbor: University of Michigan Press, 1982); William H. Goetzmann and William N. Goetzmann, *The West of the Imagination* (New York: W.W. Norton, 1986); Peter Hassrick et al., *American Frontier Life: Early Western Paintings and Prints* (New York: Abbeville Press, 1987); Anne Farrar Hyde, *An American Vision: Far Western Landscape and National Culture, 1820-1920* (New York: New York University Press, 1990).

4 Michael Mooney, ed., *George Catlin: Letters and Notes on the North America Indians* (New York: Grammercy Books, 1975), 89.

5 William H. Goetzmann and William N. Goetzmann, *The West of the Imagination* (New York: W.W. Norton, 1986), 26.

6 Catlin, *Letters and Notes*, 91.

7 "An Artist Proposes a National Park, George Catlin, 1832," in Roderick Nash, ed., *American Environmentalism: Readings in Conservation History* (New York: McGraw-Hill, 1990), 35.

8 James Fenimore Cooper, *The Pioneers* (New York: Oxford University Press, 1999), 454.

9 Michael Lofaro, ed., *Davy Crockett: The Man, the Legend, the Legacy, 1786-1986* (Knoxville: University of Tennessee Press, 1985); Mark Derr, *The Frontiersman: The Real Life and the Many Legends of Davy Crockett* (New York: Quill Books, 1993).

10 For the outstanding biography, see: Hampton Sides, *Blood and Thunder: The Epic Story of Kit Carson and the Conquest of the America West* (New York: Anchor Books, 2005).

11 Milo Quaife, ed., *Kit Carson's Autobiography* (Lincoln: University of Nebraska Press, 1966), 134–5.

Chapter 7: Warriors and Peacemakers

1 For the best accounts of wars west of the Mississippi, see: Robert Utley, *Frontiersmen in Blue: The United States Army and the Indian, 1848-1865* (Lincoln: University of Nebraska Press, 1981); Robert Utley, *Frontier*

Regulars: The United States Army and the Indian, 1866-1891, Lincoln: University of Nebraska Press, 1984); Peter Cozzens, *The Earth Is Weeping: The Epic Story of the Indian Wars for the American West* (New York: Vintage, 2017).

2 Utley, *Frontiersmen in Blue*, 42.

3 Robert Frazer, *Forts of the West* (Norman: University of Oklahoma Press, 1988).

4 Utley, *Frontiersmen in Blue*, 20.

5 Ibid., 18–19.

6 Nelson Miles, *Serving the Republic: Memoirs of the Civil and Military Life of Nelson A. Miles* (New York: Harper and Brothers Publisher, 1911), 117.

7 S.C. Gwynne, *Empire of the Summer Moon: Quanah Parker and the Fall of the Comanches, the Most Powerful Indian Tribe in American History* (New York: Scribner, 2011).

8 Albert Hurtado, *Indian Survival on the California Frontier* (New Haven, Conn.: Yale University Press, 1988); Benjamin Madley, *An American Genocide: The United States and the California Indian Catastrophe* (New Haven, Conn.: Yale University Press, 2010); Prucha, *Great Father*, 130–1.

9 Utley, *Frontiersmen in Blue*, 101.

10 Madley, *American Genocide*, 116, 127–38.

11 Hämäläinen, *The Comanche Empire*.

12 David Roberts, *Once They Moved Like the Wind: Cochise, Geronimo, and the Apache Wars* (New York: Touchstone, 1994).

13 Ray Glassley, *Pacific Northwest Indian Wars* (New York: Literary Licensing, 2011).

14 Utley, *Frontiersmen in Blue*, 175–8, 181–7.

15 Nicole Etcheson, *Bleeding Kansas: Contested Liberty in the Civil War Era* (Lawrence: University Press of Kansas, 2004).

16 Ray Billington and Martin Ridge, *Westward Expansion: A History of the American Frontier* (New York: Macmillan, 1982), 540.

17 Jay Monaghan, *Civil War on the Western Border, 1854-1865* (Lincoln: University of Nebraska Press, 1955), 17.

18 Prucha, *Great Father*, 136.

19 David Bigler, *Forgotten Kingdom: The Mormon Theocracy in the American West, 1847-1896* (Logan, Utah: Utah State University Press, 1998).

20 John Turner, *Brigham Young: Pioneer Prophet* (Cambridge, Mass.: Belknap Press, 2014).

21 David Bigler and Will Bagley, *The Mormon Rebellion: America's First Civil War, 1857-1858* (Norman: University of Oklahoma Press, 2012).

22 Sally Denton, *American Massacre: The Tragedy at Mountain Meadows, September 1857* (New York: Vintage, 2004).

23 David Konig, Paul Finkelman, and Christopher Bracey, eds, *The Dred Scott Case: Historical and Contemporary Perspectives on Law and Race* (Athens: Ohio University Press, 2010).

24 Jonathan Earle, *John Brown's Raid on Harpers Ferry: A Brief History with Documents* (New York: St. Martin's Press, 2008).

25 Michael Holt, *The Election of 1860: A Campaign Fraught with Consequences* (Lawrence: University Press of Kansas, 2017).

26 For the best overview, see: James McPherson, *Battle Cry of Freedom: The Civil War Era* (New York: Oxford University Press, 2003).

27 Jay Monaghan, *Civil War on the Western Border, 1854-1865* (Lincoln: University of Nebraska Press, 1955); Alvin Josephy, *The Civil War in the American West* (New York: Alfred Knopf, 1992).

28 Walter Pittman, *New Mexico and the Civil War* (New York: History Press, 2011).

29 Tom Dunlay, *Kit Carson and the Indians* (Lincoln: University of Nebraska Press, 2005).

30 Ray Billington and Martin Ridge, *Westward Expansion: A History of the American Frontier* (New York: Macmillan, 1982), 592.

31 Utley, *Frontiersmen in Blue*, 260.

32 Kenneth Carley, *The Dakota War of 1862* (St. Paul: Minnesota Historical Society Press, 1976).

33 Michael Oberg and Peter Olsen-Harbich, *Native America: A History* (New York: Wiley-Blackwell, 2022), 196.

34 Thom Hatch, *Black Kettle: The Cheyenne Chief Who Sought Peace but Found War* (New York: Wiley, 2004).

35 Weeks, *"Farwell, My Nation"*, 143.

36 Savoie Lottinville, ed., *The Life of George Bent, Written from His Letters* (Norman: University of Oklahoma Press, 1987), 152.

37 Duane Schultz, *Month of the Freezing Moon: The Sand Creek Massacre, November 1864* (New York: St. Martin's Press, 1990), 166.

38 Utley, *Frontier Regulars*, 4. Unless otherwise indicated all statistics in this section come from this book.

39 Mark Van de Logt, *War Party in Blue: Pawnee Scouts in the U.S. Army* (Norman: University of Oklahoma Press, 2021).

40 Bob Drury, *The Heart of Everything: The Untold Story of Red Cloud, an American Legend* (New York: Simon and Schuster, 2014).

41 Dorothy Johnson, *The Bloody Bozeman: The Perilous Trail to Montana's Gold* (New York: McGraw Hill, 1971).

42 Joseph Marshall, *The Journey of Crazy Horse: A Lakota History* (New York: Penguin, 2005).

43 Peter Cozzens, ed., *Conquering the Southern Plains: Eyewitnesses to the Indian Wars, 1865-1890* (New York: Stackpole, 2003).

44 Prucha, *Great Father*, 158.

45 Paul Wylie, *Blood on the Marias: The Baker Massacre* (Norman: University of Oklahoma Press, 2016).

46 Robert McNally, *The Modoc War: A Story of Genocide at the Dawn of America's Gilded Age* (Lincoln: University of Nebraska Press, 2021).

47 Cozzens, *Earth Is Weeping*, 153.

48 Brett Cruse, *Battles of the Red River War* (College Station: Texas A & M University Press, 2008).

49 Robert Utley, *Sitting Bull: The Life and Times of an American Patriot* (New York: Henry Holt, 2008).

50 Paul Hedren, *The Great Sioux War: 1876-77* (Lincoln: University of Nebraska Press, 1991).

51 Cozzens, *Earth Is Weeping*, 269.

52 Eliot West, *The Last Indian War: The Nez Perce Story* (New York: Oxford University Press, 2011).

53 Cozzens, *Earth Is Weeping*, 315–40.

54 "Allen Slickpoo (Nez Perce) Reviews the Nez Perce War (1877), recorded 1973," Hurtado, *Major Problems in American Indian History*, 340.

55 Utley, *Frontier Regulars*, 315.

56 Ibid., 323.

57 Virginia McConnell Simmons, *The Ute Indians of Utah, Colorado, and New Mexico* (Boulder: University of Colorado Press, 2001).

58 Paul Hutton, *The Apache Wars: The Hunt for Geronimo, the Apache Kid, and the Captive Boy Who Started the Longest War in American History* (New York: Crown, 2017).

59 Utley, *Frontier Regulars*, 192–3.

60 Ibid., 173.

61 Prucha, *Great Father*, 179.

62 Tom McHugh and Victoria Hobson, *The Time of the Buffalo* (Lincoln: University of Nebraska Press, 1979), 285.

63 Joe Starita, *"I Am a Man": Chief Standing Bear's Journey for Justice* (New York: St. Martin's Griffith, 2010).

64 Robert Mardock, *The Reformers and the American Indian* (Columbia: University of Missouri Press, 1971); Francis Prucha, ed., *Americanizing the American Indians: Writings by "Friends of the Indians," 1880-1900* (Cambridge, Mass.: Harvard University Press, 1973); Paul Prucha,

American Indian Policy in Crisis: Christian Reformers and the Indians, 1865-1900 (Norman: University of Oklahoma Press, 1976); William Hagan, *The Indian Rights Association: The Herbert Welsh Years, 1882-1904* (Tucson: University of Arizona Press, 1985); Victoria Sherer Matthes, eds, *The Women's National Indian Association: A History* (Albuquerque: University of New Mexico Press, 2015).

65 Prucha, *Great Father*, 281.

66 "Luther Standing Bear (Lakota) Recalls His Experiences at the Carlisle Indian Industrial School, 1890," Hurtado, *Major Problems in American Indian History*, 172–5.

67 Aishvarya Kavi, "Report Shows Hundreds of Native Children Died at U.S. Boarding Schools,"*New York Times*, August 1, 2024.

68 James Mooney, *The Ghost Dance Religion and the Sioux Outbreak of 1890* (Lincoln: University of Nebraska Press, 1991).

Chapter 8: Developers and Outlaws

1 J.S. Holliday, *The World Rushed In: The California Gold Rush Experience* (New York: Touchstone Books, 1981), 33.

2 Rodman Paul, *California Gold: The Beginning of Mining in the Far West* (Lincoln: University of Nebraska Press, 1965); Edward Dolnick, *Rush: America's Fevered Quest for Fortune, 1848-1853* (New York: Little, Brown, 2014).

3 Patricia Nelson Limerick, *Something in the Soil: Legacies and Reckonings in the New West* (New York: W.W. Norton, 2000), 215–18.

4 John Boesesnecker, *Gold Dust and Gunsmoke: Tails of Gold Rush Outlaws, Gunfighters, Lawmen, and Vigilantes* (New York: Wiley, 2000).

5 Kevin Starr, *Americans and the California Dream, 1850-1915* (New York: Oxford University Press, 1973); Kevin Starr, *Inventing the Dream: California through the Progressive Era* (New York: Oxford University Press, 1985).

6 Turrentine Jackson, *Wagon Roads West: A Study of Federal Road Surveys and Construction in the Trans-Mississippi West, 1846-1869* (Berkeley: University of California Press, 1952); Forest Hill, *Roads, Rails, and Waterways: The Army Engineers and Early Transportation* (Norman: University of Oklahoma Press, 1957).

7 Ray Billington and Martin Ridge, *Westward Expansion: A History of the American Frontier* (New York: Macmillan, 1982), 576.

8 Ibid., 641.

9 Marc Reisner, *Cadillac Desert: The American West and Its Disappearing Water* (New York: Viking, 1986), 114.

10 Allan Bogue, "An Agricultural Empire," Milner, *Oxford History of the American West*, 279.

11 White, *New History of the American West,* 143; Robert Athearn, *The Mythic West in Twentieth Century America* (Lawrence: University Press of Kansas, 1986), 29; Billington and Ridge, *Westward Expansion,* 644. For overviews of the transformation, see: Gilbert Fite, *The Farmers' Frontier, 1865-1900* (New York: Holt, Rinehart, and Winston, 1966); Donald Pisani, *From the Family Farm to Agribusiness: The Irrigation Crusade in California and the West* (Berkeley: University of California Press, 1984); Rodman Paul, *The Far West and Great Plains in Transition, 1859-1900* (Norman: University of Oklahoma Press, 1998).

12 " Allan Bogue, "An Agricultural Empire," Milner, *Oxford History of the American West,* 296; Billington and Ridge, *Westward Expansion,* 636.

13 Billington and Ridge, *Westward Expansion,* 636.

14 Julius Grodinsky, *Transcontinental Strategy: A Study of Businessmen* (Philadelphia: University of Pennsylvania Press, 1962); Oscar Winther, *The Transportation Frontier: Trans-Mississippi West, 1865-1890* (New York: Holt, Rinehart, and Winston, 1964); Stephen Ambrose, *Nothing Like It in the World: The Men Who Built the Transcontinental Railroad, 1863-1869* (New York: Simon and Schuster, 2000).

15 White, *New History of the American West,* 145.

16 Ibid., 252, 256.

17 Ibid., 244.

18 Clark Spence, *British Investments and the American Mining Frontier, 1860-1901* (Ithaca,, N.Y.: Cornell University Press, 1959); Rodman Paul, *Mining Frontiers of the Far West, 1848-1880* (New York: Holt, Rinehart, Winston, 1963); Richard, Lingenfelter, *The Hardrock Miners: A History of the Mining Labor Movement in the American West, 1863-93* (Berkeley: University of California Press, 1974); Richard Peterson, *The Bonanza Kings: The Social Origins and Business Behavior of Western Mining Entrepreneurs, 1870-1900* (Lincoln: University of Nebraska Press, 1977); Michael Malone, *The Battle for Butte: Mining and Politics on the Northern Frontier, 1864-1906* (Seattle: University of Washington Press, 1981); Carl Mayer and George Riley, *Public Domain, Private Domain: A History of Public Mineral Policy in America* (San Francisco: Sierra Club Books, 1985);

Duane Smith, *Mining America: The Industry and the Environment, 1800-1980* (Lawrence: University Press of Kansas, 1987).

19 "A Federal Agent Assesses Mining's Impact on the Indians, 1853," in Carolyn Merchant, ed., *Major Problems in American Environmental History* (New York: D.C. Heath, 1993), 253.

20 White, *New History of the American West,* 309.

21 John Opie, "Environmental History of the West," in Gerald Nash and Richard Etulain, eds, *The Twentieth Century West: Historical Interpretations* (Albuquerque: University of New Mexico Press, 1989), 215.

22 Tom McHugh and Victoria Hobson, *The Time of the Buffalo* (Lincoln: University of Nebraska Press, 1979); Andrew Isenberg, *The Destruction of the Bison* (New York: Cambridge University Press, 2001).

23 Richard White, "Animals and Enterprise," in Clyde Milner, Carol O'Connor, and Martha Sandweiss, eds, *The Oxford History of the American West* (New York: Oxford University Press, 1994), 248.

24 David Dary, *Entrepreneurs of the Old West* (Lincoln: University of Nebraska Press, 1986), 217.

25 Ibid., 218.

26 Eric Dolin, *Fur, Fortune, and Empire: The Epic History of the Fur Trade in America* (New York: W.W. Norton, 2010), 309.

27 David Smits, "The Frontier Army and the Destruction of the Buffalo: 1865-1883,"*Western Historical Quarterly*, vol. 25, no 3, (1994), 317, 330.

28 "Plenty Coups Mourns the Vanishing Buffalo, Recorded in 1950," Merchant, *Major Problems in American Environmental History*, 304.

29 Robert Dykstra, *The Cattle Towns: A Social History of the Kansas Cattle Trading Centers of Abilene, Ellsworth, Wichita, Dodge City, and Caldwell, 1867-85* (New York: Atheneum, 1976).

30 Douglas Branch, "The Long Drive North," in Philip Durham and Everett Jones, eds, *The Western Story: Fact, Fiction, and Myth* (New York: Harcourt, Brace, Jovanovich, 1975), 22.

31 Dary, *Entrepreneurs of the Old West*, 224.

32 Kenneth Porter, "The Labor of Negro Cowboys," Milner, *Major Problems in the History of the American West*, 344.

33 Thomas Cox, *Mills and Markets: A History of the Pacific Coast Lumber Industry to 1900* (Seattle: University of Washington Press, 1974); Andrew Prouty, *More Deadly than War: Pacific Coast Logging, 1827-1981* (New York: Garland Publishing, 1982); David Clary, *Timber and the Forest Service* (Lawrence: University Press of Kansas, 1983).

34 Richard Etulain and Michael Malone, *The American West: A Modern History, 1900 to the Present* (Lincoln: University of Nebraska Press, 2007), 27.

35 White, *New History of the American West*, 259.

36 Roger McGrath, "Violence on a Mining Frontier," Milner, *Major Problems in the History of the American West*, 386, 391.

37 Richard Brown, *No Duty to Retreat: Violence and Values in American History* (Norman: University of Oklahoma Press, 1994). For other excellent overviews of frontier violence, see: Richard Slotkin, *Regeneration through Violence: The Mythology of the American Frontier, 1600-1860* (New York: Harper Perennial, 1973); Richard Slotkin, *The Fatal Environment: The Myth of the Frontier in the Age of Industrialization, 1800-1890* (Middletown, Conn.: Wesleyan University Press, 1985); Richard Slotkin, *Gunfighter Nation: The Myth*

of the Frontier in Twentieth Century America (Norman: University of Oklahoma Press, 1992); Eugene Hollon, *Frontier Violence: Another Look* (New York: Oxford University Press, 1974); Richard Brown, *Strain of Violence: Historical Studies of American Violence and Vigilantism* (New York: Oxford University Press, 1974); Roger McGrath, *Gunfighters, Highwaymen, and Vigilantes: Violence on the Frontier* (Berkeley: University of California Press, 1984); Richard Drinnon, *Facing West: The Metaphysics of Indian Hating* (Norman: University of Oklahoma Press, 1997).

38 Julian Ralph, *Our Great West: A Study of the Present Conditions and Future Possibilities of the New Commonwealths and Capitals of the United States* (New York: Harper Brothers, 1893), 263–4.

39 Bill O'Neal, *Encyclopedia of Western Gunfighters* (Norman: University of Oklahoma Press, 1979).

40 Ibid., 8, 10.

41 Ibid., 5–6.

42 Robert Utley, *High Noon in Lincoln: Violence on the Western Frontier* (Albuquerque: University of New Mexico Press, 1987).

43 Tom Clavin, *Tombstone: The Earp Brothers, Doc Holliday, and the Vendetta Ride from Hell* (New York: St. Martin's Press, 2020).

44 Richard Prassel, *The Western Peace Officer: A Legacy of Law and Order* (Norman: University of Oklahoma Press, 1972).

45 Clavin, *Tombstone*, 62.

46 White, *New History of the American West*, 332–3.

47 Richard Brown, "Violence," Milner, *Oxford History of the American War*, 412–13.

48 Robert Chandler, "Friends in Time of Need: Republican and Black Civil Rights in California during the Civil War," *Arizona and the West*, vol. 24, no. 4 (Winter 1982), 39–40.

49 White, *New History of the American West*, 187.

50 Marion Goldman, *Gold Diggers and Silver Miners: Prostitution and Social Life on the Comstock Lode* (Ann Arbor: University of Michigan Press, 1979); Anne Buller, *Daughters of Joy, Sisters of Misery: Prostitutes in the American West, 1865-90* (Urbana: University of Illinois Press, 1985).

51 "Frederick Law Olmsted on the Value of Parks, 1865," Merchant, *Major Problems in American Environmental History*, 384–5.

52 Ferdinand Hayden, "The Wonder of the West: More About the Yellowstone," *Scribners Monthly*, vol. 3 (February 1872), 396.

53 Earl Pomeroy, *In Search of the Golden West: The Tourist in Western America* (New York: Alfred Knopf, 1957).

54 Lesley Poling-Kempes, *The Harvey Girls: Women Who Opened the West* (New York: Da Capo, 1989).

Chapter 9: Artists and Writers

1 William Nester, *The Old West's First Power Couples: The Fremonts, the Custers, and Their Epic Quest for Manifest Destiny* (Tucson: Rio Nuevo Publisher, 2020); Bruce Rosenberg, *Custer and the Epic of Defeat* (University Park: Penn State University Press, 1973); Vine Deloria, *Custer Died for Your Sins: An Indian Manifesto* (Norman: University of Oklahoma Press, 1988); Brian Dippie, *Custer's Last Stand: The Anatomy of an American Myth* (Lincoln: University of Nebraska Press, 1994).

2 Christian Bold, "Malaeska's Revenge or, The Dime Novel Tradition in Popular Literature," in Richard Aquila, ed., *Wanted Dead or Alive: The American West in Popular Culture* (Urbana: University of Illinois Press, 1996), 22.

3 Josiah Royce, "Fremont,"*Atlantic*, vol. 90, no. 10 (October 1890), 555, 548–57.

Chapter 10: Boomers and Busters

1 Gerald Nash, *The American West in the Twentieth Century: A Short History of an Urban Oasis* (Englewood Cliffs, N.J.: Prentice Hall, 1973); Peter Wiley and Robert Gottlieb, *Empires in the Sun: The Rise of the New American West* (New York: Putnam, 1982); Gerald Nash, *The American West Transformed* (Bloomington: University of Indiana Press, 1985); Gerald Nash and Richard Etulain, eds, *The Twentieth Century West: Historical Interpretations* (Albuquerque: University of New Mexico Press, 1989); Gerald Nash, *The Federal Landscape: An Economic History of the Twentieth Century West* (Tucson: University of Arizona Press, 1999); Patricia Nelson Limerick, *Something in the Soil: Legacies and Reckoning in the New West* (New York: W.W. Norton, 2000); Richard Etulain and Michael Malone, *The American West; A Modern History, 1900 to the Present* (Lincoln: University of Nebraska Press, 2007); Robert Dorman, *A Hell of a Vision: Regionalism and the Modern American West* (Tucson: University of Arizona Press, 2012); Sarah Deutsch and Richard Etulain, *Making a Modern U.S. West: The Contested Terrain of a Region and Its Border, 1898-1940* (Lincoln: University of Nebraska Press, 2022).

2 Billington and Ridge, *Westward Expansion*, 663, 664.

3 Gene Clanton, *Populism: The Human Preference in America, 1890-1900* (Boston: Twayne Publishers, 1990).

4 Samuel Hays, *Conservation and the Gospel of Efficiency: The Progressive Conservation Movement, 1890-1920* (Cambridge, Mass.: Harvard University Press, 1959); Dorceta Taylor, *The Rise of the American Conservation Movement: Power, Privilege, and Environmental Protection* (Durham, N.C.: Durham University Press, 2016).

5 John Clayton, *Natural Rivals: John Muir, Gifford Pinchot, and the Craton of America's Public Lands* (New York: Pegasus, 2020).

6 "The Birth of 'Conservation,' Gifford Pinchot, 1947, 1910," in Nash, *American Environmentalism*, 76–9.

7 Stephen Fox, *John Muir and His Legacy: The American Conservation Movement* (Boston: Little, Brown, 1982).

8 Kim Heacox, *An American Idea: The Making of the National Parks* (Washington D.C.: National Geographic, 2009), 85.

9 Michael Cohen, *History of the Sierra Club, 1892-1970* (San Francisco: Sierra Club Books, 1982).

10 Roderick Nash, ed., *American Environmentalism: Readings in Conservation History* (New York: McGraw-Hill, 1990), 94, 97.

11 Roderick Nash, *Wilderness and the American Mind* (New Haven, Conn.: Yale University Press, 1982), 137.

12 William Nester, *Theodore Roosevelt and the Art of American Power: An American for All Time* (New York: Lexington Books, 2019); Douglas Brinkley, *The Wilderness Warrior: Theodore Roosevelt and the Crusade for America* (New York: Harper Perennial, 2010).

13 Nash, *Wilderness and the American Mind*, 150.

14 "Publicizing Conservation at the White House, Theodore Roosevelt, 1909," Nash, *American Environmentalism*, 84–9.

15 William Kahrl, *Water and Power: The Conflict Over Los Angeles' Water Supply in the Owens Valley* (Berkeley: University of California Press, 1983).

16 Reisner, *Cadillac Desert*, 87.

17 White, *New History of the American West*, 234.

18 Allan Derickson, *Workers' Health, Workers' Democracy: The Western Miners' Struggle, 1891-1925* (Ithaca, N.Y.: Cornell University Press, 1986).

19 White, *New History of the American West*, 281.

20 Melvyn Dubofsky, *We Shall Be All: A History of the Industrial Workers of the World* (Urbana: University of Illinois Press, 2000).

21 James Hunt, *Pancho Villa and Black Jack Pershing: The Punitive Expedition in Mexico* (New York: Praeger, 2007); Jeff Guinn, *War on the Border: Villa, Pershing, the Texas Rangers, and an American Invasion* (New York: Simon and Schuster, 2022).

22 Drake Hokanson, *The Lincoln Highway: Main Street Across America* (Iowa City: University of Iowa Press, 1999).

23 Quinta Scott and Susan Croce Kelly, *Route 66: The Highway and People* (Norman: University of Oklahoma Press, 1988).

24 Etulain and Malone, *American West*, 44.

25 Alfred Runte, *National Parks: The American Experience* (Lincoln: University of Nebraska Press, 1987).

26 Etulain and Malone, *American West*, 33–4.

27 Laton McCartney, *The Teapot Dome Scandal: How Big Oil Bought the Harding White House and Tried to Steal the Country* (New York: Random House, 2008).

28 White, *New History of the American West*, 436.

29 Ray Billington and Martin Ridge, *Westward Expansion: A History of the American Frontier* (New York: Macmillan, 1982), 693, 695.

30 Etulain and Malone, *American West*, 19.

31 Norris Hundley, *Water and the West: The Colorado River Compact and the Politics of Water in the American West* (Berkeley: University of California Press, 1973).

32 Scott Ellsworth, *Death in a Promised Land: The Tulsa Race Riot of 1921* (Baton Rouge: Louisiana State University Press, 1992).

33 Walter Stein, *California and the Dust Bowl Migration* (Westport, Conn.: Greenwood Press, 1973); Donald Worster, *The Dust Bowl: The Southern Plains in the 1930s* (New York: Oxford University Press, 1979).

34 The Balance, GDP by Year, Thebalancemoney.co/us-gdp-by-year-3305542.

35 Billington and Ridge, *Westward Expansion*, 696.

36 Richard Lowitt, *The New Deal and the West* (Bloomington: University of Indiana Press, 1984).

37 Nash, *American West Transformed*, 5.

38 Gerald Nash, *The American West Transformed: The Impact of the Second World War* (Bloomington: University of Indiana Press, 1985), vii.

39 Theodore Saloutos, *The American Farmer and the New Deal* (Ames: Iowa State University Press, 1982).

40 William Rowley, *U.S. Forest Service Grazing and Rangelands: A History* (College Station: Texas A & M University Press, 1985).

41 Michael Hiltzik, *Colossus: The Turbulent, Thrilling Saga of the Building of Hoover Dam* (New York: Free Press, 2011).

42 Graham Taylor, *The New Deal and American Indian Tribalism: The Administration of the Indian Reorganization Act, 1934-45* (Lincoln: University of Nebraska Press, 1980).

43 Kenneth Philp, *John Collier's Crusade for Indian Reform, 1920-1954* (Tucson: University of Arizona Press, 1977).

44 Patricia Nelson Limerick, *The Legacy of Conquest: The Unbroken Past of the American West* (New York: W.W. Norton, 1987), 204.

45 Gerald Nash, *World War II and the West: Reshaping the Economy* (Lincoln: University of Nebraska Press, 1990).

46 White, *New History of the American West*, 498; Nash, *American West Transformed*, 25–6.

47 Nash, *American West Transformed*, 19–21.

48 Ibid., 21–2.

49 Ibid., 179.

50 White, *New History of the American West*, 498.

51 Karen Anderson, *Wartime Women: Sex Roles, Family Relations, and the Status of Women during World War II* (Westport, Conn.: Greenwood Press, 1981); Sherna Gluck, *Rosie the Riveter Revisited: Women, the War, and Social Change* (Boston: Twayne Publishers, 1987); Richard Craig, *The Bracero Program: Interest Groups and Foreign Policy* (Austin: University of Texas Press, 1971).

52 Nash, *American West Transformed*, 56, 59.

53 White, *New History of the American West*, 515.

54 Allison Bernstein, *American Indians and World War II: Toward a New Era in Indian Affairs* (Norman: University of Oklahoma Press, 1991); Doris Paul, *The Navajo Code Talkers* (New York: Dorrance, 1998).

55 Maurizio Mazon, *The Zoot Suit Riots: The Psychology of Symbolic Annihilation* (Austin: University of Texas Press, 1984.

56 Unless otherwise noted, statistics come from "Roger Daniels's Quantitative Note on the Force Migration of Japanese Americans, 1942-1946," Milner, *Major Problems in the History of the American West*, 550–3.

57 Richard Reeves, *Infamy: The Shocking Story of the Japanese American Internment in World War II* (New York: Picador, 2016).

58 "Public Opinion Poll on Japanese Internment," United States Holocaust Museum, exhibition.ushmann.org/americans-and-the-holocaust/main/us-public-opinion-on-japanese-americans-1942.

59 Gerald Nash, *The American West in the Twentieth Century: A Short History of an Urban Oasis* (Englewood Cliffs, N.J.: Prentice Hall, 1973); Lawrence Larsen, *The Urban West at the End of the Frontier* (Lawrence: University Press of Kansas, 1978); John Reps, *Cities of the American West: A History of Frontier Urban Planning* (Princeton, N.J.: Princeton University Press, 1979); Carl Abbott, *The New Urban America: Growth and Politics in the Sunbelt* (Chapel Hill: University of North Carolina Press, 1981); Richard Bernard and Bradley Rice, *Sunbelt Cities: Politics and Growth since World War II* (Austin: University of Texas Press, 1983).

60 "Pesticides, Rachel Carson, 1962," Nash, *American Environmentalism*, 194.

61 Richard Slotkin, *Gunfighter Nation: The Myth of the Frontier in Twentieth Century America* (Norman: University of Oklahoma Press, 1998), 2.

62 "President John Kennedy Assesses the Environment, 1963," Merchant, *Major Problems in American Environmental History*, 497–8.

63 Peter Mathiesson, *In the Spirit of Crazy Horse* (New York: Viking, 1983).

64 Prucha, *Great Father*, 342.

65 Charles Mann, *1491: New Revelations of the Americas before Columbus* (New York: Vintage, 2011), 394.

66 "Hopi Leaders on the Desecration of Their Sacred Lands, 1970," Merchant, *Major Problems in American Environmental History*, 500–02.

67 Roderick Nash, *Wilderness and the American Mind* (New Haven, Conn.: Yale University Press, 1982); Frederick Turner, *Beyond Geography: The Western Spirit against the Wilderness* (New Brunswick: Rutgers University Press, 1992); Max Oelschlaeger, *The Idea of Wilderness: From Prehistory to the Age of Ecology* (New Haven, Conn.: Yale University Press, 1993); Vause Zevoloff, William McVaugh, and Samuel Zevoloff, eds, *Wilderness Tapestry: An Eclectic Approach to Preservation* (Reno: University of Nevada Press, 1992); Michael Johnson, *Hunger for the Wild: America's Obsession with the Untamed West* (Lawrence: University Press of Kansas, 2007); Craig Allin, *The Politics of Wilderness Preservation* (Anchorage: University of Alaska Press, 2008).

68 "Aldo Leopold Proposes a Land Ethic, 1949," Merchant, *Major Problems in American Environmental History*, 455.

69 Aldo Leopold, "The Wilderness and Its Place in Forest Recreational Policy,"*Journal of Forestry*, vol. 19, no. 7 (1921), 179.

70 Nash, *Wilderness and the American Mind*, 203.

71 Ibid., 216–17.

72 "The Meaning of Wilderness for American Civilization, Wallace Stegner, 1960," Nash, *American Environmentalism*, 182–6.

73 Nash, *Wilderness and the American Mind*, 222.

74 "The National Environmental Policy Act, 1969," Merchant, *Major Problems in American Environmental History*, 498.

75 "The State of the Environment, Council on Environmental Quality, 1970," Nash, *American Environmentalism*, 224.

76 Nash, *Wilderness and the American Mind*, 309.

Chapter 11: Artists and Writers

1 For an overview, see: Richard Etulain, *Re-imagining the Modern American West: A Century of Fiction, History, and Art* (Tucson: University of Arizona Press, 1996). For literature, see: Stephen Fender, *Plotting the Golden West: American Literature and the Rhetoric of the California Trail* (New York: Cambridge University Press, 1981); Helen Winter Stauffer and Susan J. Rosowski, *Women and Western American Literature* (Troy, N.Y.: Whitstone, 1982); Harold Simonson, *Beyond the Frontier: Writers, Western Regionalism, and a Sense of Place* (Fort Worth: Texas Christian University, 1989). For art, see: Emily Ballew Neff, *The Modern West: Landscapes, 1890-1950* (New Haven, Conn.: Yale University Press, 2015).

2 Louis Warren, *Buffalo Bill's America: William Cody and the Wild West Show* (New York: Viking, 2006).

3 Don Russell, *The Wild West, or A History of the Wild West Shows* (Austin: University of Texas Press, 1970), 121–7.

4 Kristine Frederiksson, *American Rodeo: From Buffalo Bill to Big Business* (College Station: Texas A & M University Press, 1985).

5 William H. Goetzmann and William N. Goetzmann, *The West of the Imagination* (New York: W.W. Norton, 1986), 238.

6 Peggy and Harold Samuels, *Frederick Remington: A Biography* (New York: Doubleday, 1982), 307.

7 Goetzmann, *West of the Imagination*, 228.

8 For Turner's works, see: John Faragher, *Rereading Frederick Jackson Turner* (New Haven, Conn.: Yale University Press, 1994); Frederick Jackson Turner, *The Frontier in American History* (New York: Dover Publications, 1996). For books on Turner and his influence, see: Ray Billington, *The Genesis of the Frontier Thesis: A Study in Historical Creativity* (San Marino, Calif.: Huntington Library, 1971); George Taylor, ed., *The Turner Thesis: Concerning the Role of the Frontier in American History* (Lexington, Mass.: Heath, 1972); Ray Billington, *Frederick Jackson Turner: Historian, Scholar, Teacher* (New York: Oxford University Press, 1973).

9 Turner, *Frontier in American History*, 3, 12.

10 Etulain, *Re-Imagining the Modern American West*, 42.

11 Philip Durham and Everett Jones, eds, *The Western Story: Fact, Fiction, and Myth* (New York: Harcourt, Brace, Jovanovich, 1975); Robert Milton, *The Novel of the American West* (Lincoln: University of Nebraska Press, 1980); Richard Etulain, *A Bibliographical Guide to the Study of Western Literature* (Lincoln: University of Nebraska Press, 1982); Fred Erisman and Richard Etulain eds, *Fifty Western Writers: A Bio-Bibliographical Sourcebook* (Westport, Conn.: Greenwood, 1982); John Cawelti, *Six-Gun Mystique* (Bowling Green, Ohio: Bowling Green University Press, 1984); Thomas Lyon et al., *A Literary History of the American West* (Fort Worth: Texas Christian University Press, 1987); Jane Tompkins, *West of Everything: The Inner Life of Westerns* (New York: Oxford University Press, 1992); Forest Robinson, *Having It Both Ways: Self-subversion in Western Popular Classics* (Albuquerque: University of New Mexico Press, 1993); Lee Mitchell, *Westerns: Making the Man in Fiction and Film* (Chicago: University of Chicago Press, 1996); William Handley, *Marriage, Violence, and the Nation in the American Literary West* (New York: Cambridge University Press, 2002).

12 George Fenin and William Everson, *The Western from Silents to Cinerama* (New York: Orion Press, 1962); Scott Simmon, *The Invention of the Western Film: A Cultural History of the Genre for the First Half Century* (New York: Cambridge University Press, 2003); Jennifer McMahan and Steve Csaki, *The Philosophy of the Western* (Lexington: University of Kentucky Press, 2010); Richard Aquila, *The Sagebrush Trail: Western Movies and Twentieth Century America* (Tucson: University of Arizona Press, 2015).

13 Lois Palken Rudnick, *Mabel Dodge Luhan: New Woman, New Worlds* (Albuquerque: University of New Mexico Press, 1984); Lois Palken Rudnick, *Utopian Vistas: The Mabel Dodge Luhan House and the American Counterculture* (Albuquerque: University of New Mexico Press, 1996).

14 Rudnick, *Utopian Vistas*, 7–8.

15 Benita Eisler, *O'Keefe and Stieglitz: An American Romance* (New York: Doubleday, 1991); Roxanne Robinson, *George O'Keefe: A Life* (New York: Brandeis University Press, 2020).

16 Mary Street Alinder, *Ansel Adams: A Biography* (New York: Bloomsbury, 2014).

17 Ray Billington and Martin Ridge, *Westward Expansion: A History of the American Frontier* (New York: Macmillan, 1982).

18 Tompkins, *West of Everything*, 3.

19 Louis L'Amour, *Heller with a Gun: A Novel* (New York: Fawcett Books, 1955), 15.

20 Louis L'Amour, *Education of a Wandering Man* (New York: Bantam, 1990).

21 Rudnick, *Utopian Vistas*, 217.

22 Joseph McBride, *Searching for John Ford: A Life* (New York: St. Martin's, 2001).

23 Ray White, "The Good Guys Wore White Hats: The B-Western in American Culture," in Aquila, *Wanted Dead or Alive*, 135.

24 Tompkins, *West of Everything*, 5; Gary Yoggy, "Prime Time Bonanza!: The Western on Television," in Aquila, *Wanted Dead or Alive*, 161.

Chapter 12: Reds and Blues

1 Andrew Gelman, *Red State, Blue State, Rich State, Poor State* (Princeton, N.J.: Princeton University Press, 2009); Matt Grossman, *Red State Blues: How the Conservative Revolution Stalled in the States* (New York: Cambridge University Press, 2019); Steve Kornacki, *The Red and the Blue: The 1990s and the Birth of Political Tribalism* (New York: Ecco Press, 2019).

2 Fergus Bordewich, *Killing the White Man's Indian: Reinventing Native Americans at the End of the Twentieth Century* (New York: Anchor, 1997); Winona LaDuke, *All Our Relations: Native Struggles for Land and Life* (New York: Haymarket Books, 2016).

3 ncrc.org/racial_weath_snapshot_native_Americans.

4 James Klas, "NIGC 2021 Revenue—Behind the Numbers,"*Indian Gaming*, September 13, 2022.

5 Ian Hoffman, "Supreme Court Adoption Case May Threaten Tribes Sovereignty,"*New York Times*, November 7, 2022; Abbie Vansickle, "Supreme Court Rules for Tribes,"*New York Times*, June 16, 2023.

6 Simon Romero, "Cherokees Asking U.S. to Honor 1835 Treaty for House Delegate,"*New York Times*, November 4, 2022.

7 United States Congressional Research Service: Federal Land Ownership Overview and Data, website.

8 Thomas Frank, *What's the Matter with Kansas?: How Conservatives Won the Heart of America* (New York: Henry Holt, 2005).

9 Richard Lam and Michael McCarthy, *The Angry West: A Vulnerable Land and Its Future* (Boston: Houghton Mifflin, 1982); William Graf, *Wilderness Preservation and the Sagebrush Rebellions* (New York: Rowman and Littlefield, 1990); Frederick Turner, *Beyond Geography: The Western Spirit against the Wilderness* (New Brunswick: Rutgers University Press, 1992); McGreggor Cawley, *Federal Land, Western Anger: The Sagebrush Rebellion and Environmental Politics* (Lawrence: University Press of Kansas, 1993): John Smith, *Saints, Sinners, and Sovereign Citizens: The Endless War over the West's Public Lands* (Las Vegas: University of Nevada Press, 2020).

10 Lou Cannon, *President Reagan: The Role of a Lifetime* (New York: Public Affairs, 2000).

11 David Helvarg, *The War against the Greens: The Wise Use Movement, the New Right, and Anti-Environmental Violence* (San Francisco: Sierra Books, 1994), 8, 359. Kenneth Stern, *A Force upon the Plain: The American Militia Movement and the Politics of Hate* (Norman: University of Oklahoma Press, 1997), 22.

12 Stern, *Force upon the Plain*, 22.

13 Ibid., 39.

14 James Tabor and Eugene Gallagher, *Why Waco?: Cults and the Battle for Religious Freedom in America* (Berkeley: University of California Press, 1995); Dick Reavis, *The Ashes of Waco: An Investigation* (New York: Simon and Schuster, 1995).

15 Mark Hamm, *Apocalypse in Oklahoma: Waco and Ruby Ridge Revenged* (Boston: Northeastern University Press, 1997).

16 Stern, *Force Upon the Plain*, 245.

17 Lou Michael and Dan Herback, *American Terrorist: Timothy McVeigh and the Oklahoma City Bombing* (New York: Diane Publishers, 2003), last chapter. For the best analysis, see: Andrew Gumbai and Roger Charles, *Oklahoma City: What the Investigation Missed and Why It Still Matters* (New York: William Morrow, 2012).

18 Robert Shogun, *The Fate of the Union: America's Rocky Road to Political Stalemate* (Boulder, Colo.: Westview Press, 1998), 187. Ted Daniels, "Another Standoff: The Montana Freemen,"*Millennial Prophecy Report* (April 1996), 1–4; Mark Pitcavage, "Every Man a King: The Rise and Fall of the Montana Freemen,"*The Militia Watchdog,* online at http://www.militia-watchdog.org/freemen.htm; Jean Rosenfeld, "The Justus Freeman Standoff: The Importance of the Analysis of Religion in Avoiding Violent Outcomes," in Catherine Wessinger, ed., *Millennialism, Persecution, and Violence* (Syracuse, N.Y.: Syracuse University Press, 2000).

19 Ted Daniels, "Another Standoff: The Montana Freemen,"*Millennial Prophecy Report* (April 1996), 1–4; Mark Pitcavage, "Every Man a King:

The Rise and Fall of the Montana Freemen,"*The Militia Watchdog*, online at http://www.militia-watchdog.org/freemen.htm; Jean Rosenfeld, "The Justus Freeman Standoff: The Importance of the Analysis of Religion in Avoiding Violent Outcomes," in Catherine Wessinger, ed., *Millennialism, Persecution, and Violence* (Syracuse, N.Y.: Syracuse University Press, 2000).

20 Kim Severson, "Number of U.S. Hate Groups Is Rising,"*New York Times*, March 8, 2012.

21 David Barstow, "The Tea Party Movement Lights Fuse for Rebellion by the Right,"*New York Times*, February 15, 2010; "The Second Wave: The Return of the Militias," Southern Poverty Law Center, August 1, 2009.

22 Betsy Gaines Quammen, *American Zion: Cliven Bundy, God, and Public Lands* (New York: Torrey House, 2020).

23 Timothy Egan, "Deadbeat on the Range,"*New York Times*, April 18, 2014.

24 "Earth First! Advocates Ecotage, 1987," Merchant, *Major Problems in American Environment History*, 527–31.

25 "51 Years of Data: K-12 School Shooting Statistics: What Everyone Should Know,"*Campus Safety Magazine*, January 28, 2020.

26 Michael Waldman, *The Second Amendment: A Biography* (New York: Simon and Schuster, 2015): Jennifer Tucker et al., *A Right to Bear Arms?: The Contested Role of History in the Contemporary Debate on the Second Amendment* (Washington D.C.: Smithsonian Institute Press, 2019).

27 Glenn Hassler, Salvador Rizzo, and Meg Kelly, "Trump's False or Misleading Claims Total 30,573 over 4 Years,"*Washington Post*, January 24, 2021.

28 For the most powerful criticisms by an African American scholar, see: John McWhorter, *Losing the Race: Self-Sabotage in Black America* (New York: Harper Perennial, 2001): John McWhorter, *Woke Racism: How a New Religion Has Betrayed Black America* (New York: Portfolio, 2021). For Trumpian criticism of Critical Race Theory, see: James Lindsay, *Race Marxism: The Truth about Critical Race Theory and Praxis* (Orlando: New Discourses, 2020). For the Black Live Movement riot damage, see: Jennifer Kingson, "Exclusive: $1 Billion-Plus Riot Damage Is Most Expensive in Insurance History,"*Axios*, September 16, 2020.

29 "46 Months Since the Jan. 6 Attack on the U.S. Capitol,"*U.S. Attorney for the District of Columbia*, November 6, 2024, website.

30 Alex Traub, "Tribal Groups Will Join U.S. to Manage Ancestral Lands,"*New York Times*, June 22, 2022.

31 Coral Davenport, Lisa Friedman, and Christopher Flavelle, "Biden Vows Protection, but Not Monument Status, for Sacred Land,"*New York Times*, December 2, 2022.

Chapter 13: Fires and Waters

1 Christopher Flavelle, "New Measures of Climate Toll: Disasters Are Now Common,"*New York Times,* November 7, 2022.

2 Ballotpedia.org/Superfund_sites_in_the_United_States.

3 Ralph Vartabedian, "A Poisonous Cold War Legacy That Defies a Solution,"*New York Times,* May 31, 2023.

4 Richard Bartlett, *Yellowstone: A Wilderness Besieged* (Tucson: University of Arizona Press, 1988); Alston Chase, *Playing God in Yellowstone: The Destruction of America's First National Park* (New York: Harper, 1987); Alfred Runte, *Yosemite: The Embattled Wilderness* (Lincoln: University of Nebraska Press, 1990).

5 Kenneth Frederic and James Hanson, *Water for Western Agriculture* (Washington D.C.: Resources for the Future, 1982); Donald Pisani, *From the Family Farm to Agribusiness: The Irrigation Crusade in California and the West* (Berkeley: University of California Press, 1984); Donald Worster, *Rivers of Empire: Water, Aridity, and the Growth of the American West* (New York: Pantheon Books, 1985); Marc Reisner, *Cadillac Desert: The American West and Its Disappearing Water* (New York: Viking, 1986).

6 Christopher Favelle and Jack Healy, "Eye on Water, Arizona Caps New Housing,"*New York Times,* June 2, 2023.

7 William Ashworth, *Ogallala Blue: Water and Life on the Great Plains* (New York: W.W. Norton, 2006).

8 Norris Hundley, *Water and the West: The Colorado River Compact and the Politics of Water in the American West* (Berkeley: University of California Press, 1975).

9 Henry Fountain, "Painful Deadline Nears in Colorado River Basin,"*New York Times,* July 22, 2022; Winston Choi-Schagrin, "Water Levels Have Fallen to Dire Low in Lake Mead,"*New York Times,* July 23, 2022; Henry Fountain, "States Curbed From Draining A Frail Lifeline,"*New York Times,* August 17, 2022.

10 Christopher Favelle, "A Breakthrough Deal to Keep the Colorado River from Going Dry, for Now,"*New York Times,* May 22, 2023.

11 Norris Hundley, *Dividing the Waters: A Century of Controversy between the United States and Mexico* (Berkeley: University of California Press, 1966).

12 Reisner, *Cadillac Desert,* 477.

13 Ibid., 8.

14 Ibid., 482.

15 Christopher Flavelle, "As the Great Salt Lake Dries Up, Utah Faces an Environmental Nuclear Bomb,"*New York Times,* June 7, 2022.

16 Simon Romero, "Thousands Lost Everything by Fire Set by Forest Service,"*New York Times,* June 23, 2022.

17 Thomas Fuller and Livia Albeck-Ripka, "Yosemite's Paradox: Cutting the Trees to Save the Park,"*New York Times*, July 28, 2022.

18 McKenna Oxenden, "Forest Service Takes Emergency Steps to Protect Sequoias from Wild Fires,"*New York Times*, July 25, 2022.

19 Remy Tumin,, "Trip to World's Tallest Tree Could Now End in Jail Time,"*New York Times*, August 3, 2022.

20 Oliver Whang, "The Missing Mammal that Might Have Saved California's Kelp Forest,"*New York Times*, December 5, 2022.

21 Catrin Einhorn, "Monarch Butterfly Joins Endangered List,"*New York Times*, July 22, 2022.

22 Mark Walker and Chris Cameron, "Clearing a Path to the Sea to Save the Chinook Salmon,"*New York Times*, August 16, 2022.

23 "Inhofe, James," Follow the Money, followthemoney.org/entry-details?aid=10,938,141.

24 Richard White, *It's Your Misfortune and None of My Own: A New History of the American West* (New York: Oxford University Press 1991), 57.

25 Edward Abbey, "Even the Bad Guys Wear White Hats: Cowboys, Ranchers, and the Ruin of the West,"*Harpers* (January 1986), vol. 272, no. 1628, 51–5.

Chapter 14: Artists and Writers

1 Hilarie Sheets, "What Would Donald Judd Do?,"*New York Times*, August 14, 2022.

2 Joshua Hunt, "Groundwork: Cannupa Hanska Luger Is Upholding Long-held Ideas about What Native American Art Should Look Like,"*New York Times Magazine*, June 19, 2022.

3 Arthur Lebow, "Finding a Kind of Poetry in the Bleakness,"*New York Times*, July 15, 2022.

4 Patricia Nelson Limerick, *Legacy of Conquest: The Unbroken Past of the American West* (New York: W.W. Norton, 1987).

5 Clay Risen, "Roger Welsch, 85, Who Was Called America's Premier Storyteller, Dies,"*New York Times*, October 23, 2022.

6 Alex Williams, "Tim Giago, 88, Is Dead; Journalist Who Fought for Native Americans,"*New York Times*, July 29, 2022.

7 Clay Risen, "Baxter Black, 77, Dies; Popular Cowboy Poet Who Elevated Genre,"*New York Times*, June 26, 2022.

8 James Poniewozik, "In 'Yellowstone' the Land Votes,"*New York Times*, November 13, 2022; Russ Douthat, "Right Wing or Woke?: The Complicated Politics of Yellowstone,"*New York Times*, February 25, 2023.

9 Philip Montgomery, "Last Man Standing,"*New York Times Magazine*, August 21, 2022, 31.

10 Dayton Duncan and Ken Burns, *Country Music: An Illustrated History* (New York: Knopf Illustrated, 2010).

Chapter 15: Legacies

1 Frank Bergon and Zeese Papanikolas, eds, *Looking Far West: The Search for the American West in History, Myth, and Literature* (New York: American Library, 1978), 59.

2 Josiah Gregg, *The Commerce of the Prairies* (Lincoln: University of Nebraska Press, 1967), 325–6.

3 Mark Twain, *Adventures of Huckleberry Finn* (New York: Random House, 1996), 363.

4 Patricia Nelson Limerick, *The Legacy of Conquest: The Unbroken Past of the American West* (New York: W.W. Norton, 1987), 291.

5 Richard Slotkin, *Regeneration through Violence: The Mythology of the American Frontier, 1600-1860* (New York: Harper Perennial, 1996); Richard Slotkin, *The Fatal Environmental: The Myth of the Frontier in the Age of Industrialization, 1800-1890* (Middletown, Conn.: Wesleyan University Press, 1986); Richard Slotkin, *Gunfighter Nation: The Myth of the Frontier in Twentieth Century America* (Norman: University of Oklahoma Press, 1998). See also: Henry Nash Smith, *Virgin Land: The American West as Symbol and Myth* (Cambridge, Mass.: Harvard University Press, 1950); Robert Athearn, *The Mythic West in Twentieth Century America* (Lawrence: University of Kansas Press, 1986); William H. Goetzmann and William N. Goetzmann, *The West of the Imagination* (New York: W.W. Norton, 1986).

6 Slotkin, *Gunfighter Nation*, 5.

7 William Nester, *From Mountain Man to Millionaire: The "Bold and Dashing Life" of Robert Campbell* (Columbia: University of Missouri Press, 2011).

BIBLIOGRAPHY

Books

Abbott, Carl, *The New Urban America: Growth and Politics in the Sunbelt*, Chapel Hill: University of North Carolina Press, 1981.

Alinder, Mary Street, *Ansel Adams: A Biography*, New York: Bloomsbury, 2014.

Allen, John, *Passage through the Garden: Lewis and Clark and the Image of the American Northwest*, Urbana: University of Illinois Press, 1975.

Allin, Craig, *The Politics of Wilderness Preservation*, Anchorage: University of Alaska Press, 2008.

Ambrose, Stephen, *Undaunted Courage: Meriwether Lewis, Thomas Jefferson and the Opening of the West*, New York: Simon and Schuster, 1996.

Ambrose, Stephen, *Nothing Like It in the World: The Men Who Built the Transcontinental Railroad. 1863-1869*, New York: Simon and Schuster, 2000.

Anderson, Fred, *The Crucible of War: The Seven Years War and the Fate of Empire in British North America, 1754-1766*, New York: Vintage, 2000.

Anderson, Karen, *Wartime Women: Sex Roles, Family Relations, and the Status of Women during World War II*, Westport, Conn.: Greenwood Press, 1981.

Anderson, Nels, *Desert Saints: The Mormon Frontier in Utah*, Chicago: University of Chicago Press, 1969.

Aquila, Richard, ed., *Wanted Dead or Alive: The American West in Popular Culture*, Urbana: University of Illinois Press, 1996.

Aquila, Richard, *The Sagebrush Trail: Western Movies and Twentieth Century America*, Tucson: University of Arizona Press, 2015.

Armitage, Susan, and Elizabeth Jameson, *The Women's West*, Norman: University of Oklahoma Press, 1987.

Arrington, Leonard, *Great Basin Kingdom: An Economic History of the Latter Day Saints, 1830-1900*, Cambridge, Mass.: Harvard University Press, 1958.

Arrington, Leonard, *Brigham Young: American Moses*, Urbana: University of Illinois Press, 1986.

Arrington, Leonard, and Davis Bitton, *The Mormon Experience: A History of the Latter-Day Saints*, Urbana: University of Illinois Press, 1992.

Ashworth, William, *Ogallala Blue: Water and Life on the Great Plains*, New York: W.W. Norton, 2006.

Athearn, Robert, *William Tecumseh Sherman and the Settlement of the West*, Norman: University of Oklahoma Press, 1956.

Athearn, Robert, *The Mythic West in Twentieth Century America*, Lawrence: University of Kansas Press, 1986.

Atkins, Damon, and William Bauer, *We Are the Land: A History of Native California*, Berkeley: University of California Press, 2021.

Bannon, John, *The Spanish Borderlands Frontier, 1513-1821*, Albuquerque: University of New Mexico Press, 1990.

Barbour, Barton, *Fort Union and the Upper Missouri Fur Trade*, Norman: University of Oklahoma Press, 2001.

Barraclough, Laura, *Charros: How Mexican Cowboys Are Remapping Race and American Identity*, Berkeley: University of California Press, 2014.

Barrera, Mario, *Race and Class in the Southwest: A Theory of Racial Inequality*, Notre Dame, Ind.: Notre Dame University Press, 1979.

Bartlett, Richard, *Yellowstone: A Wilderness Besieged*, Tucson: University of Arizona Press, 1988.

Bauer, Jack, *The Mexican War, 1846-1848*, Lincoln: University of Nebraska Press, 1992.

Bergon, Frank and Zeese Papanikolas, eds, *Looking Far West: The Search for the American West in History, Myth, and Literature*, New York: American Library, 1978.

Bergreen, Laurence, *Columbus: The Four Voyages, 1492-1504*, New York: Penguin, 2012.

Berkhofer, Robert, *Salvation and the Savage: An Analysis of Protestant Missions and American Indian Response, 1787-1862*, Lexington: University Press of Kentucky, 2014.

Bernard, Richard, and Bradley Rice, *Sunbelt Cities: Politics and Growth since World War II*, Austin: University of Texas Press, 1983.

Bernstein, Allison, *American Indians and World War II: Toward a New Era in Indian Affairs*, Norman: University of Oklahoma Press, 1991.

Bernstein, Irving, *A Caring Society, the New Deal, the Workers, and the Great Depression: A History of American Workers, 1933-41*, Boston: Houghton Mifflin, 1985.

Bigler, David, *Forgotten Kingdom: The Mormon Theocracy in the American West, 1847-1896*, Logan, Utah: Utah State University Press, 1998.

Bigler, David, and Will Bagley, *The Mormon Rebellion: America's First Civil War, 1857-1858*, Norman: University of Oklahoma Press, 2012.

Billington, Ray, *The Genesis of the Frontier Thesis: A Study in Historical Creativity*, San Marino, Calif.: Huntington Library, 1971.

Billington, Ray, *Frederick Jackson Turner: Historian, Scholar, Teacher*, New York: Oxford University Press, 1973.

Billington, Ray, *Land of Savagery, Land of Promise: The European Image of the American Frontier in the Nineteenth Century*, New York: W.W. Norton, 1981.

Billington, Ray, and Martin Ridge, *Westward Expansion: A History of the American Frontier*, New York: Macmillan, 1982.

Blackhawk, Ned, *Violence over the Land: Indians and Empires in the Early American West*, Cambridge, Mass.: Harvard University Press, 2008.

Blackhawk, Ned, *The Rediscovery of America: Native Peoples and the Unmaking of U.S. History*, New Haven, Conn.: Yale University Press, 2023.

Blouet, Brian, and Frederick Luebke, eds, *The Great Plains in Transition: Environment and Culture*, Lincoln: University of Nebraska Press, 1979.

Boesesnecker, John, *Gold Dust and Gunsmoke: Tails of Gold Rush Outlaws, Gunfighters, Lawmen, and Vigilantes*, New York: Wiley, 2000.

Bolton, Eugene, *Spanish Borderlands: A Chronicle of Florida and the Southwest*, New Haven, Conn.: Yale University Press, 1921.

Bordewich, Fergus, *Killing the White Man's Indian: Reinventing Native Americans at the End of the Twentieth Century*, New York: Anchor, 1997.

Bradford, William, *Of Plymouth Plantation*, New York: Modern Library, 1981.

Brands, H.W., *Dreams of El Dorado: A History of the American West*, New York: Basic Books, 2020.

Brinkley, Douglas, *The Wilderness Warrior: Theodore Roosevelt and the Crusade for America*, New York: Harper Perennial, 2010.

Brooks, George, ed., *The Southwest Expeditions of Jedediah Smith: His Personal Account of the Journey to California*, Lincoln: University of Nebraska Press, 1989.

Brown, Daniel, *The Indifferent Stars Above: The Harrowing Saga of the Donner Party*, New York: Mariner Books, 2015.

Brown, Dee, *The American West*, New York: Touchstone, 1995.

Brown, Dee, *Bury My Heart at Wounded Knee: An Indian History of the American West*, New York: Holt, 2007.

Brown, Jennifer, *Strangers in Blood: Fur Trade Company Families in Indian Country*, Vancouver: University of British Columbia, 1980.

Brown, Richard, *Strain of Violence: Historical Studies of American Violence and Vigilantism*, New York: Oxford University Press, 1974.

Brown, Richard, *No Duty to Retreat: Violence and Values in American History*, Norman: University of Oklahoma Press, 1994.

Buller, Anne, *Daughters of Joy, Sisters of Misery: Prostitutes in the American West, 1865-90*, Urbana: University of Illinois Press, 1985.

Burke, Flannery, *A Land Apart: The Southwest and the Nation in the Twentieth Century West*, Tucson: University of Arizona Press, 2017.

Cabeza de Vaca, Alvar Nunez, *Chronicle of the Narvaez Expedition*, New York: Penguin, 2002.

Campbell, Joseph, *The Hero with a Thousand Faces*, New York: MJF Books, 1949.

Cannon, Lou, *President Reagan: The Role of a Lifetime*, New York: Public Affairs, 2000.

Cantrell, Gregg, *Stephen F. Austin: Empresario of Texas*, Austin: Texas State Historical Association, 2016.

Carley, Kenneth, *The Dakota War of 1862*, St. Paul: Minnesota Historical Society Press, 1976.

Castillo, Richard del, *La Familia: Chicano Families in the Urban Southwest, 1948 to the Present*, Notre Dame, Ind.: Notre Dame University Press, 1984.

Cawelti, John, *Six-Gun Mystique*, Bowling Green, Ohio: Bowling Green University Press, 1984.

Cawley, McGreggor, *Federal Land, Western Anger: The Sagebrush Rebellion and Environmental Politics*, Lawrence: University Press of Kansas, 1993.

Cerami, Charles, *Jefferson's Great Gamble: The Remarkable Story of Jefferson, Napoleon, and the Men behind the Louisiana Purchase*, Naperville, Ill.: Sourcebook, 2003.

Cervantes, Fernando, *Conquistadores: A New History of Spanish Discovery and Conquest*, New York: Viking, 2021.

Chan, Sucheng, *This Bittersweet Soil: The Chinese in California Agriculture, 1860-1910*, Berkeley: University of California Press, 1986.

Chase, Alston, *Playing God in Yellowstone: The Destruction of America's First National Park*, New York: Harper, 1987.

Chipman, Donald, *Spanish Texas, 1519-1821*, Austin: University of Texas Press, 1992.

Clanton, Gene, *Populism: The Human Preference in America, 1890-1900*, Boston: Twayne Publishers, 1990.

Clark, Ella, *Indian Legends from the Northern Rockies*, Norman: University of Oklahoma Press, 1989.

Clark, Robert, ed., *The Frontier Challenge: Responses to the Trans-Mississippi West*, Lawrence: University Press of Kansas, 1971.

Clary, David, *Timber and the Forest Service*, Lawrence: University Press of Kansas, 1983.

Clavin, Tom, *Tombstone: The Earp Brothers, Doc Holiday, and the Vendetta Ride from Hell*, New York: St. Martin's Press, 2020.

Clayton, John, *Natural Rivals: John Muir, Gifford Pinchot, and the Craton of America's Public Lands*, New York: Pegasus, 2020.

Clokey, Richard, *William H. Ashley: Enterprise and Politics in the Trans-Mississippi West*, Norman: University of Oklahoma Press, 1990.

Coffman, Edward, *The Old Army: A Portrait of the American Army in Peacetime, 1784-1898*, New York: Oxford University Press, 1986.

Cohen, Michael, *History of the Sierra Club, 1892-1970*, San Francisco: Sierra Club Books, 1982.

Cox, Thomas, *Mills and Markets: A History of the Pacific Coast Lumber Industry to 1900*, Seattle: University of Washington Press, 1974.

Cozzens, Peter, ed., *Conquering the Southern Plains: Eyewitnesses to the Indian Wars, 1865-1890*, New York: Stackpole, 2003.

Cozzens, Peter, *The Earth Is Weeping: The Epic Story of the Indian Wars for the American West*, New York: Vintage, 2017.

Cozzens, Peter, *Tecumseh and the Prophet: The Heroic Struggle for America's Heartland*, New York: Vintage, 2021.

Craig, Richard, *The Bracero Program: Interest Groups and Foreign Policy*, Austin: University of Texas Press, 1971.

Crevecoeur, J. Hector St. John de, *Letters from an American Farms and Sketches of Eighteenth Century America*, New York: Penguin Classics, 1986.

Crittenden, Hiram, *The American Fur Trade of the Far West*, 2 vols (1935), Lincoln: University of Nebraska Press, 1986.

Cronon, William, George Miles, and Jay Gitlin, eds, *Under an Open Sky: Rethinking America's Western Past*, New York: W.W. Norton, 1993.

Crosby, Alfred, *The Columbian Exchange: The Biological and Cultural Consequences of 1492*, New York: Praeger, 2003.

Cruse, Brett, *Battles of the Red River War*, College Station: Texas A & M University Press, 2008.

Daehnke, Jon, *Chinook Resilience: Heritage and Cultural Revitalization on the Lower Columbia River*, Seattle: University of Washington Press, 2017.

Dale, Harrison, *The Explorations of William Ashley and Jedediah Smith, 1822-1829*, Lincoln: University of Nebraska Press, 1991.

Daniels, Roger, *The Politics of Prejudice: The Anti-Japanese Movement in California and the Struggle for Japanese Exclusion*, Berkeley: University of California Press, 1962.

Daniels, Roger, *Asian American Chinese and Japanese in the United States since 1950*, Seattle: University of Washington Press, 1988.

Dary, David, *Entrepreneurs of the Old West*, Lincoln: University of Nebraska Press, 1986.

Dary, David, *The Santa Fe Trail: Its History, Legends, and Lore*, New York: Penguin, 2000.

Davies, Nigel, *Voyageurs to the New World*, Albuquerque: University of New Mexico Press, 1979.

De Bruhl, Marshall, *Sword of San Jacinto: A Life of Sam Houston*, New York: Random House, 1993.

De Tocqueville, Alexis, *Democracy in America*, Chicago: University of Chicago Press, 2000.

De Voto, Bernard, *The Year of Decision: 1846*, Boston: Houghton Mifflin, 1942.

De Voto, Bernard, *Across the Wide Missouri* (1947), Boston: Houghton Mifflin, 1975.

Deloria, Philip, *Playing Indian*, New Haven, Conn.: Yale University Press, 2022.

Deloria, Vine, *Custer Died for Your Sins: An Indian Manifesto*, Norman: University of Oklahoma Press, 1988.

Denton, Sally, *American Massacre: The Tragedy at Mountain Meadows, September 1857*, New York: Vintage, 2004.

Derickson, Allan, *Workers' Health, Workers' Democracy: The Western Miners' Struggle, 1891-1925*, Ithaca, N.Y.: Cornell University Press, 1986.

Derr, Mark, *The Frontiersman: The Real Life and the Many Legends of Davy Crockett*, New York: Quill Books, 1993.

Deutsch, Sarah, *No Separate Refuge: Culture, Class, and Gender on an Anglo-Hispanic Frontier, 1880-1940*, New York: Oxford University Press, 1987.

Deutsch, Sarah, and Richard Etulain, *Making a Modern U.S. West: The Contested Terrain of a Region and Its Border, 1898-1940*, Lincoln: University of Nebraska Press, 2022.

Devevan, William, ed., *The Native Population of the Americas in 1492*, Madison: University of Wisconsin Press, 1992.

Diamond, Jared, *Guns, Germs, and Steel: The Fates of Human Societies*, New York: W.W. Norton, 1999.

Dickason, Olive Patricia, *Canada's First Nations: A History of Founding Peoples from Earliest Times*, Norman: University of Oklahoma Press, 1992.

Dippie, Brian, *Custer's Last Stand: The Anatomy of an American Myth*, Lincoln: University of Nebraska Press, 1994.

Dodds, Gordon, *The American Northwest: A History of Oregon and Washington*, Arlington Heights, Ill.: Forum Press, 1986.

Dolin, Eric Jay, *Fur, Fortune, and Empire: The Epic History of the Fur Trade in America*, New York: W.W. Norton, 2010.

Dolnick, Edward, *Rush: America's Fevered Quest for Fortune, 1848-1853*, New York: Little, Brown, 2014.

Dorman, Robert, *A Hell of a Vision: Regionalism and the Modern American West*, Tucson: University of Arizona Press, 2012.

Doti, Lynne Pierson, and Larry Schweikart, *Banking in the American West: From the Gold Rush to Deregulation*, Norman: University of Oklahoma Press, 1991.

Drinnon, Richard, *Facing West: The Metaphysics of Indian Hating*, Norman: University of Oklahoma Press, 1997.

Drumm, Stella M., ed., *Down the Santa Fe Trail and into Mexico: The Diary of Susan Shelby Magoffin, 1846-1847*, Lincoln: University of Nebraska Press, 1982.

Drury, Bob, *The Heart of Everything: The Untold Story of Red Cloud, an American Legend*, New York: Simon and Schuster, 2014.

Drury, Clifford, *Marcus and Narcissa Whitman and the Opening of Old Oregon*, Glendale, Calif. A.H. Clark Publisher, 1973.

Dubofsky, Melvyn, *We Shall Be All: A History of the Industrial Workers of the World*, Urbana: University of Illinois Press, 2000.

Dunbar-Ortiz, Roxanne, *An Indigenous People's History of the United States*, New York: Beacon Press, 2015.

Dunlay, Tom, *Kit Carson and the Indians*, Lincoln: University of Nebraska Press, 2005.

Duran, Eduardo, and Bonnie Duran, *Native American Postcolonial Psychology,* Albany: State University of New York Press, 1995.

Durham, Philip, and Everett Jones, eds, *The Western Story: Fact, Fiction, and Myth,* New York: Harcourt, Brace, Jovanovich, 1975.

Dutton, Bertha, *American Indians of the Southwest,* Albuquerque: University of New Mexico Press, 1975.

DuVal, Kathleen, *Native Nations: A Millenium in North America,* New York: Random House, 2024.

Dykstra, Robert, *The Cattle Towns: A Social History of the Kansas Cattle Trading Centers of Abilene, Ellsworth, Wichita, Dodge City, and Caldwell, 1867-85,* New York: Atheneum, 1976.

Earle, Jonathan, *John Brown's Raid on Harpers Ferry: A Brief History with Documents,* New York: St. Martin's Press, 2008.

Eblen, Jack, *The First and Second United States Empires: Governors and Territorial Governments, 1784-1912,* Pittsburgh: University of Pittsburgh Press, 1969.

Eisenhower, John, *So Far From God: The U.S. War with Mexico, 1846-1848,* New York: Doubleday, 1989.

Eisler, Benita, *O'Keefe and Stieglitz: An American Romance,* New York: Doubleday, 1991.

Ellsworth, Scott, *Death in a Promised Land: The Tulsa Race Riot of 1921,* Baton Rouge: Louisiana State University Press, 1992.

Emerson, Thomas, and Barry Lewis, eds, *Cahokia and the Hinterland,* Urbana: University of Illinois Press, 1990.

Erisman, Fred, and Richard Etulain, eds, *Fifty Western Writers: A Bio-Bibliographical Sourcebook,* Westport, Conn.: Greenwood, 1982.

Etcheson, Nicole, *Bleeding Kansas: Contested Liberty in the Civil War Era,* Lawrence: University Press of Kansas, 2004.

Etulain, Richard, *A Bibliographical Guide to the Study of Western Literature,* Lincoln: University of Nebraska Press, 1982.

Etulain, Richard, ed., *Writing Western History: Essays on Major Western Historians,* Albuquerque: University of New Mexico Press, 1991.

Etulain, Richard, *Re-imagining the Modern American West: A Century of Fiction, History, and Art,* Tucson: University of Arizona Press, 1996.

Etulain, Richard, and Michael Malone, *The American West: A Modern History, 1900 to the Present,* Tucson: University of Arizona Press, 2007.

Fagan, Brian, *The Great Journey: The Peopling of Ancient America,* London: Thames and Hudson, 1987.

Fahey, John, *The Inland Empire: Unfolding Years, 1879-1929,* Seattle: University of Washington Press, 1986.

Faragher, John, *Women and Men on the Overland Trail,* New Haven, Conn.: Yale University Press, 1979.

Faragher, John, *Daniel Boone: The Life and Legend of an American Pioneer,* New York: Henry Holt, 1992.

Faragher, John, ed., *Rereading Frederick Jackson Turner*, New Haven, Conn.: Yale University Press, 1994.

Faragher, John, and Robert Hine, *Frontiers: A Short History of the American West*, New Haven, Conn.: Yale University Press, 2008.

Fedewa, Marilyn, *Maria of Agreda: Mystical Lady in Blue*, Albuquerque: University of New Mexico Press, 2010.

Fender, Stephen, *Plotting the Golden West: American Literature and the Rhetoric of the California Trail*, New York: Cambridge University Press, 1981.

Fehrenbach, T.R., *Comanches: The History of a People*, New York: Anchor Books, 2003.

Fenin, George, and William Everson, *The Western from Silents to Cinerama*, New York: Orion Press, 1962.

Fernandes, Raul, *The United States-Mexico Border: A Politico-Economic Profile*, Notre Dame, Ind.: Notre Dame University Press, 1977.

Fidel, Stuart, *The Prehistory of the Americas*, New York: Cambridge University Press, 1987.

Fine, Kerry, et al., *Weird Westerns: Race, Gender, Genre*, Lincoln: University of Nebraska Press, 2020.

Fischer, David Hackett, *Champlain's Dream: The European Founding of North America*, New York: Simon and Schuster, 2008.

Fite, Gilbert, *The Farmers' Frontier, 1865-1900*, New York: Holt, Rinehart, and Winston, 1966.

Fixico, Donald, *The American Indian Mind in a Linear World: American Indian Studies and Traditional Knowledge*, New York: Routledge, 2003.

Flores, Dan, *The Natural West: The Environmental History of the Great Plains and Rocky Mountains*, New York: Oxford University Press, 2003.

Flores, Dan, et al., *American Serengeti: The Last Big Animals of the Great Plains*, Lawrence: University Press of Kansas, 2016.

Fox, Stephen, *John Muir and His Legacy: The American Conservation Movement*, Boston: Little, Brown, 1982.

Frank, Thomas, *What's the Matter with Kansas?: How Conservatives Won the Heart of America*, New York: Henry Holt, 2005.

Frazer, Ian, *Great Plains*, New York: Farrar, Straus, and Giroux, 1989.

Frazer, Robert, *Forts and Supplies: The Role of the Army in the Economy of the Southwest, 1846-1861*, Albuquerque: University of New Mexico Press, 1983.

Frazer, Robert, *Forts of the West*, Norman: University of Oklahoma Press, 1988.

Frederic, Kenneth, and James Hanson, *Water for Western Agriculture*, Washington D.C.: Resources for the Future, 1982.

Frederiksson, Kristine, *American Rodeo: From Buffalo Bill to Big Business*, College Station: Texas A & M University Press, 1985.

Gamble, Lynn, *The Chumash World at European Contact: Power, Trade, and Feasting among Complex Hunter-Gatherers*, Berkeley: University of California Press, 2017.

Garcia, Mario, *Mexican-Americans: Leadership, Ideology, and Identity, 1930-1960*, New Haven, Conn.: Yale University Press, 1989.

Garreau, Joel, *The Nine Nations of North America*, Boston: Houghton Mifflin, 1982.

Gastil, Raymond, *Cultural Regions of the United States*, Seattle: University of Washington Press, 1975.

Gelman, Andrew, *Red State, Blue State, Rich State, Poor State*, Princeton, N.J.: Princeton University Press, 2009.

Gerhard, Peter, *The North Frontier of New Spain*, Princeton, N.J.: Princeton University Press, 1982.

Gilbert, Bill, *Westering Man: The Life of Joseph Walker*, Norman: University of Oklahoma Press, 1989.

Glanz, Dawn, *How the West Was Drawn: American Art and the Settling of the Frontier*, Ann Arbor: University of Michigan Press, 1982.

Glassley, Ray, *Pacific Northwest Indian Wars*, New York: Literary Licensing, 2011.

Gluck, Sherna, *Rosie the Riveter Revisited: Women, the War, and Social Change*, Boston: Twayne Publishers, 1987.

Goetzmann, William, *Army Exploration in the American West, 1803-1863*, New Haven, Conn.: Yale University Press, 1959.

Goetzmann, William, *Exploration and Empire: The Explorer and the Scientist in the Winning of the American West*, New York: Alfred Knopf, 1966.

Goetzmann, William H., and William N. Goetzmann, *The West of the Imagination*, New York: W.W. Norton, 1986.

Goldman, Marion, *Gold Diggers and Silver Miners: Prostitution and Social Life on the Comstock Lode*, Ann Arbor: University of Michigan Press, 1979.

Goodman, Jeffrey, *American Genesis: The American Indian and the Origins of Modern Man*, New York: Summit Books, 1981.

Gottlieb, Roger, ed., *This Sacred Earth: Religion, Nature, Environment*, New York: Routledge, 1996.

Gowans, Fred, *Rocky Mountain Rendezvous: A History of the Fur Trade Rendezvous, 1825-1840*, Layton, Utah: Peregrine Books, 1985.

Graf, William, *Wilderness Preservation and the Sagebrush Rebellions*, New York: Rowman and Littlefield, 1990.

Green, Donald, *Land of the Underground Rain: Irrigation on the Texas High Plains, 1910-1970*, Austin: University of Texas Press, 1973.

Greenburg, Joseph, *Language in the Americas*, Stanford, Calif.: Stanford University Press, 1987.

Greg, Josiah, *The Commerce of the Prairies*, Lincoln: University of Nebraska Press, 1967.

Grodinsky, Julius, *Transcontinental Strategy: A Study of Businessmen*, Philadelphia: University of Pennsylvania Press, 1962.

Grossman, Matt, *Red State Blues: How the Conservative Revolution Stalled in the States*, New York: Cambridge University Press, 2019.

Guarneri, Carl, and David Alvarez, *Religion and Society in the American West*, Lanham, Maryland: University Press of America, 1987.

Guinn, Jeff, *War on the Border: Villa, Pershing, the Texas Rangers, and an American Invasion*, New York: Simon and Schuster, 2022.

Gumbai, Andrew, and Roger Charles, *Oklahoma City: What the Investigation Missed and Why It Still Matters*, New York: William Morrow, 2012.

Gutierrez, Ramon, *When Jesus Came the Corn Mothers Went Away*, Palo Alto, Calif.: Stanford University Press, 1991.

Gwynne, S.C., *Empire of the Summer Moon: Quanah Parker and the Fall of the Comanches, the Most Powerful Indian Tribe in American History*, New York: Scribner, 2011.

Hagan, William, *The Indian Rights Association: The Herbert Welsh Years, 1882-1904*, Tucson: University of Arizona Press, 1985.

Hall, Thomas, *Social Change in the Southwest, 1350-1880*, Lawrence: University Press of Kansas, 1989.

Hämäläinen, Pekka, *The Comanche Empire*, New Haven, Conn.: Yale University Press, 2008.

Hamm, Mark, *Apocalypse in Oklahoma: Waco and Ruby Ridge Revenged*, Boston: Northeastern University Press, 1997.

Handley, William, *Marriage, Violence, and the Nation in the American Literary West*, New York: Cambridge University Press, 2002.

Harris, Matthew, and Jay Buckley, eds, *Zebulon Pike, Thomas Jefferson, and the Opening of the West*, New York: Oxford University Press, 2021.

Hassrick, Peter et al., *American Frontier Life: Early Western Paintings and Prints*, New York: Abbeville Press, 1987.

Hassrick, Royal, *The Sioux*, Norman: University of Oklahoma Press, 1964.

Hatch, Thom, *Black Kettle: The Cheyenne Chief Who Sought Peace but Found War*, New York: Wiley, 2004.

Hays, Samuel, *Conservation and the Gospel of Efficiency: The Progressive Conservation Movement, 1890-1920*, Cambridge, Mass.: Harvard University Press, 1959.

Heacox, Kim, *An American Idea: The Making of the National Parks*, Washington D.C.: National Geographic, 2009.

Hedren, Paul, *The Great Sioux War: 1876-77*, Lincoln: University of Nebraska Press, 1991.

Heitshu, Sara, and Thomas Marshall, *Native American Studies: A Guide to Reference and Information Studies*, New York: Libraries Press, 2007.

Helvarg, David, *The War against the Greens: The Wise Use Movement, the New Right, and Anti-Environmental Violence*, San Francisco: Sierra Books, 1994.

Heyerdahl, Thor, *Early Man and the Ocean: A Search for the Beginnings of Navigation and Seaborne Civilizations*, New York: Vintage, 1980.

Hickey, Donald, *The War of 1812: A Forgotten Conflict*, Urbana: University of Illinois Press, 1990.

Hietala, Thomas, *Manifest Destiny: American Exceptionalism and Empire*, Ithaca, N.Y.: Cornell University Press, 2002.

Hill, Forest, *Roads, Rails, and Waterways: The Army Engineers and Early Transportation*, Norman: University of Oklahoma Press, 1957.

Hiltzik, Michael, *Colossus: The Turbulent, Thrilling Saga of the Building of Hoover Dam*, New York: Free Press, 2011.

Hine, Robert, *The American West: An Interpretive History*, Boston: Little, Brown, 1984.

Hine, Robert, John Faragher, and Jon Coleman, *The American West: A New Interpretive History*, New Haven, Conn.: Yale University Press, 2017.

Hofstadter, Richard, *The American Political Tradition*, New York: Alfred Knopf, 1948.

Hokanson, Drake, *The Lincoln Highway: Main Street Across America*, Iowa City: University of Iowa Press, 1999.

Holliday, J.S., *The World Rushed In: The California Gold Rush Experience*, New York: Touchstone, 1981.

Hollon, Eugene, *Frontier Violence: Another Look*, New York: Oxford University Press, 1974.

Holt, Michael, *The Election of 1860: A Campaign Fraught with Consequences*, Lawrence: University Press of Kansas, 2017.

Hughes, Thomas, *Networks of Power: Electrification in Western Society, 1880-1930*, Baltimore: Johns Hopkins University Press, 1983.

Hundley, Norris, *Dividing the Waters: A Century of Controversy between the United States and Mexico*, Berkeley: University of California Press, 1966.

Hundley, Norris, *Water and the West: The Colorado River Compact and the Politics of Water in the American West*, Berkeley: University of California Press, 1975.

Hunt, James, *Pancho Villa and Black Jack Pershing: The Punitive Expedition in Mexico*, New York: Praeger, 2007.

Hurtado, Albert, *Indian Survival on the California Frontier*, New Haven, Conn.: Yale University Press, 1988.

Hurtado, Albert, and Peter Iverson, eds, *Major Problems in American Indian History*, Lexington, Mass.: D.C. Heath, 1994.

Hutton, Paul, *Phil Sheridan and His Army*, Lincoln: University of Nebraska Press, 1985.

Hutton, Paul, *The Apache Wars: The Hunt for Geronimo, the Apache Kid, and the Captive Boy Who Started the Longest War in American History*, New York: Crown, 2017.

Hyde, Anne F., *An American Vision: Far Western Landscape and National Culture, 1820-1920*, New York: New York University Press, 1990.

Hyde, Anne F., *Empires, Nations, and Families: A New History of the North American West*, New York: Ecco, 2012.

Hyde, Anne F., *Born of Lakes and Plains: Mixed-Descent Peoples and the Making of the American West*, New York: W.W. Norton, 2023.

Hyde, Lewis, ed., *The Essays of Henry D. Thoreau*, New York: Farrar, Straus, and Giroux, 2002.

Isenberg, Andrew, *The Destruction of the Bison*, New York: Cambridge University Press, 2001.

Isenberg, Nancy, *Fallen Founder: The Life of Aaron Burr*, New York: Viking, 2007.

Jackson, Donald, *Thomas Jefferson and the Stony Mountains: Exploring the West from Monticello*, Norman: University of Oklahoma Press, 1993.

Jackson, W. Turrentine, *Wagon Roads West: A Study of Federal Road Surveys and Construction in the Trans-Mississippi West, 1846-1869*, Berkeley: University of California Press, 1952.

Jacobs, Margaret, *White Mother to a Dark Race: Settler Colonialism, Maternalism, and the Removal of Indigenous Children in the American West and Australia, 1880-1940*, Lincoln: University of Nebraska Press, 2011.

Jeffrey, Julie Roy, *Frontier Women: The Trans-Mississippi West, 1840-1880*, New York: Hill and Wang, 1979.

John, Elizabeth, *Storms Brewed in Other Men's Worlds: The Confrontation of Indians, Spanish, and French in the Southwest, 1540-1795*, College Station: Texas A & M Press, 1975.

Johnson, Dorothy, *The Bloody Bozeman: The Perilous Trail to Montana's Gold*, New York: McGraw Hill, 1971.

Johnson, Michael, *New Westers: The West in Contemporary American Culture*, Lawrence: University Press of Kansas, 1996.

Johnson, Michael, *Hunger for the Wild: America's Obsession with the Untamed West*, Lawrence: University Press of Kansas, 2007.

Josephy, Alvin, *The Civil War in the American West*, New York: Alfred Knopf, 1992.

Josephy, Alvin, ed., *America in 1492: The World of the Indian People before the Arrival of Columbus*, New York: Vintage, 1992.

Josephy, Alvin, *Nez Perce Country*, Lincoln: University of Nebraska Press, 2007.

Jung, Carl, *Man and His Symbols*, New York: Dell Publishing, 1968.

Kahrl, William, *Water and Power: The Conflict Over Los Angeles' Water Supply in the Owens Valley*, Berkeley: University of California Press, 1983.

Kaufman, Polly Welts, *Women Teachers on the Frontier*, New Haven, Conn.: Yale University Press, 1984.

Kidwell, Clara Sue, *Native American Studies*, Lincoln: University of Nebraska Press, 2005.

Knaut, Andrew, *The Pueblo Revolt of 1680: Conquest and Resistance in Seventeenth Century New Mexico*, Norman: University of New Mexico Press, 1995.

Koch, Adrienne, and William Peden, eds, *The Life and Selected Writings of Thomas Jefferson*, New York: Modern Library, 1998.

Konig, David, Paul Finkelman, and Christopher Bracey, eds, *The Dred Scott Case: Historical and Contemporary Perspectives on Law and Race*, Athens: Ohio University Press, 2010.

Koot, Christian, *Empire at the Periphery: British Colonists, Anglo-Dutch Trade, and the Development of the British Atlantic, 1621-1713*, New York: New York University Press, 2015.

Kornacki, Steve, *The Red and the Blue: The 1990s and the Birth of Political Tribalism*, New York: Ecco Press, 2019.

LaDuke, Winona, *All Our Relations: Native Struggles for Land and Life*, New York: Haymarket Books, 2016.

Lam, Richard, and Michael McCarthy, *The Angry West: A Vulnerable Land and Its Future*, Boston: Houghton Mifflin, 1982.

L'Amour, Louis, *Heller with a Gun: A Novel*, New York: Fawcett Books, 1955.

L'Amour, Louis, *Education of a Wandering Man*, New York: Bantam, 1990.

Larsen, Lawrence, *The Urban West at the End of the Frontier*, Lawrence: University Press of Kansas, 1978.

Lass, William, *A History of Steamboating on the Upper Missouri*, Lincoln: University of Nebraska Press, 1962.

Lavender, David, *Bent's Fort*, New York: Doubleday, 1954.

Leach, Douglas, *Roots of Conflict: British Armed Forces and Colonial Americans, 1677-1763*, Chapel Hill: University of North Carolina Press, 1986.

Lingenfelter, Richard, *The Hardrock Miners: A History of the Mining Labor Movement in the American West, 1863-93*, Berkeley: University of California Press, 1974.

Limerick, Patricia Nelson, *The Legacy of Conquest: The Unbroken Past of the American West*, New York: W.W. Norton, 1987.

Limerick, Patricia Nelson, Clyde Milner, and Charles Rankin, eds, *Trails: Toward a New Western History*, Norman: University of Oklahoma Press, 1991.

Limerick, Patricia Nelson, *Something in the Soil: Legacies and Reckoning in the New West*, New York: W.W. Norton, 2000.

Lindsay, James, *Race Marxism: The Truth about Critical Race Theory and Praxis*, Orlando: New Discourses, 2020.

Linklater, Andro, *An Artist in Treason: The Extraordinary Double Life of General James Wilkinson*, New York: Walker Publishing Company, 2009.

Lofaro, Michael, ed., *Davy Crockett: The Man, the Legend, the Legacy, 1786-1986*, Knoxville: University of Tennessee Press, 1985.

Lombard, Anne, *Colonial America: A History to 1763*, New York: Wiley Blackwell, 2011.

Long, Jess, *Duel of Eagles: The Mexican and U.S. Fight for the Alamo*, New York: William Morrow, 1990.

Lottinville, Savoie, ed., *The Life of George Bent, Written from His Letters*, Norman: University of Oklahoma Press, 1987.

Lowitt, Richard, *The New Deal and the West*, Bloomington: University of Indiana Press, 1984.

Luebke, Frederick, *Ethnicity on the Great Plains*, Lincoln: University of Nebraska Press, 1980.

Lyall, Victoria, and Teresita Romo, eds, *Traitor, Survivor, Icon: The Legacy of La Malinche*, New Haven, Conn.: Yale University Press, 2022.

Lyon, Thomas et al., *A Literary History of the American West*, Fort Worth: Texas Christian University Press, 1987.

Mack, Shirley Boteler, *Dreaming with the Ancestors: Black Seminole Women in Texas and Mexico*, Norman: University of Oklahoma Press, 2021.

Madley, Benjamin, *An American Genocide: The United States and the California Indian Catastrophe*, New Haven, Conn.: Yale University Press, 2010.

Madsen, Axel, *John Jacob Astor: America's First Millionaire*, New York: John Wiley, 2001.

Mails, Thomas, *The Mystic Warriors of the Plains*, New York: Barnes and Noble Books, 1991.

Mails, Thomas, *The People Called Apache*, New York: BDD Illustrated Books, 1993.

Malone, Michael, *The Battle for Butte: Mining and Politics on the Northern Frontier, 1864-1906*, Seattle: University of Washington Press, 1981.

Malone, Michael, ed., *Historians and the American West*, Lincoln: University of Nebraska Press, 1983.

Maltby, William, *The Rise and Fall of the Spanish Empire*, New York: Red Globe Press, 2008.

Mann, Charles, *1491: New Revelations of the Americas before Columbus*, New York: Vintage, 2011.

Mardock, Robert, *The Reformers and the American Indian*, Columbia: University of Missouri Press, 1971.

Marshall, Joseph, *The Journey of Crazy Horse: A Lakota History*, New York: Penguin, 2005.

Matthes, Victoria Sherer, ed., *The Women's National Indian Association: A History*, Albuquerque: University of New Mexico Press, 2015.

Matthiesson, Peter, *In the Spirit of Crazy Horse*, New York: Viking, 1983.

Matthiessen, Peter, *Indian Country*, New York: Fontana, 1986.

Maybury-Lewis, David, *Manifest Destinies and Indigenous Peoples*, Cambridge, Mass.: Harvard University Press, 2009.

Mayer, Carl, and George Riley, *Public Domain, Private Domain: A History of Public Mineral Policy in America*, San Francisco: Sierra Club Books, 1985.

Mazon, Maurizio, *The Zoot Suit Riots: The Psychology of Symbolic Annihilation*, Austin: University of Texas Press, 1984.

McBride, Joseph, *Searching for John Ford: A Life*, New York: St. Martin's, 2001.

McCartney, Laton, *The Teapot Dome Scandal: How Big Oil Bought the Harding White House and Tried to Steal the Country*, New York: Random House, 2008.

McCullough, David, *The Pioneers: The Heroic Story of the Settlers Who Brought the American Ideal West*, New York: Simon and Schuster, 2020.

McGinnis, Anthony, *Counting Coup and Cutting Horses: Intertribal Warfare on the Northern Plains, 1738-1889*, Evergreen, Colo.: Evergreen Press, 1990.

McGrath, Roger, *Gunfighters, Highwaymen, and Vigilantes: Violence on the Frontier*, Berkeley: University of California Press, 1984.

McHugh, Tom and Victoria Hobson, *The Time of the Buffalo*, Lincoln: University of Nebraska Press, 1979.

McKibben, Bill, *The End of Nature* (1996), New York: Random House, 2006.

McMahan, Jennifer and Steve Csaki, *The Philosophy of the Western*, Lexington: University of Kentucky Press, 2010.

McNally, Robert, *The Modoc War: A Story of Genocide at the Dawn of America's Gilded Age*, Lincoln: University of Nebraska Press, 2021.

McPherson, James, *Battle Cry of Freedom: The Civil War Era*, New York: Oxford University Press, 2003.

McWhorter, John, *Losing the Race: Self-Sabotage in Black America*, New York: Harper Perennial, 2001.

McWhorter, John, *Woke Racism: How a New Religion Has Betrayed Black America*, New York: Portfolio, 2021.

Meinig, D.W., *The Great Columbian Plain: A Historical Geography, 1805-1910*, Seattle: University of Washington Press, 1968.

Meinig, D.W., *Imperial Texas: An Interpretative Essay in Cultural Geography*, Austin: University of Texas Press, 1969.

Meinig, D.W., *Southwest: Three Peoples in Geographical Change, 1600-1970*, New York: Oxford University Press, 1972.

Merchant, Carolyn, ed., *Major Problems in American Environmental History*, New York: D.C. Heath, 1993.

Merk, Frederick, *Manifest Destiny and Mission in American History: A Reinterpretation*, New York: Vintage, 1995.

Merry, Robert, *A Country of Vast Designs: James K. Polk, the Mexican War, and the Conquest of the American Continent*, New York: Simon and Schuster, 2009.

Michael, Lou, and Dan Herback, *American Terrorist: Timothy McVeigh and the Oklahoma City Bombing*, New York: Diane Publishers, 2003.

Miles, Nelson, *Serving the Republic: Memoirs of the Civil and Military Life of Nelson A. Miles*, New York: Harper and Brothers Publisher, 1911.

Milner, Clyde, ed., *Major Problems in the History of the American West*, Lexington, Mass.: D.C. Heath, 1989.

Milner, Clyde, Carol O'Connor, and Martha Sandweiss, eds, *The Oxford History of the American West*, New York: Oxford University Press, 1994.

Milner, Clyde, ed., *A New Significance: Re-envisioning the History of the American West*, New York: Oxford University Press, 1996.

Milton, Robert, *The Novel of the American West*, Lincoln: University of Nebraska Press, 1980.

Mihesuah, Devon, *Indigenous American Women: Decolonization, Empowerment, Activism*, Lincoln: University of Nebraska Press, 2003.

Mitchell, Lee, *Westerns: Making the Man in Fiction and Film*, Chicago: University of Chicago Press, 1996.

Monaghan, Jay, *Civil War on the Western Border, 1854-1865*, Lincoln: University of Nebraska Press, 1955.

Montejano, David, *Anglos and Mexicans in the Making of Texas, 1836-1986* Austin: University of Texas Press, 1987.

Mooney, James, *The Aboriginal Population of America North of Mexico*, Washington D.C.: Smithsonian Institute, 1928.

Mooney, James, *The Ghost Dance Religion and the Sioux Outbreak of 1890*, Lincoln: University of Nebraska Press, 1991.

Mooney, Michael, ed., *George Catlin: Letters and Notes on the North America Indians*, New York: Grammercy Books, 1975.

Morgan, Dale, *Jedediah Smith and the Opening of the West*, Lincoln: University of Nebraska Press, 1964.

Morgan, Robert, *Lions of the West: Heroes and Villains of Westward Expansion*, New York: Shannon Ravenal Book, 2012.

Moulton, Gary, ed., *The Definitive Journals of Lewis & Clark*, 9 vols, Lincoln: University of Nebraska Press, 2002.

Mountjoy, Shane, *Manifest Destiny: Westward Expansion*, New York: Chelsea House, 2009.

Myres, Sandra, *Westering Women and the Frontier Experience, 1800-1915*, Albuquerque: University of New Mexico Press, 1982.

Napersteck, Martin, *Sex and Manifest Destiny: The Urge that Drove Americans Westward*, Jefferson, N.C.: McFarland and Company, 2012.

Nash, Gerald, *The American West in the Twentieth Century: A Short History of an Urban Oasis*, Englewood Cliffs, N.J.: Prentice Hall, 1973.

Nash, Gerald, *The American West Transformed: The Impact of the Second World War*, Bloomington: University of Indiana Press, 1985.

Nash, Gerald, *World War II and the West: Reshaping the Economy*, Lincoln: University of Nebraska Press, 1990.

Nash, Gerald, *Creating the West: Historical Interpretations, 1890-1990*, Albuquerque: University of New Mexico Press, 1991.

Nash, Gerald, *The Federal Landscape: An Economic History of the Twentieth Century West*, Tucson: University of Arizona Press, 1999.

Nash, Gerald, and Richard Etulain, eds, *The Twentieth Century West: Historical Interpretations*, Albuquerque: University of New Mexico Press, 1989.

Nash, Roderick, *Wilderness and the American Mind*, New Haven, Conn.: Yale University Press, 1982.

Nash, Roderick, ed., *American Environmentalism: Readings in Conservation History*, New York: McGraw-Hill, 1990.

Neff, Emily Ballew, *The Modern West: Landscapes, 1890-1950*, New Haven, Conn.: Yale University Press, 2015.

Nester, William, *The Great Frontier War: Britain, France, and the Imperial Struggle for North America, 1607-1755*, Westport, Conn.: Praeger, 2000.

Nester, William, *The First Global War: Britain, France, and the Fate of North America, 1756-1775*, Westport, Conn.: Praeger, 2000.

Nester, William, *"Haughty Conquerors": Amherst and the Great Indian Uprising of 1763*, Westport, Conn.: Praeger, 2000.

Nester, William, *The Arikara War: The First Plains Indian War, 1823*, Missoula, Mont.: Mountain Press Publishing Company, 2001.

Nester, William, *The Frontier War for American Independence*, Mechanicsburg, Penn.: Stackpole Books, 2004.

Nester, William, *The Revolutionary Years, 1775-1789: The Art of American Power during the Early Republic*, Washington D.C. Potomac Books, 2011.

Nester, William, *From Mountain Man to Millionaire: The "Bold and Dashing Life" of Robert Campbell*, Columbia: University of Missouri Press, 2011.

Nester, William, *George Rogers Clark: "I Glory in War"*, Norman: University of Oklahoma Press, 2012.

Nester, William, *The Hamiltonian Vision, 1789-1800: The Art of American Power during the Early Republic*, Washington D.C.: Potomac Books, 2012.

Nester, William, *The Jeffersonian Vision, 1801-1815: The Art of American Power during the Early Republic*, Washington D.C.: Potomac Books, 2013.

Nester, William, *The Age of Jackson and the Art of American Power, 1815-1848*, Washington D.C.: Potomac Books, 2013.

Nester, William, *The French and Indian War and the Conquest of New France*, Norman: University of Oklahoma Press, 2014.

Nester, William, *The Struggle for Power in Colonial America, 1607-1776*, New York: Lexington Books, 2019.

Nester, William, *Theodore Roosevelt and the Art of American Power: An American for All Time*, New York: Lexington Books, 2019.

Nester, William, *The Old West's First Power Couples: The Fremonts, the Custers, and Their Epic Quest for Manifest Destiny*, Tucson: Rio Nuevo Publishers, 2020.

Nichols, Roger, ed., *American Frontier and Western Issues: A Historiographical Review*, New York: Greenwood Press, 1986.

Nofi, Albert, *The Alamo and the Texas War of Independence: Heroes, Myths, and History*, New York: Da Capo Press, 2001.

Novak, Barbara, *Nature and Culture: American Landscape and Painting, 1825-1875*, New York: Oxford University Press, 1995.

Oberg, Michael and Peter Olsen-Harbich, *Native America: A History*, New York: Wiley-Blackwell, 2022.

Oelschlaeger, Max, *The Idea of Wilderness: From Prehistory to the Age of Ecology*, New Haven, Conn.: Yale University Press, 1993.

Oglesby, Richard, *Manuel Lisa and the Opening of the Missouri Fur Trade*, Norman: University of Oklahoma Press, 1984.

O'Neal, Bill, *Encyclopedia of Western Gunfighters*, Norman: University of Oklahoma Press, 1979.

Opie, John, *The Law of the Land: 200 Years of American Farmland Policy*, Lincoln: University of Nebraska Press, 1987.

Parkman, Francis, *The Discovery of the West*, Boston: Little, Brown, 1860.

Parry, J.H., *The Age of Reconnaissance: Discovery, Exploration, and Settlement, 1450-1650*, Berkeley: University of California Press, 1982.

Parry, J.H., *The Spanish Seaborne Empire*, Berkeley: University of California Press, 1990.

Paul, Doris, *The Navajo Code Talkers*, New York: Dorrance, 1998.

Paul, Rodman, *Mining Frontiers of the Far West, 1848-1880*, New York: Holt, Rinehart, Winston, 1963.

Paul, Rodman, *California Gold: The Beginning of Mining in the Far West*, Lincoln: University of Nebraska Press, 1965.

Paul, Rodman, *The Far West and Great Plains in Transition, 1859-1900*, Norman: University of Oklahoma Press, 1998.

Peckham, Howard, *The Colonial Wars, 1689-1762*, Chicago: University of Chicago Press, 1964.

Pena, Jose Enrique de la, *With Santa Anna in Texas: A Personal Narrative of the Revolution*, College Station: Texas A & M Press, 1997.

Peterson, Richard, *The Bonanza Kings: The Social Origins and Business Behavior of Western Mining Entrepreneurs, 1870-1900*, Lincoln: University of Nebraska Press, 1977.

Petrik, Paula, *No Step Backward: Women and Family on the Rocky Mountain Mining Frontier*, Helena: Montana Historical Society Press, 1987.

Philp, Kenneth, *John Collier's Crusade for Indian Reform, 1920-1954*, Tucson: University of Arizona Press, 1977.

Pisani, Donald, *From the Family Farm to Agribusiness: The Irrigation Crusade in California and the West*, Berkeley: University of California Press, 1984.

Pittman, Walter, *New Mexico and the Civil War*, New York: History Press, 2011.

Pletcher, David, *The Diplomacy of Annexation: Texas, Oregon, and the Mexican War*, Columbia: University of Missouri Press, 1973.

Poling-Kempes, Lesley, *The Harvey Girls: Women Who Opened the West*, New York: Da Capo, 1989.

Pomeroy, Earl, *The Territories and the United States, 1861-1890: Studies in Colonial Administration*, Philadelphia: University of Philadelphia Press, 1947.

Pomeroy, Earl, *In Search of the Golden West: The Tourist in Western America*, New York: Alfred Knopf, 1957.

Pomeroy, Earl, *The Pacific Slope: A History of California, Oregon, Washington, Idaho, Utah, and Nevada*, New York: Alfred Knopf, 1965.

Potter, Tiffany, ed., *Ponteach, or the Savages of America, a Tragedy*, Toronto: University of Toronto Press, 2010.

Prassel, Richard, *The Western Peace Officer: A Legacy of Law and Order*, Norman: University of Oklahoma Press, 1972.

Prouty, Andrew, *More Deadly than War: Pacific Coast Logging, 1827-1981*, New York: Garland Publishing, 1982.

Prucha, Francis, ed., *Americanizing the American Indians: Writings by "Friends of the Indians," 1880-1900*, Cambridge, Mass.: Harvard University Press, 1973.

Prucha, Paul, *American Indian Policy in Crisis: Christian Reformers and the Indians, 1865-1900*, Norman: University of Oklahoma Press, 1976.

Prucha, Paul, *A Bibliographical Guide to the History of Indian-White Relations in the United States*, Chicago: University of Chicago Press, 1977.

Prucha, Paul, *The Great Father: The United States Government and the American Indians*, Lincoln: University of Nebraska Press, 1986.

Quaife, Milo, ed., *Kit Carson's Autobiography*, Lincoln: University of Nebraska Press, 1966.

Ralph, Julian, *Our Great West: A Study of the Present Conditions and Future Possibilities of the New Commonwealths and Capitals of the United States*, New York: Harper Brothers, 1893.

Reavis, Dick, *The Ashes of Waco: An Investigation*, New York: Simon and Schuster, 1995.

Reeves, Paul, and Ardis Parshall, eds, *Mormonism: A Historical Encyclopedia*, Santa Barbara, Calif.: ABC-CLIO, 2010.

Reeves, Richard, *Infamy: The Shocking Story of the Japanese American Internment in World War II*, New York: Picador, 2016.

Reid, John, *Contested Empire: Peter Skene Ogden and the Snake River Expeditions*, Norman: University of Oklahoma Press, 2002.

Reisner, Marc, *Cadillac Desert: The American West and Its Disappearing Water*, New York: Viking, 1986.

Rensink, Brenden, *The North American West in the Twenty-First Century*, Lincoln: University of Nebraska Press, 2022.

Reps, John, *Cities of the American West: A History of Frontier Urban Planning*, Princeton, N.J.: Princeton University Press, 1979.

Riley, Carroll et al., eds, *Man Across the Sea: Pre-Columbian Contacts*, Austin: University of Texas Press, 1971.

Riley, Glenda, *Women and Indians on the Frontier*, Albuquerque: University of New Mexico Press, 1984.

Riley, Glenda, *Female Frontier: A Comparative View of Women on the Prairie and the Plains*, Lawrence: University Press of Kansas, 1988.

Roberts, David, *Once They Moved Like the Wind: Cochise, Geronimo, and the Apache Wars*, New York: Touchstone, 1994.

Robinson, Forest, *Having It Both Ways: Self-subversion in Western Popular Classics*, Albuquerque: University of New Mexico Press, 1993.

Robinson, Roxanne, *George O'Keefe: A Life*, New York: Brandeis University Press, 2020.

Ronda, James, *Lewis and Clark among the Indians*, Lincoln: University of Nebraska Press, 1984.

Ronda, James, *Astoria and Empire*, Lincoln: University of Nebraska Press, 1990.

Rosenberg, Bruce, *Custer and the Epic of Defeat*, University Park: Penn State University Press, 1973.

Ross, John, *War on the Run: The Epic Story of Robert Rogers and the Conquest of America's First Frontier*, New York: Random House, 2009.

Rowley, William, *U.S. Forest Service Grazing and Rangelands: A History*, College Station: Texas A & M University Press, 1985.

Ruby, Robert et al., *A Guide to the Indian Tribes of the Pacific Northwest*, Norman: University of Oklahoma Press, 2010.

Rudnick, Lois Palken, *Mabel Dodge Luhan: New Woman, New Worlds*, Albuquerque: University of New Mexico Press, 1984.

Rudnick, Lois Palken, *Utopian Vistas: The Mabel Dodge Luhan House and the American Counterculture*, Albuquerque: University of New Mexico Press, 1996.

Ruiz, Vicki, *Cannery Women, Cannery Lives: Mexican Women, Unionization, and the California Food Processing Industry, 1930-1950*, Albuquerque: University of New Mexico Press, 1987.

Runte, Alfred, *National Parks: The American Experience*, Lincoln: University of Nebraska Press, 1987.

Runte, Alfred, *Yosemite: The Embattled Wilderness*, Lincoln: University of Nebraska Press, 1990.

Russell, Don, *The Wild West, or A History of the Wild West Shows*, Austin: University of Texas Press, 1970.

Saloutos, Theodore, *The American Farmer and the New Deal*, Ames: Iowa State University Press, 1982.

Samuels, Peggy and Harold, *Frederick Remington: A Biography*, New York: Doubleday, 1982.

Satz, Ronald, *American Indian Policy in the Jacksonian Era*, Norman: University of Oklahoma Press, 2002.

Saxton, Alexander, *Indispensable Enemy: Labor and the Anti-Chinese Movement in California*, Berkeley: University of California Press, 1971.

Schelebecker, John, *Cattle Raising on the Plains, 1900-1961*, Lincoln: University of Nebraska Press, 1963.

Schlesier, Karl, ed., *Plains Indians, 500-1500: The Archeological Past of Historic Groups*, Norman: University of Oklahoma Press, 1994.

Schoelwer, Susan Prendergast, *Alamo Images: Changing Perceptions of a Texas Experience*, Dallas: Southern Methodist University Press, 1985.

Schultz, Duane, *Month of the Freezing Moon: The Sand Creek Massacre, November 1864*, New York: St. Martin's Press, 1990.

Scott, Quinta, and Susan Croce Kelly, *Route 66: The Highway and People*, Norman: University of Oklahoma Press, 1988.

Shipps, Jan, *Mormonism: The Story of a New Religious Tradition*, Urbana: University of Illinois Press, 1985.

Shogun, Robert, *The Fate of the Union: America's Rocky Road to Political Stalemate*, Boulder, Colo.: Westview Press, 1998.

Sides, Hampton, *Blood and Thunder: The Epic Story of Kit Carson and the Conquest of the America West*, New York: Anchor Books, 2005.

Simmon, Scott, *The Invention of the Western Film: A Cultural History of the Genre for the First Half Century*, New York: Cambridge University Press, 2003.

Simmons, Virginia McConnell, *The Ute Indians of Utah, Colorado, and New Mexico*, Boulder: University Press of Colorado, 2001.

Simms, Steven, *Ancient Peoples of the Great Basin and Colorado Plateau*, New York: Routledge, 2008.

Simonson, Harold, *Beyond the Frontier: Writers, Western Regionalism, and a Sense of Place*, Fort Worth: Texas Christian University, 1989.

Slotkin, Richard, *The Fatal Environment: The Myth of the Frontier in the Age of Industrialization, 1800-1890*, Middletown, Conn.: Wesleyan University Press, 1986.

Slotkin, Richard, *Regeneration through Violence: The Mythology of the American Frontier, 1600-1860*, New York: Harper Perennial, 1996.

Slotkin, Richard, *Gunfighter Nation: The Myth of the Frontier in Twentieth Century America*, Norman: University of Oklahoma Press, 1998.

Smith, Duane, *Mining America: The Industry and the Environment, 1800-1980*, Lawrence: University Press of Kansas, 1987.

Smith, Henry Nash, *Virgin Land: The American West as Symbol and Myth*, Cambridge, Mass.: Harvard University Press, 1950.

Smith, John, *Saints, Sinners, and Sovereign Citizens: The Endless War over the West's Public Lands*, Las Vegas: University of Nevada Press, 2020.

Smith, Michael, *Pacific Visions: California Scientists and the Environment, 1850-1915*, New Haven, Conn.: Yale University Press, 1987.

Spence, Clark, *British Investments and the American Mining Frontier, 1860-1901*, Ithaca,, N.Y.: Cornell University Press, 1959.

Spicer, Edward, *Cycles of Conquest: The Impact of Spain, Mexico, and the United States on the Indians of the Southwest, 1533-1960*, Tucson: University of Arizona Press, 1962.

Starr, Kevin, *Americans and the California Dream, 1850-1915*, New York: Oxford University Press, 1973.

Starr, Kevin, *Inventing the Dream: California through the Progressive Era*, New York: Oxford University Press, 1985.

Stallard, Patricia, *Glittering Misery: Dependents of the Indian Fighting Army*, San Rafael, Calif.: Presidio Press, 1978.

Starita, Joe, *"I Am a Man": Chief Standing Bear's Journey for Justice*, New York: St. Martin's Griffith, 2010.

Stauffer, Helen Winter, and Susan J. Rosowski, *Women and Western American Literature*, Troy, N.Y.: Whitstone, 1982.

Steckmesser, Kent, *The Western Hero in History and Legend*, Norman: University of Oklahoma Press, 1965.

Steele, Ian, *Warpaths: Invasions of North America*, New York: Oxford University Press, 1994.

Steffen, Jerome, *Comparative Frontiers: A Proposal for Studying the American West*, Norman: University of Oklahoma Press, 1980.

Stegner, Wallace, *The American West as Living Space*, Ann Arbor: University of Michigan Press, 1987.

Stein, Walter, *California and the Dust Bowl Migration*, Westport, Conn.: Greenwood Press, 1973.

Stephanson, Anders, *Manifest Destiny: American Expansionism and the Empire of Right*, New York: Hill and Wang, 1995.

Stern, Kenneth, *A Force upon the Plain: The American Militia Movement and the Politics of Hate*, Norman: University of Oklahoma Press, 1997.

Stewart, George, *U.S. 40: Cross-section of the United States of America*, Boston: Houghton Mifflin, 1953.

Sweeney, Naoise Mae, *The West: A New History in Fourteen Lives*, New York: Dutton, 2023.

Sword, Wiley, *President Washington's Indian War: The Struggle for the Old Northwest, 1790-1795*, Norman: University of Oklahoma Press, 1985.

Tabor, James, and Eugene Gallagher, *Why Waco?: Cults and the Battle for Religious Freedom in America*, Berkeley: University of California Press, 1995.

Takaki, Ronald, *Strangers from a Different Shore: A History of Asian Americans*, Boston: Little, Brown, 1989.

Taylor, Dorceta, *The Rise of the American Conservation Movement: Power, Privilege, and Environmental Protection*, Durham, N.C.: Durham University Press, 2016.

Taylor, George, ed., *The Turner Thesis: Concerning the Role of the Frontier in American History*, Lexington, Mass.: Heath, 1972.

Taylor, Graham, *The New Deal and American Indian Tribalism: The Administration of the Indian Reorganization Act, 1934-45*, Lincoln: University of Nebraska Press, 1980.

Thelen, David, ed., *Memory and American History*, Bloomington: University of Indiana Press, 1990.

Thompson, John, *Closing the Frontier: Radical Response in Oklahoma, 1889-1923*, Norman: University of Oklahoma Press, 1986.

Thornton, Russell, *American Indian Holocaust and Survival: A Population History since 1492*, Norman: University of Oklahoma Press, 1987.

Todish, Tim, ed., *The Annotated and Illustrated Journals of Major Robert Rogers*, Fleischmanns, N.Y.: Purple Mountain Press, 2002.

Tompkins, Jane, *West of Everything: The Inner Life of Westerns*, New York: Oxford University Press, 1992.

Toole, Ross, *The Rape of the Great Plains: Northwest America, Cattle and Coal*, Boston: Little, Brown, 1976.

Tucker, Jennifer, et al., *A Right to Bear Arms?: The Contested Role of History in the Contemporary Debate on the Second Amendment*, Washington D.C.: Smithsonian Institute Press, 2019.

Tucker, Spencer, ed., *The Encyclopedia of the North American Indian Wars, 1607-1890*, 2 vols, Santa Barbara, Calif.: ABC-CLIO, 2011.

Turner, Frederick Jackson, *The Frontier in American History*, New York: Dover Publications, 1996.

Turner, John, *Brigham Young: Pioneer Prophet*, Cambridge, Mass.: Belknap Press, 2014.

Twain, Mark, *Adventures of Huckleberry Finn*, New York: Random House, 1996.

Unruh, John, *The Plains Across: The Overland Emigrants and the Trans-Mississippi West, 1840-1860*, Urbana: University of Illinois Press, 1982.

Utley, Robert, *Frontiersmen in Blue: The United States Army and the Indian, 1848-1865*, Lincoln: University of Nebraska Press, 1981.

Utley, Robert, *Frontier Regulars: The United States Army and the Indian, 1866-1891*, Lincoln: University of Nebraska Press, 1984.

Utley, Robert, *The Indian Frontier of the American West, 1846-1890*, Albuquerque: University of New Mexico Press, 1984.

Utley, Robert, *High Noon in Lincoln: Violence on the Western Frontier*, Albuquerque: University of New Mexico Press, 1987.

Utley, Robert, *Lone Star Justice: The First Century of the Texas Rangers*, New York: Berkely Book, 2002.

Utley, Robert, *Sitting Bull: The Life and Times of an American Patriot*, New York: Henry Holt, 2008.

Van de Logt, Mark, *War Party in Blue: Pawnee Scouts in the U.S. Army*, Norman: University of Oklahoma Press, 2021.

Wade, Richard, *The Urban Frontier: The Rise of Western Cities, 1790-1830*, Cambridge, Mass.: Harvard University Press, 1959.

Waldman, Michael, *The Second Amendment: A Biography*, New York: Simon and Schuster, 2015.

Warren, Harris, *The Sword Was Their Passport: A History of American Filibustering in the Mexican Revolution*, Baton Rouge: Louisiana State University Press, 1943.

Warren, Louis, *Buffalo Bill's America: William Cody and the Wild West Show*, New York: Viking, 2006.

Webb, Walter Prescott, *The Great Frontier*, Boston: Houghton Mifflin, 1952.

Webb, Walter Prescott, *The Great Plains* (1931), Lincoln: University of Nebraska Press, 1981.

Weber, David, ed., *New Spain's Far Northern Frontier: Essays on Spain in the American West, 1540-1821*, Albuquerque: University of New Mexico Press, 1979.

Weber, David, *The Tao Trappers: The Fur Trade in the Far Southwest, 1540-1846*, Norman: University of Oklahoma Press, 1982.

Weber, David, *The Mexican Frontier, 1821-1846; The American Southwest*, Albuquerque: University of New Mexico Press, 1982.

Weber, David, *The Spanish Frontier in North America*, New Haven, Conn.: Yale University Press, 1992.

Weber, David and Edward Countryman, *What Caused the Pueblo Revolt of 1680?*, New York: St. Martin's Press, 1999.

Weeks, Philip, *"Farewell, My Nation": American Indians and the United States in the Nineteenth Century*, New York: John Wiley, 2016.

Weidensaul, Scott, *The First Frontier: The Forgotten History of Struggle, Savagery, & Endurance in Early America*, New York: Houghton Mifflin, 2012.

Wessinger, Catherine, ed., *Millennialism, Persecution, and Violence*, Syracuse, N.Y.: Syracuse University Press, 2000.

West, Eliot, *The Last Indian War: The Nez Perce Story*, New York: Oxford University Press, 2011.

Wheelan, Joseph, *Invading Mexico: America's Continental Dream and the Mexican War, 1846-1848*, New York: Carroll & Graf Publishers, 2007.

White, Richard, *It's Your Misfortune and None of My Own: A New History of the American West*, Norman: University of Oklahoma Press, 1991.

Wiley, Peter, and Robert Gottlieb, *Empires in the Sun: The Rise of the New American West*, New York: Putnam, 1982.

Winther, Oscar, *The Transportation Frontier: Trans-Mississippi West, 1865-1890*, New York: Holt, Rinehart, and Winston, 1964.

Wishart, David, *The Fur Trade of the American West, 1807-1840*, Lincoln: University of Nebraska Press, 1992.

Worster, Donald, *Rivers of Empire: Water, Aridity, and the Growth of the American West*, New York: Oxford University Press, 1992.

Wright, Louis, *Culture on the Moving Frontier*, Bloomington: University of Indiana Press, 1955.

Wrobel, David, *The End of American Exceptionalism: Frontier Anxieties from the Old West to the New Deal*, Lawrence: University Press of Kansas, 1993.

Wrobel, David, *America's West: A History, 1890-1950*, New York: Cambridge University Press, 2017.

Wunder, John, *Inferior Courts, Superior Justice: A History of Justices of the Peace*, Westport, Conn.: Greenwood, 1979.

Wyckoff, William, *How to Read the American West: A Field Guide*, Seattle: University of Washington Press, 2014.

Wylie, Paul, *Blood on the Marias: The Baker Massacre*, Norman: University of Oklahoma Press, 2016.

Zevoloff, Vause, William McVaugh, and Samuel Zevoloff, eds, *Wilderness Tapestry: An Eclectic Approach to Preservation*, Reno: University of Nevada Press, 1992.

Articles

Baritz, Loren, "The Idea of the West," *American Historical Review*, vol. 66, no. 3 (April 1966), 618–40.

Chandler, Robert, "Friends in Time of Need: Republican and Black Civil Rights in California during the Civil War," *Arizona and the West*, vol. 24, no. 4 (Winter 1982), 39–40.

Degler, Carl, "Why Historians Change their Minds," *Pacific Historical Review*, vol. 45, no. 2 (May 1976), 167–84.

Gruhn, Ruth, "Linguistic Evidence in Support of the Coastal Route of Earliest Entry into the New World,"*Man*, Volume 23, Number 2 (1988), 77–100.

Hayden, Ferdinand, "The Wonder of the West: More About the Yellowstone,"*Scribners Monthly–*, vol. 3 (February 1872), 396.

Hutton, Paul, "From the Little Big Horn to Little Big Man: The Changing Image of the Western Hero in Popular Culture,"*Western Historical Quarterly*, vol. 7, no. 1 (January 1976), 19–45.

Huyser, Kimberly, "Data and American Indian Identity,"*Sage–*, vol. 19, no. 3 (2020), 10–15.

Kroeber, Alfred, "Native American Population,"*American Anthropologist*, vol. 36, no. 1 (January-March 1934), 1–25.

Leopold, Aldo, "The Wilderness and Its Place in Forest Recreational Policy,"*Journal of Forestry*, vol. 19, no. 7 (1921), 718–21.

Nugent, Walter, "Frontiers and Empires in the Late Nineteenth Century,"*Western Historical Quarterly*, vol. 20, no 4 (November 1989), 393–408.

Pomeroy, Earl, "Toward a Reorientation of Western History: Continuity and Environment,"*Mississippi Valley Historical Review*, vol. 41, no. 4 (March 1955), 579–600.

Royce, Josiah, "Fremont,"*Atlantic*, vol. 90, no. 10 (October 1890), 548–57.

Smits, David, "The Frontier Army and the Destruction of the Buffalo: 1865-1883,"*Western Historical Quarterly*, vol. 25, no 3 (1994), 312–28.

INDEX